RELIGIOUS FREEDOM

RELIGIOUS FREEDOM

Rights and Liberties under the Law

MELVIN I. UROFSKY

A B C ☯ C L I O

Santa Barbara, California • Denver, Colorado • Oxford, England

Copyright © 2002 by Melvin I. Urofsky

All rights reserved. No part of this publication may be reproduced, stored in a retrieval system, or transmitted, in any form or by any means, electronic, mechanical, photocopying, recording, or otherwise, except for the inclusion of brief quotations in a review, without prior permission in writing from the publishers.

Library of Congress Cataloging-in-Publication Data

Urofsky, Melvin I.
  Religious Freedom: rights and liberties under the law / Melvin I. Urofsky
    p. cm. — (America's Freedoms)
Includes bibliographical references and index.
  ISBN 1-57607-312-2 (harcover: alk. paper)
  1. Freedom of religion—United States—History. 2. Church and state—United States—History. I. Title. II. Series.
  KF4783 .U76 2002
  342.73'0852—dc21
                                        2002002819

07 06 05 04 03   10 9 8 7 6 5 4 3 2

ABC-CLIO, Inc.
130 Cremona Drive, P.O. Box 1911
Santa Barbara, California 93116-1911

This book is printed on acid-free paper.
Manufactured in the United States of America

For
Jerry and Marcia LaMaskin
and
Jack and Marilyn Spiro,
incomparable dinner companions

CONTENTS

SERIES FOREWORD

America's Freedoms promises a series of books that address the origin, development, meaning, and future of the nation's fundamental liberties, as well as the individuals, circumstances, and events that have shaped them. These freedoms are chiefly enshrined explicitly or implicitly in the Bill of Rights and other amendments to the Constitution of the United States and have much to do with the quality of life Americans enjoy. Without them, America would be a far different place in which to live. Oddly enough, however, the Constitution was drafted and signed in Philadelphia in 1787 without a bill of rights. That was an afterthought, emerging only after a debate among the foremost political minds of the day.

At the time, Thomas Jefferson was in France on a diplomatic mission. Upon receiving a copy of the proposed Constitution from his friend James Madison, who had helped write the document, Jefferson let him know as fast as the slow sailing-ship mails of the day allowed that the new plan of government suffered one major defect—it lacked a bill of rights. This, Jefferson argued, "is what the people are entitled to against every government on earth." Madison should not have been surprised at Jefferson's reaction. The Declaration of Independence of 1776 had largely been Jefferson's handiwork, including its core statement of principle:

We hold these truths to be self-evident, that all men are created equal, that they are endowed by their Creator with certain unalienable Rights, that among these are Life, Liberty, and the pursuit of Happiness. That to secure these rights, Governments are instituted among Men, deriving their just powers from the consent of the governed.

Jefferson rejected the conclusion of many of the framers that the Constitution's design—a system of both separation of powers among the legislative, executive, and judicial branches, and a federal division of powers between national and state governments—would safeguard liberty. Even when combined with elections, he believed strongly that such structural checks would fall short.

Jefferson and other critics of the proposed Constitution ultimately had their way. In one of the first items of business in the First Congress in 1789, Madison, as a member of the House of Representatives from Virginia, introduced amendments to protect liberty. Ten were ratified by 1791 and have become known as the Bill of Rights.

America's Bill of Rights reflects the founding generation's understanding of the necessary link between personal freedom and representative government, as well as their experience with threats to liberty. The First Amendment protects expression—in speech, press, assembly, petition, and religion—and guards against a union of church and state. The Second Amendment secures liberty against national tyranny by affirming the self-defense of the states. Members of state-authorized local militia—citizens primarily, soldiers occasionally—retained a right to bear arms. The ban in the Third Amendment on forcibly quartering troops in houses reflects the emphasis the framers placed on the integrity and sanctity of the home.

Other provisions in the Fourth, Fifth, Sixth, Seventh, and Eighth amendments safeguard freedom by setting forth standards that government must follow in administering the law, especially regarding persons accused of crimes. The framers knew firsthand the dangers that government-as-prosecutor could pose to liberty. Even today, authoritarian regimes in other lands routinely use the tools of law enforcement—arrests, searches, detentions, as well as trials—to squelch peaceful political opposition. Limits in the Bill of Rights on crime-fighting powers thus help maintain democracy by demanding a high level of legal scrutiny of the government's practices.

In addition, one clause in the Fifth Amendment forbids the taking of private property for public use without paying the owner just compensation, and thereby limits the power of eminent domain, the authority to seize a person's property. Along with taxation and conscription, eminent domain is one of the most awesome powers any government can possess.

The Ninth Amendment makes sure that the listing of some rights does not imply that others necessarily have been abandoned. If the Ninth offered reassurances to the people, the Tenth Amendment was designed to reassure the states that they or the people retained those powers not delegated to the national government. Today, the Tenth is a remainder of the integral role states play in the federal plan of union that the Constitution ordained.

Despite this legacy of freedom, however, we Americans today sometimes wonder about the origin, development, meaning, and future of our liberties. This concern is entirely understandable, because liberty is central to the idea of what it means *to be American.* In this way, the United States stands apart from virtually every other nation on earth. Other countries typically define their national identities through a common ethnicity, origin, ancestral bond, religion, or history. But none of these accounts for the American identity. In terms of ethnicity, ancestry, and religion, the United States is the most diverse place on earth. From the beginning, America has been a land of immigrants.

Neither is there a single historical experience to which all current citizens can directly relate: someone who arrived a decade ago from, say, southeast Asia and was naturalized as a citizen only last year is just as much an American as someone whose forebears served in General George Washington's army at Valley Forge during the American War of Independence (1776–1783). In religious as in political affairs, the United States has been a beacon to those suffering oppression abroad: "the last, best hope of earth," Abraham Lincoln said. So, the American identity is ideological. It consists of faith in the value and importance of liberty for each individual.

Nonetheless, a longstanding consensus among Americans on the *principle* that individual liberty is essential, highly prized, and widely shared hardly assures agreement about liberty *in practice.* This is because the concept of liberty, as it has developed in the United States, has several dimensions.

First, there is an unavoidable tension between liberty and restraint. Liberty means freedom: we say that a person has a "right" to do this or that. But that *right* is meaningless unless there is a corresponding *duty* on the part of others (such as police officers and elected officials) not to interfere. Thus, protection of the liberty of one person necessarily involves restraints imposed on someone else. This is why we speak of a *civil* right or a *civil* liberty: it is a claim on the behavior of another that is enforceable through the legal process. Moreover, some degree of order (restrictions on the behavior of all) is necessary if everyone's liberties are to be protected. Just as too much order crushes freedom, too little invites social chaos that also threatens freedom. Determining the proper balance between freedom and order, however, is more easily sought than found. "To make a government requires no great prudence," declared English statesman and political philosopher Edmund Burke in 1790. "Settle the seat of power; teach obedience; and the work is done. To give freedom is still more easy. It is not necessary to guide; it only requires to let go the rein. But to form a *free government;* that is, to temper together these opposite elements of liberty and restraint in one consistent work, requires much thought; deep reflection; a sagacious, powerful, and combining mind."

Second, the Constitution does not define the freedoms that it protects. Chief Justice John Marshall once acknowledged that the Constitution was a document "of enumeration, and not of definition." There are, for example, lists of the powers of Congress in Article I, or the rights of individuals in the Bill of Rights, but those powers and limitations are not explained. What is the "freedom of speech" that the First Amendment guarantees? What are "unreasonable searches and seizures" that are proscribed by the Fourth Amendment? What is the "due process of law" secured by both the Fifth and Fourteenth Amendments? Reasonable people, all of whom favor individual liberty, can arrive at very different answers to these questions.

A third dimension—breadth—is closely related to the second. How widely shared is a particular freedom? Consider voting, for example. One could write a political history of the United States by cataloging the efforts to extend the vote or franchise to groups such as women and nonwhites that had been previously excluded. Or, consider the First Amendment's freedom of speech. Does it include the expression of *all* points of view or merely *some?* Does the same amendment's protection of the "free exercise of religion" include all faiths, even obscure ones that may seem weird or even irritating? At different times questions like these have yielded different answers.

Similarly, the historical record contains notorious lapses. Despite all the safeguards that are supposed to shore up freedom's foundations, constitutional protections have sometimes been worth the least when they have been desperately needed. In our history the most frequent and often the most serious threats to freedom have come not from people intent on throwing the Bill of Rights away outright, but from well-meaning people who find the

Bill of Rights a temporary bother, standing in the way of some objective they want to reach.

There is also a question that dates to the very beginning of American government under the Constitution. Does the Constitution protect rights not spelled out in, or fairly implied by, the words of the document? The answer to that question largely depends on what a person concludes about the source of rights. One tradition, reflected in the Declaration of Independence, asserts that rights predate government and that government's chief duty is to protect the rights that everyone naturally possesses. Thus, if the Constitution is read as a document designed, among other things, to protect liberty, then protected liberties are not limited to those in the text of the Constitution but may also be derived from experience, for example, or from one's assessment of the requirements of a free society. This tradition places a lot of discretion in the hands of judges, because in the American political system, it is largely the judiciary that decides what the Constitution means. Partly due to this dynamic, a competing tradition looks to the text of the Constitution, as well as to statutes passed consistent with the Constitution, as a *complete* code of law containing *all* the liberties that Americans possess. Judges, therefore, are not free to go outside the text to "discover" rights that the people, through the process of lawmaking and constitutional amendment, have not declared. Doing so is undemocratic because it bypasses "rule by the people." The tension between these two ways of thinking explains the ongoing debate about a right to privacy, itself nowhere mentioned in the words of the Constitution. "I like my privacy as well as the next one," once admitted Justice Hugo Black, "but I am nevertheless compelled to admit that government has a right to invade it unless prohibited by some specific constitutional provision." Otherwise, he said, judges are forced "to determine what is or is not constitutional on the basis of their own appraisal of what laws are unwise or unnecessary." Black thought that was the job of elected legislators who would answer to the people.

Fifth, it is often forgotten that at the outset, and for many years afterward, the Bill of Rights applied only to the national government, not to the states. Except for a very few restrictions, such as those in section 10 of Article I in the main body of the Constitution, which expressly limited state power, states were restrained only by their individual constitutions and state laws, not by the U.S. Bill of Rights. So, Pennsylvania or any other state, for example, could shut down a newspaper or barricade the doors of a church without violating the First Amendment. For many in the founding generation, the new central government loomed as a colossus that might threaten liberty. Few at that time thought that individual freedom needed *national* protection against *state* invasions of the rights of the people.

The first step in removing this double standard came with ratification of the Fourteenth Amendment after the Civil War in 1868. Section 1 contained majestic, but undefined, checks on states: "*No State* shall make or enforce any law which shall abridge the privileges or immunities of citizens of the United States; nor shall any *State* deprive any person of life, liberty, or property, without due process of law; nor deny to any person with in its jurisdiction the equal protections of the laws" (emphasis added). Such vague language begged for interpretation. In a series of cases mainly between 1920 and 1968, the Supreme Court construed the Fourteenth Amendment to include within its meaning almost every provision of the Bill of Rights. This process of "incorporation" (applying the Bill of Rights to the states by way of the Fourteenth Amendment) was the second step in eliminating the double standard of 1791. State and local governments became bound by the same restrictions that had applied all along to the national government. The consequences of this development scarcely can be exaggerated because most governmental action in the United States is the work of state and local governments. For instance, ordinary citizens are far more likely to encounter a local police officer than an agent of the Federal Bureau of Investigation or the Secret Service.

A sixth dimension reflects an irony. A society premised on individual freedom assumes not only the worth of each person but citizens capable of rational thought, considered judgment, and measured actions. Otherwise democratic government would be futile. Yet, we lodge the most important freedoms in the Constitution precisely because we want to give those freedoms extra protection. "The very purpose of a Bill of Rights was to . . . place [certain subjects] beyond the reach of majorities and officials and to establish them as legal principles to be applied by the courts," explained Justice Robert H. Jackson. "One's right to life, liberty, and property, to free speech, a free press, freedom of worship and assembly, and other fundamental rights may not be submitted to vote; they depend on the outcome of no elections." Jackson referred to a hard lesson learned from experience: basic rights require extra protection because they are fragile. On occasion, people have been willing to violate the freedoms of others. That reality demanded a written constitution.

This irony reflects the changing nature of a bill of rights in history. Americans did not invent the idea of a bill of rights in 1791. Instead it drew from and was inspired by colonial documents such as the Pennsylvania colony's Charter of Liberties (1701) and the English Bill of Rights (1689), Petition of Right (1628), and Magna Carta (1215). However, these early and often unsuccessful attempts to limit government power were devices to protect the many (the people) from the few (the English Crown). With the emergence of democratic political systems in the eighteenth century, however, political power shifted from the few to the many. The right to rule belonged to the person who received the most votes in an election, not necessarily to the firstborn, the wealthiest, or the most physically powerful. So the focus of a bill of rights had to shift too. No longer was it designed to shelter the majority from the minority, but to shelter the minority from the majority. "Wherever the real power in a Government lies, there is the danger of oppression," commented

Madison in his exchange of letters with Jefferson in 1788. "In our Government, the real power lies in the majority of the Community, and the invasion of private rights is *chiefly* to be apprehended, not from acts of government contrary to the sense of its constituents, but from acts in which the Government is the mere instrument of the major number of the Constituents."

Americans, however, do deserve credit for having discovered a way to enforce a bill of rights. Without an enforcement mechanism, a bill of rights is no more than a list of aspirations: standards to aim for, but with no redress other than violent protest or revolution. Indeed this had been the experience in England with which the framers were thoroughly familiar. Thanks to judicial review—the authority courts in the United States possess to invalidate actions taken by the other branches of government which, in the judges' view, conflict with the Constitution—the provisions in the Bill of Rights and other constitutionally protected liberties became judicially enforceable.

Judicial review was a tradition that was beginning to emerge in the states on a small scale in the 1780s and 1790s and that would blossom in the U.S. Supreme Court in the nineteenth century and twentieth centuries. "In the arguments in favor of a declaration of rights," Jefferson presciently told Madison in the late winter of 1789 after the Constitution had been ratified, "you omit one which has great weight with me, the legal check which it puts into the hands of the judiciary." This is the reason why each of the volumes in this series focuses extensively on judicial decisions. Liberties have largely been defined by judges in the context of deciding cases in situations where individuals thought the power of government extended too far.

Designed to help democracy protect itself, the Constitution ultimately needs the support of those—the majority—who endure its restraints. Without sufficient support among the people, its freedoms rest on a weak foundation. The earnest hope of *America's Freedoms* is that this series will offer Americans a renewed appreciation and understanding of their heritage of liberty.

Yet there would be no series on America's Freedoms without the interest and support of Alicia Merritt at ABC-CLIO. The series was her idea. She approached me originally about the series and was very adept at overcoming my initial hesitations as series editor She not only helped me shape the particular topics that the series would include, but guided me toward prospective authors. As a result, the topic of each book has been matched with the most appropriate person as author. The goal in each instance as been to pair topics with authors who are recognized teachers and scholars in their field. The results have been gratifying. A series editor could hardly wish for authors who have been more cooperative, helpful, and accommodating.

Donald Grier Stephenson, Jr.

Preface and Acknowledgments

The book in your hands was written before the horrendous events of September 11, 2001, but I believe that the history of religious freedom in the United States has a greater meaning to Americans in the wake of that tragedy. Newspapers, periodicals, and television programs have been full of stories and analyses of why fundamentalist Muslims hate Americans, and in many of those analyses, the answer has been religious belief. The type of open, free society enjoyed in the United States, in which religion is a matter of private conscience, offends those who believe that their religion calls for conformity to a specific set of divinely inspired rules, which dictate not only the mode and content of religious worship, but how people live their everyday lives as well. Clearly September 11 was not just about religious differences, but many of the other issues, such as globalization and western cultural dominance, also resonate with those who oppose the West in general, and the United States in particular, on religious grounds.

For those of us who live in the United States, and who worship in hundreds of different ways or not at all, the model proposed by fundamentalists of any religion—be they Christian, Jewish, Muslim, or Hindu—is not only offensive but worrisome as well. As I have tried to show in the pages that follow, religious freedom in the United States developed not out of high idealism but out of practical necessity. Many of the settlers who came to North America in the seventeenth and eighteenth centuries wanted to establish a unitary church, and indeed tried to do so. But the great variety of religious beliefs among those who came, along with the immense expanse of open land on the frontier, made a single established church impossible. Aware of the religious wars that had raged for centuries in Europe, the American colonists first came to a position of religious tolerance, and then in the First Amendment to one of religious freedom.

This did not mean that everyone then agreed or continues to agree on exactly what the Establishment and Free Exercise Clauses mean, and in the last six decades the dispute over their meaning has been at the heart of constitutional debate. While most Americans, with the exception of a few fringe elements, believe in religious freedom, they differ over what this means. For some, the First Amendment mandates a complete separation of church and state in every way possible. For others, it merely means that if the government wants to aid religion, then it must do so in a nondiscriminatory manner, with the benefits available to all sects. In practice, the government assists religion in a number of ways, such as tax exemptions, but has avoided any policy that smacks of making one religion, or even one faith, official. In a world where people still kill each other because of religious differences, the United States has been blessedly free of such bloodshed.

This does not mean that people do not want religion to play a greater role in our everyday life, and that question has in fact been one of the great public policy debates of the last two decades. For the most part, that discussion has been carried on in a civil manner, even if it is occasionally marred by inflated rhetoric. Most importantly, it has been carried on within the parameters of the First Amendment, with a recognition that the Supreme Court is the ultimate arbiter of the U.S. Constitution. So long as that understanding is shared by Americans of all faiths, we can hope to avoid the type of religious extremism that led to the catastrophe on September 11th.

While the author always bears full responsibility for what has been written, the transition from a computer file to a book requires massive assistance from others, and there are several people I want to thank. I am indebted to D. Grier Stephenson, Jr., for inviting me to do this volume in the series. It gave me a chance to take some of the work I had done in the history of the First Amendment and present it in a coherent form. At ABC-CLIO it was a pleasure to work once again with Alicia Merritt, senior acquisitions editor, and Melanie Stafford, senior production editor, who have mastered the fine art of getting an author through the production process with minimal psychic stress. Rebecca Ritke did the copyediting in a thoughtful and careful way that made the manuscript much better for her efforts, while James F. Van Orden relieved me of the task of doing the "Key People, Laws, and Events" section that is so useful in a reference book. I would be remiss if I did not also mention the debt I owe to students who over the years have shared their insights into religion and religious freedom in the constitutional history and law courses I have taught.

The volume is dedicated to four longtime friends. My wife Susan and I have known Marcia and Jerry LaMaskin and Marilyn and Jack Spiro for more than a quarter century. Whatever our other commitments, we manage—sometimes with difficulty—to dine out together every few months. We have attended each other's families' life cycle events, and indeed, view them as part of our extended family. This book is a token of that friendship, and we hope to keep dining out with them for years to come.

Melvin I. Urofsky
Richmond, Virginia

1

INTRODUCTION

*T*HE CONSTITUTIONAL LIFE of the nation can be read in the volumes of *U.S. Reports,* which detail more than two centuries of Supreme Court interpretations of the various clauses and commands of the Constitution drafted in Philadelphia in 1787 and amended occasionally since. The cases tell us which issues came before the Court and how the justices decided them. Yet despite this detailed record, we all too often lose track of the critical insight that real people, men and women, brought these cases to the high court in hopes of vindicating what they saw as the rights guaranteed to them as American citizens. For example, we know that when law enforcement officers arrest people, the officers must read them their rights, and at trial the accused must have an attorney. These rights were enunciated by the Court in two landmark cases, *Gideon v. Wainwright* (1963) and *Miranda v. Arizona* (1966); they are studied by every law student and are familiar to the general public because of the numerous police and prosecution series on television. But how many people know about the two men behind these cases, Clarence Earl Gideon and Ernesto Miranda? Without them, there would be no "Miranda warnings" or effective right to counsel.

I

The same is true of the many cases testing the meaning of the two religion clauses in the First Amendment. This book explores and analyzes many of those decisions, describes the litigants, and focuses on the importance of the rulings in developing the right to religious freedom in the United States. So by way of introduction, let us look at two people whose adherence to their faiths led them to carry their individual battles all the way to the Supreme Court. Daniel Weisman won his case; Al Smith did not—but even despite his loss, the case led to a further refinement in meaning of the religion clauses.

At the beginning of the twenty-first century, many nations are looking at the constitutional model of the United States as an example of how to order their own affairs and to protect the rights of their citizens. It is hard for many Americans to believe that the rights we take for granted are still missing in much of the world; and we are appalled and frightened at the lengths to which religious zealots will go, especially in the Middle East, in the name of a god. But these realities should not surprise us: In the Middle Ages, the Catholic Church led one crusade after another to wrest the Holy Land back from the hands of "infidels," and tens of thousands of people lost their lives in the process. When Martin Luther nailed his ninety-five theses on the door of Wittenburg Cathedral in 1517, he plunged Europe into two centuries of religious warfare.

Many early pilgrims to the United States came for religious purposes, but not for the type of religious freedom we associate today with the First Amendment. They came so that they could worship freely—not to allow other groups, which they believed to be in error, to worship as well. The colonies and later the country first developed religious toleration and then freedom not because particular sects stopped believing they alone knew the true word of God, but because so many different groups came in search of a better life. In one of the most famous ideas in U.S. history, Frederick Jackson Turner suggested that the western frontier, with its great expanse of free land, shaped the nature of democracy in the United States. In a variation on this thesis, the frontier, with its wide open spaces, made it possible for different religious groups to live peacefully; they learned tolerance as a necessity, and then turned it into a virtue. Even if not all groups today are willing to acknowledge that there may be more than one path to God, most Americans think that individuals have a right to decide their own beliefs and practices, and that government has no business interfering with religious matters.

Government noninterference is the heart and soul of the Constitution's two religion clauses: the Establishment Clause, which bans government establishment of any one religious belief or church above others; and the Free Exercise Clause, which forbids government interference in people's religious lives. Neither of these clauses is absolute: Government has been and continues to be involved with religion in many areas; and there are clear limits on how far one may take one's religious beliefs. This book will examine those ties and limits through the stories of people whose faith led them to the Supreme Court.

DANIEL WEISMAN

Daniel Weisman and his family are typical middle-class Americans who a little more than a decade ago captured the nation's and the Supreme Court's attention when they stood up for a principle in which they strongly believed—the full separation of church and state.

Like many other religious minorities, Jews over their long history have learned to fear a fusion of religion and government, when one particular religious group gains control of the apparatus of the state. The results have always been persecution of minorities, often accompanied by violence and bloodshed. For groups like this, the United States has been a beacon of religious freedom precisely because the Constitution forbids any government establishment of religion. The Warren Court in the 1960s, in a series of famous decisions, seemed to erect a high wall between church and state, outlawing mandatory school prayer (*Engel v. Vitale* [1962]) and compulsory Bible reading (*Abington v. Schempp* [1963]), and striking down a religion-based law prohibiting the teaching of evolution (*Epperson v. Arkansas* [1968]).

The Weismans and other true separationists think this means that there should be no prayer either in daily classes or at special events such as graduations. Prayer, in their view, cannot be anything but sectarian, even if it is couched in supposedly neutral terms. Too often, insensitive ministers appearing at public gatherings have uttered prayers that were sectarian in tone and substance and offensive to those not of their faith. Although one might argue that a prayer at a graduation ceremony is different from mandated prayer in classes, the fact of the matter is that it puts the same burden on those who would rather not pray. Because of the nature of the gathering, it is difficult for them not to witness the prayer. Walking out would be embarrassing and would mark them as outsiders, and standing with their heads bowed while attempting to ignore the prayer would be equally uncomfortable and would make them feel hypocritical. Many religious believers consider prayer a private conversation with God; if it is to be done as a communal exercise, then it should be done in a church, synagogue, or mosque. Of course, people with no religious beliefs or faith have even greater cause to subscribe to a strict separation of church and state, and especially object to prayers at public events.

Yet prayer has been a staple of American life since the colonial era; and although it may no longer start the school day, it is still present in many state-related events. Most state legislatures invite rabbis, priests, and ministers to offer a prayer at the beginning of each day's session. The marshal of the Supreme Court calls those in attendance to rise and pay heed, and then declares "God save this honorable Court!" For many people, the issue is not the wording of the prayer, but rather that a prayer acknowledges the role God plays in our everyday life. This is not a new belief, nor is it limited to any one sect; it is shared by Jews, Christians, Muslims, and others who worship a deity. Moreover, it has also been a staple of American political philosophy that civic virtue, the basis of responsible citizenship, includes a healthy respect for religion and reliance on God. The fact that one can pray in private is irrelevant; to deny the public place of prayer is to deny the role of God in American life.

In 1986, at the Weismans' oldest daughter's graduation from Nathan Bishop Middle School in Providence, Rhode Island, a Baptist minister had delivered an extremely sectarian prayer. Angered, Daniel and Vivien Weisman complained in a letter to Robert E. Lee, the school principal, telling him that the Supreme Court had outlawed school prayer. Lee never answered the letter. He believed that the *Engel* decision applied only to daily prayer; the Court had never addressed prayers at special ceremonies. When Deborah Weisman's turn came to graduate in 1988, Lee, still the Bishop Middle School principal, decided to placate the family by inviting Rabbi Leslie Gutterman of Temple Beth-El in Providence to deliver the opening and closing prayers at the graduation.

Lee failed to understand that the Weismans objected not only to a sectarian prayer but to any prayer. Four days before the graduation ceremony Daniel Weisman, on behalf of his fourteen-year-old daughter Deborah and with the assistance of the Rhode Island American Civil Liberties Union (ACLU), went into the U.S. District Court seeking a temporary restraining order barring school officials from including either an invocation or a benediction in graduation ceremonies. The court denied the motion for lack of adequate time to consider it.

Rabbi Gutterman had earlier accepted Lee's invitation and had received from him a pamphlet prepared by the National Conference of Christians and Jews entitled "Guidelines for Civic Occasions." The pamphlet suggested that public prayers at nonsectarian events such as graduations be composed with "inclusiveness and sensitivity," but acknowledged that "prayer of any kind may be inappropriate on some civic occasions." Rabbi Gutterman, following the advice of the pamphlet, delivered the following prayers:

Invocation:

God of the Free, Hope of the Brave:
For the legacy of America where diversity is celebrated and the rights of minorities are protected, we thank You. May these young men and women grow up to enrich it.
For the liberty of America, we thank You. May these new graduates grow up to guard it.
For the political process of America in which all its citizens may participate, for its court system where all may seek justice we thank You. May those we honor this morning always turn to it in trust.
For the destiny of America we thank You. May the graduates of Nathan Bishop Middle School so live that they might help to share it.
May our aspirations for our country and these young people, who are our hope for the future, be richly fulfilled.
Amen.

Benediction:

O God, we are grateful to You for having endowed us with the capacity for learning which we have celebrated on this joyous commencement.
Happy families give thanks for seeing their children achieve an important milestone. Send Your blessings upon the teachers and administrators who helped prepare them.
The graduates now need strength and guidance for the future; help them to understand that we are not complete with academic knowledge alone. We must each strive to fulfill what You require of us all: To do justly, to love mercy, to walk humbly.

We give thanks to You, Lord, for keeping us alive, sustaining us
    and allowing us to reach this special, happy occasion.
Amen.

Although the benediction included quotes from the prophet
Micah and from the traditional Jewish prayer of thanksgiving, no
one could argue that it failed to meet the recommendations of
inclusiveness and sensitivity. And yet it offended the Weismans,
who even though attendance was not required, had gone to the
ceremony like other proud parents, wanting to see their child
graduate.

After the graduation, the Weismans went back to the district
court to seek a permanent injunction barring future prayers at
public school graduations. The district court granted the injunction on the grounds that the action of the school officials endorsed
religion and thus violated the Establishment Clause of the First
Amendment. The Court of Appeals for the First Circuit affirmed
the lower court decision, and the Supreme Court agreed to hear
the case.

Many observers wondered whether the conservative majority
that Ronald Reagan had put on the bench had the votes needed to
overturn *Engel.* This was the great hope of the social conservatives
who had become the backbone of the Republican Party, and also
the hope of the Bush administration, which filed a brief urging the
justices to allow prayer in public school.

But by a 5–4 vote, the Court rejected the Bush administration's
plea, refusing to abandon precedent. Justice Anthony Kennedy's
majority opinion reaffirmed previous rulings and held that
prayers at public school graduations, no matter how nonsectarian
in nature, violated the Constitution.

The fact that Kennedy wrote the opinion surprised many people, since he previously had given every appearance of being firmly in the conservative camp. In an earlier case, a dissenting
Kennedy had urged the Court to abandon judicially imposed
restrictions on religious activities in schools. But Kennedy's latest

opinion indicated that he had changed his mind about the coercive nature of even a supposedly "neutral" prayer:

> The lessons of the First Amendment are as urgent in the modern world as in the eighteenth century when it was written. One timeless lesson is that if citizens are subjected to state-sponsored religious exercises, the State disavows its own duty to guard and respect that sphere of inviolable conscience and belief which is the mark of a free people. To compromise that principle today would be to deny our tradition and forfeit our standing to urge others to secure the protections of that tradition for themselves.

The Weisman case is far from the last word on school prayer, but it gives us a good indication of how the Court has viewed the Establishment Clause. Although the Court in recent years has been split between strict separationists and accommodationists (discussed in Chapter 3), the basic notion shared by both sides is that government cannot favor one religion over another, or favor a situation in which those who do not share the majority viewpoint are treated unequally. But as we shall see, the question that must be answered is whether in protecting the rights of Daniel Weisman and others like him, we are treading on the rights of those who continue to believe that religion plays a necessary and legitimate role in civic society.

AL SMITH

Al Smith is a member of the Klamath tribe of southern Oregon, a tribe with the dubious distinction of having been ruled out of existence by a vote of Congress in the 1950s. Born into a relatively intact family and culture, he was, like thousands of other Native American children, torn away from his home and sent to a boarding school where he could learn to be an "American." There teachers ensured that he learned nothing of his native language, history, or religion. Although he did well at the school, when he graduated he had no skills, and he lived on Portland's skid row, became an alcoholic, and did some jail time. In 1957 Al Smith began to turn his life around: he sobered up and began to look for something spiritual to which he could cling. The white man's religion meant nothing to him, but he remembered his grandmother going through the house every night before going to bed, chanting a prayer in Klamath. Al Smith began to pray to the Creator, without, as he admitted, understanding very much about it.

Over the next twenty years his life came together, and he found rewarding work helping other Indian people deal with alcohol and drug-abuse problems. Despite what the Bureau of Indian Affairs said about the existence of his people, Smith saw himself as a Klamath Indian, and in the fall of 1975 he returned to live in the Klamath Basin. There he finally began to learn about Native American spirituality and rituals, and he brought this knowledge to bear in his new job at Sweathouse Lodge, a treatment center for Native Americans that utilized a blend of the Alcoholics Anonymous twelve-step program and Indian rituals. He also joined the Native American Church, a loose confederation of groups with different rituals and beliefs, whose ceremonies often include the use of peyote, a hallucinogenic extract of certain cactus plants.

Al Smith began to find out about peyote, but was worried about whether the Peyote Road was right for him. He had been sober for a quarter of a century, and from his work in the treatment center he knew how easy it was for someone to fall back into alcohol abuse. He had made a new life for himself, and he did not want to jeopardize it. But he saw that some of his clients who ingested peyote actually did better in their treatments and seemed to have a firmer grasp of what they needed to do. Finally, in 1979, he took the peyote sacrament at a ceremony on the Makah Reservation in northwestern Washington State. He did not fall off the wagon, and he began to see the benefits of the Peyote Road in helping him to become a better person.

By then Smith was working at the Douglas County Council on Alcohol and Drug Abuse Prevention and Treatment (ADAPT). There he met Galen Black, a white man and recovering alcoholic who had discovered Native American spirituality and wanted to partake of it. In many ways, Black's determination to try the Peyote Road led to Smith's involvement in a legal battle over the ritual use of peyote. Although Smith had used peyote, like most users he did so sparingly and only at certain rituals. Moreover, he knew that Oregon law listed peyote as a proscribed substance, and thus he had been discreet about his own involvement in Native American Church rituals. Smith finally agreed to take Black to a meeting; but when Smith got sick, Black went on his own. He ingested the peyote, had what he described as an overwhelming religious experience, and then told many people about it.

On September 19, 1983, John Gardin, the director of ADAPT, called Black into his office and suspended him from his job. Gardin then called Smith in and asked him whether he had attended the peyote meeting as well. Smith said that he would go to a meeting if invited but that he had not gone. Gardin informed him that he was forbidden under ADAPT policy to use peyote at any time, and if he did so he would be terminated. Gardin saw himself as defending the integrity of ADAPT's policy of total abstinence from drugs and alcohol; but Smith recalled leaving the meeting and saying to himself, "I can't go to church?"

A few weeks later Gardin offered Black a choice of entering a treatment program and returning to a lower-level job, resigning, or being fired. Black accused the director of racist discrimination and was fired on the spot. Gardin began pressing Smith for reassurances that he had not used any drugs, and treated him with suspicion. Although Smith had not looked for a fight, he and his wife agreed that he could not abandon the rituals of his people. In

March 1984 he got an invitation to a large Native American gathering at Coos Bay, where there would be a peyote ceremony. On Friday he informed Gardin that he would be going, and the following Monday Smith was called into the director's office first thing in the morning. Did he take peyote? Gardin asked. Yes, Smith replied, "I took the sacred sacrament and prayed for you and the rest of you sick mothers." Gardin fired him and told him to clear out his desk by the end of the day.

Smith did not know what work he would do next, but he knew what he had to do in the short term. He went down to the county office building and filled out forms for unemployment compensation to tide him over until he found a new job. Much to his surprise, a few days later he received a letter from the employment division denying him unemployment compensation. His employer opposed payment, the letter said, because of a "willful violation of the standards of behavior that an employer has the right to expect of an employee." It was at this point that Smith really got mad, and his anger led him eventually to the U.S. Supreme Court.

In the mid-1980s, if one approached a professor of constitutional law at any American law school and laid out the facts of Al Smith's case, the response would likely have been: "That's a no-brainer. *Sherbert v. Verner* governs." In that case in 1963, the Supreme Court held that a state could not condition the availability of unemployment insurance on an individual's willingness to forgo conduct required by his religion.

Sherbert v. Verner arose in South Carolina where a Seventh-Day Adventist had been discharged from her job because she would not work on Saturday. Her refusal to work on her Sabbath made it almost impossible for her to find other employment, and as a result the state denied her unemployment compensation. State law barred benefits to workers who refused, without "good cause," to accept suitable work when offered. She sued, claiming that the denial of benefits violated her free exercise of religion as guaranteed by the First Amendment.

Justice William J. Brennan framed the question in this way: What compelling interest did the state have, in denying benefits to Ms. Sherbert, that would justify the curtailment of a constitutionally protected right? He found none, and the Court held that states had to make reasonable accommodations to the religious beliefs of their citizens.

Sherbert illustrates the tension that often exists between the two religion clauses. If one takes a strict view of the Establishment Clause, then South Carolina had acted properly in its initial determination. The law was the law, and bending it for the sake of one group put that denomination in a favored position, thus creating a form of establishment. On the other hand, such an approach meant that certain groups would be disadvantaged and would have to compromise their religious practices because of state action—a violation of the Free Exercise Clause.

Subsequent cases in the 1980s validated the *Sherbert* ruling. In *Thomas v. Review Board, Indiana Employment Security Division* (1981), a case factually similar to *Sherbert,* the Court reversed Indiana's denial of unemployment compensation to a Jehovah's Witness who quit his job in a munitions plant because of his religious objections to war. Interestingly, the only dissenter was Justice William Rehnquist, who believed that the Court had read the Free Exercise Clause too broadly and who urged that *Sherbert* be overruled. In *Hobbie v. Unemployment Appeals Commission of Florida* (1987), the Court required the state to pay benefits to a man whose religious beliefs had changed during the course of his employment. In *Frazee v. Illinois Employment Security Department* (1989), the three prior cases were applied to an applicant who refused to accept work on Sunday, not because of his membership in any established church or sect, but only on his claim that "as a Christian he could not work on the 'Lord's Day.'"

Given this progression of cases, one might well have assumed that Galen Black and Al Smith would have prevailed in their suit to force Oregon to pay them unemployment compensation benefits, and in fact, initially they did. They claimed that the Supreme Court had interpreted the Free Exercise Clause to mean that state unemployment insurance could not be conditional on an individual's willingness to forgo conduct required by his religion, when that conduct was otherwise legal. Smith and Black argued that the same rule should apply to them, even though the Oregon law made ingestion of peyote illegal, because the Oregon law itself was unconstitutional. The Oregon Supreme Court agreed and overturned the ruling, holding that the First Amendment bars criminal punishment of good-faith religious use of peyote.

The state appealed, primarily on the grounds that the earlier cases had not dealt with criminal activity. Although many western states and the federal government provided exemptions for peyote when used in religious ceremonies, Oregon did not, and in the eyes of state officials, this made a big difference. In addition, the Court that would hear the case was far more conservative than its predecessors, less willing to give the Free Exercise Clause a broad reading, and had proven far from receptive to previous claims brought by Native Americans.

In its first term the Rehnquist Court had heard a Free Exercise claim involving a challenge to the federal government's plan to build a highway and permit timber harvesting in areas that had sacred value to Indian tribes. In *Lyng v. Northwest Indian Cemetery Protective Association* (1988), Justice Sandra Day O'Connor spoke for a 5–3 majority that conceded that the activities would interfere with tribal pursuit of spiritual fulfillment. But, she argued, the government's plans neither coerced the members into violating any of their religious tenets nor penalized any religious activity. This sophistic reasoning, which ignored the basis of the Free Exercise claim, relied on a 1986 decision in *Bowen v. Roy,* which had upheld the government's assignment of a Social Security number to an Indian child over the protest of her parents, who believed that the number would "rob" the little girl of her soul. In his dissent, Justice Brennan found the majority's reliance on *Bowen* "altogether remarkable." In that case the issue had been one of internal government record-keeping and had had a limited effect. Logging and road building in or near sacred grounds, on the other hand, had potentially far-reaching negative effects on Native American religions—effects, Brennan warned, that could possibly destroy them. (In the end, the road was not built, because Native Americans used their political influence to stop it.)

Justice Scalia, writing for a bare majority of the Court in *Oregon v. Smith,* took an extremely narrow view of the Free Exercise Clause. Going all the way back to the 1879 case of *Reynolds v. United States,* he argued that religion could never be used as an excuse for violating "an otherwise valid law regulating conduct that the state is free to regulate." Justice O'Connor, joined in part by Brennan, Marshall, and Blackmun, sharply criticized the Court for abandoning the balancing test. Moreover, by denying the applicants the opportunity to challenge a general criminal law on Free Exercise grounds, the majority had cut out "the essence of a free exercise claim." The mere fact that this statute involved a criminal statute did not mean that it did not burden religious freedom. Nonetheless, O'Connor joined in the result because she believed the state had a compelling interest under the balancing test, namely its effort to wage a war on drugs.

What is one to make of the *Smith* decision? On the one hand, practically every religious group in America angrily protested, and their ire led Congress to pass the Religious Freedom Restoration Act, which in turn prompted a constitutional confrontation between Congress and the Court that the Court easily won.

The State of Oregon could certainly have been more responsive to the practices of the Native American Church. Peyote is not heroin or cocaine, and of all government efforts to control hallucinogenic substances, the peyote program is the most successful. The cacti that produce the peyote button grow in a small desert area of the southwestern United States and northern Mexico. It is a limited crop, and only certain tribes are allowed to harvest and process the buttons. Only particular tribes and recognized groups such as the Native American Church may buy peyote, and its ritual use is strongly contained. There is no evidence that it is addictive, or that people under its influence commit crimes or endanger themselves or others.

But we do live in a federal system, in which each state is free to establish—within the broader constitutional framework—rules by which its citizens shall live. One can decry the lack of sensitivity to Native American ritual, but in fact the state law did not specifically target peyote ceremonies. To some extent, the law is on the books as part of a larger policy against drugs, and as a warning that Oregon will not tolerate certain behaviors just because they are purported religious practices. (About this time the state was embroiled in a major controversy with a charismatic Hindu leader named Bhagwan Shree Rajneesh, whose followers had taken over an Oregon town by moving in and voting themselves into office, which soon led to a dictatorship. The State of Oregon was not going to allow that sort of thing to happen under the rubric of religious freedom.) Oregon is, by the way, one of the most progressive states in the nation, and it has long been in the forefront of many reform movements; at present, it is the only state that has approved physician-assisted suicide.

This was the problem facing the Court: It was one thing to say that a state could not deny benefits otherwise available simply because some people's religious beliefs created an administrative problem. The actual costs to the state were minimal, and no major policy had to be revised to accommodate the few persons involved. But if the Court struck down the state's peyote law on Free Exercise grounds, then, given current headlines, it was going to have to revisit an issue it had first faced in the 1870s, polygamy. A group of resurgent fundamentalist Mormons have not only revived the practice of polygamy but have been open—almost brazen—in letting the world know about it. If one can argue an exemption from one criminal law on Free Exercise grounds, then why not an exemption from others as well?

The Smith case shows, as we shall see in greater detail in Chapter 4, that the Free Exercise Clause, although one of the noblest statements in the Bill of Rights, is not an unlimited right. How far the Court is willing to go in interpreting its meaning is often a very good reflection of just how open and tolerant is the general society.

CONCLUSION

These two cases, like most issues that go to the high court, are not easy. If, in reading the pages that follow, one gets confused and believes that there is no clear line of jurisprudence regarding either the Establishment Clause or the Free Exercise Clause, that is understandable. The courts have attempted to walk a fine line protecting those rights guaranteed by the Constitution yet at the same time to show some sensitivity to the wishes of the majority. If the results have not satisfied all of the people all of the time, they have at least established a climate of constitutional protection of minorities and individual dissenters. As Justice Holmes reminded us in regard to the Free Speech Clause, freedom of speech is not for the speech we like, but for the speech we hate. The same is true of the religion clauses.

REFERENCES

Brownstein, Alan E. 2000. "Prayer and Religious Expression at High School Graduation: Constitutional Etiquette in a Pluralistic Society." *Nexus* 5: 61.

Epps, Garrett. 2001. *To an Unknown God: Religious Freedom on Trial.* New York: St. Martin's Press.

Long, Carolyn N. 2000. *Religious Freedom and Indian Rights: The Case of Oregon v. Smith.* Lawrence: University Press of Kansas.

Sherry, Suzanna. 1992. "Lee v. Weisman: Paradox Redux." *Supreme Court Review* (1992) 123.

2

ORIGINS AND
DEVELOPMENT

*T*HE DEVELOPMENT of religious freedom—the liberty to believe or not to believe according to the dictates of one's own conscience, free from the pressures or sanctions of the state—is relatively recent in humankind's history. There have been societies that permitted, in varying degrees, deviations from the state-sanctioned and enforced religion; but such toleration depended upon the whim of the majority or of the rulers and could be withdrawn as easily as it had been given. Religious freedom requires, above all else, the divorce of a nation's religious life from its political institutions; and this separation of church and state, as it is called, is also of recent vintage. One of the great social revolutions that accompanied America's rebellion against England and the adoption of the Constitution and Bill of Rights was the formal separation of church and state, first by the former colonies and then by the federal government. By embedding this idea, and the accompanying notion of a full freedom of religious exercise, in the Constitution, the founding generation transformed what had been at best a temporary privilege into a protected right. That does not mean that religious freedom as we

know it today fully existed in 1791; but the seeds had been plant-
ed. The great flowering of those germinal ideas would come in the
twentieth century.

ORIGINS

In ancient tribal societies the strongest warrior not only made the
political decisions (when to hunt or move or go to war) but also
served as the shaman, the intermediary between the people and
their gods. It appears that at all times the secular function out-
weighed the religious, and even after the development of separate
rulers and priests, the political power dominated (Pfeffer, 1953, 4).
As late as the Greek and Roman empires, people believed in
numerous gods, each one having a particular function or domain.
For example, Poseidon/Neptune ruled the waters, and Ares/Mars
was the god of war. As the Greeks and Romans conquered other
peoples, they did not insist on their new subjects accepting their
gods. Rather, they merely added the local deities to their own pantheon, although clearly in a subsidiary position. After all, if one
ascribed victory to the gods, then obviously the gods of the vic-
tors were more powerful than those of the losers.

But although this tolerance of other gods and practices may
seem very modern, both the Greeks and Romans insisted that
their citizens and subjects pay the proper homage to the gods.
Athens condemned Socrates to drink the hemlock because, among
other "crimes," he preached unorthodox religious views, neglect-
ed the city's gods, and engaged in novel religious practices. In
both empires no division existed between state and church, and
the latter clearly served the interests of the former. Augustus held
not only the title "Caesar" but "Pontifex Maximus" (high priest)
as well, and his grand plans for enlarging the Roman empire
included the revival and restoration of religion to a high estate.

No doubt a polytheistic religion can easily afford tolerance. After
all, if there are multiple gods, then adding a few more and allowing

people to pay homage to the deities of their choice is no great hardship. But monotheistic religions pose a different problem. If one believes that there is only one god, then there can be no competing deities or practices. The God of the Hebrews makes no bones about this. "I am the Lord your God," he tells them, speaking through Moses at Mount Sinai, "and you shall have no other gods before Me" (Exodus 20:2–3). When Moses came down from the mountain and found people worshiping the golden calf, he ordered the immediate slaying of the three thousand idolaters (Exodus 32:28). For a long time the ancient Hebrews practiced theocracy, a form of government in which priests/prophets led the people. The monarchy was first established under Saul; and by the time of the third king, Solomon, religion already had become a handmaiden to the needs of the state. Yet the theocratic element never disappeared. Despite the great power of King David, Nathan the prophet publicly chastised him for causing Uriah the Hittite's death so that the king could take Bathsheba for a wife (2 Sam. 12:1–15). A priest/prophet led the Maccabean revolt against the Greeks.

The important legacy of Judaism in this area is the idea of one true god, which by definition excludes all other gods, all other religions, and all other practices as false and not to be tolerated. If one truly believes that Jehovah is *melekh malchai hamlachim*, the King of the kings of kings, the creator of the universe and the giver of life and the law, then how can one calmly say that others are free to follow their false gods, false beliefs, and false practices? This legacy was passed directly to Christianity, which even more than Judaism has been a proselytizing religion that compels conformity. At one time, Christians not only believed that there should be only one religion in a state (i.e., Christianity) but also that all citizens must adhere to that religion, and that those who refuse to do so, or who do so halfheartedly, should be compelled to conform, even on pain of death.

Originally Christianity could do little about nonbelievers, since for its first three centuries it was a minor and often despised and persecuted sect. Ironically, it got its chance to become the dominant religion of the Roman Empire thanks to the Edict of Milan, issued by the coemperors Constantine and Licinius in 312 or 313. The edict abrogated all restrictions on religious worship, and provided that "liberty of worship shall not be denied to any, but that the mind and will of every individual shall be free to manage divine affairs according to his own choice" (Pfeffer, 1953, 12). Christians would no longer suffer under laws directed against their faith, and all other faiths would be free as well. This condition, however, lasted less than a century. By 346 the state had ordered the closing of all non-Christian temples, and the death penalty awaited anyone caught sacrificing to other gods. By 392 the Christian triumph in Rome was complete, and an edict by Theodosius that year forbade even the simplest offerings to household gods.

Religious unity and conformity marked the triumph of Christianity in Europe for the next thousand years. Judaism was barely tolerated, and increasingly heavy burdens were laid upon Jewish communities, which remained ever the target of zealots eager to convert Jews to the true faith. Church officials single-mindedly hunted down those who failed to conform to official dogma, branding them heretics and often burning them at the stake. Church fathers such as Augustine, who in his youth had praised the virtues of tolerance and heterodoxy, called for strict conformity to orthodox teachings, and asked officials of the state to help expurgate dissidence. Better that they should be severely punished and made to repent than that they should die in error and therefore unsaved. A hallmark of the Christian middle ages, religious unity was seen as a necessity for a stable social order and for the proper worship of God.

A few—very few—argued for a different view of society; but for the most part their voices went unheard and their writings were branded as heresy. Marsilius of Padua denied to the church and to its officials any coercive power over individual conscience, and even claimed they had no right to excommunicate people from the communion of Christianity because they believed in God differently from the manner prescribed by the Church. His book *Defensor Pacis,* published in 1314, went little noticed at the time, but its arguments would be revived first in the Protestant Reformation and later by modern scholars of religious liberty.

In the middle ages, however, the views of Thomas Aquinas, the great schoolmaster of Catholicism, and Augustine dominated, and the Inquisition, with papal blessing, went about its bloody business of finding and punishing heretics. The papal bull *Ad extirpanda,* issued by Pope Innocent IV in 1252, officially approved torture as a means of forcing those accused to recant and to name others who shared their heretical beliefs. The most infamous of all the inquisitions, the one in Spain, did not come into being until 1480, but it became the largest and most powerful of all the agencies of enforced conformity. As late as 1781 it was still burning heretics at the stake, and it did not go out of business until 1834 (Pfeffer, 1953, 20).

One might expect the Protestant Reformation to have led to some toleration; and in fact one can find in the writings of Martin Luther and John Calvin some passages that plead for tolerance and freedom of conscience. But in those areas where Protestants gained control, they soon proved as zealous and conformist as the Catholic Church they had so recently opposed. This should not be surprising, since Luther never objected to the notions that there is only one true faith, that all other faiths must be eradicated, and that in any state there can be only one church. As long as one believes these things, then whatever the dominant religion may be, it will essentially act as did the Protestants, the Catholics, and the ancient Hebrews (as well as the Muslims, following their sweep across the Arabian peninsula and Africa) before them.

The Protestant Reformation did, however, split the religious unity of Europe. Some areas, such as the Italian States and Spain, became even more Catholic, driving out all traces of Protestantism. Few countries became completely Protestant; but in Switzerland and some of the German states, a triumphant Reformation made the practice of Catholicism impossible. In some countries, religious differences led to bitter civil wars, many of which lasted for decades. James Madison had this history in mind when he wrote that "torrents of blood have been spilt in the world in vain attempts of the secular arm to extinguish religious discord, by proscribing all differences in religious opinion" (Alley, 1985, 59; see also James Madison, "Memorial and Remonstrance" [1786], in Chapter 6). Only in Holland did the competing religious sects so balance each other that by the seventeenth century the good burghers had adopted a live-and-let-live policy that permitted not only Catholics and Protestants but Jews as well to live in a spirit of mutual toleration. The Americans of the Revolutionary generation knew of the situation in Holland. Their contrasting actions were dictated primarily by their experience as British colonial subjects.

HISTORY

Great Britain, like all other medieval Catholic countries, had an established church—that is, a church sanctioned and supported by the state to the exclusion of all others; and English kings and bishops paid fealty to the pope as Christ's vicar on earth. The Protestant Reformation that shook northern Europe at first seemed not to touch England; the young monarch, Henry VIII, urged on by his devout bride, Katherine of Aragon, proved so forceful a champion of Catholicism that he earned the title "defender of the faith." But when Henry wanted to put aside Katherine and take Anne Boleyn as his wife, the Church proved unwilling to accommodate him. So he threw over the Church of Rome in England, and in its place he established the Church of England, with a rite that greatly resembled that of Rome but with himself at its head. The so-called "English Reformation" unloosed the forces of

Protestantism, advocates of which demanded a "cleansing" of the Church of England to eliminate its papist remnants.

After Henry's death, his daughter Mary ascended to the throne. She had never forgiven Henry for divorcing her mother, Katherine; and although Mary paid lip service to the Anglican Church, she had remained a devout Catholic. Now she intended to bring England back into the orb of the "true" Church. She initiated a brutal campaign in which many Protestants were imprisoned, fled the country, or were burned at the stake. Fortunately for England, Mary's reign was short, and her successor, Elizabeth I, reestablished the Anglican Church. But Elizabeth, who had feared for her life during Mary's reign, had no desire to impose the type of conformity sought either by Mary or the medieval church. She sought, as she put it, "no window into a man's soul," and so long as individuals did not disturb the social peace, she cared little about their form of worship. Catholics under Elizabeth's rule suffered a number of disabilities due to Britain's rivalry with Spain, but these were nothing like what Mary had imposed on Protestants during her tenure. During Elizabeth's long reign, moreover, the forces of reform grew stronger. The so-called "Marian exiles," who had fled the country for Holland during her sister's rule, returned preaching a "purified" Church of England—hence the name "Puritans." When James VI of Scotland (home of a rigorous Protestant church) succeeded Elizabeth as James I in 1603, the reformers thought their time had come.

But James had had enough of the dour Scots Presbyterianism, and like Elizabeth, he had no desire to impose uniformity of worship in his realm. He bickered constantly with the Puritan reformers, and the only satisfaction he gave them was permission for a new English translation of the Bible, the great King James version. During his reign the colonization of North America began, and both Anglicans and Puritans took their visions of the godly community to the New World. What is important, in terms of religion in America, is that all of the new settlers believed in an established church, and soon after they set up their colonies, they established their churches. A famous document of this development is *New England's First Fruits*, a 1643 pamphlet describing the early years of the Massachusetts Bay Colony, whose author wrote, "After God had carried us safe to New England . . . we had builded our houses, provided necessities for our livelihood, reared convenient places for God's worship, and settled the civil government" (Wright, 1957, 116).

From the settlement of Jamestown in 1607 until the American Revolution, the British colonies in North America, with few exceptions, had established churches. In New York and the southern colonies the Church of England enjoyed the same status as it had in the mother country, and in New England various forms of Congregationalism dominated. These colonies consistently discriminated against Catholics, Jews, and even dissenting Protestants, although the mother country, in the Act of Toleration of 1689, following the English Civil War and the accession of William and Mary to the throne in the Glorious Revolution of 1688, exempted most Protestant dissenters from the Church of England and from the penal laws that enforced its establishment.

In 1656 the General Court of Massachusetts Bay forbade the presence of Quakers in the colony. Should any be found, they were to be jailed, whipped, and deported. But the Quakers were persistent. So the following year the legislature ordered that banished male Quakers who returned should lose one ear; if they returned a second time, the other ear. Females who came back were to be "severely" whipped. On a third return, males and females alike should "have their tongues bored through with a hot iron." But the Quakers kept coming; so in 1658 the General Court prescribed death by hanging, the same penalty imposed upon Jesuits and other Catholic priests who returned after banishment (Noonan, 1998, 51). Between 1659 and 1661, one woman—Mary Dyer—and three men were indeed hanged for this cause on Boston Common.

As late as 1774, at a time when the colonists were strongly protesting British infringements on their rights, the Reverend

Isaac Backus, leader of the Massachusetts Baptists, informed the governor and council that eighteen Baptists had been jailed in Northampton, during the coldest part of the winter, for refusing to pay taxes for the support of the town's Congregational minister (Levy, 1994, 4). That same year, James Madison wrote to a friend: "That diabolical, hell-conceived principle of persecution rages among some. . . . There are at this time in the adjacent county not less than five or six well-meaning men in close jail for publishing their religious sentiments, which in the main are very orthodox. . . . So I must beg you to . . . pray for liberty of conscience for all" (Bradley, 1987, 31).

Yet from the very beginning of settlement, pressures against establishment and conformity grew, especially in the northern colonies. As early as 1645 a majority of the deputies in the Plymouth General Court wanted "to allow and maintain full and free tolerance of religion to all men that would preserve the civill peace and submit until government; and there was no limitation or exception against Turke, Jew, Papist, Arian, Socinian, Nicholaytan, Familist, or any other, etc." The governor refused to allow the resolution to come to a vote. Nonetheless, Plymouth throughout its existence retained a spirit of moderation, in stark contrast to neighboring Massachusetts. In 1645 the four Puritan colonies of New Haven, Connecticut, Massachusetts, and Plymouth formed the United Colonies, primarily for mutual defense against the Indians. But the Massachusetts Puritans also wanted the organization to act as a barrier against "error and blasphemy," especially the tolerance for diverse views enjoyed in Plymouth (Curry, 1986, 18–19).

If Plymouth appeared lax, Rhode Island stood outside the pale. After banishment from Massachusetts for heresy, Roger Williams founded a new colony that allowed an environment of almost total religious liberty. Williams has been characterized as a prophet of modernity, and for his actions in this regard he certainly deserves that title. But as a number of scholars have pointed out, Williams was quintessentially a man of his time, seeking fervently the one true religion. What differentiated him from Cotton Mather and the New England Divines was his belief that he had not found that one true faith; and so long as he had not, then he could not impose his will on others or force them to believe in a particular manner. The full extent of his faith can be seen in the fact that Rhode Island welcomed not only Quakers (the only sanctuary they had before the founding of Pennsylvania) but Jews as well (Curry, 1986, 191–194). Williams not only favored freedom of conscience, but he opposed religious establishment, and he did so in the belief that establishment harmed not only the civil society but religion as well. He was one of the few in the seventeenth-century colonies to make this argument (Levy, 1994, 228).

Although formal establishments lasted until 1776, in effect the colonies had to allow some degree of religious toleration. The first settlers came from a relatively homogeneous background; but within a short time the New World was luring immigrants from all over the British Isles as well as from northern and western Europe. They came not because America offered any greater religious freedom than they enjoyed at home but because of economic opportunity and the promise of land. Not all of them shared the Congregational faith of the Puritans or the Anglican views of the middle and southern colonists. Baptists, Jews, Catholics, Lutherans, and other new arrivals began to protest the exaction of taxes for a church they did not attend, and of conformity to a faith they did not share.

It is beyond the scope of this book to examine the protests in every colony; but the activities of the Baptists in Virginia are of especial importance, because they led to a landmark event in American religious liberty.

FOUNDING PRINCIPLES

At the beginning of the Revolution, Virginia, like many other states, disestablished the Church of England, which the colonists identified with the hated royal government. Although the Virginia constitution of 1776 did not explicitly address the religious establishment, it guaranteed to every person equality in the free exercise of religion. This wording was thanks in large part to the work of James Madison. But Madison could not get the convention to adopt a clause providing for the full separation of church and state, much to the disappointment of the largest dissenting group in the state, the Baptists; other dissenting groups, especially conservatives in the Tidewater, still adhered to the state-supported Anglican faith (soon to be rechristened Episcopalianism). Yet, although the latter believed that tax monies should support religion, they thought taxes ought not go to just one sect but should be used to support all (Protestant Christian) churches equally.

In 1779 the Virginia legislature considered two conflicting bills. Thomas Jefferson had written the first, a "Bill for Religious Freedom," which provided, among other things, "that no man shall be compelled to frequent or support any religious worship, place, or ministry whatsoever." Jefferson believed religion to be a personal matter between an individual and God and therefore beyond the reach of the civil government. He did not limit religious freedom to Protestant sects or even to Christians but extended it to all groups, considering it one "of the natural rights of mankind" (Malone, 1948, 278). In contrast, Patrick Henry's "Bill concerning Religion" proposed a general tax assessment, declared Christianity the "established religion" of Virginia, and provided articles of faith to which church members had to subscribe in order to be incorporated as an established church. Henry's bill, in effect, made Christianity the official religion of the Commonwealth, but allowed all Christian churches to share in the tax proceeds (Levy, 1994, 61).

The Assembly was not willing to go as far as Jefferson proposed; and protests, especially from the Baptists, prevented the enactment of Henry's bill as well. The issue remained controversial for several years until the Presbyterian clergy, who had previously been opposed to a general assessment, changed their minds, and having grown eager to get tax revenues for their churches, endorsed Henry's bill. So in 1784, Henry, who had a substantial Presbyterian constituency, introduced "A Bill Establishing a Provision for Teachers of the Christian Religion." The bill retained the idea of a general assessment as well as of a plural establishment, and it initially had the support of Episcopalians, Methodists, and Presbyterians as well as a majority of the Assembly. But James Madison managed to postpone deliberations and helped elect Henry governor, thus removing him from the Assembly. Madison also managed to postpone the final decision until after the 1785 election, so that the members could see how their constituents felt about the issue.

That year Madison also presented his own views to the people, in his tract "Memorial and Remonstrance against Religious Assessments" (Hutchinson, 1962, 8:298–304; see Chapter 6). Like Jefferson, Madison argued that the essentially private and voluntary nature of religion should not be subject to government in any manner. Even if Henry claimed that his bill did not establish a religion, a tax assessment was just that—an establishment of religion—and it should therefore be opposed, no matter how mild or beneficent it appeared. Madison's argument caught fire, and when the Assembly met that fall it found more than one hundred petitions signed by upwards of 11,000 Virginians opposing the assessment. Some came from individuals, and others, from Presbyterian, Baptist, and Quaker churches. One by an anonymous author garnered a large number of signers who declared themselves "evangelical Christians believing deeply in the principle of voluntary support." The debate Madison stirred up caused many people who had previously supported Henry's assessment bill, including George Washington, to change their minds (Levy, 1994, 68; Miller, 1986, Parts I and II).

The election that November returned an Assembly that was completely opposed to Henry's bill and receptive to Madison's resurrection of the older bill for religious freedom, authored by Thomas Jefferson (now American minister to France). Although

the Assembly refused to go along with all of Jefferson's philosophical preamble, it kept the substantive articles he had proposed. Under its provisions, no one would be forced to attend or
support any religious worship or church, or be in any way punished for failure to do so. The first line, moreover, summed up the
Jeffersonian view: "Whereas Almighty God hath created the mind
free; that all attempts to influence it by temporal punishments or
burthens, or by civil incapacitations, tend only to beget habits of
hypocrisy and meanness; and are a departure from the plan of the
Holy author of our religion . . . . All men shall be free to profess,
and by argument to maintain, their opinion in matters of religion,
and that the same shall in no wise diminish, enlarge, or affect their
civil capacities" (see Virginia Statute for Religious Freedom
[1786], in Chapter 6).

The Virginia Statute for Religious Freedom was the first of Virginia's laws, and it was one of three achievements that Jefferson
wished to be remembered for, along with the Declaration of Independence and the founding of the University of Virginia. As Jefferson's biographer so aptly noted, "After more than a century and
a half it remains an ineffaceable landmark of human liberty; and
men of any land would do well to turn to it at any time that persecution for opinion may rear its ugly head" (Malone, 1948, 280).

But as advanced as Virginia was, its sister states lagged far
behind until well after the Revolution. Although several states disenfranchised the Anglican Church, they maintained restrictions
on Catholics and Jews, imposed a test oath for office-holding, and
continued to finance the religious activities of churches and ministers through taxation. Eventually, however, the ideals Jefferson
had set forth were triumphantly vindicated.

THE CONSTITUTION

Virginia enacted the Statute for Religious Freedom one year
before James Madison went to Philadelphia to help draft the Con-

stitution. The fact that a state had enacted such a sweeping statement of liberty fit well with the general view during the drafting of the Articles of Confederation that matters of individual rights ought to be left completely to the states. As John Adams wrote: "I hope that [the Confederation] Congress will never meddle with religion further than to say their own prayers, and to fast and to give thanks once a year. Let every colony have its own religion without molestation" (Urofsky, 1986, 2). In the most important statute enacted under the Articles, the Northwest Ordinance of 1787, Congress affirmed that "the fundamental principles of civil and religious liberty ... form the basis whereon true republics, their laws and constitutions are erected." In the pact that Congress made with the new states to be carved out of the territory, the first article guaranteed that "no person, demeaning himself in a peaceable and orderly manner, shall ever be molested on account of his mode of worship, or religious sentiment." However, another clause noted, "Religion, morality and knowledge being necessary to good government and the happiness of mankind, schools and the means of education shall be forever encouraged." To implement this goal, the ordinance set aside tracts of lands for schools and churches. If Congress decided that some of the proceeds from the sale of public lands should actually go to supporting churches, then the money would be apportioned according to the number of adherents of each denomination. Congress also set aside some 10,000 acres of land for the United Brethren (or Moravians), in anticipation of their "civilizing the Indians" who lived on that land, supposedly by Christianizing them (Finkelman, 2000, 387).

The Constitution itself did little to advance the cause of religious freedom in general, although religious tests for federal office are prohibited by Article VI, Section 3—the only reference to religion in the entire document. This federal practice contrasts markedly with those in several of the states. Delaware, for example, required every public official to swear, "I do profess faith in

God the Father, and in Jesus Christ His only Son, and in the Holy Ghost, one God, blessed for evermore, and I do acknowledge the holy scriptures of the Old and New Testaments to be given by divine inspiration" (Poore, 1877, 1:276).

During the debates over ratification, a few people defended the idea of a test; however, many more wanted the Constitution to provide definite guarantees of religious liberty. Jefferson, then in Paris, upon receiving a copy of the Constitution from Madison, wrote that on the whole "there is a great mass of good in it," but "a bill of rights is what the people are entitled to against every government on earth... & what no just government should refuse, or rest on inference" (Rutland, 1983, 129).

Several states in effect ratified the Constitution on condition that it be amended to include a bill of rights, and to this task James Madison applied his considerable talents in the first Congress to meet under the new Constitution. From his labors came the ten amendments ratified in 1791 and known collectively as the Bill of Rights. The first of these amendments reads:

> Congress shall make no law respecting an establishment of religion, or prohibiting the free exercise thereof; or abridging the freedom of speech, or of the press; or the right of the people peacefully to assemble and to petition the Government for redress of grievances.

The bundling of these various rights within a single amendment is far more than an act of literary economy. All of the rights described in the First Amendment deal with the right of the people to express themselves, to be free of state coercion in voicing their political and religious beliefs, their ideas, and even their complaints. One should remember that at the time when Madison drafted these amendments, religion and religious beliefs were important political issues. Madison had to win a *political* fight to get the Statute of Religious Freedom enacted, and similar political fights took place in other states as well. Not surprisingly, many of the First Amendment cases that have come before the Supreme Court since then have cut across the artificially imposed categories of speech and press and religion to deal more generally with the limits of governmental power to restrict a person's mind, and with the untrammeled right of expression.

The First Congress, the same one that approved the First Amendment, also reenacted the Northwest Ordinance. The Congress steadfastly identified education with religious education, as can be seen in its provisions for educating the Indians— one of the few educational efforts in which the federal government directly involved itself. Civilizing the natives meant propagating the gospel among them, an assumption that long dominated the federal government's view of and relations with the various tribes. In 1803 the Jefferson administration negotiated a treaty with the Kaskaskia Indians that included a provision that the United States support a Roman Catholic priest for seven years and erect a church for the tribe. Throughout the nineteenth century, Congress regularly appropriated funds to support reservation schools run by missionaries from several Christian sects.

DEVELOPMENT

Although today we place much of the credit for religious freedom on the First Amendment, in its own time the adoption of the Virginia Statute for Religious Freedom in 1786 marked a major step away from state support and enforcement of one particular religious belief and toward an open, tolerant society in which each individual could practice his or her own faith without fear of governmental coercion. Important and revolutionary as the disestablishment of the Anglican Church may have appeared at the time, the greater significance of the Statute lay in its assumption that religious matters were of a totally personal nature, beyond the legitimate scope of the state. Thomas Jefferson expressed this view when he wrote to his friend Martha Bayard Smith in 1816: "I never told my own religion, nor scrutinized that of another. I never attempted to make a convert, nor wished to change another's creed. I never judged the religion of others . . . for it is in our own lives and not our words that our religion must be read" (Adams, 1983, 376). The past two hundred years have seen the playing out of this idea, of keeping government and religion separate so as to allow each person the right to believe or not to believe, according to the dictates of individual conscience. This is not to say that religious prejudice has been absent in the United States. Catholics, Jews, and other groups have been the victims of discrimination; but this discrimination has been neither endorsed nor enforced by the state. Legal discrimination lasted a little while after the Revolution, and then faded away.

In the period between the Declaration of Independence and the establishment of government under the Constitution, several states moved in the direction of greater religious freedom. None went so far as Virginia (except Rhode Island, a pioneer in protecting individual conscience), and some resisted the trend. New England states continued to use tax monies for Protestant churches until the 1820s. Well before the Civil War, however, disestablishment and individual religious freedom had become hallmarks of the new nation, perhaps the brightest flame in the torch of opportunity that beckoned millions of immigrants from the Old World to the New. This did not mean that the United States was irreligious. As Justice William O. Douglas later wrote, "We are a religious people whose institutions presuppose a Supreme Being" (*Zorach v. Clauson* [1952]). As we shall see in the next chapters, it has been impossible to separate totally state action and individual conscience. The history of Jefferson's idea has been a constant reevaluation of where the line between church and state should be drawn. This has not been an easy task, and Justice Lewis F. Powell Jr., a great admirer of Thomas Jefferson, remarked that "Jefferson's metaphoric 'wall of separation' between Church and State has become 'as winding as the famous serpentine wall' he designed at the University of Virginia" (*Committee for Public Education and Religious Liberty v. Nyquist* [1973]).

The spirit of liberty that suffused the Declaration of Independence spread into several of the new states in the form of bills of rights, nearly all of which included references to religious freedom. Virginia, in fact, adopted its Declaration of Rights a few days before the Continental Congress proclaimed independence from Great Britain. Pennsylvania also quickly asserted the "unalienable right" of all men to worship God "according to the dictates of their own consciences and understanding," and condemned compulsory public worship and the required support of religion. But although no one who acknowledged "the being of God" should suffer loss of civil rights because of religious belief or practice, the new state constitution did establish such an acknowledgment as part of a test oath for membership in the Assembly. Would-be officeholders also had to declare their belief in the divine inspiration of the Old and New Testaments. In other words, these clauses usually removed disabilities from Catholics, but left atheists, Jews, and other non-Christians in a distinctly inferior position.

North Carolina's bill of rights, also adopted in 1776, disestablished the Anglican Church, but limited officeholders to Protestants and—perhaps echoing fears of the Catholic clericalism so well-known in Europe—precluded clergymen who occupied pulpits from holding any state office. Not until 1835 was the word *Protestant* changed to *Christian.* Jews continued to be excluded from office until 1868, when the post–Civil War constitutional revision finally did away with any reference to Christianity, although applicants for office still had to affirm their belief in God.

New York came closest to Virginia and Rhode Island in establishing religious freedom. The New York constitution of 1777 guaranteed the free exercise of "religious profession and worship . . . without discrimination or preference," although John Jay, later the nation's first chief justice, attempted unsuccessfully to limit the rights of Catholics, whom many Protestants at the time believed owed their primary loyalty to the Vatican. Jay did succeed in pushing through a requirement that all applicants for citizenship (a matter of state control until the Fourteenth Amendment was adopted in 1868) renounce "all allegiance and subjection to all and every foreign king, prince, potentate and State, in all matters ecclesiastical as well as civil." New York also excluded the clergy from public office, and although it disestablished the Anglican Church, it allowed the church to retain earlier royal grants of land. In 1784 a constitutional revision revoked these grants, but anti-Catholic prejudice then triumphed in the establishment of test oaths, which were not repealed until 1806.

In New York and the southern states the Anglican Church was relatively easily abandoned, as it long had been identified with the royal government; but in New England the established Congregational churches were of local origin, and their interests were strongly defended by influential elites. Connecticut did not write a new constitution in the revolutionary era, nor did it disestablish the churches; and not until 1818 did the state finally adopt a new constitution that included a religious freedom clause. Massachusetts, which had the most conservative declaration of rights of the thirteen original states, also did not disestablish the church despite a clause declaring that "no subordination of any one sect or denomination to another [should] ever be established by law." In fact, the state constitution of 1780 included a clause on the duty of religious worship, and disqualified Catholics from holding public office. How strongly the sentiment ran in New England in favor of tax support of religion can be seen in the comments of New Hampshire Senator Paine Wingate during a discussion of the state's proposed new constitution:

> By this paragraph in the Constitution it is admitted that it is for the public civil welfare and prosperity to support the Protestant teachers of reli-

gion, and that every member of society is bound to contribute his proportion for the general good of the whole; for the same reasons that
schools, and other means of useful instruction are supported at the public expense, and for the general benefit although each individual may not
immediately receive the same degree of advantage. (Bradley, 1987, 23)

Disestablishment, even in those states favorable to the idea, did
not always proceed smoothly. The Church of England was far
more than a parish church, and it held many large tracts of land,
called glebe lands, that had been given to it either by the Crown or
by colonial proprietors for support of the clergy and of good
works. Could a state deprive a religious corporation of its property as part of the state's disestablishment of religion? Courts in
general protected the religious corporation as well as property
rights, but their reasoning was often perplexing. Take, for example, Joseph Story's opinion in *Terrett v. Taylor* (1815), growing
out of a series of 1802 Virginia laws aimed at depriving the Episcopal Church (the successor to the Church of England) of special
privileges. One act held that all land belonging to the Church of
England at the time of the dissolution of British rule in 1776
devolved upon the people of the state, and it authorized the over-
seers of the poor to take the glebe lands when vacant and use the
proceeds for nonreligious purposes.

The Episcopal Church sued and eventually won in the U.S.
Supreme Court. There was little in either the Constitution or U.S.
common law relating to church rights to property, but there was a
general belief in property rights, both by individuals and compa-
nies. Justice Joseph Story construed that notion of property to
include religious bodies as well. The ruling that religious corporations had clear property rights that could not be infringed upon
by the state was reaffirmed a few years later in *Society for the
Propagation of the Gospel in Foreign Parts v. New-Haven* (1823),
and established a clear precedent for similar disputes over church-
owned property.

Most states, at the same time as they disestablished the Anglican Church, enacted a variety of constraints on other groups, primarily on Catholics, Jews, and nonbelievers. Maryland and South Carolina recognized Christianity in their constitutions, and several states passed legislation requiring citizens to contribute to religion although allowing them the choice of which church to support. Test oaths were also common. One can certainly discern a trend toward greater freedom of religion; but the revolutionary generation for the most part still considered religion so important a part of civil life as to justify some degree of state coercion for its support. Witness the third article of the Massachusetts constitution of 1780:

As the happiness of a people and the good order and preservation of civil government essentially depend upon piety, religion, and morality, and as these cannot be generally diffused through a community but by the institution of the public worship of God and of public instructions in piety, religion, and morality: Therefore, To promote their happiness and to secure the good order and preservation of their government, the people of this commonwealth have a right to invest their legisla ture with power to authorize and require, the several towns, parishes, precincts, and other bodies-politic or religious societies to make suitable provision, at their own expense, for the institution of the public worship of God and for the support and maintenance of public Protestant teachers of piety, religion and morality in all cases where such provision shall not be made voluntarily.

Religious tests for public office remained in effect in some states until after the Civil War. In many places one had to swear to a belief in a Christian religion—a requirement that barred Jews from public office. Maryland, however, allowed Jews to qualify by taking a special oath that they believed in a future state of rewards and punishments. Some states also debarred Catholics and atheists. Alexis de Tocqueville recorded a court case in which an atheist's testimony was rejected because he could not swear the appropriate oath. Gradually, however, the test oath disappeared in most of the country, not only for public office but for jury duty as well. The Oregon constitution of 1859, for example, prohibited religious tests for jurors and witnesses, and also forbade putting any questions to a witness regarding religious beliefs, lest it "affect the weight of his testimony." The Supreme Court finally declared test oaths unconstitutional in *Torcaso v. Watkins* (1961).

Today we would consider a law excluding the clergy from public office a violation of civil liberties, but Americans of the late eighteenth and early nineteenth centuries saw this as one means of separating church and state. Restrictions of this type appeared most frequently in the older, seaboard states, which remembered the days of established churches and ministerial meddling in politics. The younger, transmontane states, which had never known the problems of establishment or clerical politicking, rarely utilized this restraint. By the eve of the Civil War, most states had abandoned the practice.

Americans of the revolutionary and postrevolutionary generations were not opposed to religion, and in fact sought the fullest freedom for each person to worship as he or she chose. But the vast majority never believed in total separation of religion and the state, but only desired that the government should not favor one denomination above others. In what some people today consider a gross violation of the First Amendment, states and localities have always granted tax exemptions to church-owned property used for religious purposes. The practice began when government routinely offered preferences and direct support to religion, because the church provided theological support to maintain civil harmony. Since the adoption of separation, defenders of the tax exemption have pointed to the social, cultural, and philanthropic work of religious agencies to justify the policy. A true separation of church and state would, of course, do away with the practice; but most Americans see it as a harmless method of supporting religion and other not-for-profit institutions, and since all denominations can benefit, no one group receives any preference.

During the nineteenth century many states also enforced laws against blasphemy, on the grounds that by offending religious-minded people, blasphemy disturbed the public peace. In New York, for example, the state constitution guaranteed religious freedom, but a proviso added "the liberty of conscience hereby granted shall not be so construed as to excuse acts of licentiousness, or justify practices inconsistent with the peace and safety of the state." Chancellor Kent relied on this proviso in *People v. Ruggles* (N.Y. 1811) to uphold the conviction of a man who claimed that Jesus Christ was a bastard and his mother a whore. "We are a Christian people," the court declared, "and the morality of the country is deeply engrafted upon Christianity" (Finkelman, 2000, 43, 317).

In the most famous such case of the nineteenth century, Massachusetts imprisoned Abner Kneeland, a free-thinker who had published statements "scandalous, impious, obscene, blasphemous and profane . . . concerning God." A number of prominent churchmen, although obviously not in sympathy with Kneeland's views, nonetheless petitioned for his pardon on the grounds that his religious views had been restrained. The work for which Kneeland had been indicted and convicted was a near-academic piece in which he contrasted his own pantheistic views with those of the Universalist Church. But according to Chief Justice Lemuel Shaw, the very denial of a divine existence, regardless of the overall theological construct, was *per se* blasphemous (*Commonwealth v. Kneeland* [1838]; Levy, 1973, *passim*). Some states still have such laws on their books but have not enforced them for decades.

The most serious interference by state governments with religious liberty came in the form of restrictions on Catholics, Jews, and atheists. Test oaths have already been mentioned; but these groups suffered under other restrictions as well. Anti-Catholic sentiment in the United States stemmed directly from the post-Refor-

mation prejudices of western Europe, which viewed the Church in
Rome as a threat to secular independence. The Church in Europe
had been and would continue to be involved in affairs of the state,
for Church doctrine held that its responsibility for the care of souls
extended into all domains, temporal as well as spiritual. No one
could overlook the extensive political activity of many high church
figures, such as the Medici popes, Cardinal Richelieu in France, or
Cardinal Wolsey in England. By the time of the American colonization, the fear of a worldwide Catholic conspiracy directed from
St. Peter's had become a staple of Protestant thought, and it would
not truly disappear from the United States until the second half of
the twentieth century. (See, for example, "Alfred E. Smith On
Catholicism and Patriotism [1927]," and "John F. Kennedy on
Church and State [1960]," both in Chapter 6.)

For Catholics, an important struggle during the nation's early
decades involved the Church hierarchy's control over all aspects
of religious affairs, including church property—a practice that ran
counter to the American tradition of local, lay ownership of congregational tangibles. Most states passed special incorporation
laws to provide for supervision of church buildings and property
by lay-elected trustees; the Catholic Church insisted that its bishops determine such use and disposition. Pope Pius VII addressed
this issue directly in *Non Sine Magno* (1822), in which he wrote to
Bishop Marechal of Philadelphia that goods "which are offered
for divine worship, and for the support of the church, and its ministers, fall under the power of the Church," and that "since Bishops by divine ordination are those who are placed over the
church, therefore they cannot be excluded from the care, disposition, and supervision of these goods." Although the Church continued to press for clerical control, in the end it had to abandon
the effort; whatever might be said about state interference with
religion, the tradition of local, lay control triumphed in America.

Unfortunately, harsh and intemperate words were said on both
sides of this long-simmering dispute that inflamed existing preju-

dice and played into the hands of a rising anti-Catholic movement in the second quarter of the nineteenth century. The religious and secular press carried one article after another on such topics as "Is Popery Comparable with Civil Liberty?" Many of the writers well exceeded the limits of truth and decency. In the 1830s, a young girl dismissed from her job at the Ursuline convent in Charlestown, Massachusetts, told lurid and false tales of alleged goings-on within the convent walls that spread like wildfire. The town fathers then refused permission to bury two Catholic children in the Bunker Hill cemetery, stating that health regulations permitted the interment of Protestants but not of Catholics! On the night of 11 August 1834, a mob attacked the convent and burned it to the ground. The accused ringleaders were acquitted of the charge of arson by a local jury. When the bishop applied to the state legislature for funds to rebuild the convent, a new wave of anti-Catholic sentiment spread across the state.

Perhaps no other religious issue in the pre–Civil War era so inflamed public passion as the Catholic drive to secure public funds for parochial schools. In Europe, state support of religious schools was commonplace; in countries where both Protestants and Catholics operated academies, the state normally gave money to both, to be distributed on a per-student basis. In America at this time, however, the principle of separation precluded such support. In its state constitution of 1818, Connecticut became the first state to bar explicitly public funds for religious education. Connecticut's action became a model for other states, all of which adopted a similar constitutional prohibition. Congress in 1876 nearly adopted the Blaine Amendment, which would have prohibited the appropriation of state or federal funds to support religious education. Although President Grant endorsed the amendment, it failed to pass. It was reintroduced twenty more times over the next sixty years, and failed each time. In 1895, Congress at last approved a rider to an appropriation bill stating that public funds "should not be used for education in sectarian institutions."

Despite this language, Congress continued to support church-related schools on Indian reservations, claiming that the tribal trust funds were not public monies. The Supreme Court approved the practice in *Quick Bear v. Leupp* (1908), finding it neither a violation of the First Amendment nor of the 1895 statute (Finkelman, 2000, 387).

Catholics correctly claimed that state-supported public schools implicitly taught Protestant religious principles. In 1854, for example, the Supreme Court of Maine upheld a decision to expel an Irish Catholic child from a school for refusing to participate in a Protestant religious exercise (*Donahue v. Richards*). Public schools routinely taught from the King James version of the Bible, and the religious epigrams in the widely used Webster Speller embodied Protestant views. In the 1830s and 1840s the Catholic Church, primarily through its teaching orders, established numerous primary schools in order to protect Catholic children from the suspected proselytizing influence of public schools. By the 1850s, Catholic parochial schools made up the largest system of religious schools in the country, and so it remains today. During this same period, the drive for expansion of tax-supported common schools, led by Horace Mann of Massachusetts, gained enormous ground, and the Catholic hierarchy reasoned that since it shared the burden of teaching children, it should also share in tax revenues allocated for education.

Accompanied by a growing Catholic immigration to the United States, the parochial school issue triggered a massive nativist movement against what was perceived to be the Pope's attempt to gain control of the country. Various political parties sprang up, committed to thwarting the alleged papist conspiracy. Anti-Catholic revolts occurred in several cities, including Philadelphia, the "city of brotherly love," as lurid stories circulated widely about the evils of the Church and the persecution it inflicted on those attempting to escape its clutches. The climax came in the Know-Nothing Party, which grew out of the nativist Order of the Star Spangled Banner. Article II of the 1856 Know-Nothing platform declared that the party's object was "to resist the insidious policy of the Church of Rome, and other foreign influences against the institutions of our country, by placing in all offices . . . none but native-born Protestant citizens" (Johnson, 1978, 22–23).

The Know-Nothing Party declined as rapidly as it had arisen. Responsible citizens recognized the danger of religious bigotry carried to such extremes. As former president John Tyler of Virginia wrote to his son, the Know-Nothing hatred of Catholics seemed unfounded, for "that sect seems to me to have been particularly faithful to the Constitution of the country, while their priests have set an example of noninterference in politics." Abraham Lincoln also denounced the Know-Nothings, and declared that if the movement gained ground, he would prefer to move to Russia, "where despotism can be taken pure, and without the base alloy of hypocrisy" (Urofsky, 1986, 4). The anti-Catholic sentiment faded, however, as public attitudes focused more and more on the evil of slavery and the Civil War it caused.

Fortunately, anti-Catholic prejudice did not achieve statutory expression, although Congress and the state legislatures received a flood of petitions urging them to "do something" about the Papists. Moreover, Catholics won an important victory in 1813 for themselves and for the cause of religious liberty. A Jesuit priest, Father Anthony Kohlmann, had been handed stolen goods by a thief after the culprit had repented and confessed his sins, and Father Kohlmann had then returned the property to its rightful owner. The police summoned Father Kohlmann and wanted him to name the burglar. He refused, claiming that he could not repeat information given to him under the seal of confession. An essential component of Catholic doctrine is the sacrament of confession; and for centuries, matters discussed by priest and penitent in the confessional booth had been considered sealed and beyond the reach of secular inquiry.

In the court case that followed, the four judges of the Court of General Sessions of New York City, as well as the counsels for both sides, were Protestant. In his argument in defense of Father Kohlmann, Richard Riker interpreted religious freedom in a very broad sense, one that modern readers will find familiar. Since at that time the First Amendment did not apply to the states, Riker based his argument on the free exercise provision of the New York State constitution. "Religious liberty was the great object which they had in view," he declared:

> They felt that it was the right of every human being, to worship God according to the dictates of his own conscience. They intended to secure, forever, to all mankind, without distinction or preference, the free exercise and enjoyment of religious profession and worship. They employed language commensurate with that object. It is what they have said. . . .
>
> Now, where is the liberty of conscience to the Catholic, if the priest and the penitent be thus exposed? Has the priest the liberty of conscience, if he thus be coerced? Has the penitent the liberty of conscience, if he is to be dragged into a court of justice, to answer for what has passed in confession? . . . Do they freely enjoy the sacrament of penance? If this be the religious liberty, which the [New York] constitution intended to secure—it is perplexing as the liberty which, in former times, a man had of being tried by the water ordeal, where, if he floated he was guilty—if he sunk he was innocent. (Urofsky, 1986, 15–16)

The court unanimously upheld the principle of confessional sanctity; and in 1828 the New York legislature gave statutory enforcement to the old common law doctrine of priest-penitent confidentiality. Over the years, other states have enacted similar laws. The Supreme Court of Nebraska, in *Hill v. State* (1901), upheld that state's statute, declaring that confession must be made "in confidence of the relation and under such circumstances as to imply that it should forever remain a secret in the breast of the confidential advisor." Although Catholics alone have confession as a rite, the idea of confidentiality surrounding communications between a person and his or her spiritual adviser, be it priest, minister, rabbi, or imam, has long been accepted in both statutory and common law in most of the country. What started as a defense of one religion's practices spread to enhance the freedom of conscience for all. Slowly the Old World view of Catholics as disloyal pawns of a foreign potentate began to fade, although anti-Catholic prejudices remained evident through the middle decades of the twentieth century, especially during the candidacies of two Catholics for the presidency, Alfred E. Smith in 1928 and John F. Kennedy in 1960.

Although Protestants did not fear a Jewish conspiracy (in fact, the early Puritans admired Judaism), Jews also suffered from centuries-long religious bigotry. The New World, because it was "born free," did not have to overthrow the medieval institutions that had sanctioned anti-Semitism; nonetheless, seeds of prejudice did cross the Atlantic, and the small Jewish communities that dotted the seaboard had to overcome their fruits. And like the Catholics, Jews received aid from Protestants who firmly believed that in the United States no room existed for the type of religious persecution so prevalent in Europe. "Happily, the Government of the United States," as George Washington told the Jewish community of Newport, "which gives to bigotry no sanction, to persecution no assistance, requires only that they who live under its protection should demean themselves as good citizens" (Fitzpatrick, 1931, 31:93–94). Jefferson and Madison offered similar assurances that in this country religious freedom—not tyranny—would be the rule.

But many Americans considered this a Protestant Christian country, and if they feared a Catholic conspiracy, they felt less than comfortable with Jews as well. In Maryland, as in other states, the postrevolutionary Bill of Rights was a stride toward religious freedom, but only for Christians. In 1818, Thomas Kennedy, a devout Christian, began the fight to extend religious liberty to Jews as well. He could not get the so-called Jew bill passed by the legislature until 1822; and because the bill involved a constitutional amendment, it had to pass the subsequent assembly as well. Religious toleration thus became the central issue of the 1823 election, and nativists, already upset by the growing Catholic presence in America (despite the fact that Maryland had been founded as a Catholic refuge), came out to defeat Kennedy and the bill.

Perhaps because Jews were so small a group, or because other states looked upon Jews as good citizens, or because the blatant prejudice offended many citizens, the case for Jewish rights received strong support from other states. Newspaper editorials called upon Maryland to redeem itself. The influential *Niles Register* wrote: "Surely, the day of such things has passed away and it is abusive of common sense, to talk about republicanism, while we refuse liberty of conscience in matters so important as those which have relation to what a man owes his Creator" (Urofsky, 1986, 5). The pressure had its effect, and Maryland gave full political and religious rights to Jews in 1826 (Eitches, 1971, *passim*). Within a year, Solomon Etting and Jacob Cohen successfully ran for the Baltimore City Council. By the Civil War, only North Carolina and New Hampshire still restricted Jewish rights, and those disabilities disappeared in 1868 and 1877 respectively.

On the federal level, the bill establishing a government for the District of Columbia included provisions for chartering churches but, probably due to an oversight, did not mention non-Christian houses of worship. There had been no Jewish community in Washington at the time of its founding; but by the 1850s a small congregation had come into existence, and it petitioned Congress for an act allowing it to build a synagogue. Senator Lewis Cass of Michigan championed the cause, and called the existing act with its limitations to Christian churches "an act of gross injustice, and . . . a disgrace to our jurisprudence" (Urofsky, 1986, 5). Had there been a test case, a court might well have found the old law in violation of the First Amendment; but Congress quickly remedied the defect.

Jews did, however, suffer from one form of state-sponsored discrimination, namely the enforcement of Sunday closing laws, the "blue laws" common in many American states and cities. These laws posed an economic burden on observant Jews, who could not, because of their religious scruples, work on Saturday. Even less observant Jews found it irksome that the Christian weekly calendar was applied to all. Beginning in 1816, Jews went to court to challenge such laws in Virginia, South Carolina, Maryland, Ohio, Pennsylvania, Louisiana, and elsewhere, but their efforts were in vain (Diner, 1992, 151). Many Americans probably did not even recognize the discrimination implicit in such laws, seeing the United States as a Christian nation and therefore believing that its citizens ought to rest on the Lord's Day (Przbyszewski, 2000, *passim*). The Sunday blue laws eventually were repealed—not because of pressure from Jewish lawsuits, but because national habits changed as women entered the marketplace in the 1960s, and families needed Sunday for shopping and errands. As late as 1961, a divided Supreme Court upheld Sunday closing laws, interpreting them as a legitimate exercise of the state's police power in its efforts to assure one and all a day of rest (*Braunfeld v. Brown*).

By the Civil War, then, the idea of religious freedom had expanded significantly from the early issue of disestablishment. Nearly all states had adopted and implemented bills of rights to provide individual liberty of conscience and, despite a pervasive sense that America was primarily a Protestant Christian nation, had removed civil and political disabilities from Catholics and Jews. The federal government, bound by the First Amendment, had never attempted to intrude into religious matters, and in religious matters as in political affairs, the United States appeared to those suffering from oppression in the Old World, as Lincoln put it, as "the last best hope of freedom."

After the war, however, the United States underwent significant economic, social, and demographic changes, and with them came new problems of religious freedom. With the passage of the Fourteenth Amendment in 1868, the strictures of the First Amendment gradually came to be applied to the states as well. New questions relating to religious freedom arose, questions that might well have seemed incomprehensible to the founding generation; and as Alexis de Tocqueville noted long ago, in America nearly all important issues ultimately become judicial questions. Starting in the latter part of the nineteenth century, and with ever greater frequency in the twentieth, the courts had to resolve difficult questions relating to the meaning of the two religion clauses in the Fourteenth Amendment. How they answered these questions will be explored in the next two chapters.

REFERENCES

Adams, Dickinson W., ed. 1983. *Jefferson's Extracts from the Gospels.* Princeton: Princeton University Press.

Alley, Robert S., ed. 1985. *James Madison on Religious Liberty.* Buffalo, NY: Prometheus Books.

Bradley, Gerard V. 1987. *Church-State Relationships in America.* Westport, CT: Greenwood Press.

Curry, Thomas J. 1986. *The First Freedoms: Church and State in America to the Passage of the First Amendment.* New York: Oxford University Press.

Diner, Hasia R. 1992. *A Time for Gathering: The Second Migration, 1820–1880.* Baltimore: Johns Hopkins University Press.

Eitches, Edward. 1971. "Maryland's Jew Bill." *American Jewish Historical Quarterly* 60: 258–279.

Finkelman, Paul, ed. 2000. *Religion and American Law: An Encyclopedia.* New York: Garland.

Fitzpatrick, John C., ed. 1931–1944. *The Writings of George Washington.* 39 vols. Washington, DC: Government Printing Office.

Hutchinson, William T., et al., eds. 1962–1981. *The Papers of James Madison.* 17 vols. Chicago: University of Chicago Press.

Johnson, Donald Bruce. 1978. *National Party Platforms, 1840–1976.* Rev. ed. 2 vols. Urbana: University of Illinois Press.

Levy, Leonard W. 1994. *The Establishment Clause: Religion and the First Amendment.* 2d ed. Chapel Hill: University of North Carolina Press.

Levy, Leonard W., ed. 1973. *Blasphemy in Massachusetts: Freedom of Conscience and the Abner Kneeland Case—A Documentary History.* New York: Da Capo Press.

Malone, Dumas. 1948. *Jefferson the Virginian.* Boston: Little, Brown & Company.

Miller, William Lee. 1986. *The First Liberty: Religion and the American Republic.* New York: Alfred A. Knopf.

Noonan, John T., Jr. 1998. *The Lustre of Our Country: The American Experience of Religious Freedom.* Berkeley: University of California Press.

Pfeffer, Leo. 1953. *Church, State, and Freedom.* Boston: Beacon Press.

Poore, Benjamin Perley, ed. 1877. *The Federal and State Constitutions, Colonial Charters, and Other Organic Laws of the United States.* 2 vols. Washington, DC: Government Printing Office.

Przybyszewski, Linda. 2000. "The Religion of a Jurist: Justice David J. Brewer and the Christian Nation." *Journal of Supreme Court History* 25: 228–242.

Rutland, Robert Allen. 1983. *The Birth of the Bill of Rights, 1776–1791.* Rev. ed. Boston: Northeastern University Press.

Urofsky, Melvin I. 1986. *Two Hundred Years of Mr. Jefferson's Idea: The Expansion of Religious Freedom in the United States.* Richmond: Virginia Department of Education.

West, John G., Jr. 1996. *The Politics of Revelation and Reason: Religion and Civil Life in the New Nation.* Lawrence: University Press of Kansas.

Wright, Louis B. 1957. *The Cultural Life of the American Colonies, 1607–1763.* New York: Harper & Row.

3

THE ESTABLISHMENT
CLAUSE

HE FIRST AMENDMENT to the Constitution contains the following instructions concerning the government's activity with regard to religion: "Congress
shall make no law respecting an establishment of religion, or prohibiting the free exercise thereof." The first of these injunctions is
known as the Establishment Clause (examined closely in this
chapter), and the second, as the Free Exercise Clause (discussed in
Chapter 4). For most of the first 150 years following the adoption
of the Bill of Rights, Congress obeyed the first injunction; as a
result, very few cases implicated the Establishment Clause, and
those had little value as legal precedent. This situation began to
change in 1947, after the Supreme Court ruled that both religion
clauses applied not only to the federal government but also to the
states. Justice Hugo L. Black, in his majority ruling in *Everson v.
Board of Education*, expounded at length on the historical development of religious freedom in the United States, and concluded:

> The "establishment of religion" clause of the First Amendment means
> at least this: Neither a state nor the Federal Government can set up a

church. Neither can pass laws which aid one religion, aid all religions, or prefer one religion over another. Neither can force nor influence a person to go to or remain away from church against his will or force him to profess a belief or disbelief in any religion. No person can be punished for entertaining or professing religious beliefs or disbeliefs, for church attendance or nonattendance. No tax in any amount, large or small, can be levied to support any religious activities or institutions, whatever they may be called, or whatever form they may adopt to teach or practice religion. Neither a state nor the Federal Government can openly or secretly, participate in the affairs of any religious organization or groups and vice versa. In the words of [Thomas] Jefferson, the clause against establishment of religion by law was intended to erect "a wall of separation between church and State."

In this paragraph we find the root rationale for nearly every religion case decided by the Court in the past fifty years, whether it involves the Establishment Clause (the government is accused of performing a religious function) or the Free Exercise Clause (the government is accused of restricting individuals' adherence to some practice). And with that rationale, *Everson* began one of the most contentious public policy debates of our time: namely, whether the Establishment Clause forbade any and all governmental aid to religion, or whether it allowed aid on a nonpreferential basis (that is, money could be given, provided the government did not give any sect preference over the others).

HISTORICAL ORIGINS

Nearly all scholars believe that at its adoption in 1791, the Establishment Clause in the minds of the American people clearly meant that the government could not prefer a single church over all others. This went further than a simple prohibition of the establishment of one denomination as the official church of the state, as the Church of England had been and still was in the mother country. People as diametrically opposed philosophically on this issue as James Madison and Patrick Henry agreed on the meaning of establishment: "When Madison spoke of prohibiting a 'national' religion, he was not opening the door to the federal government's aid to religion in general. When Henry called for a ban on the establishment of one sect 'in preference to others,' he was not proposing that the federal government have the power to tax for a national general assessment" (Curry, 1986, 213). This is not to say that all American citizens and states agreed on whether there should be state support of religion; rather, no matter what their point of view, they agreed on what an establishment of religion meant. They also agreed that the Establishment and Free Exercise clauses taken together meant that the new national government should have no power over religion in *any* matter.

Scholars today for the most part agree that even as Americans of the time defined establishment as a preference of government for one religion, they also did not approve of nonpreferential government aid. Although modern proponents of nonpreferentialism have pointed to a number of eighteenth-century sources to support their position, scholars overwhelmingly agree that this is a "fundamentally defective interpretation" of the Establishment Clause by advocates who are "innocent of history but quick to rely on a few historical facts" (Levy, 1986, 91). The Americans who drafted and ratified the First Amendment had no knowledge of nonpreferentialism; the colonial experience had been that of established churches, one denomination sanctioned by and supported by the government. At the same time, Justice Black's evocation of Thomas Jefferson's "wall of separation" metaphor suffers equally from historical anomalies. As a result, the debate's constant appeal to history may have limited value, telling us less about what the founding generation believed than about where current advocates stand on governmental aid.

Both separationists (those who believe that there should be no aid in any form to any religious body) and accommodationists (those who argue that aid can be given on a nonpreferential basis) start from the flawed assumption that those who drafted and ratified the First Amendment's Establishment Clause recognized and differentiated between preferential and nonpreferential schemes of governmental aid to religion. The appeal to history at the very least requires that those involved in the two debates—the one taking place in the twentieth and twenty-first centuries, and the other in the eighteenth—be arguing about the same things. Just because eighteenth-century Americans agreed that establishment meant no government preference to a single sect, it does not follow that they also agreed that this implied government could provide aid to religion on a nonpreferential basis. Neither does it mean that they agreed that government could not provide *any* aid to religion.

Much of the argument for nonpreferentialism centers on the debate in the Senate over the wording of the amendment. James Madison had drafted the original amendments in the House of Representatives, and the relevant phrase had simply been that "Congress shall make no law establishing religion." The Senate rejected this wording, and in its place adopted an amendment reading "Congress shall make no law establishing articles of faith or modes of worship." Advocates of nonpreferentialism rely on this proposal to argue that most members of Congress, in both houses, wanted only to bar the government from preferring one religion above all others, but did not oppose government aid to religion given out in a nonpreferential manner. This would make sense except for the fact that everyone—Federalists and Antifederalists alike—agreed that the federal government should have no role whatsoever to play in religious matters, and that the religion clauses had but one purposes: to reinforce that prohibition. It is illogical and flies against historical fact to assume that people who fervently opposed any governmental role in religion would nonetheless favor allowing the government to provide aid to one and all (Levy, 1994, 94–104).

This argument is reinforced if we look at states like New Jersey, Delaware, and North Carolina that not only adopted provisions opposing the establishment of any particular religion but also barred the state from supporting religion on any basis. As Robert Curry has noted, "History provides not a speck of evidence to show that, in accepting a definition of establishment of religion as a government preference for one religion over others, Americans signaled a willingness to accept the idea of government assistance to religion on a broader, nonpreferential basis—that, although government could not prefer one religion, it could support all religions" (Finkelman, 2000, 164).

Moreover, although the First Amendment prohibited Congress from establishing a religion, it did not prohibit the states from doing so; and if one hopes to find any evidence that the founding generation supported nonpreferential aid, then one could look at the states, which had the option to provide such aid. But in each instance where one finds a state extending support, the record shows that the practice was not new—as nonpreferentialism would have been—but the extension of customs dating from the colonial era. Massachusetts and other New England states (with the exception of Rhode Island) provided funds for Congregational churches according to the selections made in individual towns. Anglicans could designate their taxes for the Anglican (now Episcopalian) church. Baptists and Quakers were exempted from the tax; they did not pay it, nor did they receive any funds. This practice, which was established before the Revolution and continued long after the ratification of the First Amendment, bears little resemblance to the modern notion of nonpreferentialism.

A more striking instance of how the revolutionary generation viewed religion and the public purse can be seen in Virginia. After the disestablishment of the Anglican Church, Patrick Henry led a drive by which certain tax revenues would be distributed to churches according to the wishes of the taxpayer; that is, Baptists could direct their pro rata funds to Baptist churches, Episcopalians to their church, etc. This produced one of the great policy debates of the nation's early years, with James Madison heading the opposition through the justly famous "Memorial and Remonstrance," which in turn led to the adoption of Thomas Jefferson's bill for religious freedom (see James Madison, "Memorial and Remonstrance" [1786]; and the Virginia Statute for Religious Freedom [1786], both in Chapter 6).

Although one can safely conclude that the founding generation opposed the use of public funds to support either an established church or all churches nonpreferentially, this does not mean that they opposed religion. In fact they saw religion as one—perhaps the chief—basis of public virtue, which in turn was the foundation of good citizenship. At the time of the adoption of the Constitution and the Bill of Rights, the vast majority of Americans were Protestant Christians. Although belonging to many denominations, they nonetheless shared certain basic assumptions, such as that Sunday was the Lord's Day and should be a day of rest. Public prayer, in schools and at almost every public gathering, was taken for granted, and the fact that a state assembly or the U.S. House of Representatives began each session with a prayer or a reading from the Bible seemed the most natural thing in the world. Early Americans perceived no wall of separation between religion and the state, or even between the sphere of religious matters and that of secular concerns. In times of crisis and of thanksgiving, the state not only could but should declare a day of prayer. This was part of the culture, and no one gave a second thought to it. But they clearly drew a distinction between the cultural intertwining of religion and the state, and the financial support of religion by the state. Thomas Jefferson may have seen total separation as a democratic ideal, but that view would have found little support among his contemporaries.

A view more reflective of how people in the late eighteenth and early nineteenth centuries viewed the interaction between government and religion may be found in the writings of Justice Joseph

Story, who is considered the greatest constitutional theorist of the early Republic. His *Commentaries on the Constitution* went through many editions, and both lawyers and judges considered this work authoritative in interpreting the meaning of the Constitution. In his *Commentaries,* Justice Story wrote, "The right of a society or government to interfere in matters of religion will hardly be contested by any persons, who believe that piety, religion, and morality are intimately connected with the well being of the state, and indispensable to the administration of civil justice." The various aspects of a religion, including the promulgation of doctrine, the belief in a future of rewards and punishments, the cultivation of individual morality, "can never be a matter of indifference to any well ordered community.... It is impossible for those, who believe in the truth of Christianity, as a divine revelation, to doubt, that it is the especial duty of government to foster, and encourage it among all the citizens and subjects" (see Chapter 6). But the "real difficulty," as Story acknowledged, involved ascertaining the appropriate limits of that governmental interference. Although most Americans today would not agree with Story's approval of extensive government involvement with religion, we are still debating the nature of the boundary between the two.

If accommodationists have distorted the historical record in their efforts to gain nonpreferential state support, separationists are equally guilty of misreading the past. In *Everson* Justice Black produced a historical record that seemingly left no room for either financial support or for cultural intertwining; and the debate since then has in many ways played variations on the themes that Black first enunciated in *Everson.*

Yet the *Everson* decision contained an interesting twist. The New Jersey statute in question had authorized school districts to make rules providing transportation for students, "including the transportation of school children to and from school other than a public school, except such school as is operated for profit." One local board had allowed reimbursement to parents of parochial school students for fares paid by their children on public buses when going to and from school. A taxpayer in the district had challenged the payments as a form of establishment.

After his lengthy review of the history and language of the clauses, which implied that no form of aid—direct or indirect— could be tolerated under the Establishment Clause, Justice Black concluded that the reimbursement plan did not violate the First Amendment, which required only that

> the state be a neutral in its relations with groups of religious believers and nonbelievers; it does not require the state to be their adversary. . . . [The] legislation, as applied, does no more than provide a general program to help parents get their children, regardless of their religion, safely and expeditiously to and from accredited schools.
>
> The First Amendment has erected a wall between church and state. That wall must be kept high and impregnable. We could not approve the slightest breach. New Jersey has not breached it here.

The opinion evoked dissenting views from four members of the Court. Justice Robert Jackson noted that Black, after marshaling every argument in favor of a total separation of church from state, weakly allowed that no breach of the wall had occurred. "The case which irresistibly comes to mind as the most fitting precedent," Jackson noted, tongue in cheek, "is that of Julia who, according to Byron's reports, 'whispering "I will ne'er consent,"—consented.'" Justice Wiley Rutledge traced the logic of Black's historical argument to the inevitable conclusion that if "the test remains undiluted as Jefferson and Madison made it, [then] money taken by taxation from one is not to be used or given to support another's religious training or belief, or indeed one's own. The prohibition is absolute." Despite the 5–4 vote, all nine members of the Court agreed with Black's larger theory—that the Establishment Clause required a total separation of church and state, and that this prohibition applied not only to Congress but to the states as well—

even though some of them disagreed with his application of that theory in this particular case.

Black's position was based on the principle of neutrality. One might easily fail to distinguish this principle from that of nonpreferentialism, but in fact the two are significantly different. In a nonpreferential milieu, the state may give out monies and leave it to the churches to decide how to use those funds, within certain broad parameters. In a neutral environment, the state makes a particular benefit available and allows everyone to use it. In this instance the benefit was subsidized transportation for schoolchildren; and while everyone knew that the overwhelming majority of beneficiaries attended Roman Catholic schools, in fact anyone whose children attended a private school could avail themselves of the benefit. Under this theory, Black could adhere to the separation metaphor and still recognize that in certain areas the state could play a role that affected religion, provided it did so in a fair, consistent, and neutral manner, and if it did not provide funds directly to religious activities.

The application of the religion clauses to the states—known as the "incorporation" of the First Amendment through the Due Process Clause of the Fourteenth Amendment—raised a number of issues that neither Black nor his colleagues considered in *Everson*. Congress had been prohibited from either establishing a religion or interfering with the free exercise of religion; and with the exception of its treatment of the Mormons (see Chapter 4), it had adhered to the intent of the Framers. But implicit in the Constitution and in the First Amendment had been the assumption that although Congress had no role to play in religion, the states did have such a role. As we have seen, a number of states had continued to fund churches after the Revolution, had imposed test oaths, and had discriminated against Jews, Catholics, and atheists.

Even though most of those practices had disappeared by 1947, both the mental proclivity and the opportunity for greater interaction between church and state still existed in the state governments. Nearly all of the cases that we will examine in this chapter involve efforts by the states to provide some form of support, financial or otherwise, to church-related endeavors—usually to schools. Although in the nineteenth century Protestant America looked askance at Catholic schools, by the late twentieth century Catholics and Jews had become more assimilated into the mainstream culture, and many people believed that if states had the responsibility to support education, then for the benefit of the children it made sense to support religious schools. In addition, the physical presence of churches and synagogues in towns and cities made interaction inevitable. Everyone assumed that the local police would help out with traffic at funerals or after services, that religious buildings would be exempt from property taxes, and so on. Whatever the Supreme Court said about a wall of separation, most Americans knew that in their hometown that wall had a lot of holes in it.

By the time the Court heard its next religion cases, Justice Black had apparently moved to the position Rutledge had suggested: that the prohibition had to be absolute. In a 1948 decision, *McCollum v. Board of Education,* the Court struck down a "released-time program" in Illinois, in which classrooms in the public schools were used for one hour of religious instruction per week. Local churches and synagogues could send instructors to teach the tenets of their religion to students whose families approved. Children whose parents did not want them to participate continued their secular studies during this hour. To Justice Black, writing for the 8–1 majority, the issue could not have been clearer. "Not only are the state's tax-supported public school buildings used for the dissemination of religious doctrines, the State also affords sectarian groups an invaluable aid in that it helps to provide pupils . . . through use of the state's compulsory public school machinery." This was the first case in which the Supreme Court used the Establishment Clause to strike down a state law.

Felix Frankfurter concurred separately, in part because he did not want the opinion to rely on *Everson,* in which he had dissented. In his opinion, Frankfurter made it very clear that he believed the rule applied only to the Illinois system, where religious classes actually met in public school facilities. This close intertwining of a clearly religious activity with the public school precincts gave the religious instruction the imprimatur of the state, and this constituted the violation of the First Amendment. Underlying Frankfurter's opinion, although not explicit in it, was his view of the public school as an Americanizing and unifying force, a place where children of all backgrounds develop a common American identity and outlook. He feared that religious education in the schools would destroy this force for cohesion and in its place put divisiveness (Urofsky, 1991a, 168). He also recognized, however implicitly, the cultural role religion played in American life; he favored that as well, but not in the schools.

Responses to the decision varied. The Attorney General of Virginia, Lindsay Almond, declared that released-time programs, even those that used public classroom space, might continue, a ruling applauded both by school officials and by church leaders. In northern states where the released-time program followed the Illinois model, with religious instruction taking place in school classrooms, there appears to have been general compliance with the Court's decision. But where local officials could differentiate between the Illinois model and their own, no matter how fine the distinction, the programs remained in operation (Wasby, 1970, 127).

Four years after *McCollum,* the Court issued what might be called its first "accommodationist" ruling on the Establishment Clause, that is, one in which it tried to accommodate the needs of religion by bending, however slightly, the absolute bar that Black had spoken of in *Everson* and *McCollum.* To continue the released-time program, a number of states had moved religious instruction off school property; New York officials, for example, established times in which students left the school grounds and went to nearby religious facilities for instruction. Taxpayers challenged the program on grounds that it still involved the state in promoting religion. The authority of the school supported participation in the program; public school teachers policed attendance; and normal classroom activities came to a halt so that students in the program would not miss their secular instruction.

Justice William O. Douglas's opinion for the six-member majority in *Zorach v. Clauson* indicated that the Court had heard the public outcry over the *McCollum* decision, in that he went out of his way to assert that the Court was not antagonistic to religion. "We are," he intoned, "a religious people whose institutions presuppose a Supreme Being." Although the First Amendment prohibition against an establishment of religion was "absolute," this did not mean that "in every and all respects there shall be a separation of Church and State." He went on to argue that historically the Amendment had been interpreted in a "common sense" manner, because a strict and literal view would lead to unacceptable conclusions: "Municipalities would not be permitted to render police or fire protection to religious groups. Policemen who helped parishioners into their places of worship would violate the Constitution." Such a view would make the state hostile to religion, a condition also forbidden by the First Amendment.

Douglas distinguished between the Illinois and New York programs primarily on the basis that the former had taken place on school property (a direct aid forbidden by the Constitution) and the latter off the school grounds (indirect assistance not forbidden). Justices Black, Jackson, and Frankfurter dissented. Black put the issue in its bluntest form: New York "is manipulating its compulsory education laws to help religious sects get pupils. This is not separation but combination of Church and State." Justice Jackson, who sent his own children to private church schools, objected as strenuously. The schools did not close down during the released-time period but suspended teaching so that students who did not choose to attend religious instruction would not get ahead of the "churchgoing absentees." The school, with all the power of the state behind it, thus "serves as a temporary jail for a pupil who will not go to Church."

These first three modern opinions, *Everson, McCollum,* and *Zorach,* left very little clear, other than that the religion clauses now applied to the states as well as to the federal government. In all three cases the majority as well as the dissenters had seemingly subscribed to the "wall of separation" metaphor and to the absolute nature of the First Amendment prohibitions; but they had disagreed on how "absolute" the separation had to be. Justice Black, after fudging in *Everson,* moved to an absolutist view that characterized his interpretation of the First Amendment for the remaining two decades through which he sat on the high court. Justice Douglas, who joined Black in that view, also abandoned the temporizing stance he uncharacteristically took in *Zorach.* It appeared likely, therefore, that a majority of the Court would take a strict stand when the next case came before it. And that case touched on a theme near and dear to many Americans—the daily prayers that began the public school day.

SCHOOL PRAYERS

For many years, ritual marked the beginning of each school day all across America. Teachers led their charges through the pledge of allegiance, a short prayer, singing of "America" or "The Star-Spangled Banner," and possibly some readings from the Bible. The choice of ritual varied according to state law, local custom, and the preferences of individual teachers or principals. But most Americans saw nothing wrong with this; it constituted part of America's historical heritage, an important cultural artifact of, as Justice Douglas wrote, "a religious people whose institutions presuppose a Supreme Being." In New York, the statewide Board of Regents had prepared a "nondenominational" prayer for use in the public schools. The brief invocation read: "Almighty God, we acknowledge our dependence upon Thee, and we beg Thy blessings upon us, our parents, our teachers and our Country." After one district had directed that the prayer be recited each day, a group of parents challenged the edict as "contrary to the beliefs, religions, or religious practices of both themselves and their children." The New York Court of Appeals, the state's highest tribunal, upheld the school board, providing that it did not force any student to join in the prayer over a parent's objection.

The Supreme Court, however, reversed this decision in *Engel v. Vitale* (1962). In his opinion for the 6–1 majority, Justice Black (who had taught Sunday school for more than twenty years) held that the entire idea of state-mandated prayer, no matter how religiously neutral, was "wholly inconsistent with the Establishment Clause." A prayer by any definition constituted a religious activity, and the First Amendment "must at least mean that [it] is no part of the business of government to compose official prayers for any group of the American people to recite as part of a religious program carried on by government." Black went on to explain what he saw as the philosophy behind the Establishment Clause:

> [Although] these two clauses may in certain instances overlap, they forbid two quite different kinds of governmental encroachment upon religious freedom. The Establishment Clause, unlike the Free Exercise Clause, does not depend upon any showing of direct governmental compulsion and is violated by the enactment of laws which establish an official religion whether those laws operate directly to coerce nonobserving individuals or not. . . . When the power, prestige and financial support of government is placed behind a particular religious belief, the indirect coercive pressure upon religious minorities to conform to the prevailing officially approved religion is plain. But the purposes underlying the Establishment Clause go much further than that. [Its] most immediate purpose rested on the belief that a union of government and religion tends to destroy government and degrade

religion. [Another] purpose [rested upon] an awareness of the historical fact that governmentally established religions and religious persecutions go hand in hand.

Black believed that the content of the prayer, its actual words,
and its alleged denominational neutrality had no relevance to the
case. Prayer was by nature religious, and in promoting prayer the
state had violated the Establishment Clause, fostering a religious
activity that the state itself determined and sponsored. The actual
test that Black would apply, however, remained unclear. The
Court apparently did not rely on or require a finding of coercion
to support an Establishment Clause violation. Nor did the Court
find that the prayer furthered the interests of any one denomination. Rather, Black's majority opinion focused almost entirely on
the state's promotion of religious practices in the public school,
and he concluded that this activity by itself violated the First
Amendment.

Justice Douglas concurred with the decision, but his opinion
shows how far he had traveled both from *Everson* and *Zorach*. He
acknowledged that the former case seemed "in retrospect to be
out of line with the First Amendment," and further, that "Mr. Justice Rutledge stated in dissent what I think is desirable First
Amendment philosophy." The man who had approvingly noted
the practice of starting sessions of the Court or of legislative bodies with prayers was arguing that even those prayers ought to be
ruled unconstitutional. Douglas had come to believe that a violation of the Establishment Clause might be entailed not only in an
establishment of religion but even in the government's financing
of a religious activity. Only Potter Stewart dissented. He quoted
Douglas's *Zorach* opinion that "we are a religious people whose
institutions presuppose a Supreme Being." The practice in New
York and elsewhere did no more than recognize "the deeply
entrenched and highly cherished spiritual traditions of our
Nation," as did the opening of Court and Congress with prayer.

The *Engel* decision unleashed a firestorm of conservative criticism against the Court that, although it has abated from time to time, has never died out. In the eyes of many, the Court had struck at a traditional practice that served important social purposes even if it occasionally penalized a few nonconformists or eccentrics. Taken in concert with the Court's recent decisions regarding segregation, it appeared as if Chief Justice Earl Warren and his colleagues were hell-bent on overturning decades, even centuries, of cherished American values. One newspaper headline screamed "COURT OUTLAWS GOD." An outraged Billy Graham thundered, "God pity our country when we can no longer appeal to God for help!" Francis Cardinal Spellman of New York denounced *Engel* as striking "at the very heart of the Godly tradition in which America's children have for so long been raised" (Weaver, 1967, 261; Schwartz, 1983, 441).

The level of abuse heaped upon the Warren Court for this decision reached its peak in Congress. "They put the Negroes in the schools," Representative George W. Andrews of Alabama complained, and "they have driven God out" (Murphy, 1972, 392). Senator Sam Ervin of North Carolina charged that the Supreme Court "has made God unconstitutional," and Congressman Williams of Mississippi condemned the decision as "a deliberately and carefully planned conspiracy to substitute materialism for spiritual values and thus to communize America" (Pfeffer, 1967, 469). In an obvious swipe at the Court, the House of Representatives voted the following September to place the motto "In God We Trust" behind the Speaker's chair, and a number of congressmen and senators introduced constitutional amendments to reverse the ruling (Beaney and Beiser, 1964, 478).

The Court had its champions as well. Liberal Protestant and Jewish agencies saw the decision as a significant move to divorce religion from meaningless public ritual and to protect its sincere practice. The National Council of Churches, a coalition of liberal and orthodox denominations, praised the *Engel* decision for protecting minority rights, and the Anti-Defamation League applauded the "splendid reaffirmation of a basic American principle" (Sorauf, 1976, *passim*). President John F. Kennedy, who had been the target of vicious religious bigotry in the 1960 campaign (from many of the same groups that attacked the Court), urged Americans to support the decision. He commented at a news conference (*New York Times*, 28 June 1962, 12):

> We have, in this case, a very easy remedy. And that is, to pray ourselves. And I would think that it would be a welcome reminder to every American family that we can pray a good deal more at home, we can attend our churches with a good deal more fidelity, and we can make the true meaning of prayer much more important in the lives of all of our children.

The President's commonsense approach captured the Court's intent in *Engel*. The majority did not oppose either prayer or religion but did believe that the Framers had gone to great lengths to protect individual freedoms in the Bill of Rights. To protect the individual's freedom of religion, the state could not impose any sort of religious requirement, even in an allegedly "neutral" prayer. As soon as the power and prestige of the government are placed behind any religious belief or practice, according to Justice Black, "the inherently coercive pressure upon religious minorities to conform to the prevailing officially approved religion is plain."

The firestorm unleashed by *Engel* only increased when the Court handed down its decision in *Abington v. Schempp* the following year. This case involved a challenge to a Pennsylvania law requiring that "at least ten verses from the Holy Bible shall be read, without comment, at the opening of each public school on each school day." The law also stated, "Any child shall be excused from such Bible reading, or attending such Bible reading, upon the written request of his parent or guardian." In addition, the students were to recite the Lord's Prayer in unison. This time Justice Tom Clark, normally considered a conservative, spoke for the 8–1 majority in striking down the required Bible reading. He built upon Black's comment in *Engel* that the neutrality commanded by the Constitution stemmed from the bitter lessons of history, which recognized that a fusion of church and state inevitably led to persecution of all but those who adhered to the official orthodoxy.

Recognizing that the Court would be confronted with additional Establishment Clause cases in the future, Clark attempted to set out rules by which lower courts could determine when the constitutional barrier had been breached. He recommended the following test:

> What are the purpose and the primary effect of the enactment? If either is the advancement or inhibition of religion then the enactment exceeds the scope of legislative power as circumscribed by the Constitution. That is to say that to withstand the strictures of the Establishment Clause there must be a secular legislative purpose and a primary effect that neither advances nor inhibits religion.

In this last sentence, Clark set out the first two prongs of what would later be known as the *Lemon* tripartite test, which the Court has used to evaluate all Establishment Clause challenges. The legislation (1) had to have a secular purpose, and (2) it could neither advance nor inhibit religion. (The third prong, added in *Lemon v. Kurtzman* [1971], prohibited excessive entanglement between the government and the religious agency.) Clark also sought some criteria for distinguishing between the two religion clauses. The Establishment Clause prohibited state sponsorship of religious activities, whereas the Free Exercise Clause prohibited state compulsion. "The distinction between the two clauses is apparent—a violation of the Free Exercise Clause is predicated on coercion while the Establishment Clause violation need not be so attended."

In this case there had been no formal coercion, since students could be excused from the exercises, but Clark correctly noted that nonparticipating students inevitably called attention to themselves by their absence and thus invited retribution in the form of peer ostracism. Justice William J. Brennan in his concurrence quoted his teacher, Felix Frankfurter: "Non-conformity is not an outstanding characteristic of children. The result is an obvious pressure upon children to attend." The Court apparently held that the coercion needed to trigger a Free Exercise claim might be indirect, resulting from the situation created by the government's actions.

In response to Justice Stewart's criticism that in protecting the religious freedom of a few dissenters the Court violated the free exercise rights of the majority who wanted to read the Bible (an early and telling example of how the two religion clauses can sometimes be in conflict), Clark declared that the Court

> cannot accept that the concept of neutrality, which does not permit a State to require a religious exercise even with the consent of the majority of those affected, collides with the majority's right to free exercise of religion. While the Free Exercise Clause clearly prohibits the use of state action to deny the rights of free exercise to anyone, it has never meant that the majority could use the machinery of the State to practice its beliefs.

Only Stewart dissented. He argued against both the necessity and the desirability of having a single constitutional standard. "Religion and government must interact in countless ways," most of which were harmless and should not be subject to a "doctrinaire reading of the Establishment Clause." He chastised the majority for violating the Free Exercise claims of those who wished their children to start the school day with exposure to the Bible. Stewart also objected to the majority's assumption that every involvement by the state necessarily led to coercion; such an assumption would cast suspicion on every type of activity in which one might find some religious component, and he wanted to shift the burden of proof from a presumption of coercion to an actual showing that it had occurred.

Stewart's dissent reflected the feeling of many people that their rights had been restricted for the sake of a few kooks. Moreover, the Court seemed to say (despite Clark's specific assurances to the contrary) that the Bible could no longer be read in the schools. Americans had been reading the Bible ever since the Puritans had established schools in Massachusetts in the 1630s; generations of settlers had taught their children to read, poring over the Bible by the light of oil lamps. Public officials from the president down often took the oath of office with one hand on the Bible. How could it be religious coercion to require schoolchildren to hear a few verses from the Good Book each day? One still finds many people who cannot understand why the Court should find the Bible so threatening.

The discussion might begin with the question "Which Bible?" Most statutes or regulations called for the King James version of the Bible, which is anathema to Catholics. Jews object not only to the New Testament but also to the translation of certain passages in the Old Testament. Leaving aside the poetic qualities of this seventeenth-century masterpiece, it is riddled with errors in translation from the ancient Hebrew and Greek, and many of the resulting passages are unacceptable under current dogma in several Protestant sects. Given the patterns of recent immigration, one might well ask whether the Koran or any one of several far eastern texts might also be demanded in some schools.

Another consideration is that whether one uses the King James or the Revised Standard or the Douay or the Jewish Publication Society or the Good News version, one is dealing with a book that is essentially a religious appliance. It is designed to promote belief and faith, and that is what every Jewish and Christian sect uses it for. It is the Good Book, the Holy Scriptures, and its official reading over the school public address system cannot fail but to remind listeners of its reading from the pulpit as part of a religious service.

The fact that a majority—even a large majority—is not affronted by prayer in the school or Bible reading is, to a large extent, irrelevant in constitutional adjudication. The purpose of the Bill of Rights is not to protect the majority, but the minority. As Oliver Wendell Holmes once said of freedom of speech, it is not for the speech we agree with, but for the speech we detest. Freedom of religion, like freedom of speech, does protect the majority as well as the minority; but we need not invoke it when nearly everyone is Protestant and subscribes to middle-class values. The protection of the First Amendment is invoked when the majority attempts to use the power of the state to enforce conformity in speech or in religious practice. Very often, to protect that one dissident, that one disbeliever, the majority may be discomfited; that is the price the Founding Fathers declared themselves willing to pay for religious freedom.

Civil libertarians also express concern about state agencies, especially schools, advocating particular religious doctrines or practices as society grows ever more heterogeneous. Those who do not accept the norms of the majority, as Justice Sandra Day O'Connor wrote in a later case, "are outsiders, not full members of the political community" (*Wallace v. Jaffree* [1985]). The dissenters are merely tolerated, because of their religion or lack of it, and they are made to feel like inferior members of society—a situation the Framers wanted to avoid.

Finally, although fundamentalist religious groups attacked the Court's decisions in *Engel* and in *Schempp*, many mainstream religious bodies soon came to see that the Court had actually promoted religion rather than subverted it. The framers of the renowned "Memorial and Remonstrance" that Virginia Baptists addressed to the General Assembly in 1785 believed that not only the state's antagonism but also its efforts at assistance could damage religion and religious liberty. Their intellectual descendants have argued along similar lines, believing that the state can never help religion but only hinder it. To establish any form of state-sanctioned religious activity in the schools threatens to introduce denominational hostility. Moreover, the sincere believer does not need the state to do anything for him except leave him alone; those with confidence in their faith do not need Caesar's assistance to render what is due to God.

EVOLUTION AND CREATIONISM

One might describe the cases arising from school prayer and Bible reading as instances in which a benign majority unthinkingly imposed its views, unaware that the results restricted the religious freedom of a minority. In the third major Establishment Clause case of the Warren Court, however, a local majority deliberately attempted to establish its views as official dogma, in defiance of what the rest of the country believed.

One of the most famous battlegrounds of the 1920s between the forces of tradition and modernism was the Scopes "Monkey Trial" in Dayton, Tennessee. The legislature had passed a bill outlawing the teaching of evolution in the state's schools. Civic boosters in Dayton had gotten a young teacher named John Scopes to test the law, and the American Civil Liberties Union then provided a lawyer for Scopes. To sleepy Dayton came William Jennings Bryan to thunder against science and uphold the literal interpretation of the Bible, and Clarence Darrow, the greatest trial lawyer of his time, who spoke for science, reason, and intellectual toleration. Darrow exposed Bryan as a narrow-minded bigot, but the local jury still convicted Scopes. The Tennessee Supreme Court reversed the conviction on a technicality, which forestalled Darrow's plan to appeal to the Supreme Court. The law therefore remained on the Tennessee statute books. Similar laws could be found in other "Bible Belt" states, but they remained essentially unenforced and in many cases nearly forgotten (Larson, 1997, *passim*).

An Arkansas statute forbade teachers in state schools to teach the "theory or doctrine that mankind ascended or descended from a lower order of animals." An Arkansas biology teacher, Susan Epperson, sought a declaratory judgment on the constitutionality of this statute (Irons, 1988, 205–230). The Arkansas Supreme Court, aware of anti-evolution sentiment within the state, evaded the constitutional issue entirely by expressing "no opinion" on "whether the Act prohibits any explanation of the theory of evolution or merely prohibits teaching that the theory is true."

Whatever the nature of its specific prohibition, the law ran afoul of the Constitution. The Court voted unanimously to strike down the Arkansas statute as a violation of the Establishment Clause. Justice Abe Fortas concluded that the Arkansas law "selects from the body of knowledge a particular segment which it proscribes for the sole reason that it is deemed to conflict with a particular religious doctrine, that is, with a particular interpretation of the Book of Genesis by a particular religious group." The Court, having found what it considered sufficiently narrow grounds on which to base a ruling, ignored the larger issues of academic freedom.

Justices Black and Stewart concurred in the result, although they considered the statute void due to vagueness. In addition, Black pointed to several "troublesome" First Amendment questions that in his view had been raised by the majority opinion. For example, would a state law that forbade all teaching of biology be constitutionally different from one that compelled a teacher to teach that only one particular theory were true? Black argued that it would; but he also asserted that no case could be made for a teacher's constitutional right to teach theories—be they economic, political, sociological, or religious—that the school's elected and appointed managers did not want discussed. Black's comments along these lines foreshadowed a number of issues that would come before the Court again in later years.

Black's most interesting point involved the question of whether the majority opinion actually achieved the constitutional desideratum of "religious neutrality." If the people of Arkansas considered evolutionary theory anti-religious, did the Constitution nonetheless require the state to permit the teaching of such a doctrine? Had the Court infringed on "the religious freedom of those who consider evolution anti-religious doctrine?" The record did not indicate whether Arkansas schools taught a literal reading of the Genesis creation story. If they did not, then could the state law prohibiting the teaching of evolution be considered a neutral statute, if it removed a contentious issue from the classroom? He saw no reason "why a State is without power to withdraw from its curriculum any subject deemed too emotional and controversial for its public schools."

Black's reasoning, or rather its obverse, proved the vehicle by which anti-evolutionists in Arkansas and elsewhere sought to bypass the *Epperson* ruling a generation later. Instead of removing biology and evolutionary theory from the schools, they added "creation science," which advocated the Biblical narrative as supported by allegedly scientific evidence, and required that any school that taught evolution had to give "equal time" in the classroom to "creation science."

Louisiana's Balanced Treatment Act of 1982 reached the Supreme Court in *Edwards v. Aguillard* (1987). Justice Brennan spoke for a 7–2 majority in striking down the statute as a violation of the Establishment Clause. He denounced the stated purpose of the law—to advance academic freedom—as a sham, since the sponsors of the bill had made it quite clear during the legislative debate that they wanted to inject religious teachings into the public schools. As Brennan phrased it, the predominant purpose was "to advance the religious viewpoint that a supernatural being created mankind," and to make the science curriculum conform with that religious viewpoint. The evidence showed that the primary purpose of the bill had been to advance a particular religious doctrine, and by that fact alone, that the law violated one prong of the *Lemon* test and was therefore unconstitutional.

Justice Lewis Powell, joined by Sandra Day O'Connor, concurred. Powell also traced the history of the law, but in greater detail than did the majority opinion, and came to the conclusion that the act did not withstand constitutional scrutiny. But Powell wanted to emphasize that if by coincidence a harmony existed between material taught in a public school and the doctrines of some religions, that by itself would not violate the Constitution. The First Amendment is not implicated unless some entity attempts to use the schools to advance a particular religious belief.

Only Justice Antonin Scalia, joined by Chief Justice William Rehnquist, dissented. Scalia has never been big on legislative history as a means of statutory interpretation, and he objected to the supposed intent of the framers of the law as a reason for nullifying it. He looked only at the statute, and in doing so saw nothing that exceeded the legitimate bounds of state authority or conflicted with the Constitution.

The *Epperson* and *Aguillard* cases are two of only four decisions in which the high court has invalidated a law under the Establishment Clause because of a clear lack of secular purpose. The other two are *Stone v. Graham* (1980), in which the Court struck down a law requiring schools to post the Ten Commandments, and *Wallace v. Jaffree* (1985), another case in which a law that seemed neutral turned out on closer examination to be an effort to reintroduce prayer into the public schools. In Alabama there had been three laws designed to provide a moment of silence. The first merely indicated that there should be silence; the second allowed students to meditate silently or to pray; and the third required teachers to lead prayers when students requested them. (These cases are discussed in greater detail below.)

These cases raise interesting questions and implicate some Free Exercise issues as well. Should a law be voided merely because it lacks a secular purpose, with no other Establishment Clause objection in view? For example, if the legislation for the moment of silence indicated that students could do what they wanted during that moment, so long as they did it quietly, and that they could pray during that period, should that by itself be enough to nullify the law? As a teacher, I know that students often pray in my class, usually before an exam. I personally do not see this as a violation of the First Amendment, since there is no coercion, it is done silently, and no one makes a big deal of it. If that sentiment is embodied in a law, does it cross the line?

There are many initiatives that have religious purposes to them. The Prohibition movement grew out of a religious crusade; and the presence of many ministers surely lent more than a tinge of religiosity to the civil rights movement. Efforts to limit abortion are driven by religious objections to the practice, as is the opposition to stem cell research. The overt religiosity of Joseph Lieberman in the 2000 presidential campaign offended some Americans but appealed to many others. As Michael McConnell suggests, a constitutional interpretation that looks down on religiously inspired policies makes second-class citizens of those to whom religion is a key element in civic life, whose view in this regard was common to our nation's founding generation (McConnell, 1992, 115). It is unlikely that the issue will go away. As in the cases of school prayer and Bible reading, the true believers will keep seeking some way to get their views grafted onto the school curriculum.

AID TO PAROCHIAL SCHOOLS

At about the same time that the Court was expanding the reach of the Establishment Clause in regard to state laws, the federal government raised new problems through its greatly increased aid to education programs. In January 1965, Lyndon B. Johnson proposed $1.5 billion in grants to primary and secondary schools, both public and private, secular and parochial. With Johnson exerting all of his famed political arm-twisting, the Elementary and Secondary Education Act passed both houses of Congress by wide margins, and the president signed it into law in April. By 1968 Congress was funneling more than $4 billion a year into elementary and secondary schools. Part of this sum went to church-related schools with high percentages of children from low-income families. The aid to those schools immediately drew accusations of a First Amendment violation, and opponents set about finding a way to challenge the act in the courts.

The Supreme Court had first encountered the problem of federal aid to religious institutions in *Bradfield v. Roberts* (1899), in which it had sustained a federal appropriation for the construction of a public ward in a hospital owned and operated by a nursing order of the Roman Catholic Church. The Court did not address the issue of whether aid to religious institutions is permissible, because it held that the hospital did not constitute a religious body. In the 1947 *Everson* case, the Court had upheld a form of state aid the primary purpose of which had been to benefit children. The Johnson administration hoped to prevent a challenge to the act from coming before the Court, and it defeated an effort by Senator Sam Ervin of North Carolina to amend the measure so as to allow taxpayer suits to test its constitutionality. (Under the doctrine of *Frothingham v. Mellon* [1923], taxpayers lacked standing to challenge the government's disposition of its tax revenues.)

In *Flast v. Cohen* (1968), however, Chief Justice Warren reversed a lower court ruling based on *Frothingham* and permitted a taxpayer to initiate a suit against the law. The policy considerations behind the earlier decision no longer applied, and in any event, the "barrier should be lowered when a taxpayer attacks a federal statute on the ground that it violates the Establishment and Free Exercise clauses of the First Amendment." By this decision, the Chief Justice ensured that the Supreme Court would have a significant voice in the debate over educational policies. Although most of those cases did not reach the Court until after Warren retired, the late 1960s saw the enactment of dozens of state and federal programs to aid education, many of which included parochial schools as beneficiaries. In the cases testing these laws, opponents would argue that they violated the Establishment Clause, and supporters would rely on the child benefit theory that had been enunciated in *Everson.*

The Warren Court itself heard only one of these cases: a challenge to a 1965 New York law mandating that local school boards furnish textbooks from a state-approved list to nonprofit private schools within their jurisdictions. Technically, the boards merely "loaned" the books and retained title to them; in fact, the books would remain in possession of the private schools until the school boards wrote them off for wear and tear. In *Board of Education v. Allen* the Court upheld the law on what today is known as the pupil benefit theory, which derived directly from Justice Black's opinion in *Everson.* The loan of the texts, according to Justice Byron White, did not aid religion, but benefited the individual student, whether at a public or parochial school, and that, he claimed, had been the primary intent of the legislature. Given these facts, the Court found no violation of the Establishment Clause.

White's opinion drew strong protests from Black and Douglas, and a partial dissent from Harlan. Black claimed that the New York arrangement represented exactly the type of involvement he had warned about in *Everson.* Douglas entered a lengthy opinion that argued the centrality of textbooks in education and the intrinsically sectarian nature of parochial schools. But White had not gone as far as the dissenters charged; in an opinion described as "laconic" and "cloudy," he left the door open for the Court to reverse itself without embarrassment. White handed down no grand rulings on the meaning or scope of the Establishment Clause, only narrow approval of a particular program.

Because there had been so little Establishment Clause jurisprudence before 1953, the Warren Court dealt with the question almost as if it were a blank slate; as a result, its landmark decisions on prayer, Bible reading, and the teaching of evolution in the schools captured public attention and struck many Americans, especially those who believed that religion belonged in schools, as wrong. As the Court moved to the right with the appointments made by Richard Nixon, Ronald Reagan, and George Bush, political and religious conservatives expected, indeed demanded, that the Court reject these earlier rulings. Some members of the Court appeared quite willing to do so, and espoused an accommodationist view based on what came to be known as a jurisprudence of original intent. Original intent, and what the religion clauses actually meant, occupied a central place in popular and academic debates over the Court in the last three decades of the twentieth century.

Justice Black in *Everson v. Board of Education* (1947) had expounded at length on the historical development of the Establishment Clause and had concluded that the clause against establishment of religion by law had been intended to erect "a wall of separation between church and State." Black's opinion became the basis for all Establishment Clause cases for the next fifty years. It also opened the door to the flourishing debate over the original intent of the Framers in drafting not only the First Amendment but the Constitution as a whole, and how justices today ought to interpret that document.

Edwin Meese, who served as attorney general in the second Reagan administration, led the campaign for a strict adherence to what he called a "jurisprudence of original intention," in which the courts would determine exactly what the Framers had meant, and interpret the Constitution accordingly. He believed that the Founders had left a clear record of exactly what they meant when they had drafted the Constitution and the first ten amendments, and that the current court had to follow that intent in its interpretations. Meese and other conservatives also believed that this original intent had never been to establish a high wall of separation, but rather to foster cooperation between church and state in such a way that no sect received preferential treatment over another (Meese, 1985, 23, 26).

Aside from the question of historical justification, at the core of the problem is one's view of the Constitution and its role in American government (Ely, 1980, *passim*). Advocates of original intent believe that the vision of the Framers is as good today as it was two hundred years ago and that any deviation from that view is an abandonment of the ideals that have made this country free and great. Defenders of judicial activism agree that courts ought not amend the Constitution, but believe that for the document to remain true to the intent of the Framers, it must be interpreted in the light of two lamps: the spirit of the Framers and the realities of modern society. They believe that the founding generation never intended to put a straitjacket on succeeding generations; rather, they set out a series of ideals, expressed through powers and limitations, and deliberately left details vague so that those who came after them could apply those ideals to the world they lived in. This debate has framed the high court's handling of religion cases since the early 1980s.

The jurisprudence of strict separation espoused by Justices Black, Douglas, Warren, and Brennan has certainly been eroded. Yet despite the presence on the bench of such strong accommodationists as Justices Warren Burger, Rehnquist, and Scalia, in many areas the ideal of strict separation is still strong.

Following the Elementary and Secondary Education Act of 1965, Congress and the states passed dozens of educational aid programs that benefited parochial schools. The question is whether these programs violated the First Amendment. One should keep in mind that even the most absolutist champions of separation recognize that some accommodations must be made in the interest of furthering the goals of the Free Exercise Clause. On the other hand, strong advocates of accommodation recognize that some separation, perhaps even a great deal, is required to make sure that religion does not take over government, nor government, religion.

Purists call for a total wall of separation forbidding any form of governmental aid, even passive support such as tax exemptions. They claim that any aid leads to entanglement: the government is obliged to ensure that its money is spent lawfully and effectively, and therefore it must be involved in church affairs whenever religiously affiliated agencies receive state or federal aid. At the other end of the spectrum are those who insist that the First Amendment never meant that the government could not aid churches. They see the Establishment Clause as no more than a prohibition against the government's favoring one denomination over the others. The wall of separation, they claim, is no more than Jefferson's personal belief, a belief that the Framers did not espouse. (The phrase appears nowhere in the Constitution or Bill of Rights.) By this view, all state aid to parochial schools is legitimate, provided that it is available on an equal basis to all denominations.

THE *LEMON* TEST

The Warren Court's decisions had made it clear that parochial schools could not expect state aid for the teaching of religion, but *Allen* held out the hope that they might receive government money for secular subjects. Under the pupil benefit rule, the Court had upheld bus transportation and the loan of textbooks; might not this philosophy be extended to cover the actual costs of instruction in history, mathematics, or science? The launching of Sputnik in 1957 triggered an enormous public clamor for better education, and many parents, dissatisfied with the public schools, saw religious schools as an attractive alternative. Why shouldn't tax monies be used to support school systems that provided good education to children? The students, and not religious doctrine, would benefit. This argument commanded the support of a number of justices during the Burger years, and in some cases it found a majority.

The Warren Court had handed down two tests in Establishment Clause cases—legislation had to have a secular purpose, and it had to neither advance nor inhibit religion. In *Walz v. Tax Commission* (1970), the Court added a third. The case involved a challenge to the real estate tax exemptions traditionally granted by state and local governments to property used solely for religious purposes. Chief Justice Burger wrote for a near unanimous Court (only Justice Douglas dissented), justifying the exemption as an effort to promote free exercise by sparing religion the burden placed on private profit-making institutions. In his opinion, though, Burger warned against "an excessive government entanglement with religion." One year later, the Chief Justice added this entanglement rule to the first two, thereby devising the three-pronged test that governed all subsequent Establishment Clause cases.

Meanwhile, Rhode Island enacted legislation providing supplemental salary payments to parochial school instructors who taught secular subjects. Pennsylvania had in place a somewhat different scheme, in which the state "purchased" secular educational "services" from private and parochial schools. Both plans specifically prohibited payment for religious education, and required use of state-approved texts for secular subjects. In *Lemon v. Kurtzman* (1971) the Court struck down both state plans on the grounds that they violated the Establishment Clause.

Chief Justice Burger set out what became known as the *Lemon* test: "First, the statute must have a secular legislative purpose; second, its principal or primary effect must be one that neither advances nor inhibits religion; finally the statute must not foster an excessive government entanglement with religion." The Chief Justice's opinion could not have pleased strict separationists more; for in examining the two schemes, he hit upon nearly every objection raised by those opposed to state aid. His statement that "government is to be entirely excluded from the area of religious instruction and churches excluded from the affairs of government" seemed a solid buttress for the wall of separation. Moreover, in talking about the political divisiveness that might develop along religious lines, Burger echoed James Madison's views in the 1785 "Memorial and Remonstrance."

In articulating the three-pronged test, the Chief Justice seemed to be sending several messages. First, he was signaling that proponents of the pupil benefit theory could not rely on the limited application of that doctrine in *Everson* and *Allen* to justify further support. Second, he was providing lower courts a clear and easily applied constitutional rule that could be used in an anticipated flood of litigation resulting from literally hundreds of state and federal programs.

The Court, however, also indicated that it would apply the rule in a discretionary manner; on the same day it handed down *Lemon,* it also decided *Tilton v. Richardson,* in which it approved federal construction grants to church-related colleges for buildings devoted exclusively to secular purposes. With somewhat questionable reasoning, a plurality of the Court held that religious indoctrination was not a substantial purpose of these schools, and that college students were not as susceptible to religious teachings as younger pupils. Applying the *Lemon* test, the Chief Justice did not find excessive entanglement, because only minimal inspection would be needed to ensure the secular usage of the buildings.

The Burger Court now had its rule, and one that could be used either to prohibit or approve state aid to religious schools. In cases over the next fifteen years, nearly every majority and minority opinion invoked the *Lemon* rule, often with strikingly opposite conclusions. Some of this unpredictability stemmed from shifting alignments among the justices; but by the early 1980s, one could find three fairly distinct groupings on the bench.

Justices John Paul Stevens, Brennan, and Thurgood Marshall most strongly supported separation, and believed the *Lemon* test too permissive. Stevens suggested abandoning the test altogether and resurrecting "the 'high and impregnable' wall between church and state constructed by the Framers of the First Amendment." At the other extreme stood Justices White and Rehnquist, frequently joined by the Chief Justice. White proved the most consistent supporter of aid to parochial education, and apparently had no qualms about public money indirectly supporting religious instruction. In the middle stood Justices Harry Blackmun, Lewis Powell, and Potter Stewart, who often split on whether the *Lemon* test had been violated or whether it was even applicable.

THE BURGER COURT AND SCHOOL AID

Although the Supreme Court has wide discretion over which cases it chooses to accept, in a broader sense its agenda is set by society. Growing pressure from advocacy groups seeking to strengthen parochial schools led sympathetic legislatures to enact laws providing that aid. Following the 1971 cases, state governments tried a variety of measures either to meet the *Lemon* criteria or to get around them. State aid was an issue the Court could not avoid.

In the spring of 1972, with four Nixon appointees on the bench, the Court ruled on a variety of state efforts to aid religious education. In *Levitt v. Committee for Public Education and Religious Liberty*, Chief Justice Burger spoke for an 8–1 Court in striking down a New York law designed to reimburse nonpublic schools for services mandated by the state. One provision of the statute allowed for the disbursement of $28 million on a per capita basis, with no requirement that the schools account for the monies or show any relationship between the monies received and the actual costs. The Court had no difficulty here, since New York had failed to establish any safeguards to ensure that the services were in fact completely secular and fully divorced from religious instruction.

Justice Powell delivered three other Establishment Clause decisions that came down the same day as *Levitt*. Powell had quickly established himself as the Court's resident authority on education because of his extensive experience on the Richmond city and Virginia state boards of education; he also appreciated the legacy of two other Virginians, James Madison and Thomas Jefferson, regarding the separation of church and state.

In the first case it appeared that Powell would join White as an accommodationist, when he spoke for a 6–3 majority in upholding the South Carolina Educational Facilities Authority Act in *Hunt v. McNair*. The state had created a bond authority similar to that already in existence in many other states, to help colleges finance badly needed construction. Under the scheme, the authority issued bonds to finance the project; the school then conveyed title to the authority, which held it until the school had paid off the debt. Unlike some other states, South Carolina permitted the authority to finance construction at church-related schools; but the statute specifically prohibited support for buildings to be used for any form of sectarian instruction or religious services. In addition, the authority's power to intervene in school management was strictly limited to ensuring that adequate financial arrangements existed to pay off the debt. For the majority of the Court, these provisions met the *Lemon* test.

Powell upheld the statute, and did so under *Lemon*, at the same time refining the primary effect test to make the rule more precise. A program would now be considered to have a primary effect of advancing religion if the school receiving aid were so sectarian in nature that it would be impossible to isolate its secular functions. State aid to fund a primarily sectarian activity in an otherwise secular setting would also be considered a constitutional violation. Powell then used this analysis in *Committee for Public Education and Religious Liberty v. Nyquist* to strike down all three sections of a New York law aimed at supporting various forms of aid to parochial schools.

One provision provided between $30 and $40 per student per year to maintain and repair facilities of schools in low-income areas. Relying on *Tilton*, Powell ruled that if "the State may not erect buildings in which religious activities are to take place, it may not maintain or renovate them when they fall into disrepair." The second section of the law provided tuition grants of $50 to $100 per pupil for families with annual incomes under $5,000. Again, Powell ruled that the state may not do indirectly what it is forbidden to do directly. A state could not make outright grants to parochial schools; neither could it make indirect payments in the form of tuition assistance. The third provision allowed tax credits for families with annual incomes between $5,000 and $25,000. Powell again looked past the form to the substance: Tax credits, like the tuition grants, would aid institutions pervasively sectarian in nature; thus, this provision also violated the *Lemon* test.

Although separationists applauded this decision, they misunderstood Powell if they considered him firmly in their camp. Previous cases did allow for some forms of public aid to sectarian institutions, and Powell believed that total separation was neither possible nor desirable:

> As a result of these decisions and opinions, it may no longer be said that the Religion Clauses are free of "entangling" precedents. Neither, however, may it be said that Jefferson's metaphoric "wall of separation" between Church and State has become "as winding as the famous serpentine wall" he designed at the University of Virginia.

The basic premise remained intact, and the burden always rested upon the state to prove that excessive entanglement did not result from its aid. Neither Powell nor the majority of the Burger Court accepted the notion that Douglas and Black had espoused, that the First Amendment required a total separation. The Establishment Clause decisions do not satisfy the desire for a simple black-letter test; they are pragmatic efforts to find some way to permit limited aid without subverting the intent of the First Amendment. As a result, the Burger Court majority tended to state broad principles, such as the *Lemon* test, and then focus on the particular facts of the case.

In *Meek v. Pittenger* (1975), for example, the Court dealt with another Pennsylvania effort to bypass the *Lemon* entanglement barrier. A new statute allowed public school employees to provide to students in private schools an extensive range of services such as counseling, speech and hearing therapy, and testing for exceptional or disadvantaged pupils. The state, in addition, provided material and equipment such as maps, overhead projectors, and laboratory supplies. Pennsylvania claimed that the new law did not entangle the state in the affairs of religion, because public school employees would provide the services, and because the materials and equipment were related entirely to secular subjects.

With Justice Stewart writing for the majority, the Court struck down all but one provision of the law. To observe the Establishment Clause requirements, the state would have to ensure that none of the public school teachers taught religion, whether in math or history; and there would be excessive entanglement if the state had to oversee its own people to make sure they remained religiously neutral. Although Stewart certainly addressed the facts of the case, his reasoning appears more than a little sophistic. Public school teachers are not supposed to teach religion in any event, so why would the state have to exercise any more, or any less, supervision of a math teacher to make sure she did not teach religious doctrine in St. Joseph's than in P.S. 35? The Court also struck down the material aid, with the exception of textbook loans, which it upheld on the basis of *Allen*.

But the near unanimity of *Levitt* had been shattered. Stewart spoke for only a plurality of the Court in his decision; Brennan, Marshall, and Douglas joined him in those parts that struck down the aid, but they dissented in the approval of the textbook loans. Brennan called it a "pure fantasy" to believe that the loan program did not benefit the school. Chief Justice Burger and Justice Rehnquist joined White, who until then had been the chief and often the lone accommodationist on the bench, in strong dissent. Henceforth there would be at least three members of the Court willing to allow at least limited public support for religious schools. And at least two members of the majority, Blackmun and Powell, believed that aid in certain forms might not violate the Establishment Clause.

Taking its cue from this decision, Ohio carefully crafted a plan whereby public school personnel performed speech, hearing, and other diagnostic services on parochial school premises and provided remedial and therapeutic services off premises. In addition, the state furnished textbooks for secular subjects, and reimbursed private schools for materials, equipment, and field trips. The state drew a parallel between these services and programs and those that it provided to all public school pupils in Ohio; by moving the remedial services off of parochial school grounds, it believed that it avoided the entanglement problem.

A divided Court agreed in *Wollman v. Walter* (1977). Teaching religion, a main fear in these cases, is less likely to take place in administering a standardized test or in diagnosing a learning problem. Any form of regular classroom activity, even in remedial programs or secular subjects, seemed to open the possibility of proselytizing. Powell, Blackmun, Stewart, and John Paul Stevens (who took Douglas's seat in 1975) accepted the state's argument that remedial services off of school grounds avoided the entanglement problem. They were joined by the three accommodationists, Burger, Rehnquist, and White. Brennan and Marshall found a constitutional violation no matter where the state offered remedial services to parochial school students, and Brennan took a strict separationist stance that even denied the validity of the diagnostic services. The divisions on the Court confounded those who sought some simple rule; for many, the Court's decisions often seemed to rely on hair-splitting.

A Resurgence of Fundamentalism

Fundamentalist religious groups constituted a highly vocal part of the conservative coalition that carried Ronald Reagan into the White House in the 1980 election. Reagan shared the platform at fundamentalist Christian rallies with Jerry Falwell, called himself a "born-again Christian," and declared that "it is an incontrovertible fact that all the complex and horrendous questions confronting us at home and worldwide have their answer in that single book"—the Bible. Reagan also announced that he had "a great many questions" about evolution, and believed the biblical version of creation ought to be taught in the schools as well as Darwinian theory. Reagan promised Catholic groups that when he became president he would ask Congress for legislation authorizing tax credits to those paying for private tuition.

Once Reagan was in office, these issues were put on the back burner; but throughout the eight years of his presidency, he seemed more than willing to lend his support to fundamentalist demands, especially the demand for a constitutional amendment to permit prayer in schools. Reagan called for a return to "that old time religion and that old time Constitution," and charged that the First Amendment had been twisted "to the point that freedom of religion is in danger of becoming freedom from religion." In addition, the new president espoused what he called a "pro-religion" program, which included financial support for religious schools. A proposal to provide tuition tax-credits, similar to the New York plan struck down by the Court in *Nyquist,* received a vigorous endorsement from the administration.

But despite the presence of an articulate accommodationist bloc, the Court's rulings from the time that Burger became chief justice in 1969, throughout the 1970s, had reinforced rather than repudiated the separationist doctrine that had been expounded during the Warren years. The government could not support religious practices or institutions; government had to be neutral in its dealings with religions; and government had to avoid excessive entanglement in the management or activities of secular programs in religious schools. This adherence to separation received confirmation in the first church-state case of the 1980s, *Stone v. Graham* (1980), in which the Court summarily voided a Kentucky statute requiring the posting of the Ten Commandments in all of the state's public schools. Only Justice Rehnquist dissented. Burger, Blackmun, and Stewart noted their dissatisfaction with the summary reversal of the state court decision, without, however, indicating their views on the merits of the case.

Mr. Dooley's old aphorism, that the Court follows the election returns, seemed to be sustained in a series of cases in the early 1980s, when the accommodationist wing of the Court apparently gained ascendancy. In *Committee for Public Education and Religious Liberty v. Regan* (1980), Justice White, who had been the only dissenter in the *Lemon* case, wrote for a 5–4 majority in upholding a New York statute authorizing reimbursement to private and religious schools for performing testing and reporting services required under state law. The law differed from the Ohio statute in that it provided direct cash payments to the schools. Justice White utilized the tripartite *Lemon* test, and pronounced that the law met the standards. Four members of the Court disagreed, however, and Justice Blackmun called the majority opinion "a long step backwards in the inevitable controversy that emerges when a state legislature continues to insist on providing public aid to parochial schools."

The following year the Court heard a Free Speech case that had Establishment ramifications. The University of Missouri at Kansas City had refused to permit the use of its buildings for religious services or religious teaching. An evangelical Christian student club challenged the regulation on First Amendment and equal protection grounds, and the Court agreed. In *Widmar v. Vincent*, Justice Powell took a fairly standard First Amendment approach for an 8–1 majority. Given that the university allowed its buildings to serve as a forum in general, it could not prohibit their use on content grounds; the fact that a particular group wanted to engage in religious speech did not matter.

The university had not been attempting to stifle religion but had been concerned that because it was a state agency, religious activities on its premises might be construed as violating the separation of church and state. The Court ignored this concern, and Powell's opinion emphasized that the decision had been based on the First Amendment's speech and associational rights. But religious groups quickly saw the wedge they wanted; if they portrayed their religious activities as protected speech (invoking the Free Speech Clause), then they might be able to reintroduce prayer, Bible reading, and the like into primary and secondary schools. Efforts to achieve this goal ran aground in the lower courts, which continued to perceive such activities as religious. Fundamentalists won a partial victory in 1984, however, when Congress provided limited "equal access" for religious clubs to hold meetings in public schools, even if those meetings frequently assumed the character of religious services.

The sympathetic Reagan administration increased its efforts to secure support for religious schools at the state level. The failure of the Burger Court to enunciate a firm standard led legislatures to seek some way to distinguish their forms of aid from those proscribed by the Court. In the *Nyquist* case, the Court had invalidated a New York law allowing tax credits for private and parochial school tuition, as well as tuition grants. Minnesota passed a law providing for a deduction from state taxable income of up to $700 on tuition paid not only for children in private schools but also for those in public schools.

The accommodationists on the Court upheld the Minnesota plan in *Mueller v. Allen* (1983). Justice Rehnquist (who had dissented in *Nyquist*), along with Burger and White, now had a majority. They were joined by the Court's newest member, Justice O'Connor, and most surprisingly, by Justice Powell, who had written the *Nyquist* opinion. Rehnquist based his decision on the fact that the tuition exemption was available to all parents, and was but one of many deductions allowed by state law; by extending these benefits to all groups, the state thus met the "effects" prong of the *Lemon* test, in that the law did not work either to advance or to inhibit religion. Rehnquist casually dismissed the entanglement criterion, which had played so important a role in previous cases, implying that it mattered only when direct financial subsidies were being paid to parochial schools or their teachers.

The accomodationists seemed to gain strength in the next few terms. Chief Justice Burger, in *Marsh v. Chambers* (1983), spoke for a 6–3 Court in holding that paid legislative chaplains, and prayers at the start of each session of the Nebraska legislature, did not violate the Establishment Clause. Just as Justice Black had elaborated a long historical analysis to justify his view of a wall of separation, so now Burger went back to show that the Framers of the First Amendment had been aware of such practices and had not objected to them, and that opening prayers had been a staple of national, state, and local government since the founding of the Republic.

Although both the majority and dissenting opinions character-ized the holding as "narrow . . . careful . . . [with] a limited ratio-nale [that] should pose little threat" to the Establishment Clause, the Chief Justice's opinion could be read as implying that the same rationale might be applied in other areas. He compared the Nebraska practice with the Court's earlier decisions on blue laws as "simply a tolerable acknowledgement of beliefs widely held among people of this country." If one took this reasoning, might it not as well be applied to school prayer and Bible reading, prac-tices that had even longer histories than prayer at the opening of legislative sessions? The First Amendment, and the Bill of Rights in general, had been adopted to protect minorities from majoritar-ian tyranny; the Burger opinion implied that the majority's will should be given greater latitude.

This reading was implicitly affirmed the following term when the Court by a 5–4 vote upheld the placement, at public expense, of a crèche—the Christmas nativity scene—in front of the city hall in Pawtucket, Rhode Island. Many Americans, no matter what their faith or their views of the First Amendment, would agree that there could hardly be a more religious symbol than a crèche. Nor could one imagine any activity more likely to run counter to all the values enunciated by the Court in regard to the Establishment Clause since 1947, or more likely to flunk all of the criteria of Burger's own *Lemon* test—it was not a secular activity, it advanced religious ideas, and it entangled the government in religion. Moreover, even if one took all of the arguments used by the accommodationists to justify previous decisions—free speech, secular benefits, historical exceptions—none of them applied to this case. Public monies were being expended to support an openly religious display.

The majority opinion in *Lynch v. Donnelly* (1984) is the most extreme accommodationist position taken by the Burger Court, and it upset and dismayed legal scholars and laypersons alike. Burger's opinion—that the Constitution "affirmatively mandates" accommodation—stood more than three decades of Establishment Clause jurisprudence on its head. The Chief Justice referred to his earlier decision in *Marsh v. Chambers* to prove that the Framers had intended that there be public support for some activities religious in nature; but he did not make clear the connection between a chaplain's prayer at an opening session of Congress, and a local government's display of a crèche. Other activities that supported his view of an affirmative mandate included the Court's released-time decision in *Zorach v. Clauson;* coins bearing the motto "In God We Trust"; the phrase "one nation under God" in the pledge of allegiance; and paintings with religious messages on display in the National Gallery of Art in Washington.

Burger's application of the *Lemon* test was even more fanciful. He placed the crèche "in the context of the Christmas season," and thus found that it had a secular purpose in depicting "the historical origins of this traditional event long recognized as a National Holiday." Its primary effect did not benefit religion or Christianity, nor did the Court find any administrative entanglement in religious affairs. Since there had been no direct subsidy to a religious agency, the Court had no need to enquire into "potential political divisiveness." In essence, Christmas, according to the opinion, should be viewed not as a religious holiday but as a secular festival.

In his dissent Justice Brennan noted that the acknowledgment of a deity in public ceremonies or on coins was very different from the active endorsement of an event considered holy by Christians whatever their particular denomination. The exhibition of works of art that happened to have religious motifs also could hardly be considered a government endorsement of religion. Brennan's opinion differed most significantly from that of the Chief Justice in its sensitivity to the meaning of the crèche. Although the Christmas season has taken on a secular aspect that is especially evident in the materialism of the shopping malls, its essence is the birth of Christ, and Brennan caught quite clearly the importance of such a symbol to Christians and non-Christians alike:

> The essence of the crèche's symbolic purpose and effect is to prompt the observer to experience a sense of simple awe and wonder appropriate to the contemplation of one of the central elements of Christian dogma—that God sent His son into the world to be Messiah. Contrary to the Court's suggestion, the crèche is far from a mere representation of a "particular historic religious event." It is, instead, best understood as a mystical re-creation of an event that lies at the heart of the Christian faith. To suggest, as the Court does, that such a symbol is merely "traditional" and therefore no different from Santa's house or reindeer is not only offensive to those for whom the crèche has profound significance, but insulting to those who insist for religious or personal reasons that the story of Christ is in no sense a part of "history" nor an unavoidable element of our national "heritage."

The crèche decision carried a message that it is doubtful had been intended by the Chief Justice, namely that those who did not subscribe to such "national" symbols—such as atheists, Muslims, Hindus, and Jews—did not belong to the community. Many Christians who, like Justice Brennan, recognized the deep spiritual significance of the crèche, objected to the majority's debasing of the religious aspects of Christmas. A spokesperson for the National Council of Churches complained that the Court had put Christ "on the same level as Santa Claus and Rudolph the Red-Nosed Reindeer." Soon many cars sported bumper stickers urging, "Keep Christ in Christmas." For scholars, the decision seemed to constitute a major breach in the wall of separation, a breach that might not be reparable. Reports of the wall's demise, however, proved premature.

Another Effort to Reinstate School Prayer

Separationists found little to cheer about during the early 1980s other than *Larkin v. Grendel's Den* (1982), a decision that struck down a silly Massachusetts statute giving schools and churches power to veto applications for liquor licenses at sites within five hundred feet of the school or church premises. The chief justice held that the law gave both real and symbolic benefit to churches, enmeshed churches in the affairs of government, and created potential divisiveness along religious lines, therefore violating the *Lemon* rule. In fact, as Justice Rehnquist (the lone dissenter) pointed out, Massachusetts had originally imposed an absolute ban on all taverns and later decided that its objective—maintaining neighborhood peace—might be better served if schools and churches that objected to having saloons as neighbors initiated a complaint.

Although separationists approved of the *Larkin* decision, they viewed the apparent shift of Justice Powell to the accommodationist wing, and the arrival of Justice O'Connor, with dread. They were surprised when the Court handed down a series of decisions during its 1984 term strongly reaffirming its commitment to a wall of separation.

The first case involved the highly emotional issue of school prayer. Fundamentalist groups had never accepted the Court's 1962 *Engel* ruling, and the resurgence of the religious right in the 1970s led to a number of efforts to overturn the decision by constitutional amendment or to bypass it with new statutes. In Alabama, the legislature passed a law in 1978 requiring elementary school classes to observe a period of silence "for meditation" at the beginning of the school day. Three years later it amended the law and called upon the teacher to announce "that a period of silence not to exceed one minute in duration shall be observed for meditation or voluntary prayer." The following year saw another change, this time authorizing any teacher or professor in any of the state's public educational institutions to lead "willing students" in a prescribed prayer that recognized "Almighty God" as the "Creator and Supreme Judge of the World."

State Senator Donald G. Holmes made no secret, either in the legislative debate or in the District Court hearings afterward, of exactly what he had in mind in regard to the 1981 measure:

Gentlemen, by passage of this bill by the Alabama Legislature our children in this state will have the opportunity of sharing in the spiritual heritage of this state and this country. The United States as well as the State of Alabama was founded by people who believe in God. *I believe this effort to return voluntary prayer* to our public schools for it returns us to the original position of the writers of the Constitution. This local philosophy and belief [have led] hundreds of Alabamians [who] have urged my continuous support for permitting school prayer. Since coming to the Alabama Senate I have worked hard *on this legislation to accomplish the return of voluntary prayer to our public schools and return to the basic moral fiber.* (Urofsky, 1991, 60)

Separationists challenged all three statutes, but the Supreme Court decided the merits only of the 1981 version, with its formula for either "meditation or voluntary prayer." The original statute, with its "pure" moment of silence and no legislative mandate to teachers, could easily have been interpreted as having a secular intent. The alteration, with its direction that teachers should announce that the time could be spent in prayer, had been acknowledged by the sponsor and by the District Court as having a religious motivation—to return "voluntary prayer to our public schools." This would certainly violate the first prong of the *Lemon* test, if that test still had any meaning after the Chief Justice's interpretation of it in the crèche case (*Lynch v. Donnelly* [1984]).

Speaking for a 6–3 majority, over the separate objections of Burger, White, and Rehnquist, Justice Stevens struck down the Alabama statute in *Wallace v. Jaffree* (1985) and reaffirmed the vitality of the *Lemon* test. Had the case been decided half a decade earlier, commentators would have given it little thought. The decision relied on *Engel* as precedent, and employed a fairly straightforward *Lemon* analysis. But given the accommodationist decisions of the previous terms, Stevens decided to reexamine some of the assumptions that had guided the Court since *Everson.*

The growing complexity of Establishment Clause cases, and the wide latitude within which the *Lemon* test could be applied, had led to dissatisfaction both in the academic community and on the Court. Justice O'Connor had raised these issues in her concurrence in *Lynch,* and Stevens now adopted some of her comments in redefining the "purpose" section of the *Lemon* test. The rule had previously been interpreted to ask whether there had been a secular or a religious purpose behind the bill. O'Connor had suggested that there might be *both* secular and religious purposes, and that the existence of a secular purpose would not by itself be sufficient to turn away a challenge on grounds of religious establishment. Stevens, quoting from O'Connor, now stated, "It is appropriate to ask whether the government's actual purpose is to endorse or disapprove of religion."

In another step away from accommodation, the majority held that the Court would look beyond the words of the statute, and at the actual practices or pronouncements of the State. This brought forth an angry dissent from Justice Rehnquist, who in essence said that the Court should accept the terms of the statute on its face value; if it said it had a secular purpose, then the Court should accept that the law had a secular purpose. The Chief Justice also dissented, being aroused to ire by the part of Stevens's opinion that rejected the accommodationist view Burger had set forth in *Lynch*.

Perhaps most important, a majority of the Court rejected two basic challenges to post-*Everson* jurisprudence. Judge W. Brevard Hand in his District Court opinion had held that the Constitution imposed no obstacle to Alabama's establishment of a state religion. Had this view been articulated in 1847, it would have been considered correct; in the 1980s, however, it struck most observers as a mental and judicial aberration. The incorporation of the protections guaranteed in the Bill of Rights and their application to the states had been in progress for more than six decades; and with very few exceptions, these protections had been accepted throughout the judicial, academic, and political communities. No one on the Supreme Court supported Brevard Hand's view, and Stevens was probably responding to Rehnquist's long historical analysis, which purported that the Establishment Clause did not create any wall of separation but rather allowed government to aid religion on a nonpreferential basis. Stevens provided the strongest opinion in support of the traditional jurisprudence that the Court had issued in a number of years.

At the very end of its 1984 term, the Court handed down two important decisions on school aid—decisions that apparently signaled a return to the stricter standards that had prevailed in the 1970s. In *Grand Rapids School District v. Ball*, the Court examined a "shared time" program in which the city's public school teachers offered remedial and enrichment reading and mathematics as well as art, music, and physical education courses in 41 private schools, 40 of which were religious schools. A related "community education" program offered a variety of academic and nonacademic courses in nonpublic schools, but at the end of the regular school day. Most of the faculty members in the community program were on the staffs of the schools where the courses were offered, so most of them were religious school teachers. *Aguilar v. Felton* dealt with a federally funded New York program similar to the Grand Rapids "shared time" scheme. New York, however, had a monitoring system that it claimed insulated the program from the religious inculcation that prevailed in the surrounding church schools.

The Court invalidated both shared time programs by narrow 5–4 votes—the Grand Rapids plan, because in effect it advanced religion; and the New York scheme, because of excessive government entanglement. Chief Justice Burger and Justice O'Connor joined the majority in striking down the community education program. Justice Brennan spoke in both cases for the majority, which found the rationale of *Meek v. Pettinger* still compelling. "Teachers in such an atmosphere may well subtly (or overtly) conform their instruction to the environment in which they teach," he declared in *Grand Rapids,* "while students will perceive the instruction provided in the context of the dominantly religious message of the institution, thus reinforcing the indoctrinating effect." The Court produced no new doctrine in these cases; but the return to the basic principles of *Lemon, Nyquist,* and earlier cases evoked great relief among separationists.

THE REHNQUIST COURT AND ACCOMMODATION

By the time Warren Burger stepped down as chief justice in 1986, both separationists and accommodationists could be forgiven if they could not discern a clear pattern in the Court's decisions. One might have disagreed with the Warren Court decisions, but at least one knew where the justices stood—in support of a strict wall of separation between church and state. The few exceptions that could be found in the Warren Court's Establishment Clause jurisprudence, such as the doctrine of neutrality and the pupil benefit rule, had been limited, and were designed to allow the minimum of state aid to religious enterprises. The Burger Court, supposedly more accommodationist, had scattered its decisions all across the jurisprudential landscape, leaving no clear guidelines to state legislatures as to what they could or could not do, and aside from the *Lemon* test, giving the lower courts very little guidance on how they should evaluate a flood of state legislation.

This confusion, as far as conservative religious leaders were concerned, was no better than what they saw as the godless atheism of the Warren era. The Court, it is true, no longer spoke in the absolute tones of a Hugo Black; worse, it seemed to speak in too many voices, none of which were very clear. With Ronald Reagan's appointees, especially Rehnquist as chief justice, conservatives expected that the Court would finally reverse thirty years of error and get America—and the Constitution—back on God's track. They were to be sorely disappointed. Although the Rehnquist Court in some areas proved receptive to accommodationist arguments, a majority of the Court refused to abandon the notion of separation. It allowed some accommodation, but far from what those on the right demanded.

In *Lamb's Chapel v. Center Moriches Union Free Public School District* (1993), a local evangelical society had been denied the use of school facilities to show a six-part film featuring a psychologist who would argue in favor of "Christian family values instilled at an early age." The school board routinely allowed its facilities to be used after school hours by social, civic, and even political groups; but it claimed that if it allowed Lamb's Chapel access, it would be sponsoring a church-related activity. The sect claimed that the school district had opened its buildings to such a wide group of activities that it had become a *de facto* public forum.

Speaking for a unanimous Court, Justice White accepted the claim that the school had become a public forum. The school district had not been required to open its buildings for any after-school outside activities, he noted; but once it did, denying Lamb's Chapel equal access amounted to content discrimination. The Court held that denial of access had to be "viewpoint neutral," and the school district had failed this test. Although the Warren Court had never had to decide a case like this, its First Amendment jurisprudence would certainly have supported this notion of content neutrality.

Similarly, in *Capital Square Review Board v. Pinette* (1995), the Court struck down the denial of permission to the Ku Klux Klan to erect a large cross on Capitol Square in Columbus, Ohio. The state had designated the square a public forum, and the Court assumed that permission had been denied because of the religious symbolism of the cross. The plurality opinion by Justice Scalia rejected the state's contention that permitting the sign would have been a form of establishment. He went on to interpret the issue in terms of free speech as well, noting that the activity should be considered private religious expression, which was fully protected by the First Amendment.

Perhaps the most accommodationist decision of the Court involved funding of a Christian-oriented magazine at a state-sponsored university. Wide Awake Publications sought funding from the University of Virginia, claiming that as a student organization it should not be denied student activity funds merely because it wished to focus on religious rather than secular matters. The university denied the application, arguing that to support a proselytizing club would be to violate the Establishment Clause. In *Rosenberger v. Rector and Visitors of the University of Virginia* (1995), the Court by a 5–4 vote held that the university could not discriminate against Wide Awake. Justice Kennedy, relying on

Lamb's Chapel, declared that the case rested more on the Free Exercise Clause than the Establishment Clause, and he held that denying funds to a publication because of its orientation amounted to content discrimination.

But the opinion held more than its share of Establishment Clause comments. In dismissing the university's argument, Kennedy found that the law did not require the state in the form of the university to favor or disfavor religion in its funding of student activities through student fees. The funding program was facially neutral, and its object was to open a forum for speech and other enterprises. The university's argument also suffered from the fact that the program had given monies to other clearly religious groups, such as the Hillel Society and a Muslim student organization.

One could find other examples of accommodation in the Court's decisions both before and after *Rosenberger.* In *Bowen v. Kendrick* (1988), the Court upheld those provisions of the Adolescent Family Life Act of 1982 that authorized federal funding of a variety of public and nonpublic organizations, including those with religious affiliation, for counseling services "in the area of premarital adolescent sexual relations and pregnancy." Opponents labeled the law the "Chastity Act" and claimed that the statute violated the Establishment Clause by providing public funds to promote particular religious views. Speaking for the Court, the Chief Justice ignored the fact that one of the purposes of the act had been to fund religious groups opposed to abortion and premarital sex and to support their efforts to utilize religion-oriented counseling to attack the problem of teenage pregnancy. He rejected the claim that the law violated the *Lemon* test, and argued that any effect of advancing religion was merely "incidental and remote." To make their case, Rehnquist said, challengers of the law would have to show that federal funds went to organizations that were "pervasively sectarian" and not merely religiously affiliated or inspired.

In *Zobrest v. Catalina Foothills School District* (1993), the Court held that providing a publicly funded sign-language interpreter to a deaf student in a parochial school classroom did not violate the Establishment Clause. The case relied in large measure on the Court's decision in *Witters v. Washington Department of Services for the Blind* (1986), which had held that no violation of the First Amendment occurred when a visually handicapped person used state vocational rehabilitation money to pay tuition to a Christian college in order to prepare himself for a career in the ministry. The two decisions, especially *Zobrest,* indicated that the Court might reconsider its opinion in two closely divided 1985 cases, *Grand Rapids School District v. Ball* and *Aguilar v. Felton,* in which the Court had invalidated a popular after-school program of publicly funded remedial sessions that took place in parochial schools.

In *Agostini v. Felton* (1997), the Court by a 5–4 vote declared that the earlier decisions no longer could be squared with intervening Establishment Clause cases that gave greater leeway for the use of public funds in parochial settings. Of the justices who had decided the earlier case, *Aguilar,* O'Connor and Rehnquist had been in the minority; but now they prevailed, with the addition of Scalia, Kennedy, and Thomas. Justice Stevens, the sole remnant of the 1985 majority, now joined in dissent with Souter, Ginsburg, and Breyer.

In her opinion, Justice O'Connor addressed each of the assumptions that the earlier Court had made to reach its conclusion that the after-school program had the impermissible effect of advancing religion: first, that any public employee who works on the premises of a religious school is presumed to inculcate religion; second, that the presence of public employees on private school premises creates a symbolic union between church and state; and third, that any and all public money that directly aids the educational function of religious schools impermissibly finances religious indoctrination.

In the twelve years since *Ball* and *Aguilar,* the Court had abandoned the first presumption; it no longer assumed that public employees who set foot in a parochial school automatically were inculcating religion. It also no longer presumed that aid to any educational function in a religious school served to foster religious indoctrination. With these two assumptions gone—even if one applied the stringent standards of the *Lemon* test—the after-school program did not violate the Establishment Clause. The four dissenters, Souter, Stevens, Ginsburg, and Breyer, denied that the cases since 1986 meant that the Court's tests for violation had changed. The program had transgressed the First Amendment then, and it still did.

A final example of the accommodationist trend on the Rehnquist Court came in *Mitchell v. Helms* (2000), when a 6–3 majority upheld a federal program that placed computers and other equipment in parochial schools. However, the six members who voted for the program splintered over how far down this road they were willing to go. Justice Thomas wrote a plurality opinion joined by the Chief Justice and by Justices Scalia and Kennedy; but Justices O'Connor and Breyer, who concurred in the result, took a far narrower approach.

Those who demanded that the Court allow some accommodation could look at this series of cases with some satisfaction; but in two areas where religious conservatives wanted change, the Court sorely disappointed them. Although the famous Scopes trial in the 1920s had seemed to discredit those who rejected evolution outright, the belief in a literal reading of the account of creation in Genesis had never died among religious fundamentalists. In the 1960s they had tried to outlaw the teaching of evolution again, only to be overruled by the Warren Court in *Epperson v. Arkansas* (1968). After a more sophisticated religious bloc hit upon a new tack and labeled the Genesis version "creationism" or "creation science," the state of Louisiana passed a so-called balanced treatment act proclaiming that schools did not have to teach either creation science or evolution but that if either one was taught, then the other had to be as well.

Nearly all reputable scientists dismiss creationism—which accepts the story of Genesis literally and uncritically—as a doctrine bearing no relation to real science, which questions the validity of everything. With only Justice Scalia and the Chief Justice dissenting, Justice Brennan spoke for a 7–2 majority in *Edwards v. Aguillard* (1987), striking down the balanced treatment act. Although the Court always defers to legislative purpose in secular matters, the debate and legislative record in this instance left no doubt as to the religious purposes behind the statute. The act's primary purpose—to advance a particular religious belief—could not pass the *Lemon* test.

Opposition to the Warren Court's most famous religion clause case, the original school prayer decision in *Engel v. Vitale* (1962), also had not faded; and with a more accommodationist majority on the Court, advocates of school prayer hoped to see the case overruled. But in *Lee v. Weisman* (1992), the Court, albeit by a slim majority, reaffirmed the vitality of the wall of separation.

The case arose in Providence, Rhode Island, where the school system had for many years invited clergy of various denominations to offer prayers at graduation and promotion ceremonies. When their eldest daughter graduated from middle school in 1986, Daniel and Vivien Weisman (who are Jewish) were offended by the prayer of a Baptist minister, and they protested in a letter to school officials. They never received an answer. When their younger daughter was to graduate from the same school, the Weismans learned that a rabbi had been invited to give the blessing, apparently in an effort to appease them. The Weismans, however, had not objected just to the particular prayer, but believed that under *Engel* there should be no prayer in public school.

By a 5–4 vote, the Court refused to abandon precedent and adopt a new test in lieu of *Lemon* for Establishment Clause cases. The new centrist majority, including Justices O'Connor, Souter, and Kennedy, indicated it saw no need for a new test. Justice Kennedy's opinion reaffirmed previous rulings and held that prayers at public school graduations, no matter how nonsectarian in nature, violate the Constitution.

A few years later the Court reinforced its ban on prayers in school by an even wider margin. Advocates of school prayer hit upon the tactic of voluntarism in an attempt to bypass the strong line of precedents that ran from *Engel* to *Weisman.* If the student *voluntarily* chose to pray, then there could be no legal objection. The Santa Fe school district allowed its students to choose one student who would lead prayers before each football game. The Court, by a vote of 6–3, ruled in *Santa Fe Independent School District v. Doe* (2000) that this still amounted to an unconstitutional establishment of religion. Although some of the spectators may have been there voluntarily, the team, the cheerleaders, the band, and other students were there because they had to be in attendance, and requiring them to be in an audience with this type of prayer, according to Justice Stevens, had the same effect as *Weisman,* creating a barrier between the accepted and those outside. If one believed that the Court had sent a message in these two cases about school prayer, it then muddied the waters somewhat when in December 2001, it refused to grant certiorari to an appeal from the Eleventh Circuit that seemed to contradict its rulings, especially in the *Santa Fe* case.

Prior to the Court's decision in *Lee v. Weisman* in 1992, school officials in Duval County, Florida, routinely allowed invocations and benedictions at the county's fifteen public school graduation ceremonies. Following the decision, the school board adopted a policy of allowing high school seniors to choose, if they so decided, a fellow student to give a "brief opening and/or closing message" at graduation. That student would then decide the content of the messages without any review by school officials. Although the messages could be secular or humorous in content, they could also be religious.

At some schools the senior class elected a class "chaplain" to lead the invocations and benedictions, or to give "reflective" or "inspirational" messages. In 1998 a group of students and their parents sued, claiming that the policy violated the First Amendment's ban against an establishment of religion.

The Court of Appeals for the Eleventh Circuit upheld the policy, on the grounds that since there was no choice made by, nor censorship imposed by the school board, there was no government involvement. Under this policy students did little more than exercise their freedom of expression. On appeal the Supreme Court remanded to the circuit court with instructions to reconsider the case in light of the High Court's decision in the *Santa Fe* case.

The circuit court reheard the case, and came to the same conclusion, in *Adler v. Duval County School Board* (2001), again ruling that as long as students made the choice, there was no state coercion involved.

The Supreme Court refused to take the case, leaving the ruling intact and binding on the Eleventh Circuit, which covers several southern states. Because there was no dissent filed, and because the justices never explain why a case has been denied review, one can only speculate on why it chose this course. Perhaps it wants to see where the policy leads, and will hear the issue again in the future when the results of the policy provide a clearer factual basis. One does not really know.

But what had been a clear policy has now been muddied. The decisions in *Lee v. Weisman* and *Santa Fe Independent School District v. Doe* sent a clear message that public prayer in schools before a captive audience violated the Establishment Clause. Although it is true that a majority of the students may choose the speaker, the contents of his or her remarks may well offend a minority of the students on the same basis as it did in the other two cases. Clearly there will have to be a resolution of this issue in the not-too-distant future.

CONCLUSION

The Free Exercise Clause, which is examined more closely in the next chapter, operates primarily to protect minority groups; although it may on occasion annoy the majority, it rarely affects them. The Establishment Clause, in contrast, is designed to prevent the majority from using the resources of the state to advance particular religious beliefs. When the people's representatives enact a law carrying out the wishes of their constituents, they rarely stop to ask whether this law, in the broadest sense of the term as used by the Framers, establishes a religion—that is, favors one denomination above others. Most of the time it is not a case of Baptists attempting to use state monies for their benefit to the exclusion of Methodists. Rather, because we are still predominantly a Christian nation with a Christian culture, the violations are more cultural in nature. Since "everyone" believes in Christmas, what can be wrong with a crèche in front of city hall? Since "everyone" believes in God, what can be wrong with a prayer to the Almighty at a graduation, or better yet, at the beginning of a school day? Since "everyone" in this state believes in the literal word of God and takes the Genesis story of creation at face value, then why not prohibit that godless Darwin from contaminating our children, or at the very least give God equal time with Darwin? After all, aren't the schools supposed to be incubators of patriotism and culture and to reflect community values? Why should a community in the Ozarks have to adapt its curriculum to what some city slickers believe? After all, if they think they descended from apes, that's fine; but God created man in his own image, not in the image of a monkey, and that's what "everyone" here believes.

The problems are not easy, and it really does not matter whether one believes in the particular issue at stake. One does not have to be a creationist to sympathize with those who do believe in the literal word of the Bible and who want their children to believe that as well, and not have some crazy theory taught in school. After all, if the Supreme Court said that the Amish don't have to send their children to public school after eighth grade because it corrupts them, then isn't the majority entitled to the same protections?

The answer—and it is not a simple one—is that the Bill of Rights was intended to place constraints on the majority in order to protect the minority. This seems to fly in the face of democratic theory, which says the will of the majority is to govern. Yet the men who crafted the Constitution understood a greater truth: that in order for a majority to govern wisely and fairly, it had to be restrained. The Framers feared a tyranny of the majority even more than they loathed the perceived tyranny of George III.

For all that religious conservatives opposed the rulings of the Warren Court, they at least knew where the Court stood—on the side of separation—and that made the law clearer. They did not like the law and wanted to change it; but until that happened, they at least knew what to expect from the law. Today that certainty is gone; and the replacement of one or two members of the Court could easily tilt Establishment Clause jurisprudence farther in one direction or the other. Unfortunately, religion is an issue that evokes high emotion; and legal certainty, especially with regard to emotional issues, is all that separates social order from chaos.

References

Beaney, William M., and Edward N. Beiser. 1964. "Prayer and Politics: The Impact of *Engel* and *Schempp* on the Political Process." *Journal of Public Law* 13: 475.

Curry, Thomas J. 1986. *The First Freedoms: Church and State in America to the Passage of the First Amendment.* New York: Oxford University Press.

Ely, John Hart. 1980. *Democracy and Distrust: A Theory of Judicial Review.* Cambridge: Harvard University Press.

Finkelman, Paul, ed. 2000. *Religion and American Law: An Encyclopedia.* New York: Garland.

Irons, Peter. 1988. *The Courage of Their Convictions*. New York: Free Press.

Larson, Edward J. 1997. *Summer of the Gods: The Scopes Trial and America's Continuing Debate over Science and Religion*. New York: Basic Books.

Levy, Leonard W. 1986. *The Establishment Clause: Religion and the First Amendment*. New York: Macmillan.

————. 1994. *The Establishment Clause: Religion and the First Amendment*. 2d ed. Chapel Hill: University of North Carolina Press.

McConnell, Michael. 1992. "Religious Freedom at a Crossroads." *University of Chicago Law Review* 59: 115.

Meese, Edwin L., Jr. 1985. "Construing the Constitution." *University of California at Davis Law Review* 19: 22.

Muir, William K. 1967. *Prayer in the Public Schools*. Chicago: University of Chicago Press.

Murphy, Paul L. 1972. *The Constitution in Crisis Times, 1918–1969*. New York: Harper & Row.

Noonan, John T., Jr. 1998. *The Lustre of Our Country*. Berkeley: University of California Press.

Pfeffer, Leo. 1967. *Church, State, and Freedom*. Rev. ed. Boston: Beacon Press.

Schwartz, Bernard. 1983. *Super Chief: Earl Warren and His Supreme Court*. New York: New York University Press.

Sorauf, Francis J. 1976. *The Wall of Separation: The Constitutional Politics of Church and State*. Princeton: Princeton University Press.

Urofsky, Melvin I. 1991. *The Continuity of Change: The Supreme Court and Individual Liberties, 1953–1968*. Belmont, CA: Wadsworth.

————. 1991a. *Felix Frankfurter: Judicial Restraint and Individual Liberties*. Boston: Twayne.

Wasby, Stephen L. 1970. *The Impact of the United States Supreme Court: Some Perspectives*. Chicago: Dorsey.

Weaver, John D. 1967. *Warren: The Man, the Court, the Era*. Boston: Little, Brown.

4

THE FREE EXERCISE
CLAUSE

*I*N SOME WAYS, but only some, Free Exercise cases are easier to define than Establishment claims, because they involve the state's restriction of an individual's religious practices. There is, of course, much overlap between the First Amendment's two religion clauses. Governmental programs that are intended to help religion in general may in fact restrict the freedoms of individuals. State laws permitting school prayer and Bible reading offended the Court not just on establishment grounds but also because they limited the free exercise of those who disagreed with the mode of prayer or the version of the Bible used.

Free Exercise claims also overlap with claims to freedom of speech; several important cases prior to 1953 involved Jehovah's Witnesses, who claimed that the right to proselytize—without state regulation—was essential to the free exercise of their beliefs. In these cases, the Court's analysis concentrated almost solely on the criteria used to safeguard free speech.

Some issues are unique to Free Exercise claims. One such issue is the belief/action dichotomy enunciated by Chief Justice Morrison Waite in the Mormon bigamy case, *Reynolds v. United States*

(1879), and later applied to the Free Speech Clause. Although the First Amendment absolutely prohibits government efforts to restrict beliefs, it does not prevent the state from forbidding practices that threaten public order or safety. In the example Waite used, if a sect believed in human sacrifice, the government could do nothing to restrict that belief; but it could, without violating the Free Speech Clause, bar the actual sacrifice. The Court eventually recognized, however, that one could not divide belief and action so easily. In the 1940s it modified Waite's rule, finding that although action remained subject to regulation, it deserved some protection under Free Exercise claims.

A second problem involves limits placed by the Establishment Clause on the Free Exercise Clause. The two clauses overlap in their protection, but there are also instances where they conflict. A state's efforts to accommodate certain groups by exempting or immunizing them from general laws may also be seen as providing a preference to one sect.

Scholars have had a great deal of difficulty in identifying some overarching principle or theory that would provide a single authoritative interpretation of what free exercise of religion is. The effort to find that meaning in the words of the men who framed and ratified the First Amendment is derivative of the originalist effort to interpret the Establishment Clause so as to allow aid to religion, and it suffers from the same weaknesses. We do not really know what they meant, since the nation, as well as the condition of religion, have changed greatly over the centuries. Steven Smith has argued that the search for a fundamental principle explaining religious freedom is doomed to failure, because every understanding inescapably entails some theory of religion, and there is absolutely no agreement in this country about theology. Adopt one view, he declares, and you have betrayed others with equal claims. The preference of one religious or secular position over another is exactly what modern theories of religious freedom seek to avoid (Smith, 1995, 68).

Just as in Establishment Clause cases, the Supreme Court is far from unified on what principles to apply in interpreting the Free Exercise Clause. Bette Evans has suggested that there are at least four "partial accounts" used by the Court (Evans, 1997, 16ff.). The first and most common is the notion of protecting individual choice. Evans points to Justice John Paul Stevens's comment in *Wallace v. Jaffree* (1985) that "the individual freedom of conscience protected by the First Amendment embraces the right to select any religious belief or none at all. . . . [R]eligious beliefs worthy of respect are the product of free and voluntary choice by the faithful." The problem with this view is that in its emphasis on the individual, it neglects what we may call the communal aspects of religion: not just the formal worship in particular churches, synagogues, or mosques, but the way religion permeates the national culture. Perhaps the most outspoken critic of this individualist view is Stephen Carter, who believes that the emphasis on each person's right to choose has trivialized religion (Carter, 1993, 14–15).

The second theory is that of protecting the sanctity of individual religious conscience. A person must not only be free to choose; but having made a choice, he or she must be safe in following the dictates of conscience. Judge Learned Hand, in a conscientious objector case during World War II, wrote about how religious belief often finds reason inadequate as a guide to life, and how "conscience categorically requires the believer to disregard elementary self interest and to accept martyrdom in preference to transgressing its tenets" (*United States v. Kauten* [2nd Cir. 1943]). In this view the emphasis is not on the choices one makes (which religion to follow) but rather on the obligations imposed by conscience; not on whether I shall be a Catholic or a Jew or a Mormon, but on what obligations that choice imposes on me, and whether I will be able to meet those demands without fear of the state. The problem with this view, as Douglas Laycock has pointed out, is that it defines religion in terms that are far too narrow, merely as a list of "thou shalt not" rules; as long as the government does not interfere with these, then many people think that is the end of the issue. That is much too limited a view of religion. What we need to ask instead is, What are the positive commands of the religion, and how does the Free Exercise Clause deal with them? It is relatively easy to say that a state cannot penalize a woman whose religion forbids her to work on Sunday (*Sherbert v. Verner* [1963]); it is quite another to permit a man to have several wives (*Reynolds v. United States* [1879]) or to use a prohibited substance (*Employment Division, Oregon Department of Human Resources v. Smith* [1990]) on the grounds that his religion commands him to do so. The latter decisions would involve a far more serious commitment to free exercise (Laycock, 1990, 24–26).

The third view is that by separating the state from all religious matters, we protect the state from religious controversies. To understand the merits of this view, one need not be a student of history and know that Europe was wracked for centuries by bitter combat between warring religious groups; one need only be aware of current events in Afghanistan, a country devastated by decades of religious warlordism and enforced state theocracy under the rule of the Taliban. John Locke, whose essays on toleration greatly influenced the Revolutionary generation, was reacting to a century of religious warfare in England when he wrote that religious toleration was essential to civil peace, and that government could function best without involvement in religious controversy. In terms of Supreme Court decisions, one should here recall the three prongs of the *Lemon* test, discussed in the previous chapter. The third prong—avoiding excessive entanglement between religion and government—addresses the fear that close ties between the two will work to the advantage of neither. This makes religious toleration a prudential matter; we allow a full range of freedom in order to keep religion and government separate. There is no need to call in the state if one is already free to believe.

One should note that the Free Exercise Clause, like the Free Speech Clause, is not aimed at the majority; it was specifically designed to protect dissident sects from government under the control of the mainstream religions. Several commentators have pointed out that no single Free Speech case has ever reached the high court from a mainstream Christian religious practitioner. The value of protecting minorities will become ever more apparent as the cultural diversity of the American population continues to increase through the twenty-first century.

If we value religious freedom, then we cannot protect government from religion without protecting religion from government. Madison not only sought to prevent the establishment of one dominant religion; he also wanted to keep the government out of all religious controversies. The Framers had both experience and knowledge of how potent a weapon government could be in the hands of religion and vice versa, and they would brook no such alliance. But they faced the same problem then that we face today: How can government neutrality in religious matters be achieved and defended, given the strong role traditionally played by religion in American civic life? The emphasis on individualism in American culture has tended to negate this role over time, as has the notion that government should be concerned only with secular matters. Yet religion remains very important to many Americans as part of the civic culture, and it is pointless to pretend that government today is completely uninvolved with religion.

Evans posits a fourth view in seeing the Free Exercise Clause "as a way of protecting independent sources of meaning and full and equal citizenship within the polity" (Evans, 1997, 37). In other words, it fosters pluralism by allowing each person and each group full play of their ideas and faiths. Although we tend to think of the colonies as having been settled primarily from the British Isles, in fact by 1776 immigrants had arrived from Scandinavia, western and central Europe, and (involuntarily) Africa. Although the new country was nowhere near as pluralistic as the

United States is at the beginning of the twenty-first century, it was a hodgepodge of a far greater number of nationalities and religions than were in England and other European nations. Evans makes a compelling case that the intellectual cross-fertilization that we need to remain a vibrant and democratic society is only possible if one of the most important aspects of each person's life—religious belief—is left untouched by government's hand.

As one reads the cases below, one will see all of these theories played out. Whether one or all are correct, the Free Exercise Clause has provided a remarkable degree of freedom to Americans of many varying faiths.

THE MORMONS AND POLYGAMY

As one might assume, a majority of Free Exercise cases have involved minority sects whose beliefs are significantly different from those of mainstream Protestantism or Catholicism. It might be well to recall that when the colonies declared independence and wrote their first bills of rights, they did not provide for the full religious freedom of all groups. Moreover, even Christians who did enjoy full freedom did so within limits. Those limits were reached, in the words of the 1776 Maryland constitution (see Chapter 6), when "under colour of religion, any man shall disturb the good order, peace or safety of the State, or shall infringe the laws of morality." Although that wording does not appear in the First Amendment, it remained for many years a silent part of the Free Exercise Clause, as can easily be seen from the Mormon cases.

The first appeal to the Free Exercise Clause involved adherents to the Church of Jesus Christ of Latter-Day Saints (Mormons). Joseph Smith founded the group in New York in the 1830s. Because the group's views on prophetic leadership, polygamy, and a theocratic social structure made it unpopular, Smith's followers were first driven from New York to Ohio, then to Missouri, and then to Illinois, where Smith and his brother were murdered in 1844. Led by Brigham Young, the Mormons trekked westward to the Utah territory, where they established Deseret, a Mormon kingdom in the middle of the desert.

Initially it seemed that the Mormons had finally found a place where they could live in peace, and under Young's leadership they enjoyed good relations with the neighboring Indian tribes. Although the federal government did not approve of Mormon theology or practices, the distance of Utah from Washington, and the seeming isolation of the Mormon community from mainstream society, led the federal government to leave Young and his followers alone. But after the Civil War the transcontinental railroad tied east and west together, and Utah was no longer as isolated. The government in Washington, under pressure from mainstream Christian groups, began a forty-year campaign to eradicate Mormon distinctiveness. Although the population of Utah soon reached the minimum required for statehood, Congress refused to admit Utah until the Mormons abandoned some of their practices, especially polygamy. Congress enacted a series of laws aimed at the Mormons, who then went into federal court seeking protection. Because Utah was a federal territory, the First Amendment applied there; and the Mormons made one effort after another to invoke its protections in federal courts, but to no avail.

Between 1862 and 1877 Congress enacted four major pieces of legislation aimed at the Mormons. Antislavery activist and congressional representative Justin Morrill of Vermont, best known as the father of the land grant public universities, was also the sponsor of the Morrill Anti-Polygamy Act of 1862. Under this law polygamy was a crime in any U.S. territory, punishable by fines up to $500 and imprisonment for as many as five years. The act also revoked the charter given by the Utah territorial legislature incorporating the Church of Jesus Christ of Latter-Day Saints, and annulled all acts of that legislature that supported or protected polygamy in any way.

Twelve years later, the Poland Act of 1874 did away with much of the jurisdiction of the territorial courts in Utah. It replaced the territorial courts with federal tribunals, gave process powers to U.S. marshals, and granted the U.S. Supreme Court the power to review any decision of a territorial court.

Despite these laws, polygamy thrived in Utah. Prosecutions were rare because local juries refused to convict their neighbors for an action that they condoned. As a result, in 1881, President Chester A. Arthur asked Congress to enact new legislation to deal with the problem of "procuring legal evidence sufficient to warrant a conviction [of polygamy] even in the case of the most notorious offenders." Congress responded with the Edmunds Act of 1882, which imposed civil disabilities on polygamists, depriving both polygamists and their wives of the vote (in Utah, women had enjoyed the right to vote since 1870) as well as the ability to hold public office. The law also greatly simplified prosecution for polygamy. To get around the problems caused by the legal distinction in the Morrill Act between "bigamy" and "polygamy," the Edmunds Act created a new offense, "unlawful cohabitation," for which no proof of marriage was required. All the prosecutor had to show was that a man lived in the same household with two or more women who were not his mother or daughters; a marriage license proved of little use, since the law allowed prosecutors to mix cohabitation and polygamy in the same indictment. Prosecutors could also dismiss from the jury pool for cause anyone who was or had been a polygamist, or even one who although a monogamist himself believed it acceptable to have more than one wife. Since church policy still upheld polygamy, this in effect excluded all believing Mormons from juries hearing polygamy cases.

Still the Mormons maintained the practice. In 1887 Congress passed its strongest measure yet, the Edmunds-Tucker Act. The law eliminated various evidentiary obligations on the part of prosecutors to prove polygamy, and repealed the common law proscription barring a wife from testifying against her husband in cases involving bigamy, polygamy, or unlawful cohabitation. U.S. marshals could compel witnesses to appear in court; all marriages in the territory had to be licensed and registered; and a Utah law directing that only a spouse could bring a polygamy charge in court was annulled. In addition, and for reasons that are clearly not related to the attack on polygamy, §20 completely disenfranchised Utah's women. Women married to polygamists had been disenfranchised in the 1882 Edmunds Act; now single as well as monogamous women were disenfranchised as well. Lastly, the Edmunds-Tucker Act stripped the Utah territorial assembly of much of its power, placed the state's school system under federal control, and dismantled the Mormon church. The act directed the attorney general to seize all church real estate in excess of $50,000 in value. Because the Morrill Act already had revoked the Mormon church's charter, theoretically the church could no longer own any property, and thus it was faced with the seizure of all its assets. It can hardly be doubted that had these laws been passed today, all but the provisions outlawing polygamy would have been struck down as unconstitutional. But Congress passed these laws in the latter nineteenth century, when many middle-class Protestants saw Mormon teachings and practices as a threat to social stability and morality.

The Mormons fought all of these laws in federal court, but to little effect. The judges in the district courts, as well as members of the U.S. Supreme Court, shared all of the prejudices that had led Congress to act. More importantly, the district courts had no clear Free Exercise jurisprudence to guide them; and Utah being a territory, district judges tended to defer to Congress, because the Constitution gave full control over the territories of the United States to that body and apparently placed no restrictions on its authority.

The first and still the most important case arising from these events is *Reynolds v. United States* (1879). George Reynolds had migrated to the United States from England, had become private secretary to Brigham Young, and following the dictates of his faith and conscience, had become a polygamist. In 1875 the U.S. attorney indicted him under the Morrill Act, and the court convicted Reynolds and sentenced him to two years at hard labor and a $5,000 fine. After the Utah Supreme Court upheld the conviction, Reynolds appealed to the U.S. Supreme Court, claiming that the trial court had failed to instruct the jury that a finding that he had behaved out of sincere religious belief would justify his acquittal. Relying on the First Amendment, Reynolds argued that the Free Exercise Clause supported precisely such a finding.

The Court clearly was unwilling to free Reynolds, and thus it put the stamp of constitutional approval on a practice condemned by more than 95 percent of the country. On the other hand, the Constitution did seem to give unequivocal protection to religious exercise. Chief Justice Morrison Waite finessed the problem in a way that still affects all Free Exercise cases; he drew a sharp distinction between religious belief and practice. Waite quoted Thomas Jefferson's statement that "religion is a matter which lies solely between man and his God; . . . the legislative powers of the government reach actions only, and not opinion." Following this reasoning, the Court held that "Congress was deprived of all legislative power over mere opinions, but was left free to reach actions which were in violation of social duties or subversive of good order." Polygamy, according to the Court, clearly was subversive of good order, and Congress could thus make the practice a crime.

The male chauvinism expressed by the Court, its unquestioning acceptance of a monogamistic social order, its willful ignorance of women's interests or desires, and its underlying assumption that the United States was a Protestant Christian nation might strike the modern reader as outrageous; but they fit perfectly into the mental patterns not only of nineteenth-century judges but of the entire population of the United States outside of Utah. Nonetheless, Waite's essential dichotomy has withstood the test of time;

even in a society as religiously pluralist as the modern United States, certain actions cannot possibly be justified on the grounds of free religious exercise, no matter how sincere the believer may be. Although the Court's judgments in some cases might seem needlessly severe (e.g., its affirmation of military proscriptions against the wearing of *keepahs* [skull caps] by Orthodox Jewish service personnel), for the most part its jurisprudence is sound. People may believe whatever they wish, and the government may not prosecute them, no matter how outrageous that belief may be. But if the belief leads to action that is offensive to many people and subversive of the social order, the government may limit that activity. In the nineteenth century, and even today, polygamy strikes most people as falling within that definition.

The Court then turned to cases arising from the Edmunds Act of 1882, prohibiting cohabitation. The statute did not provide definitions of cohabitation; and as one might expect of a Victorian-era document, it shied away from stating the obvious—namely that a man living with one or more women could be presumed to be having sexual intercourse with them. Angus Cannon had married three women before passage of the law; two of his three wives lived with him in separate quarters in the same house, and the third lived nearby. At his trial, Cannon claimed that after the law had been passed he had told two of his three wives and their families that he intended to obey the law and not occupy their beds or have intercourse with them, but he could not afford separate houses for all of them. After having been found guilty of cohabitation, Cannon based his appeal on the grounds that the law had been aimed at sexual relationships, and that because he had declared he would not engage in sex with two of the women, then he should have been found innocent.

The Supreme Court upheld the conviction, having dismissed Cannon's testimony as unreliable. Moreover—and in this comment one can read not only the Court's moral compass but that of the country as well—"compacts for sexual non-intercourse, easily made and easily broken, when the prior marriage relations continue to exist . . . [are] not a lawful substitute for the monogamous family which alone the statute tolerates" (*United States v. Cannon* [1886]).

The Court heard several other cases deriving from the cohabitation act. Zealous prosecutors claimed that each year a man lived with more than one woman in a house constituted a separate offense, and thus Lorenzo Snow was charged with three counts of cohabitation, all with the same women, each offense relating to a different year. By the time Snow's appeal reached the Supreme Court, prosecutors had started charging cohabitation for six-month periods as separate offenses. In one of the few victories won by Mormons, the high court found that cohabitation was a "continuous offense, having duration, and not an offense consisting of an isolated act" (*In re Snow* [1887]).

Despite this one case, for the most part the Supreme Court ignored the constant dilution of evidentiary requirements needed for conviction, so that by 1890, even if a man were living with only one of his wives and had absolutely no contact with the others, who resided apart from him, he could still be found guilty under the cohabitation statute. A man could live only with one legal wife; and the presumption seemed to be that the first woman he married occupied that position, no matter the circumstances. In addition to violations of Free Exercise, the courts seemed willing to tolerate violations of accepted due process and criminal procedure in order to stamp out polygamy: The high court upheld the exclusion of Mormons as petit as well as grand jurors (*Clawson v. United States* [1885]). In *Murphy v. Ramsey* (1884) the Court had held that the Utah Commission could disenfranchise practicing polygamists as well as bar them from holding office; and a few years later, in a case from Idaho, a state known for its anti-Mormon sentiments, the Court upheld a state constitutional provision barring Mormons from voting. In *Davis v. Beason* (1890), the Court not only justified the exclusion of practicing polygamists because they were little more than a class of criminals, but it also approved the exclusion of those who believed in polygamy or supported an organization that taught about polygamy. In a little over a decade, hatred of Mormons blinded the Court to the core holding of *Reynolds*—that belief by itself could not be punished.

In the end, the government won its battle against polygamy through economic warfare. The Morrill Act and the Edmunds-Tucker Act essentially left all of the church's real and tangible property vulnerable to confiscation. By the 1880s this property amounted to a considerable amount.

Under its original charter, issued by the Assembly of the State of Deseret in 1851, the church had vast powers, none of which were subject to judicial review. Over the years, in part due to the theocratic nature of Mormon society, the church became a major business force in Utah, and as a result of Mormon communal doctrines, it held a major portion of the group's collective wealth. The seizure of these assets would not only harm the church but would deal a devastating blow to the community. In July 1887 the U.S. attorney for Utah went into court seeking an order to dissolve the church as a corporate entity and to recover all property held by the church except for real property acquired before 1862 (the date of the Morrill Act) and valued at less than $50,000.

Here the Mormons should have been on sound constitutional ground; for ever since *Dartmouth College v. Woodward* (1819), the sanctity of corporate charters had been held inviolate. Although the Contracts Clause of the Constitution applied to states, one might have inferred from the Court's defense of property rights in this era that under the Fifth Amendment's Due Process Clause that same prohibition would have held against the federal government. But even if Congress had the right to nullify the charter, the property should have reverted to the church's membership and not to the United States.

However, the Court disagreed with each of these contentions in *The Late Corporation of the Church of Jesus Christ of Latter-Day Saints v. United States* (1890). It held that the property had been donated to the church to promote public and charitable purposes but instead the church had used it to spread polygamy, an evil and illegal activity. By depriving the church of its property, Congress was doing no more than redirecting the use of the property to its original charitable purposes. To justify this argument, the Court invoked the ancient common law doctrine of cy pres. If a charitable trust could not be fulfilled according to its terms, the state would apply it to those purposes most nearly like that of the original intent. The Mormon Church's continued adherence to polygamy made it impossible to return the money to its members, since that would only continue its use for illegal purposes. The majority opinion by Justice Brewer likened polygamy to barbarism and dismissed out of hand Mormon claims to religious freedom. Brewer described the plenary powers of Congress to legislate for the territories in truly sweeping terms.

Chief Justice Fuller, joined by Field and Lamar, dissented. They agreed that Congress could try to erase polygamy through criminal sanctions, but they argued that it had no authority to confiscate the property either of persons or of corporations that might have been guilty of criminal practices. "I regard it of vital consequence," Fuller wrote, "that absolute power should never be conceded as belonging under our system of government to any one of its departments."

The Court remanded the case to the territorial court for final disposition of property. While this court was considering the issue, the Mormon Church officially abandoned polygamy in October 1890. Church president Wilford Woodruff issued a manifesto declaring that he was prepared to submit to the laws of the United States and that he strongly urged all members of the church to do so as well. This action, however, did not move the Utah Supreme Court, which refused to give the assets back and named a trustee to oversee the property for the maintenance of church structures and the relief of the poor. Eventually Congress, satisfied with its victory, and perhaps influenced by Fuller's dissent, passed a resolution returning the church's personal property in 1894 and its real property two years later.

Congress had won its war against polygamy, and in so doing had seriously crippled the Mormon Church. Aside from the seizure of real and personal property, there had been 1,004 convictions for unlawful cohabitation and 31 for polygamy. Moreover, under Mormon doctrine only men who were morally worthy and financially able to support large families could marry more than one woman. Thus the attack on polygamists was also an attack on the Mormon leadership, and it had a devastating effect on the lives of many people. Wives who refused to testify against their husbands often wound up in jail. Many men either went into hiding or obeyed federal law and lived with only one wife, leaving numerous women abandoned and their children fatherless. Federal agents criss-crossed the Utah territory looking for polygamists, disrupting communities and invading the privacy of homes (Finkelstein, 2000, 324).

One can see how great the anti-Mormon sentiment was in the latter nineteenth century, and how far the Mormon vision of a theocratic society differed from that of mainstream Protestant America. Yet one wonders whether the Mormon plan would have been acceptable at any time in our history—even today, when pluralism is so much in vogue. There has been a resurgence of polygamy in Utah, a counterpart to the resurgence of conservative religion in other parts of the country. But whereas the Christian Right and Orthodox Judaism are seen as respectable, public opinion still runs strongly against polygamy. Even in a nation as devoted to religious freedom as the United States, the limits to freedom are apparent.

JEHOVAH'S WITNESSES AND THE FLAG SALUTE

Undoubtedly the most famous of the Free Exercise cases involved Jehovah's Witnesses and their refusal to salute the American flag;

but that was only one of many cases that the Witnesses took to court. As one scholar has noted, religious freedom in the United States owes a great debt to Jehovah's Witnesses (Waite, 1944, 209).

Charles Taze Russell founded the sect of Jehovah's Witnesses in 1868. At age 16, Russell, who was raised as a Congregationalist, had decided that all religions were wrong and had started his own Bible study group. Known initially as Russellites, he and his followers considered Jehovah alone—not the Trinity—the one true God. They believed that the answers to all questions in life could be found in close scrutiny and faithful adherence to biblical texts. In 1884 the group was incorporated in Pennsylvania as the Watchtower Bible and Tract Society, dedicated to the dissemination of biblical truth in various languages. The group did not choose "Jehovah's Witnesses" as its name until 1931. By then its adherents firmly believed that as a religious obligation they had to spread the word of God by selling or giving away their publications, by speaking on street corners, and by going door-to-door in residential neighborhoods.

Russell died in 1916, and "Judge" Joseph Franklin Rutherford, former general counsel, took over as president and remained the group's leader until his death in 1942. In the quarter century of Rutherford's tenure the Witnesses were banned in many parts of the world and became one of the most persecuted religious groups in the United States. The reason can easily be found in the Witnesses' total rejection of patriotism and their sole adherence to a literal interpretation of the Bible. In his last book, published in 1917, Russell denounced patriotism as "a narrow-minded hatred of other people," and claimed that there was no justification for it in the New Testament. As a result the government indicted and secured convictions of Rutherford and other Society officials under the 1917 Espionage Act, on grounds that they had attempted to cause insubordination in the military. Although an appeals court upheld the conviction and the sentence of twenty years' imprisonment, the case was later reversed and remanded, and eventually the U.S. attorney general exonerated the defendants.

The prosecution of Rutherford, however, did lead to the Witnesses' first encounter with the Supreme Court. During Rutherford's trial, Agnes Hudgings, a Witness, refused to cooperate as a witness for the government, and she was held in contempt of court. However, in *Ex parte Hudgings* (1919), the Supreme Court ruled that the district court had no authority to adjudge a witness guilty of contempt solely because the judge thought she was willfully refusing to testify truthfully; nor did it have the power to jail the witness until she gave evidence that the court deemed truthful.

Between the two world wars, animosity toward the Witnesses increased. This antipathy did not result from theological doctrine per se but from the constant proselytizing that lay at the core of the Witnesses' faith; they believed that God required them to go out and spread the Word. Unfortunately, much of the word they spread, and many of the tracts they distributed, included attacks on mainstream Catholic and Protestant churches and their leaders. Rutherford called the Roman Catholic Church "the old harlot" and condemned it for the bloody sins it had committed in perversion of God's word. The playing of a recording of his pamphlet *Enemies* led to a series of cases in the late 1930s and early 1940s through which the meaning of the Free Exercise Clause was expanded and the clause was incorporated through the Fourteenth Amendment so as to apply to the states.

The first Witness cases successfully challenged local ordinances that prohibited distribution of pamphlets or door-to-door solicitation without local officials' permission (*Lowell v. City of Griffin* [1938]; *Schneider v. Irvington* [1939]). The Court decided both these cases on traditional First Amendment speech grounds rather than on the Free Exercise Clause; but in *Schneider,* Justice Owen J. Roberts took the first step toward a Free Exercise interpretation by implementing Justice Harlan Fiske Stone's famous *Carolene Products* footnote, calling on courts to scrutinize any regulation of personal rights with heightened attention.[1] Then in 1940 the high court in *Cantwell v. Connecticut* gave the Witnesses their first victory based on the Free Exercise Clause. Roberts, for a unanimous bench, struck down a state law that prohibited solicitation of money for any charitable or religious cause without prior approval by the secretary of the public welfare council, who alone could determine whether the applicants represented a legitimate religion. The state had the power to license solicitors, Roberts noted, even for religious causes, but the arbitrary power lodged in the secretary created an impermissible censorship over religion.

Roberts, however, reiterated the doctrine first enunciated by Chief Justice Morrison Waite in *Reynolds v. United States* (1879), the nineteenth-century Mormon case that differentiated belief from action. The First Amendment provided absolute freedom to believe, but it did not provide equal protection for action—even action taken for religious purposes. In the latter case, courts had to balance the activity against the effects it had on others, to balance individual rights against the needs of society. Shortly afterwards, the Court showed just how relative that balance could be in the most famous of the wartime religion cases: those involving Jehovah's Witnesses' opposition to the flag salute.

Flag saluting ceremonies in schools began during wartime. New York passed its mandatory salute statute in 1898, soon after the United States declared war on Spain. Only five more states had adopted similar measures before World War I; but in 1919 the American Legion began a national campaign to secure mandatory flag salute ceremonies in all schools. By 1935, eighteen states had such statutes, and hundreds of school districts in other states compelled students to join in the morning ceremony (Irons, 1988, 16).

The Gobitas family (a local court clerk's mistaken notation of "Gobitis" remained on the record through the Supreme Court hearings) lived in the small mining town of Minersville, Pennsylvania, where close to 90 percent of residents were Roman Catholic. Walter Gobitas, a town native, had been a Catholic until he became a member of the Jehovah's Witnesses in 1931. His two school-age children, twelve-year-old Lillian and ten-year-old William, had participated in their school's flag salute at first; but in 1935 they stopped doing so, because of their faith. Jehovah's Witnesses objected to the flag salute because of their literal reading of Exodus 20:4–5, by which they equated the salute with bowing down to graven images. The school superintendent, Charles Roudabush, met several times with the Gobitas family, trying to get the parents to direct their children to salute the flag; when they continued to refuse, he expelled Lillian and William from school in 1935. Walter Gobitas, with the help of the American Civil Liberties Union (ACLU), took the school board to court and won, first in federal district court and then again in the circuit court of appeals. In his opinion in the appellate court, Judge William S. Clark, a Republican, expressed deep scorn for compulsory flag salutes. Such a practice, he declared, "happens to be abhorrent to the particular love of God of the little girl and boy now seeking our protection." Faced with two losses, the school board decided not to pursue the matter further; but then several "patriotic" groups offered to underwrite its expenses. And so the Minersville School District appealed to the Supreme Court. Much to its surprise, the Court granted certiorari (Irons, 1988, 20).

The case presented no new questions to the Court: Whether or not a state could compel schoolchildren to salute the American flag had been an issue in twenty states between 1935 and 1940, and had been the subject of major litigation in seven. Prior to *Minersville School District v. Gobitis* (1940), the high court had four times upheld state court decisions validating compulsory flag salute laws (Urofsky, 1997, 107). Justice Felix Frankfurter, a naturalized American citizen who took the ideals of citizenship and patriotism very seriously, had little sympathy with those who, as he saw it, refused to meet their civic obligations. During oral argument of the case on April 25, 1940, he passed a note to Frank Murphy questioning whether the Framers of the Bill of Rights "would have thought that a requirement to salute the flag violates the protection of 'the free exercise of religion'" (Fine, 1984, 185).

Chief Justice Charles Evans Hughes assigned the opinion to Frankfurter, who circulated a draft in May. William O. Douglas, who later intimated that he might have voted the other way had Justice Harlan Stone circulated his dissent earlier (Douglas, 1980, 45), endorsed not only Frankfurter's original draft but the final version as well. "This is a powerful moving document of incalculable contemporary and (I believe) historical value," he wrote, terming the opinion "a truly statesmanlike job."

Frankfurter, believing that the Court should speak unanimously, tried to get Stone not to dissent. It is worth quoting at length from his letter to Stone, because it indicates how little Frankfurter understood the implications of the Free Exercise Clause, and how limited a role he saw for the Court in effectuating the promise of free exercise (Mason, 1956, 526–527).

> Were [this] an ordinary case, I should let the opinion speak for itself. But that you should entertain doubts has naturally stirred me to an anxious re-examination of my own views, even though I can assure you that nothing has weighed as much on my conscience, since I have come on this Court, as has this case. All my bias and pre-disposition are in favor of giving the fullest elbow room to every variety of religious, political, and economic view ... [but the issue] enters a domain where constitutional power is on one side and my private notions of liberty and toleration and good sense are on the other. ... My intention was to use this opinion as a vehicle for preaching the true democratic faith of not relying on the Court for the impossible task of assuring a vigorous, mature, self-protecting, and tolerant democracy by bringing the responsibility for a combination of firmness and toleration directly home where it belongs—to the people and their representatives themselves. ... What weighs with me strongly in this case is my anxiety that, while we lean in the direction of the libertarian aspect, we do not exercise our judicial power unduly, and as though

we ourselves were legislators by holding with too tight a rein the organs of popular government.

This sense of judicial limitation showed clearly in his opinion for the 8–1 majority, where Frankfurter framed the "precise" issue in terms of judicial restraint, and called upon the Court to defer to the wisdom and prerogatives of local school authorities.

To stigmatize legislative judgment in providing for this universal gesture of respect for the symbol of our national life in the setting of the common school as a lawless inroad on that freedom of conscience which the Constitution protects, would amount to no less than the pronouncement of pedagogical and psychological dogma in a field where courts possess no marked and certainly no controlling competence.... To the legislature no less than to courts is committed the guardianship of deeply cherished liberties.

There is an almost formulaic quality to the opinion: Is the legislative end legitimate? Are the means chosen reasonable? If so, then it is not up to the courts to say that a better way exists. Therefore, if the end is legitimate and the means chosen are not unreasonable, the measure—in this case the flag salute—is constitutional. Frankfurter paid practically no attention to the Gobitas claim that First Amendment rights of free exercise of religion had been violated; and although he gave a nominal bow to balancing, he found national unity a far more pressing matter (Danzig, 1984, *passim*). One scholar has noted that this opinion was influenced directly by the events of the day: he describes it as "Felix's Fall-of-France Opinion" (Peters, 2000, 46).

Let us pause now and compare this approach to later judicial analyses based on the First Amendment. Frankfurter's lead question was whether the state has a legitimate interest; but modern courts would ask whether free exercise rights have been restricted, and if they have, whether the state had a *compelling* interest to warrant that restriction. A merely "legitimate" or even an "important" interest will not justify violation of the First Amendment. If, however, the state does have a compelling interest, then the courts will ask whether the limitation has been imposed in the least restrictive manner. The difference between the two approaches is substantial: one treats regulations of religious freedom in the same manner as economic rules, and the other elevates the rights of the individual above the administrative convenience of the state. In terms of balancing, the latter approach places far greater weight on individual liberty than on any but the most compelling governmental interest. This approach derives directly from Stone's *Carolene Products* footnote, in that it requires the courts to look more intensely at issues involving individual rights. In contrast, Frankfurter's view was that the courts must defer to legislative judgment, regardless of the issue.

Only Stone dissented from the majority opinion in *Gobitis*, and he did not decide to enter a written dissent until it was too late to circulate it among the brethren. By that time, Stone had become quite emotional about the subject, and he took the unusual step of reading his dissent aloud from the bench. In his first sentence he put his finger on the very meaning of the Free Exercise Clause: "History teaches us that there have been but few infringements of personal liberty by the state which have not been justified, as they are here, in the name of righteousness and the public good, and few which have not been directed, as they are now, at politically helpless minorities." What Stone recognized, and what Frankfurter always failed to see, was that while the political process could in many instances be relied upon to work out points of friction between mainstream groups, it would never rally to the defense of the despised minority. For that protection, groups like the Witnesses had to depend on the Constitution and the Court. As for Frankfurter's argument that the state had to teach loyalty, Stone in effect said that while loyalty is a wonderful idea, it cannot be created by compulsion and force.

Much of the liberal press applauded Stone's opinion in *Gobitis* and denounced that of Frankfurter. Harold Laski, a close friend of Frankfurter's, wrote Stone to tell him "how right I think you are . . . [and] how wrong I think Felix is." Harold Ickes, recognizing Frankfurter's concern about the war in Europe (the decision came down during the Dunkirk evacuation), thought the opinion worse than useless, "as if the country can be saved, or our institutions preserved, by forced salute of our flag by these fanatics" (Urofsky, 1997, 109).

The three most liberal members of the Court—Hugo Black, William O. Douglas, and Frank Murphy—all voted with the majority. However, from the start, Murphy was troubled by the decision. Black also did not like the law, but saw nothing in the Constitution to invalidate the measure. When the Court convened after its summer recess, Douglas told Frankfurter that Black had had second thoughts about his *Gobitis* vote. "Has Black been reading the Constitution?" Frankfurter sarcastically asked. "No," Douglas responded, "he has been reading the newspapers" (Fine, 1984, 187). Black—and everyone else—would have noted the Justice Department and ACLU reports that in the weeks following the decision, there had been hundreds of attacks on Witnesses, especially in small towns and rural areas. By the end of 1940, more than 1,500 Witnesses had been attacked and many had been beaten brutally, in more than 350 separate incidents; and this pattern of violence continued for at least two years (Peters, 2000, 10).

The first flag salute case had been one of the early struggles in the debate over how far the protection of the Bill of Rights extended to the states, and what role the courts had in determining the limits of that protection. In *Gobitis,* despite the 8–1 vote, at least three members of the majority found themselves uncomfortable with Frankfurter's narrow view of those protections; and in the next few years, this unease expanded. The Witnesses refused to compromise their beliefs despite a great deal of public scorn and even physical attacks, and they pressed for litigation to vindicate their religious practices. In *Cox v. New Hampshire* (1941), a unanimous Court upheld a state regulation requiring permits for parades—even for religious parades. The following year, the Court sustained the conviction of a Witness who had gotten into a fight after calling a city marshal "a goddamned racketeer" and "a damned fascist." Murphy, normally the Court's champion of free speech, found that these "fighting words" were outside the protection of the First Amendment (*Chaplinsky v. New Hampshire* [1942]).

The following term, the issue arose again when the Court announced its decision in *Jones v. Opelika* (1942), in which Jehovah's Witnesses had refused to pay a municipal licensing fee for peddlers, prior to selling their religious tracts. The issue was essentially the same as in *Gobitis:* the extent to which the government's acknowledged power to maintain public order impinged on the free exercise of religion. A majority voted in favor of the state; but this time, four judges dissented—Stone, Black, Douglas, and Murphy. Moreover, in an unprecedented step, the latter three appended a statement acknowledging that *Opelika* was a logical extension of *Gobitis* and admitting that they had been wrong in the earlier case. The majority opinions in both decisions, they charged, "put the right freely to exercise religion in a subordinate position in violation of the First Amendment."

By this time many Americans had begun to rethink the implications of the earlier flag salute case, especially in light of what they knew of fascism and its enmity with democracy. The flag salute could hardly compare to the repression practiced in Nazi Germany; but it did strike many people as a needless intrusion on personal liberty in the name of the state. Moreover, as practiced in many places, the American flag salute involved holding the right hand straight out—a gesture much too similar to the fascist salute for the comfort of many Americans. On the Court, Black and Frankfurter, even while disagreeing on other things, agreed that, as Frankfurter put it, the Witness cases "are probably but the curtain raisers of future problems of [great] range and magnitude" (Urofsky, 1997, 110).

After President Roosevelt named Wiley Rutledge to replace James Byrnes in 1942, the dissenters in *Opelika* had a majority. In May 1943, the Court by a 5–4 majority handed the Witnesses two victories on the same day, striking down a tax on peddlers of religious tracts *(Murdock v. Pennsylvania)* and an ordinance prohibiting door-to-door distribution of religious materials *(Martin v. City of Struthers)*. In *Murdock*, Justice Douglas described the application of the peddlers' tax to Jehovah's Witnesses as comparable to taxing a minister for the privilege of delivering a sermon. In *Struthers*, Justice Black conceded the need for some police regulation but held that the preferred position of speech and religion took precedence.

In light of the spate of attacks on Witnesses, the apparent shift in Court sentiment, and news of Hitler's "Final Solution" of the Jewish question in Europe, the Court accepted another case dealing with required flag salutes and free exercise of religion in the October 1942 term. Both the American Bar Association Committee on the Bill of Rights and the American Civil Liberties Union—two groups that rarely have been in agreement—filed amici briefs in support of the Witnesses in *West Virginia Board of Education v. Barnette* (1943). Chief Justice Stone assigned the opinion to Robert H. Jackson, who although he rarely voted for minority rights against a public interest argument, this time joined the liberals to strike down the mandatory salute. In most of the other Witness cases, the Court had relied as much upon the Speech Clause as the Free Exercise Clause. Jackson's wording of the opinion was an important step forward in defining religious freedom. In one of the most eloquent opinions of his judicial career, Jackson declared: "If there is any fixed star in our constitutional constellation, it is that no official, high or petty, can prescribe what shall be orthodox in politics, nationalism, religion or other matters of opinion or force citizens to confess by word or act their faith therein."

Frankfurter entered an impassioned dissent that, if taken literally, nearly denied the Court any role in enforcing the Bill of Rights. Despite Frankfurter's comment that he belonged to "the most vilified and persecuted minority in history," he in fact dismissed judicial protection of minorities. The Framers, he said, "knew that minorities may disrupt society." Frankfurter reiterated the formula he had used in the earlier decision, that "this Court's only and very narrow function is to determine whether within the broad grant of authority vested in legislatures they have exercised a judgment for which reasonable justification can be offered." Because of Jackson's eloquent depiction of the meaning of free exercise of religion, Frankfurter could not pass over it as lightly as he had in *Gobitis;* but he took a minimalist approach. The First Amendment provided "freedom from conformity to religious dogma, not freedom from conformity to law because of religious dogma." Claims of conscience by themselves can never justify exemption from valid laws that have a reasonable basis. As Sanford Levenson points out, because the state could always create the nexus of a reasonable justification for its action, the courts, following Frankfurter's reasoning, would never impose any serious review on state action (Levenson, 1969, 232).

The swing to the side of individual rights marked by the Witness cases did not go unprotested. The minority opinions in *Murdock* and *Struthers* emphasized the importance of the state's preservation of public order and took a relatively restricted view of the Bill of Rights. In his *Murdock* dissent, Stanley Reed argued that the Framers had intended only that freedom of speech should ensure the right to be heard and that freedom of religion should protect ritual. The First Amendment, he said, should not be interpreted to exclude speech, press, or religion from the general rules that govern society. Jackson, aside from the second flag salute case, normally voted with Frankfurter, Roberts, and Reed. His dissents indicated disenchantment with the Witnesses, whose intolerance he documented in *Douglas v. Jeannette* (1943). The

Constitution, he asserted, did not allow one religious group to ride "roughshod over others simply because their conscience told them to do so."

One more area in which Witnesses helped to forge modern Free Exercise jurisprudence involved conscientious objection. During World War I, the Witnesses had no doctrine regarding combat, and some members of the sect fought while others applied for conscientious objector (CO) status (few were granted that status). Their unpopularity in the interwar years did little to help them during World War II, and more than 4,000 Witnesses wound up in prison between 1941 and 1946—a figure representing more than two-thirds of all Americans jailed for refusing to serve.

The Selective Service Act of 1940 exempted ministers from the draft, defining a minister as "a man who customarily preaches and teaches the principles of a recognized church." The law listed the Witnesses as a recognized church, and Haydn Covington, the general counsel of the Watchtower Society, and General Lewis B. Hershey, head of the selective service system, reached an agreement that all "pioneer" Witnesses—that is, those who preached full-time—would be considered ministers of religion and draft-exempt. Those Witnesses who did not enjoy "pioneer" status were simple COs, required to report to national civil work camps, preventing them from performing the key obligation of their faith: proselytizing (Finkelman, 2000, 248).

Under the draft system, local boards had the power to grant or withhold various exemptions, such as CO status. In many parts of the country, Witnesses claimed that they had been treated unfairly by local boards, whose members despised the sect. All of the cases to reach the Supreme Court dealt with the lack of an established review process for classifications made by local boards, and the Witnesses won only two of the five decisions. In *Falbo v. United States* (1944), the Court decision did not even mention the sect, although Falbo clearly was a member. The Court ruled that given Congress's plenary power to raise an army, there was no need for judicial review of local draft board decisions. Two years later, after the war had ended, the Court reversed itself. In *Estep v. United States* (1946), it set aside the conviction of a Witness who had failed to report for induction, because he had not been allowed to challenge the board's classification during his trial.

Chief Justice Stone once quipped, "I think the Jehovah's Witnesses ought to have an endowment in view of the aid which they give in solving the legal problems of civil liberties" (Peters, 2000, 186). Certainly much credit is due to them for the cases they brought to the courts in the late 1930s and early 1940s, in which they insisted that under the Free Exercise Clause their actions— such as proselytizing and refusing to salute the flag—warranted protection against state action. Nearly all of the Free Exercise cases beginning in the early 1960s built upon these precedents.

FINDING AN ACCOMMODATION
FOR RELIGION

Just as the Jehovah's Witnesses' cases show how closely free exercise and freedom of expression are intertwined, so the Sunday blue laws show the interconnectedness of the two religion clauses. A number of states had, and some still do have, laws requiring the majority of businesses to close on Sunday. In 1961 the Court heard four cases challenging these laws as violations of the First Amendment. In three of them it refused to consider Free Exercise claims. In *McGowan v. Maryland,* Chief Justice Warren conceded that "the original laws which dealt with Sunday labor were motivated by religious forces." He rejected, however, the argument that this constituted an establishment of religion, reasoning that the current laws were merely the result of the state's desire to enforce one day of rest in seven: "The fact that this day is Sunday, a day of particular significance for the dominant Christian sects, does not bar the State from achieving its secular [goals]. Sunday is a day apart from all others. The cause is irrelevant; the fact exists."

In the companion case of *Braunfeld v. Brown,* Orthodox Jewish merchants attacked the Sunday laws on Free Exercise grounds. Their religious beliefs required them to close on Saturdays, and having their shops closed two days a week would seriously undermine their livelihood. Chief Justice Warren recited the accepted distinction between belief and action, and noted that nothing in the law forced the appellants to modify or deny their beliefs; at worst, they might have to change occupations or incur some economic disadvantages.

Warren's opinion shows a striking insensitivity, almost a callousness, toward Jewish merchants, especially when one considers the great sensitivity he showed to the plights of other minority groups. The opinion is mechanical in its recitation of previous cases setting forth the belief/action dichotomy and finding that the law affected only action. Although it is true that nearly all laws have adverse effects on some groups, the Court had imposed a closer scrutiny on laws affecting First Amendment rights. To say that the law did not affect beliefs but only made it economically difficult for adherents of Judaism to practice those beliefs, showed a complete misunderstanding of the spirit of the Free Exercise Clause.

Justices Potter Stewart and Douglas dissented, but it was Justice Brennan's objections that pointed the way toward future First Amendment jurisprudence. Brennan had no doubt that the Sunday laws imposed a great burden on Jewish merchants, forcing them to choose between their business and their religion; and this, he believed, violated the Free Exercise Clause. The state had to prove some compelling interest to justify this restriction on freedom of religion; the "mere convenience" of having everybody rest on the same day did not, in his eyes, constitute a compelling state interest. Brennan continued further: Did Pennsylvania have any options by which the state's interest in fostering one day's rest in seven would not conflict with the appellants' religious freedom? Of course it did. Of the thirty-four states with Sunday closing laws, twenty-one granted exemptions to those who in good faith observed a different day of rest. The Court, he charged, had "exalted administrative convenience to a constitutional level high enough to justify making one religion economically disadvantageous."

The same mechanical jurisprudence that governed the Sunday closing law cases can also be seen in the Burger Court's decision in *Goldman v. Weinberger* (1986). An Air Force medical officer who was an Orthodox Jew challenged a prohibition against unauthorized headgear, which prevented him from wearing a *keepah*, the traditional skullcap. What makes the decision unfathomable is that by this time the Court had moved away from the rigid stance it had taken in *Braunfeld;* and in cases such as *Sherbert v. Verner* and *Wisconsin v. Yoder*, it had adopted a much more permissive attitude toward individual religious claims. To justify the result in *Goldman*, the five-man majority relied on the Constitution's full grant of power over the military to Congress, and essentially said that if Congress wanted to make an exception, it had the power to do so. In a sharp dissent reminiscent of his *Braunfeld* dissent a quarter-century earlier, Justice Brennan wrote that wearing the skullcap with a United States military uniform "is an eloquent reminder that the shared and proud identity of U.S. servicemen embraces and unites religious and ethnic pluralism." The criticism of the majority opinion led the Air Force to rescind the rule. But although Jews wound up on the losing end in these cases, the Court's opinions later were overruled by public opinion and changing cultural values. Those opinions in any case hardly warrant the cries of some to the effect that the "Christian" Court's jurisprudence was anti-Semitic (Feldman, 1997, 247).

In his Sunday closing law dissents, Brennan not only pointed out that a commonsense solution existed; it also showed greater sensitivity to the problems that economic hardship imposed on religious freedom. The Brennan view triumphed fairly quickly. Two years after the Sunday closing law cases, the Court heard *Sherbert v. Verner* (1963), a case in which a Seventh-day Adventist in South

Carolina had been discharged from her job because she would not work on Saturday. Adele Sherbert's refusal to work on her Sabbath had prevented her from finding any other employment in the area, and the state had denied her unemployment compensation payments. South Carolina law barred benefits to workers who refused, without "good cause," to accept an offer of suitable work.

In what we would now term the "modern" approach to First Amendment issues, Justice Brennan posed the same question he had in *Braunfeld:* Did the state have a compelling interest sufficient to warrant an abridgement of a constitutionally protected right? This is, of course, the same question the Court asks in regard to speech restrictions, because the analytical process in speech and free exercise claims is similar. Free expression of ideas is involved in religion just as it is in speech, press, assembly, or petition. One has a right to say what one believes, whether it involves political, economic, social, or religious ideas. Justices Black and Douglas over the years argued for what they termed a "preferred position" for First Amendment rights, because the two men believed these rights to be at the core of a democratic society. Only the most compelling societal need can warrant any restrictions on these rights.

Justice Brennan found no compelling interest presented by the state, and in fact the state could do little more than suggest that some applicants might file fraudulent claims alleging that they could not find work for religious reasons. Brennan did recognize, however, the difficulties that Stewart raised in his dissent: that in ruling that the state had to pay unemployment compensation benefits to Sherbert, South Carolina was favoring the adherents of a particular sect. Brennan went out of his way to indicate the very limited nature of the decision:

> In holding as we do, plainly we are not fostering the "establishment" of the Seventh-day Adventist religion in South Carolina. . . . [Nor] do we . . . declare the existence of a constitutional right to unemployment

benefits on the part of all persons whose religious convictions are the cause of their unemployment. This is not a case in which an employee's religious convictions serve to make him a nonproductive member of society. [Our] holding today is only that South Carolina may not constitutionally apply the eligibility provisions so as to constrain a worker to abandon his religious convictions respecting the day of rest.

The *Sherbert* case raised the question of whether the Constitution can be read as totally "religion-neutral" or "religion-blind." Philip B. Kurland suggested that one can find a unifying principle in the two religion clauses and that they ought to be "read as a single precept that government cannot utilize religion as a standard for action or inaction, because these clauses prohibit classification in terms of religion either to control a benefit or impose a burden" (Kurland, 1961, 1). The argument parallels the suggestion made by the first Justice Harlan that the Constitution is "color-blind"; and like that argument, it is manifestly incorrect.

Neither the Constitution nor the Court has been color-blind. Both the original Constitution and the Civil War Amendments recognized that blacks stood in a position of decided inferiority to whites; the original Constitution tended to sustain this arrangement, whereas the Amendments sought to redress the prevailing discrimination. The Court that decided *Plessy* favored the post–Civil War South's efforts to re-create a dual society; the Warren Court sought to erase the badges of discrimination.

Neutrality in religious matters, like neutrality with regard to skin color, is more an ideal than a reality in constitutional adjudication, and for the same reason. Very few issues that reach the Court can be resolved in simple ways; if the cases had been easy, the Court would not have heard them. Religion, like race, is a tangled skein, and not amenable to simplistic solutions. The Court recognized this, and from the absolutist decisions of the early Warren era, the Court moved steadily toward a jurisprudence of balancing various considerations.

CONSCIENTIOUS OBJECTORS

The question of conscientious objection had been notably absent from the high court's docket following the last of the Jehovah's Witnesses' cases in the late 1940s, and no major case grew out of the Korean conflict. But the war in Vietnam brought the issue back to the Court's docket during the later years of the Warren Court, which at that time had arguably the most liberal composition of any Court in the nation's history. Conscientious objection to war on religious grounds had already been recognized both by Congress and by the courts. But what about people who opposed war in general, not necessarily just on religious grounds, and what about those who opposed specific, "unjust" wars?

The United States has always shown a commendable sensitivity toward those with religious scruples against war. By 1784, the constitutions or bills of rights of five states, as well as the militia statutes of a majority of states, exempted religious pacifists from required service. The exemption is not surprising if we recall that many immigrants came to America to escape conscription or military service elsewhere. In more recent times, the World War I draft law provided an exemption for conscientious objectors, and the Supreme Court summarily rejected First Amendment objections to this exemption, holding it to be an appropriate exercise of legislative discretion (*Selective Draft Law Cases* [1918]). But in these cases and others, such as whether a pacifist who refused to bear arms could be denied citizenship under the Naturalization Act (*United States v. Macintosh* [1931] and *Girouard v. United States* [1946]), the Court has never held that the Free Exercise Clause requires that conscientious objector status be based on religion alone. Rather, the courts have held that Congress, with its plenary powers over both naturalization and military service, may provide for various CO exemptions without violating the First Amendment.

During World War II, Congress broadened the statutory CO exemption, and as we have seen, provided a liberal exception for ministers of religion. Following the war, Congress revised the draft law to exempt persons from military service who conscientiously opposed participation in war in any form because of their "religious training and belief" (Universal Military Training and Service Act of 1948, Section 6[j]). The statute defined "religious belief" as "belief in a relation to a Supreme Being involving duties superior to those arising from any human relation, but [not including] essentially political, sociological, or philosophical views or a merely personal moral code." Critics attacked Section 6(j) variously on Establishment, Free Exercise, and Due Process grounds, arguing that the clause did not exempt nonreligious conscientious objectors and that it discriminated among various forms of religious expression. But the unease some felt resulted from a concern over where to draw the line between the sincerely held religious beliefs of individuals and the impositions of general laws on all others. In the *Reynolds* case, Chief Justice Waite had expressed the Court's anxiety about making "doctrines of religious belief superior to the law of the land, and in effect . . . permit[ting] every citizen to become a law unto himself." Although Waite's comments related to polygamy, which a majority of Americans condemned, were they not equally applicable to exemptions from draft laws?

A number of challenges to Section 6(j) reached the courts in the early 1960s, as U.S. involvement in Southeast Asia began to escalate. In 1965 the Supreme Court heard three challenges, which it decided together as *United States v. Seeger.* Daniel Seeger claimed an exemption because of his belief in "goodness and virtue for their own sakes, and a religious faith in a purely ethical creed," and admitted to a skepticism about the existence of a God. Arno Jakobson believed in "Godness," and claimed his "most important religious law was that no man ought ever to willfully sacrifice another man's life as a means to any other end." The third litigant, Forest Britt Peter, sought CO status because the taking of human life violated his moral code. When his local draft board asked him whether that view derived from religious beliefs, Peter responded: "You could call that a belief in a Supreme Being or God. These just do not happen to be the words I use" (Johnson, 1992, 722).

The Court evaded the constitutional challenges by the simple expedient of reading the statute so broadly as to provide exemptions for all of the petitioners. Justice Tom Clark declared that Congress, by using the phrase "Supreme Being" rather than "God," meant to "embrace all religions" and to exclude only non-religious objections to military participation. Therefore, the proper test would not be adherence to a particular denomination but "whether a given belief that is sincere and meaningful occupies a place in the life of its possessor parallel to that filled by the orthodox belief in God of one who clearly qualifies for the exemption."

Whether the Congress that had passed the 1948 statute really intended this outcome is impossible to determine; but two years later, Congress ratified and in fact expanded the scope of the exemption by deleting the phrase "belief in a relation to a Supreme Being." The Warren Court, although it read the statute broadly, nonetheless evaded the First Amendment questions as well as the particular challenges raised by those opposed to the war in Vietnam.

The Burger Court continued this liberalizing trend. In *Welsh v. United States* (1970), the Court overruled a draft board that excluded agnostics, and reaffirmed the *Seeger* ruling that conscience and not religion dictated status. The Court did try to impose some rationale in *Clay v. United States* (1971), in the form of a tripartite test for claims of conscientious objection; but it took a very broad view of what constituted a "religious" claim. However, in *Gillette v. United States*, decided the same year, the Court held that the requirement that an individual seeking exemption object to war in any form excluded those who objected only to specific wars.

Guy Porter Gillette did not oppose all wars; but "spurred by deeply held moral, ethical, or religious beliefs," he refused to fight in Vietnam, and he had been arrested after he failed to report for induction. Although Catholicism and other religions have a long history of opposition to "unjust" wars, the Court found no basis in the Free Exercise Clause for allowing individuals to choose which wars they would fight and which they would oppose. Harking back to the *Reynolds* decision, Justice Thurgood Marshall, writing for a near-unanimous Court (only Justice Douglas dissented), refused to read the Free Exercise Clause as giving Gillette any special consideration because of his beliefs, no matter how sincere, about the wrongness of the American presence in Vietnam. Because Congress had plenary power to raise and maintain armed forces, Congress also had the power to institute a "fair system for determining 'who serves when not all serve.'" Any "incidental burdens" on the religious practices of selective objectors were "justified by substantial governmental interests" in military readiness. Like its predecessors, the *Gillette* Court would not constitutionalize a right of conscientious objection, selective or otherwise, under the First Amendment.

PROTECTING THE AMISH

The Burger Court's record was far more consistent with cases invoking the Free Exercise Clause than with those invoking the Establishment Clause. The Court reaffirmed the basic holding of *Sherbert v. Verner*—that a person may not be denied government benefits due to religious belief—when it reversed, by an 8-to-1 vote, Indiana's denial of unemployment compensation benefits to a Jehovah's Witness who had left his job in a munitions factory because of his religious objections to war (*Thomas v. Review Board* [1981]). But although the Free Exercise Clause requires exemption from government regulation under certain circumstances, these are not unlimited. In *United States v. Lee* (1982), the Court refused to exempt on religious grounds the Old Order Amish from paying Social Security taxes. In *Tony and Susan Alamo Foundation v. Sec-*

retary of Labor (1985), the Court rejected fundamentalist Christian claims that religious scruples prevented compliance with the minimum wage and other provisions of the Fair Labor Standards Act. The Court also sustained an Internal Revenue Service ruling denying tax-exempt charitable status to schools that practiced racial discrimination. In *Bob Jones University v. United States* (1983), Chief Justice Burger rejected the Free Exercise claim and found a compelling governmental interest in promoting racial equality.

A state's claim that compulsory education for all children is another such compelling interest would be affirmed by most Americans; yet it failed to convince the Court in *Wisconsin v. Yoder* (1972), which held that the Amish had a Free Exercise right to keep their children out of public schools. Wisconsin law required that all children between the ages of 7 and 16 attend school, and it placed the responsibility for compliance upon parents or guardians. The law did allow for instruction outside a school, but only if the state superintendent approved the alternative. The case began when Green County lost $18,000 in state aid after Amish children began attending a new Amish school. The state superintendent refused to approve the school because it would not provide "substantially equivalent education." The Amish parents were clearly guilty of a legal violation, but they also enjoyed a great deal of respect in their communities; weighing these considerations, the trial judge imposed a minimum fine of $5 on each parent. The intermediate appeals court upheld the decision, but Wisconsin's supreme court reversed it. Five of the seven justices signed a concurring opinion saying they would not support the Amish if the exemption of Amish children from the state's compulsory schooling law posed a serious threat to the public school system. More on principle than due to any opposition to the Amish, the state appealed its supreme court's decision. The U.S. Supreme Court granted certiorari, and much to everyone's surprise, handed down one of the most expansive Free Exercise rulings in its history.

The Amish objected to provisions of the state law requiring school attendance past the eighth grade. They believed—and the state did not challenge the sincerity of their belief—that sending adolescent children to public high schools would endanger their salvation. The Court recognized that the Amish marched completely out of step with contemporary society, and Chief Justice Burger affirmed their constitutional right to do so. Enforcement of the law would raise "a very real threat of undermining the Amish community and religious practices as they exist today; they must either abandon belief and be assimilated into society at large, or be forced to migrate to some other and more tolerant region." Given the relatively small number of children involved, the state's interest in educating its citizens would not suffer if it allowed the Amish an exception.

Justice Stewart concurred separately, wishing to emphasize that the case did not involve the rights of children but only those of parents to educate their children according to their religious beliefs. The record showed, he believed, that the children involved shared the religious beliefs of their parents. Byron White also concurred separately, noting that the Amish agreed to eight years of schooling and that the dispute was over the additional two years the state required; such a small difference, he believed, must be resolved in favor of the Amish.

Justice Douglas dissented on two of the three families involved, but concurred with the Court on the one child who had testified that she shared her parents' religious beliefs; he would have remanded for additional hearings on the views of the children from the other two families. Whereas Chief Justice Burger was almost effusive in praise of the Amish and their way of life, Douglas was much less admiring. If a child "is harnessed to the Amish way of life by those in authority over him and if his education is truncated, his entire life may be stunted and deformed." To Douglas the case was not about parental rights but about the rights of children to the type of education they would need to function in the world. If they received that education and then chose to remain in the Amish community, that would be a legitimate choice. But without the education, which Douglas saw as a right belonging to the child, there could be no realistic choice, because the child would not be fit to cope with the outer world.

The Court's ruling in *Wisconsin v. Yoder* gave new impetus to the home schooling movement—a development that the justices cannot have anticipated. Although there have always been parents who have taught their children at home, growing dissatisfaction with the nation's public school system, a rising urban crime rate, and the phenomenal growth of the religious right, with its suspicion of all things secular, led to tens of thousands of parents deciding to keep their children out of the public schools. Although home schooling is not limited to social and religious conservatives, they have been the backbone of the movement, and their publications have hailed the *Yoder* decision for giving their movement a constitutional imprimatur. It is doubtful that the Burger Court even considered home schooling in its deliberations, since at the time the numbers involved were insignificant. One might well point to *Yoder* and the home schooling movement as a good example of the law of unanticipated consequences.

NATIVE AMERICANS IN THE COURT

With regard to its Free Exercise jurisprudence, the Rehnquist Court will probably be remembered for its marked insensitivity to Indian beliefs. In its first term the Rehnquist Court heard a Free Exercise claim involving a challenge to the federal government's plan to build a highway and permit timber harvesting in areas that had sacred value to Indian tribes. In *Lyng v. Northwest Indian Cemetery Protective Association* (1988),[2] Justice O'Connor spoke for a 5–3 majority conceding that the activities would interfere with tribal pursuit of spiritual fulfillment but arguing that the government's plans neither coerced the members into violating any of their religious tenets nor penalized any religious activity. This sophistic reasoning, which ignored the basis of the Free Exercise claim, relied on a 1986 decision, *Bowen v. Roy,* which upheld the government's assignment of a Social Security number to an Indian child over the protest of her parents, who believed that the number would "rob" the little girl of her soul. Dissenting in *Lyng,* Justice Brennan found the majority's reliance on *Bowen* "altogether remarkable." In *Bowen* the issue had been one of internal government record-keeping and had had a limited effect. Logging and road building in or near sacred grounds, on the other hand, had potentially far-reaching negative effects on Indian religions—effects, Brennan warned, that could possibly destroy them. In the end, the road was not built, because the Indians succeeded in gathering sufficient political support to stop it.

Two years later the Court showed a similar insensitivity to Indian beliefs in *Employment Division, Oregon Department of Human Resources v. Smith* (1990). By a 5–4 vote, the Court held that the First Amendment does not bar a state from applying its general criminal prohibition of peyote to individuals who claim to use it for sacramental purposes. In addition, the majority announced that the test balancing governmental action burdening religious practices against a compelling governmental interest, first enunciated in *Sherbert v. Verner* (1963), would no longer apply in cases involving criminal laws of general applicability.

Although many western states and the federal government provided exemptions for peyote when used in religious ceremonies, Oregon did not. Two employees in a drug rehabilitation program, Alfred Smith and Galen Black, were fired from their positions because they ingested peyote at a religious ceremony of the Native American Church. The two were then denied unemployment compensation because they had been dismissed for criminal misconduct—the use of a proscribed substance (see Chapter 1 for more details). In a line of cases going back to *Sherbert v. Verner* (1963), the Supreme Court had ruled that state unemployment insurance could not be conditioned on an individual's willingness to forgo conduct required by his religion, when that conduct was otherwise legal. Smith and Black argued that the same rule should apply to them, even though the Oregon law made ingestion of peyote illegal, because the Oregon law itself was unconstitutional.

Justice Scalia, writing for a bare majority of the Court, took an extremely narrow view of the Free Exercise Clause. Going all the way back to the 1879 case of *Reynolds v. United States,* he argued that religion could never be used as an excuse for violating "an otherwise valid law regulating conduct that the state is free to regulate." Justice O'Connor, joined in part by Brennan, Marshall, and Blackmun, sharply criticized the Court for abandoning the balancing test. Moreover, by denying the applicants the opportunity to challenge a general criminal law on Free Exercise grounds, the majority had cut out "the essence of a free exercise claim." Just because this government action involved a criminal statute did not mean that that it did not burden religious freedom. Nonetheless, O'Connor joined in the result because she believed the state had a compelling interest under the balancing test: namely its effort to wage a war on drugs.

THE RELIGIOUS FREEDOM RESTORATION ACT

The general criticism of the *Smith* decision led a broad coalition of religious groups to petition Congress for a federal law that would restore a number of exemptions for religious activities. The coalition garnered strong bipartisan support, and in 1993 Congress overwhelmingly passed and President Clinton signed into law the Religious Freedom Restoration Act (RFRA). (See Chapter 6.) The statute contained a number of formal findings that "laws 'neutral' toward religion may burden religious exercise without compelling justification." The law and its accompanying legislative history could not have been blunter in its statement that the Supreme Court had been wrong in *Smith* for eliminating the requirement that government justify burdens on religious exercise imposed by facially neutral laws, and that the better interpretation had been the compelling interest test of *Sherbert*. Although popular, the RFRA was a sweeping law purporting to bind government action at all levels—federal, state, and local. In practical terms, it was an attempt to overrule a Supreme Court decision by creating a broad federal guarantee of religious freedom greater than that created by the First Amendment.

But where did Congress get its authority to pass the RFRA? Congress can "overrule" a court's interpretation of a statute by legislating more precise language; but what provision of the Constitution allowed the Congress to override the Court's interpretation of the First Amendment? Congress claimed that it was not actually overturning *Smith* but merely passing civil rights legislation—in this case, religious civil rights. In the past, Congress had passed laws creating greater rights than those embodied in the Constitution, claiming the authority to do so from Section 5 of the Fourteenth Amendment: "Congress shall have the power to enforce, by appropriate legislation, the provisions of this article." Since 1803, however, the Court had held itself to be the definitive interpreter of the Constitution. The test case to determine who would prevail arose in the small Texas city of Boerne, located some 28 miles northwest of San Antonio.

The city council had authorized the Historic Landmark Commission to prepare a preservation plan for the downtown area. In order to maintain the historic look of the area, anyone seeking to change landmarks or buildings in that area was required to get prior approval. St. Peter's Catholic Church dated from 1923, and had been built in the mission style of the area's earlier history. The parish was growing, but the sanctuary could hold only 230 worshipers, and on any given Sunday between 40 and 60 people could not be accommodated at some masses. The church sought permission to expand, but the city denied the application on the grounds that the altered structure would damage the integrity of the historic district. The archbishop brought suit, claiming that the denial of the permit violated the RFRA. *City of Boerne v. Flores* (1997) could hardly have been a better test case to demonstrate the weaknesses of the law.

The decision had less to do with religious free exercise than with federalism and the separation of powers. The Court denied that Congress had the power under Section 5 to impose upon the courts a particular constitutional interpretation. Justice Kennedy, in essence, read a civic lesson to Congress: the Court, and only the Court, would decide what the Constitution meant.

Had the Court sustained the RFRA, it would have opened a Pandora's box of litigation and problems. The church in Boerne was asking for something no one else in the downtown area could get—approval to expand and alter a historic building. Had the church been successful, what would have stopped the hardware store across the street from demanding approval for its plans to expand, under an equal protection claim that it should be treated at least the same as the church? (Justice Stevens in his concurring opinion made this point, and claimed that the RFRA violated the Establishment Clause by granting preferences for religious groups.) The Court had been insensitive in *Smith,* and for reasons that are unclear it had abandoned a perfectly usable balancing test that had been in effect for more than three decades. In their separate concurring opinions, Justices O'Connor, Souter, and Breyer indicated that they had heard the message, and argued that the *Smith* doctrine should be reconsidered.

Within a few weeks after the *Boerne* decision, the House Subcommittee on Civil and Constitutional Affairs began to hold hearings on "Protecting Religious Liberty after *Boerne v. Flores.*" On 9 June 1998, sponsors introduced the Religious Liberty Protection Act of 1998 in both the House and Senate; but legislators' attention was immediately diverted when Kenneth Starr presented his report on President Clinton, and Congress became embroiled in the House's impeachment of the president and then the Senate's exoneration of him.

On 5 May 1999 the bill was reintroduced in both houses, and they began hearings one week later. Couched in broad, at times even vague language, the bill provided that government would not substantially burden a person's religious exercise, even as the result of a neutral general law, unless the law met some compelling governmental interest. The second section of the bill applied to interstate commerce and situations where federal funds were involved, two areas normally recognized by the courts as coming within broad federal control; and its third section provided that once a person had made a prima facie case that free exercise of religion had been burdened, then the burden of proof shifted entirely to the government to prove the need for such a restraint. This last provision appears redundant, since that has been the case in First Amendment cases for decades; parts 1 and 2, however, implicated the issues raised by the Court in *Boerne* (Long, 2000, 263–265).

The House of Representatives approved the bill on 15 July 1999, but the bill died in the Senate, where constitutional considerations, as usual, played a larger role than they did in the House deliberations. Congress did, however, respond to the problems raised in the *Lyng* decision, passing the Religious Land Use and Institutionalized Person Act, which became law in September 2000. Although more modest in scope than the RFRA, this Act will probably withstand constitutional scrutiny because it deals primarily with issues over which Congress has acknowledged responsibilities, such as Indian lands and national forests.

In the meantime, efforts arose in several states to pass a state version of the RFRA. Aware of the concerns voiced in both *Smith* and *Boerne*, the state measures for the most part do little more than provide faith-based exemptions "to ensure the broadest support for religious exercise." Four states passed such measures in

1998, and nine other states were considering similar legislation. Short of promoting religion—which would, of course, violate the Establishment Clause—these for the most part innocuous measures will probably pass constitutional muster. If nothing else, the Court showed in *Boerne* how otherwise innocent and well-intentioned laws could have completely unforeseen consequences.

While Congress pondered new legislation, the Court indicated that although it would not give religious groups exemptions from general laws, it also would not countenance laws aimed specifically at inhibiting particular practices. The Santeria sect, which originated when the Yoruba people were brought to Cuba as slaves, involved an amalgam of West African religion intermixed with Roman Catholicism. Animal sacrifice (after which the animals were cooked and eaten) constituted an essential part of the group's practices. The animals were not tortured but were killed by a clean cutting of the carotid artery in the neck.

When the Santeria announced plans to open a church in Hialeah, Florida, many residents objected. The city council quickly passed a series of ordinances effectively preventing animal sacrifice within the city limits and punishing violators with fines not to exceed $500 and/or imprisonment of up to 60 days. Although masquerading as health regulations, the taped sessions of the city council clearly indicated the hostility of officials toward the Santeria as well as the fact that the ordinances had been passed specifically to keep the Santeria out of Hialeah.

In *Church of the Lukumi Babalu Aye v. City of Hialeah* (1993), the Court unanimously invalidated these regulations as a violation of the Free Exercise Clause, although the justices differed in their reasoning. Justice Kennedy, in his opinion for the Court, called the Hialeah law "religious gerrymandering"—"an impermissible attempt to target petitioners and their religious practices." The law ran afoul not only of the First Amendment but of the Fourteenth as well, in that it violated the Equal Protection Clause by singling out one group's practices.

CONCLUSION

As we have seen, much of the basic free exercise jurisprudence was developed during the World War II era by the Jehovah's Witnesses' cases, and many of the strands in these cases seemed to come together in *Sherbert v. Verner* (1963), in which the Court indicated that general rules had to give way to accommodate individual religious preferences. Although hailed as a landmark of religious toleration and openness, *Sherbert* carried within it seeds of discord. It is one thing to say that in terms of unemployment compensation administrative convenience must not outweigh the principles of religious freedom. But how far can one take this rule? Chief Justice Waite, as far back as *Reynolds v. United States* (1879), warned that the Free Exercise Clause did not give individuals license to disobey general rules on the grounds of religious belief, no matter how sincere that belief. In *Wisconsin v. Yoder* (1972) the Court seemed to ignore that injunction; yet the same justices who decided this case, only the previous year, in *Gillette v. United States* (1971), had refused to allow people to choose on the basis of religious belief which wars they would fight on behalf of their country. The Court's decision in *Oregon v. Smith* (1990) shocked many people only because it seemed so restrictive when compared to *Sherbert* and *Yoder;* but it would be a much better comparison to place it alongside *Gillette.* There are certain general laws, especially criminal laws, that must be enforced against everyone; otherwise, the social structure collapses. If people are free to ignore drug laws or conscription statutes on claims of religious belief, then acknowledging those beliefs and permitting the exemptions does in fact amount to a violation of the Establishment Clause, because even if it does not create an official religion, it does give one set of religious beliefs preference over others. That tension is part of the creativity of the First Amendment; it has led to some striking blows in behalf of despised religious minorities, and at the same time has deprived others of what they believe to be their constitutional rights. This is a debate that, one hopes, will go on forever.

NOTES

1. This relatively insignificant case is remembered primarily for a footnote that literally created a revolution in the Supreme Court's constitutional jurisprudence. Congress had passed a law prohibiting the interstate shipment of so-called filled milk, defined in the statute as skim milk "compounded with . . . any fat or oil other than milk fat." Although this was clearly special-interest legislation favoring particular parts of the dairy industry, Stone, speaking for four justices, put forward a simple test for weighing economic regulation: namely, whether the legislature had a rational basis for enacting the law. But in footnote four, inserted immediately after Stone's statement of the rational basis test, he declared that "there may be narrower scope for operation of the presumption of constitutionality when legislation appears on its face to be within a specific prohibition of the Constitution," including those of the first ten amendments that had been incorporated through the Fourteenth Amendment's Due Process Clause, and those aimed at particular religions, the integrity of the political process, or at "discrete and insular minorities." This footnote led to a new jurisprudence that emerged full-blown in the Warren Court era, in which the Court applied a very minimal "rational basis" test to all economic regulation but a much higher standard to laws affecting the guarantees of the First Amendment, especially speech, as well as to any law affecting race. The Court's role as the ultimate protector of constitutional rights was thereby confirmed.

2. Despite the title of the case, there were no burial grounds involved; the area was used traditionally for retreats and rites of passage.

REFERENCES

Arrington, Leonard. 1985. *Brigham Young: American Moses.* New York: Knopf.

Carter, Stephen. 1993. *The Culture of Disbelief.* New York: Basic Books.

Danzig, Richard. 1984. "Justice Frankfurter's Opinions in the Flag Salute Cases: Blending Logic and Psychologic in Constitutional Decisionmaking." *Stanford Law Review* 36: 675.

Evans, Bette Novit. 1997. *Interpreting the Free Exercise of Religion: The Constitution and American Pluralism.* Chapel Hill: University of North Carolina Press.

Feldman, Stephen M. 1997. *Please Don't Wish Me a Merry Christmas: A Critical History of the Separation of Church and State.* New York: New York University Press.

Fine, Sidney. 1984. *Frank Murphy: The Washington Years.* Ann Arbor: University of Michigan Press.

Finkelman, Paul, ed. 2000. *Religion and American Law: An Encyclopedia.* New York: Garland.

Firmage, Edwin B. 1989. "Free Exercise of Religion in Nineteenth-Century America: The Mormon Cases." *Journal of Law and Religion* 7: 282–313.

———. 1991. "Religion and the Law: The Mormon Experience in the Nineteenth Century." *Cardozo Law Review* 12: 765–803.

Firmage, Edwin B., and Richard C. Mangrum. 1988. *Zion in the Courts: A Legal History of the Church of Jesus Christ of Latter-Day Saints, 1830–1900.* Urbana: University of Illinois Press.

Hansen, Klaus J. 1981. *Mormonism and the American Experience.* Chicago: University of Chicago Press.

Irons, Peter H. 1988. *The Courage of Their Convictions: Sixteen Americans Who Fought Their Way to the Supreme Court.* New York: Free Press.

Johnson, John W., ed. 1992. *Historic U.S. Court Cases, 1690–1990: An Encyclopedia.* New York: Garland Publishing.

Kurland, Philip B. 1961. "Of Church and State and the Supreme Court." *University of Chicago Law Review* 29: 1.

Laycock, Douglas. 1990. "The Remnants of Free Exercise." *Supreme Court Review* 1990: 1.

Levenson, Sanford. 1969. "Skepticism, Democracy, and Judicial Restraint: An Essay on the Thought of Oliver Wendell Holmes and Felix Frankfurter." Doctoral dissertation, Harvard University.

Long, Carolyn N. 2000. *Religious Freedom and Indian Rights: The Case of Oregon v. Smith.* Lawrence: University Press of Kansas.

Manwaring, David. 1962. *Render unto Caesar: The Flag Salute Controversy.* Chicago: University of Chicago Press.

Mason, Alpheus Thomas. 1956. *Harlan Fiske Stone: Pillar of the Law.* New York: Viking Press.

Peters, Shawn Francis. 2000. *Judging Jehovah's Witnesses: Religious Persecution and the Dawn of the Rights Revolution.* Lawrence: University Press of Kansas.

Smith, Steven. 1995. *Foreordained Failure: The Quest for a Constitutional Principle of Religious Freedom.* New York: Oxford University Press.

Urofsky, Melvin I. 1997. *Division and Discord: The Supreme Court under Stone and Vinson, 1941–1953.* Columbia: University of South Carolina Press.

Waite, Edward F. 1944. "The Debt of Constitutional Law to Jehovah's Witnesses." *Minnesota Law Review* 2: 209.

5

KEY PEOPLE, CASES, AND EVENTS

Abington School District v. Schempp (1963)

This case followed *Engel v. Vitale* (1962), which outlawed a New York state prayer that was used to start the school day, and which had generated tremendous public sentiment against the Court. The question in *Schempp* was whether the Constitution forbade a reading from the Bible, without any commentary by the reader, at the start of each school day (any child could excuse himself or herself from this). Building on Black's reasoning in *Engel*, conservative Justice Tom Clark spoke for the Court in striking down the Pennsylvania statute. Clark pointed to the historical dangers of a closely related church and state, which often produced persecution for those not in the majority, and set forth the first two prongs of what nine years later would become known as the *Lemon* test. A policy must have a secular purpose and its primary effect must be neutral, meaning that it cannot effectively advance or inhibit religion. Moreover, the Free Exercise Clause prohibited state compulsion, just as the Establishment Clause prohibited state sponsorship of religious activities. Clark believed that coercion was more apt to occur when Free Exercise issues were at stake; but in this case, Clark's reasoning seems to have been predicated on a notion of peer pressure: the fact that members of the minority called attention to themselves by not participating was enough to satisfy the Court that substantial coercion existed and therefore the Bible reading was a violation of the First Amendment.

Accommodationist

Accommodationists argue that the government may aid religion as long as it does not do so to the advantage of one religion over another. Rather, aid must be given in a nonpreferential manner; what is available to one religion must be available to all.

Agostini v. Felton (1997)

This case marked a major departure from earlier First Amendment reasoning regarding the use of public funds in religious school settings, as an accommodationist bloc challenged the assumptions previously utilized in *Grand Rapids v. Ball* and *Aguilar v. Felton.* Justice O'Connor rejected the notions that any public school employee who enters a religious school should be presumed to inculcate religion (the reasoning in *Ball* and *Aguilar*); that the presence of such public employees is a symbolic union of church and state; and that all public monies that aid education in a religious setting always encourage religious indoctrination.

Aguilar v. Felton (1985)

This decision paralleled that in *Grand Rapids v. Ball,* except that congressionally provided Title I funds for remedial instruction were involved.

Bill Concerning Religion (1779)

Drafted by Patrick Henry, this bill sought to establish the Christian religion as the official religion of Virginia, and called for an equal division of tax proceeds among the various state-recognized Christian sects. It prescribed articles of faith that church members would have to recite in order for their church to be considered "official." In essence, it would have required that churches swear an oath before they could receive state funds. The bill hung in the balance for seven years before the Protestants changed their position (based on their increasing need for funding). In 1784, Henry proposed "A Bill Establishing a Provision for the Teachers of the Christian Religion," which maintained the basic premises of the Bill Concerning Religion, namely a general tax and multiple official Christian religions. James Madison stalled deliberations on this bill while gathering support for his own position (that religion should not be granted official status), effectively undermining any chance of Henry's bill's passage.

Bill for Religious Freedom (1779)

This Virginia state bill was drafted by Thomas Jefferson with the intent that personal religious choice be left fully to one's conscience. Jefferson aimed to place religion outside of the action of civil government. He sought to enlarge the scope of the religious freedom clause of the Virginia Constitution of 1776 by extending tolerance to all groups, not just Protestant Christians. He believed that such rights were inalienable to humanity and therefore merited full protection as set forth by the government.

Blue Laws

See Sunday Blue Laws.

Board of Education v. Allen (1968)

This case challenged a New York law requiring local school authorities to lend textbooks free of charge to all students in grades 7–12, including those enrolled in religious schools. The Court upheld the statute on the basis of the child-benefit theory initially articulated in the *Everson* case.

Bowen v. Kendrick (1987)

This case dealt with a portion of the Adolescent Family Life Act of 1982 that authorized federal funding to various public and private organizations, including religious groups, that provided counseling to adolescents regarding sexual relations and pregnancy. Chief Justice Rehnquist wrote for the court, stating that the Act did not fail the *Lemon* test, and so was not state establishment of religion. Any advance in religion due to the statute was "incidental and remote." This accommodationist holding set forth that mere religious affiliation did not merit the denial of funds. Rather, the threshold would be met when groups were "pervasively sectarian."

Bowen v. Roy (1986)

The Court upheld the government's issuance of a Social Security number to a Native American girl, despite her parents' belief that this act would "rob" her of her soul.

Braunfeld v. Brown (1961)

Orthodox Jewish merchants challenged blue laws as a violation of their free religious exercise, because they were forced to close their establishments on both Saturdays (for religious reasons) and Sundays (in obedience to the law), to their detriment. Chief Justice Warren utilized the belief-action dichotomy, stating that the law did not challenge their beliefs but merely affected their behavior. In his dissent, Justice Brennan argued that the state needed a compelling interest to justify a law that violated free exercise rights. Brennan's line of reasoning became very important in later cases.

Cantwell v. Connecticut (1940)

This case offered Jehovah's Witnesses their first high court victory on Free Exercise grounds. The Court overturned a state law that prohibited the solicitation of money for any charitable or religious cause without the approval of the secretary of the public welfare council. The law placed too much discretion in the hands of a public official to ban religiously motivated action. The decision was the first to apply the Free Exercise Clause to the states by way of the Fourteenth Amendment.

Child Benefit Rule

This rule was articulated in the *Everson* case. It reasoned that if the state directly aided schoolchildren on a general basis (i.e., with no preference being shown to students in religious schools), the aid was constitutionally permissible. This rule was the driving principle behind the allowance of bus transportation (in *Everson*) and loaned textbooks (in *Board of Education v. Allen*) for students at sectarian schools.

Church of the Lukumi Babalu Aye, Inc. v. City of Hialeah (1993)

Practitioners of the Santerian religion engaged in ritualistic animal sacrifice, and the city sought to block their activities with a series of ordinances disguised as health regulations. The Court unanimously found the ordinances unconstitutional because they targeted *only* religious practice and singled out religious adherents for disfavored treatment.

City of Boerne v. Flores (1997)

In this case, the Court ruled that the Congress had overstepped its constitutional bounds in enacting the Religious Freedom Restoration Act (RFRA). A Catholic church in the city had sought exemption, on RFRA grounds, from a generally applicable historic preservation ordinance in order to build an addition onto its church. The Court ducked the question of whether the church was entitled to the exemption, instead ruling that Congress could not substitute its interpretation of the Free Exercise Clause for the Court's. The Court, not Congress, must decide what the Constitution means.

Committee for Public Education and Religious Liberty v. Nyquist (1973)

The Court struck down a New York aid package for parochial schools. Justice Powell believed that the state did not have the right to do indirectly what it was prohibited to do directly, and therefore the Court would not allow aid for repair of buildings, reimbursement for families with annual incomes under $5,000, or tax credits for families in the next income bracket (up to $25,000).

Committee for Public Education and Religious Liberty v. Regan (1980)

A New York statute provided for direct monetary payments to private and religious schools for testing and reporting services as dictated by federal law. Applying the *Lemon* test, Justice White wrote for the majority that New York's statute did not violate the

Establishment Clause. The dissenting opinion penned by Justice Blackmun strongly disagreed, calling the case "a long step backwards."

Edwards v. Aguillard (1987)

In this case, the Court overturned Louisiana's Balanced Treatment Act of 1982, which decreed that creation science be taught alongside evolution. Justice Brennan cited the fact that the sponsors of the bill openly stated their intentions of injecting religion into the state schools. It thus violated the first prong of the *Lemon* test, which requires that a law be framed with a secular purpose.

Employment Division, Oregon Department of Human Resources v. Smith (1990)

This case arose out of the dismissal of two drug counselors in Oregon from their jobs after their employer learned that they had ingested peyote for religious purposes (the use of peyote for any purpose, religious or otherwise, was prohibited by state law). They filed for unemployment and were denied benefits because their dismissal from work was grounded on their "misconduct." Justice Scalia rejected the approach followed in *Sherbert v. Verner* and greatly narrowed the Free Exercise Clause, stating (on behalf of a bare 5–4 majority) that religion was not a valid excuse for ignoring "an otherwise valid law regulating conduct that the state is free to regulate." The majority worried that if one person were able to duck responsibility on Free Exercise grounds, that would open the floodgates for other, similar claims, undermining the state's ability to govern in an evenhanded and rational way on pressing societal issues. In short, this case set forth the notion that where one's spiritual practice ran counter to a law of general applicability, the law would prevail over faith. Justice O'Connor, in a separate opinion, criticized the Court for abandoning the balancing test articulated in *Sherbert v. Verner,* but then agreed with its finding, on the grounds that the state's need to combat narcotics use passed *Sherbert*'s "compelling governmental interest" test. The burden in this case was shifted to the individual whose religious beliefs were infringed, whereas in the past the burden had been on the state to show that it had a compelling interest justifying the infringement (as set forth by Justice Brennan in *Sherbert*). Because of the public outrage that followed the *Oregon v. Smith* decision, Congress passed the Religious Freedom Restoration Act (which was enacted with unanimity in the House and nearly the same in the Senate) with the intent to restore the *Sherbert* test.

Engel v. Vitale (1962)

This important case arose out of the prayer ritual that started the day at most schools for much of American history. The New York Board of Regents had created a "nondenominational" prayer to be recited at the beginning of each day in the state's schools. Justice Hugo Black issued the majority opinion invalidating the prayer, stating that any form of official religious act in schools, no matter how neutral the content of the prayer, was on its face "wholly inconsistent with the Establishment Clause." It was not what was said in the prayer but rather the act of prayer in general that Black felt was coercive in nature. He believed that the amount of power wielded by the state fostered a situation where any form of religious activity would be intimidating and pressuring toward religious minorities. Allowing this marriage of government with religion would be detrimental to both. Potter Stewart offered the only dissent, asserting that prayer had long been part of the American tradition and therefore deserved deference. Much of the public felt the same way. The ruling sparked a widespread public outcry, and the issue was readdressed the following year, in *Abington School District v. Schempp.*

Epperson v. Arkansas (1968)

This case dealt with whether states could ban the teaching of evolution in schools under the First Amendment's Establishment Clause. A biology teacher in Arkansas challenged the state's anti-evolution statute, claiming that she could not properly teach her course. Justice Abe Fortas spoke for a unanimous Court, stating that the only reason to disallow the teaching of evolution was because of the creation story in the Book of Genesis. This statute was tailored to the views of a specific religious group (consisting of the majority in the state) and therefore was a constitutionally impermissible governmental establishment of religion.

Establishment Clause

This first clause of the First Amendment of the Constitution bans the governmental establishment of a specific religion over other religions. It was included in the Bill of Rights as a safeguard against the type of oppression that colonial Americans experienced under British rule. In short, the Establishment Clause prohibits both direct instances (such as a written declaration by Congress favoring a specific religion) and indirect effects of governmental policies or laws that create or suggest establishment in practice (such as singling out religious groups for special benefits). In the *Everson* case, the Court extended its definition of establishment to include any government preference shown for religion over nonreligion.

Everson v. Board of Education (1947)

This case introduced the Supreme Court's contemporary view on the role of church and state in a democratic society in constitutional law. Here, New Jersey had authorized school boards to reimburse parents for the transportation expenses of their children attending public and nonpublic schools (including religious institutions).

The Court (5–4) applied the Establishment Clause to the states via the Fourteenth Amendment for the first time, although it upheld the reimbursement policy. Justice Hugo Black explained that the First Amendment called for neutral treatment of religious groups and for equal treatment between religion and nonreligion. Reimbursement was therefore within the permissible realm of the First Amendment. Black's opinion gave rise to the child-benefit theory, which posits that aid for the benefit of the children, not the schools, was not the same as unconstitutional funding of religious organizations. The case forms much of the foundation for the modern debate on the proper role of religion in a democratic state. Justice Black affirmed the notion of the full separation of church and state, as set forth 150 years earlier by Thomas Jefferson in his oft-quoted formulation "wall of separation." Still, as the case demonstrated, not every state activity that implicated religion would violate the First Amendment, although there was clearly a strong burden of proof to overcome when it did. The *Everson* case highlights many of the issues that characterize modern First Amendment jurisprudence, namely whether the Establishment Clause forbids all forms of governmental aid to religion (full separation principle) or whether it allows nonpreferential aid (accommodationist principle).

First Amendment

Ratified in 1791, this first article of the Bill of Rights reads: "Congress shall make no law respecting an establishment of religion, or prohibiting the free exercise thereof; or abridging the freedom of speech, or of the press; or the right of the people peaceably to assemble and to petition the Government for redress of grievances." This key amendment was the culmination of vast debate and deliberation over the proper role of religion in a democratic state. It is at the forefront of the constitutional debate regarding the limits of each of the religious freedoms guaranteed, and conversely, the ways in which the government may directly or indirectly support religion. Although this amendment speaks with stern certainty ("Congress shall make no law . . ."), its provisions are in no way absolute. Rather, they are to be safeguarded by weighing the governmental purpose behind limiting them against the freedom restricted (for instance, consider *Oregon v. Smith*). One's view of these boundaries is a clear indicator for one's views on the role of religion and its interaction with society and the government. Because of the differences in interpretation of this amendment, constitutional notions of religious freedom remain in question today.

Flast v. Cohen (1968)

As an exception to the policy against federal taxpayer suits, the Court granted a taxpayer standing to sue in order to challenge federal expenditures used for textbooks provided to religious schools, effectively allowing him to utilize the Establishment Clause to challenge this use of federal funds. This case assured the Supreme Court a position at the forefront of religious issues regarding education.

Footnote Four

In the otherwise obscure case of *United States v. Carolene Products Co.*, 304 U.S. 144 (1938), the fourth footnote suggested that in the future the Supreme Court would offer greater protection for civil liberties and civil rights, especially those enshrined in the Bill of Rights.

Free Exercise Clause

This second clause of the First Amendment was designed to prohibit governmental interference with personal religious liberty. By codifying free exercise, the framers of the Constitution intended to establish a society of toleration, unburdened by governmental interference. In most cases, however, the religious minority turns to this part of the First Amendment in the face of oppressive general laws enacted by an empowered majority. The Free Exercise Clause is the vehicle for the judicial decisions in such famous cases as *Sherbert v. Verner* and *Oregon v. Smith.*

Goldman v. Weinberger (1986)

A U.S. Air Force medical officer who was also an Orthodox Jew was prohibited by military regulations from wearing his *keepah* (traditional skullcap). He challenged the pertinent Air Force regulation as a Free Exercise violation. The Court, against strong dissent, ruled against him, utilizing the broad war power allotted to the legislature by the Constitution: only Congress could make the requested exemption.

Grand Rapids School District v. Ball (1984)

The Court examined the "shared time" program whereby the city's public school teachers offered secular enrichment instruction in 40 sectarian schools. The Court invalidated this measure by a 5–4 vote because it advanced religion. Justice Brennan offered the majority opinion, ruling that the Court's rationale in *Meek v. Pittenger* (that teachers in such situations would deliver a message to students that would be considered within the religious context) was still controlling.

Hunt v. McNair (1973)

Justice Powell wrote for a 6–3 majority validating a South Carolina statute that had created a bond authority to finance college construction, permitting funds to go to religious institutions only for buildings of a secular nature. Powell fine-tuned the *Lemon* test. A program with a primary effect of advancing religion would be one where the secular and sectarian functions could not easily be separated.

In re Snow (1887)

Of the many cohabitation cases heard around this time, this one is notable because it represents one of the few times the court sided with the Mormons. The Court stated that cohabitation could not be considered a separate offense each year it was committed, but rather was a "continuous offense."

Jay, John (1745–1829)

Coauthor of the Federalist Papers, this statesman from New York was the first Chief Justice of the United States and governor of New York. His state was relatively tolerant (it disestablished the Anglican Church and excluded clergy from public office), but Jay was not an avid spokesperson for religious toleration. He tried, unsuccessfully, to impose some limit on the rights of Catholics in the Empire State, citing the fact that many Catholics professed loyalty to the Vatican. He did succeed in establishing what amounts to a civil and religious denouncement of all foreign bodies as a condition of U.S. citizenship.

Jones v. City of Opelika (1942)

Two years after *Minersville v. Gobitis*, the court again sided with the state. In this case, Jehovah's Witnesses had refused to pay municipal licensing fees for the sale of their religious merchandise. The case was important for its dissenting opinion, in which Justices Black, Douglas, and Murphy announced that they had changed their minds about the *Gobitis* ruling, stating that the case had been "wrongly decided."

Kennedy, John F., on Church and State (1960)

This important address came during John F. Kennedy's closely contested campaign for presidency in 1960. As the only Catholic to be seriously considered for the presidency since Alfred E. Smith in 1928, Kennedy faced questions regarding whether he could remain both a devout Catholic and a loyal American (because some Americans believed Catholics aswered to the Pope). He chose to address these concerns in this speech, where he set forth his belief that the separation of church and state was absolute, rejecting the notion of a religious test for office. Although he practiced the Catholic faith in his personal life, Kennedy stated that he believed in an America that had no formal religion. Overall, his address called for universal religious tolerance and understanding and equal treatment of all religious faiths. Kennedy asked that he be judged on his record (as a senator, he had opposed the establishment of a U.S. ambassador to the Vatican, among other things) rather than on the propaganda of the time. In short, he believed that each president deserved such consideration, regardless of his personal religious choices. Kennedy insisted that his speech was dictated by his own conscience, not the church, and that the church did not speak for him, but rather he for himself. Kennedy promised that if elected, he would do all he could to safeguard the religious freedom he called for in this address. Kennedy was indeed elected, becoming the first Catholic president of the United States.

Know-Nothing Party

This short-lived party was formed in 1856 with the sole intent of filling every governmental position with Protestants, in response to the perceived influence of the Roman Catholic Church over its followers. It arose at a time of growing anti-Catholic sentiment across the country, but soon was disbanded due to the public's distrust of extreme religious bigotry.

Lamb's Chapel v. Center Moriches Union Free Public Schools District (1993)

This case arose when a school denied the use of its facilities to an evangelical society for the showing of a film series in which a psychologist called for "Christian family values instilled at an early age." Although the school board allowed after-hours use of the school by social, civil, and political groups, a unanimous Court rejected the claim that it had become a *de facto* public forum. Yet, Justice White explained, once the school did open its doors, denial of access had to be "viewpoint neutral."

Larkin v. Grendel's Den (1982)

In this separationist-oriented case, the Court overturned a Massachusetts law that gave churches and schools veto power over liquor licenses at sites within 500 feet of their premises.

The Late Corporation of the Church of Jesus Christ of Latter-Day Saints v. United States (1890)

In this case, the Court allowed Congress to deprive the Mormon church of its property, stating that the Church had taken assets that had initially been donated for public and charitable good and used them to spread polygamy. Invoking the doctrine of cy pres, the Court backed Congress, setting forth that it was redirecting the use of the property for its intended purpose. The majority rejected the Mormons' claim of religious liberty, shunning their lifestyle. Chief Justice Fuller dissented, arguing that property rights should be maintained and that Congress should not be granted such "absolute power" under any circumstances.

Lee v. Weisman (1992)

This case arose because Daniel Weisman, a strict separationist, objected to prayer at public school graduation ceremonies. A prayer had been offered at his daughter's high school graduation, and Weisman sought a permanent injunction against future prayers at graduation ceremonies. By a 5–4 vote, the Court upheld the reasoning from *Engel v. Vitale.* Justice Kennedy wrote for the majority finding that such acts violated the First Amendment of the Constitution and were impermissible due to their inherently coercive effects.

Lemon Test

See *Lemon v. Kurtzman.*

Lemon v. Kurtzman (1971)

This influential case considered whether Rhode Island and Pennsylvania laws that allowed for supplemental pay for teachers of secular subjects in private schools constituted state establishment of religion. Chief Justice Burger's opinion added a third prong to the test set forth in *Abington v. Schempp* (the first two prongs stated that the law must be secular in purpose and could not effectively advance or inhibit religion): namely that a law could not promote "excessive entanglement" of church and state. Considering the three-pronged "*Lemon* test," the Court overturned the two state laws at hand, setting forth that if a law was neutral on its face and satisfied the second prong, it created excessive entanglement, thus failing the last portion of the test. Without the entanglement, the state had no assurance that the second prong was being satisfied. Echoing Jefferson's "wall of separation," this decision enlarged *Schempp* and would be applied in later cases, including *Meek v. Pittenger, Ball,* and *Aguilar.*

Levitt v. Committee for Public Education and Religious Liberty (1973)

An 8–1 Court struck down a New York statute that allowed reimbursement to religious schools for services mandated by the state. New York had not created safeguards in order to be certain that the monies granted by the state went to a secular purpose, therefore violating the *Lemon* test.

Lynch v. Donnelly (1984)

This opinion by Chief Justice Burger is often considered the most accommodationist of his tenure because he stated that the Constitution "affirmatively mandates" accommodation. The Court allowed a privately owned Christmas display, including a crèche, to be displayed in a municipally owned park in Pawtucket, Rhode Island. Burger reasoned that the display, which included some secular holiday figures as well, was within the context of the Christmas season and reflected the nation's historical roots. This ruling ran counter to more than three decades of establishment jurisprudence. Dissenting Justice Brennan argued that Burger's reasoning relegated the crèche to a historical symbol, effectively undermining its true spiritual and mystical nature.

Lyng v. Northwest Indian Cemetery Protective Association (1988)

Justice O'Connor issued an opinion that allowed a federal plan for a highway and timber logging on sacred lands of Native Americans to proceed. The judgment effectively disregarded the free exercise rights of Native Americans. O'Connor argued that the plan did not coerce members into violating their religious tenets, or penalize their activities. She based her reasoning on *Bowen v. Roy,* even though the highway was far more devastating to Native American rights than was the issuance of Social Security numbers.

Madison, James (1751–1836)

An influential framer of the Constitution, Madison played a key role in the creation of the Bill of Rights. Madison, a Virginian, espoused the view that religious toleration was integral to democratic society. As the result of his efforts, Virginia's Constitution of 1776 provided for free exercise; however, it omitted any ban on establishment, despite Madison's efforts to enact full separation between church and state. In 1785 Madison penned the "Memorial and Remonstrance against Religious Assessments," which reiterated his reasons for believing that church and state should be kept fully separate. This writing was the foundation for his revival of Thomas Jefferson's Bill for Religious Freedom.

Marsh v. Chambers (1983)

Chief Justice Burger issued this opinion, handing a victory to accommodationists. A 6–3 Court upheld the right of states to begin their legislative sessions with prayers offered by chaplains who were on the state's payroll.

McCollum v. Board of Education (1948)

In this case, the Supreme Court for the first time invalidated a state law on Establishment Clause grounds. The case involved a "released time" program in Champaign, Illinois. In such programs, the classrooms of the public schools were turned over to religious instructors for an hour a week, for sectarian instruction of any student with parental approval. As in the *Everson* case, Justice Black spoke for the court (an 8–1 decision), stating that the use of a classroom for religious teaching clearly was state support of religion and therefore violated the First Amendment. In a concurring opinion, Justice Felix Frankfurter agreed with Black's reasoning, but made it clear that this case was distinct because the classes actually met on the public school grounds. This distinction was critical in *Zorach v. Clausen,* heard by the Court four years later.

McGowan v. Maryland (1961)

Chief Justice Warren offered the majority opinion in this case concerning Sunday blue laws. Although such laws were adopted for religious reasons, the Court found that they did not equate to establishment but rather furthered the legitimate secular goal of assuring a day of rest for workers.

Meek v. Pittenger (1975)

Pennsylvania passed a statute that allowed public school employees to provide aid to students in sectarian schools, including counseling, speech and hearing therapy, and school supplies. Justice Stewart's opinion of the Court struck down nearly all of the state statute because there was no assurance without excessive monitoring that these programs would not inculcate religion; and state monitoring would amount to inappropriate entanglement. The Court granted an exemption for textbooks, using *Allen* as its precedent.

"Memorial and Remonstrance against Religious Assessments" (1785)

In this essay James Madison asserted that religion was effectively private and voluntary in nature and that it therefore should be kept fully separate from the government. Madison wrote in response to Patrick Henry's "Bill Concerning Religion," rejecting Henry's view that Christian religious organizations should be granted taxes without prejudice. Madison believed that such an act constituted an establishment of religion and could not be tolerated in a democratic state. Madison amassed significant support for this position both among ordinary citizens and among clergy (Presbyterian, Quaker, and Baptist), effectively ending any hope for passage of Henry's bill.

Minersville School District v. Gobitis (1940)

Because they believed the flag to be a "graven image," Jehovah's Witnesses Lillian and Walter Gobitas (the case name includes a misspelling of the family's name) refused to salute the flag in elementary school and were expelled. After much internal wrangling, the Court sustained 8–1 an action to force participation in the flag salute. Justice Frankfurter argued that the ends (national unity) were legitimate, that the means chosen were reasonable, and that judges should defer to educators in such matters. Probably due to the war in Europe, the Court found national unity more important than free exercise of religion. This ruling was overturned in 1943, in *West Virginia Board of Education v. Barnette*.

Mitchell v. Helms (2000)

A 6–3 majority voted to allow a federal program that provided computers and other equipment to religious schools, although the Court was divided on how far this reasoning could be extended in other instances.

Northwest Ordinance of 1787

In this major piece of legislation passed under the Articles of Confederation, Congress affirmed the basic rights of civil and religious freedom that would apply to any new states in the new territory. However, it sent mixed signals in that it both guaranteed that no person would be persecuted for his religion, and affirmed the notion that religion was the underlying foundation of human fulfillment and of a working society. Although it tacitly offered religious guarantees, it additionally granted land to schools and churches (with Congress deciding on the final payoff of the proceeds from the sale to each denomination). This ordinance was later resurrected by the first Congress of the newly formed government, following the constitutional convention. In its latter form, it was widely used to Christianize Native Americans through education.

Oregon v. Smith (1990)

See *Employment Division, Oregon Department of Human Resources v. Smith.*

People v. Ruggles (N.Y., 1811)

This state court case arose because a man in New York had spoken blasphemously, in violation of state law, saying that Jesus Christ was a bastard and his mother was a whore. A clause in the state constitution declared that "the liberty of conscience hereby granted shall not be so construed as to excuse acts of licentiousness, or justify practices inconsistent with the peace and safety of the state." Relying on this, the state's Supreme Court of Judicature rejected the behavior of the defendant, ultimately reinforcing what the court believed was the crucial role that Christianity played in the moral nurture of the country. In sum, the defendant's behavior threatened the very glue of society by undermining Christian ideals.

Peyote

Peyote, a cactus with hallucinogenic (but not addictive) properties, is ingested in a sacramental manner by various sects of Native

American tribes. It is grown in a limited crop in the southwest for use in their religious rituals. Overall, governmental efforts have been successful in controlling its dispersal to the general public; but for years, the government has made an exception for Native Americans' religious use. Al Smith's ingestion of peyote led to the important case *Oregon v. Smith,* in which the state of Oregon upheld the denial of unemployment benefits to Smith following his dismissal from work on the grounds of his illegal use of this drug. Over time, the increasing legal acceptance for the use of peyote by Native Americans is a good example of a religion-rooted exception to a law of general application.

Quick Bear v. Leupp (1908)

Although the Congress in 1895 dictated that public funds must not be used at schools with a sectarian purpose, the Court in this case upheld support for church-related schools on Indian reservations. The Court found that such support violated neither the First Amendment's Establishment Clause nor the statutory provision the Congress had previously enacted to the contrary.

Religious Freedom Restoration Act (1993)

In response to the Court's decision in *Oregon v. Smith,* Congress stipulated in this Act that laws of general application could not burden religious practice without compelling justification. The Religious Freedom Restoration Act (RFRA) cast a wide net over all levels of government, challenging the Court's decision in *Oregon v. Smith.* The Court overruled this legislation in the *City of Boerne* case.

Reynolds v. United States (1879)

In its first major decision under the Free Exercise Clause, the Court in this case upheld the portion of the Morrill Act that criminalized polygamy in the territories even when practiced by a member of the Mormon religion. The decision was founded on Chief Justice Waite's articulation of a difference between beliefs and actions: although beliefs were not governable by the state, actions that ran counter to important state prerogatives were indeed subject to governmental restraint. This view of the Free Exercise Clause, known as the Reynolds doctrine, prevailed for decades, until it was greatly restricted by *Sherbert v. Verner* (1963). *Oregon v. Smith* (1990) went far toward reinstating the Reynolds doctrine.

Rosenberger v. Rector and Visitors of the University of Virginia (1995)

The Court here took an accommodationist view, holding in a 5–4 opinion written by Justice Kennedy that a state university could not withhold funds from a student group for the publication of a Christian magazine if those same university funds were available to support publications by nonreligious student groups. Rooted in the *Lamb's Chapel* case, the Court held that such a denial equated to content discrimination.

Santa Fe Independent School District v. Doe (2000)

In this instance, a 6–3 Court invalidated voluntary prayer before high school football games, finding that such prayer amounted to establishment.

Schneider v. Irvington (1939)

Jehovah's Witnesses' free speech challenges to restrictions on door-to-door leafleting were often successful in the early decades of the twentieth century. In this case, Justice Roberts invoked the famous *Carolene Products* Footnote Four, which called for heightened scrutiny of governmental regulation of personal rights.

Separationists

Followers of this line of reasoning believe that a full separation of church and state is necessary. For instance, prayers should not have any part in public schools in any form. Even with prayers presented in neutral terms, separationists believe that all prayer is ultimately sectarian in intent and nature. For example, Daniel Weisman felt it was absolutely inappropriate that any form of prayer be included in his daughters' graduation ceremonies, and he sought an injunction to bar any such action, which gave rise to *Lee v. Weisman* (1992).

Sherbert v. Verner (1963)

This landmark case arose when Adele Sherbert, a Seventh-day Adventist, was fired from her job because she was unwilling to work on Saturday, her Sabbath. When she filed for unemployment compensation, her claim was rejected because the state would not allow benefits unless she showed "good cause" for her inability to work. She sued on the grounds that the denial infringed her First Amendment right to free religious exercise. Justice Brennan framed the issue for the majority in terms of what compelling interest the state had in denying Sherbert unemployment benefits. Finding no justifiable reason, Brennan stated that the state of South Carolina was effectively forcing Sherbert to choose between her religion and employment. This the state could not constitutionally do, because it overly burdened her ability to practice her religion. Henceforth, state and federal governments would be constitutionally bound to grant exemptions to those whose ability to practice their religion was undermined by laws of general applicability, unless the government could demonstrate a compelling interest to the contrary. This case greatly expanded the realm of acceptable Free Exercise claims from what previously had been possible under the Reynolds doctrine. However, *Sherbert* was later undermined by *Oregon v. Smith* (1990). In response, Congress in 1993 attempted to reestablish the *Sherbert v. Verner* reasoning by means of the Religious Freedom Restoration Act (RFRA); but the RFRA was soon overturned by the Supreme Court, in *City of Boerne v. Flores*. The *Sherbert* case is a good example of the tension that exists between the Establishment and the Free Exercise clauses.

Smith, Alfred E. (1873–1944)

Smith believed strongly in the universal freedom of religious conscience. A Catholic and governor of New York, he ran for president in 1928, although he knew his chances for victory were slim. Anti-Catholic sentiment was growing in the nation during the 1920s because many Protestant Americans believed that Catholics' first loyalty was to the pope rather than to their nation. Charles Marshall published an open letter attacking the loyalty of Catholics, to which Smith bravely replied, calling Marshall's outlook unfounded. Smith stated that it did not necessarily follow that Catholics who were devoted to the church could not be loyal Americans. He cited his own Catholicism and his long career of public service as support for this assertion. He also noted that the members of the first New York cabinet espoused a variety of religious and political beliefs. Smith's letter to Marshall mirrored the notion set forth in the Virginia Statute for Religious Freedom, that religion is a private, individual matter and is not subject to state intrusion. He insisted that no Catholic decree had the power to overrule the U.S. Constitution; rather, such decrees were simply communications between the church hierarchy and lay membership. Any form of interference in matters of religion was therefore constitutionally improper.

Sunday Blue Laws

These local and statewide laws prohibiting work on Sundays were grounded in religious prescriptions of a day of rest, common to most Christian denominations; but they placed Americans espousing other beliefs at a disadvantage. Jews and Seventh-day Adventists, for example, would be forced to close their establishments on two days of the week: on Saturdays, for religious reasons; and on Sundays, as dictated by the state. Many American Jews vocally denounced these laws as inappropriate, and took their cause to the legal system; but initially they achieved no redress. When blue laws were eventually repealed, it was not because of the demands of religious dissenters but rather because the American culture of work changed as women entered the workplace. In *Braunfeld v. Brown* (1961), a divided Court upheld blue laws, stating that they were within the auspices of the state's police power, which allowed the state to assure a day of rest to all. There are places in America today where Sunday closing laws are still in effect.

Terrett v. Taylor (1815)

This case dealt with Virginia laws designed to deprive the Episcopal Church of special privileges. For instance, one act held that all land belonging to the Church of England at the time of independence would go to the people of the state; representatives of the less fortunate could then take the lands and use the profits for secular purposes. The Episcopal Church sued in order to stop such practices, and won. Justice Story wrote for the Court, basing his opinion on fundamental notions of property rights. Although this case did not deal explicitly with the religion clauses, it did go a long way in making clear that religious bodies possessed property rights that could not be revoked by the state. This line of legal reasoning was later bolstered in *Society for the Propagation of the Gospel in Foreign Parts v. New-Haven* (1823).

Test Oaths

In the religious context, test oaths are verbal pledges of allegiance to a specific religion as a rite of passage for citizenship or public office. They were widely used in the seventeenth and eighteenth centuries because of the government's ability to ascertain the individual's public religious position from them. A product of the notion that Christianity (at least, the right Christian sects) was the backbone of a well functioning, healthy society, test oaths were used to exclude Catholics, Jews, atheists, and other minorities from positions of social and political influence. Article VI of the Constitution banned religious tests for national office, and the Supreme Court outlawed their use by the states in *Torcaso v. Watkins* in 1961.

Tilton v. Richardson (1971)

This case came down on the same day as *Lemon v. Kurtzman*. It consisted of a challenge to federal construction grants to religious colleges for buildings to be used for secular purposes. Reasoning that college students are not as impressionable as younger students with regard to religious teachings, the Court allowed the grants, signaling that the *Lemon* test was not entirely inflexible.

Torcaso v. Watkins (1961)

This case challenged Maryland's requirement that officeholders declare their belief in the existence of God. The Supreme Court for the first time declared that test oaths in the states, such as those imposed in the state of New York at the instigation of John Jay, were unconstitutional.

United States v. Cannon (1886)

The Supreme Court affirmed Thomas Cannon's conviction under the Edmunds Act of 1882, which prohibited cohabitation. The Court thereby restated the importance of monogamy for the well-ordered functioning of society, discounting Cannon's claim that he had not engaged in sexual activity with the women in question.

United States v. Seeger (1965)

Section 6(j) of the Universal Military Training and Service Act of 1948 exempted from the draft conscientious objectors whose religions prohibited the taking of human life. Just as the nation's military involvement in Southeast Asia was expanding, three men claimed conscientious objector status because they did not believe in violence, without citing any direct religious beliefs. The Court evaded the constitutional issue by reading the statute broadly and granting their exemptions, effectively equating a strongly held belief with belief in what the statute called a "Supreme Being."

Virginia Constitution of 1776

Virginia's first constitution guaranteed the free exercise of religion largely as the result of James Madison's efforts, but it did not safeguard the separation of church and state. Because the constitution did not include a ban on state funding of Protestant Christian churches, it drew objections from Baptists, who were excluded from access to such funding because they were not an officially recognized Protestant sect.

Virginia Statute for Religious Freedom (1786)

This landmark Virginia state statute (the state's first law on the subject), which espoused the Jeffersonian view of religion and the state, was the result of more than a decade of heated debate. The first line set forth the tone of the law: "Whereas Almighty God hath created the mind free; that all attempts to influence it by temporal punishments or burthens, or by civil incapacitations, tend only to beget habits of hypocrisy and meanness; and are a departure from the plan of the Holy author of our religion . . . ." Jefferson believed not only that a high barrier should separate church and state, but also that separation was grounded on religious principles. In short, religious matters were of an individual nature and therefore beyond the grasp of state action, as dictated by Christian ideals. The law guaranteed that no one would face punishment either for supporting or for failing to support any specific religion. Jefferson took great pride in the passage of this law and hoped that it would become a key part of his legacy. His statute paved the way for a religiously open and tolerant society, in which persons could exercise their respective religions without governmental interference.

Wallace v. Jaffree (1985)

In this case the Court voted 6–3 against an Alabama law that called for two minutes of silence in the public school system at the beginning of each day "for meditation or voluntary prayer." Arguably the state was trying to skirt the decisions in the *Engel* and *Schempp* cases. Justice Stevens explained that by setting aside time for prayer, the state was making prayer "a favored practice" and therefore was violating the secular purpose prong of the *Lemon* test. Stevens rooted his logic in the free exercise notion that one's right to "select any religious belief or none at all" was protected under the Constitution. (The Court left open the question of whether an unspecified moment of silence would be constitutionally acceptable.) The reasoning used in this case was reaffirmed in *Lee v. Weisman,* in 1992.

Walz v. Tax Commission (1970)

The third prong of the *Lemon* test originated in this case. Certain real estate exemptions had been granted by state and local governments to not-for-profit organizations, including those owning land used solely for religious purposes. Chief Justice Burger opined that the exemption was allowable because it fostered free exercise by removing the tax burden faced by religious organizations, and that it avoided the "excessive entanglement" between church and state that otherwise would be caused by tax assessments and tax collection.

West Virginia Board of Education v. Barnette (1943)

With the nation at war with Nazi Germany, the court ruled 6–3 that a mandatory flag salute was a violation of free speech, thus overturning the *Gobitis* decision. Dissenting, Justice Frankfurter repeated his view that the Court had only a small role to play in protecting civil liberties.

Widmar v. Vincent (1981)

This free speech case with Establishment Clause overtones arose when the University of Missouri at Kansas City refused to allow the use of its buildings for religious purposes. An 8–1 Court found for an evangelical Christian student club that had challenged the school's policy on an equal protection rationale. In short, the university could not deny the use of its buildings based on the background of a group without violating their rights to engage in religious speech.

Williams, Roger (1603–1683)

Having been exiled from the colony of Massachusetts for his religious beliefs, Williams founded the colony of Rhode Island. Williams's influence helped Rhode Island become religiously tolerant, allowing its members the freedom to decide their religion, and explicitly disallowing religious establishment. Williams espoused the latter point by arguing that established religion not only curtailed the healthy functioning of civil society but also degraded religion itself. Through the establishment of Rhode Island, Williams created a microcosm of religious liberty well before such ideas were widely accepted.

Wisconsin v. Yoder (1972)

A Wisconsin law required all children between the ages of 7 and 16 to attend school. Amish children began attending a local Amish school without the approval of the school superintendent (whose county had just lost $18,000 in funding because of the loss of the Amish students). The superintendent refused approval, and the Amish families were fined. The Supreme Court found that the Amish were entitled to an exemption under the Free Exercise Clause from the requirement that their children remain in school until age 16. To compel obedience to the law would harm the Amish way of life, which in turn was central to the practice of their religion.

Witters v. Washington Department of Services for the Blind (1986)

The Court stated that a visually impaired person could use state vocational rehabilitation funds to pay tuition to a Christian college in order to become a minister without violating the Establishment Clause.

Wollman v. Walter (1977)

In response to the decision in *Meek v. Pittenger,* Ohio created a program of aid to religious schools whereby personnel would provide speech, hearing, and other diagnostic services on the premises of parochial schools, and therapeutic and remedial services off of school property. The program also provided textbooks and supplies and field trip funding for secular subjects. A divided Court agreed with the state that the various services did not create a situation of improper entanglement, and it sustained the practice. The possibility of religious topics being injected into these activities was less troublesome than it had been in *Meek,* because the teachers in this case were only administering tests and providing remedial aid. However, the Court invalidated the provisions for instructional materials and field trips.

Zobrest v. Catalina Foothills School District (1993)

James Zobrest, who is deaf, enrolled in a Roman Catholic high school in Arizona. His request to the local school district for a sign language interpreter was denied by the district even though under the Disabilities Education Act and its state counterpart he would have been entitled to one at a public school. The local school board believed that its provision of an interpreter to a student in a parochial school would be a violation of the Establishment Clause. The Court sided with Zobrest, reasoning that the aid would help the child, not the sectarian school. The Court's decision in this case exemplifies the child-benefit theory, first articulated in *Everson*.

Zorach v. Clauson (1952)

The Court's finding in this case is widely considered the first accommodationist decision regarding the Establishment Clause. The facts closely resemble those of the *McCollum* case just four years earlier: New York continued its "released time" program, with one minor adjustment: Instead of holding classes in religious instruction on the school grounds, the state gave students the option of leaving school premises and receiving formal spiritual instruction at nearby religious facilities. Taxpayers challenged this program, arguing that regardless of the locale of the instruction, it still equated to state support for religion. Writing for the majority, Justice William Douglas argued that the American people are inherently religious and that the First Amendment, although absolute, did not call for an impenetrable boundary between church and state. Rather, he asserted, the First Amendment had been interpreted in a "commonsense" manner, because a strict separationist view would violate the First Amendment by encouraging state hostility toward religious groups, thereby violating guarantees of free exercise. The key distinction for Douglas was the location of the assistance to religion: religious teaching on school grounds directly supported religion, whereas off-site religious instruction constituted only indirect assistance, which, in Douglas's view, was permissible. Justice Black dissented, chastising Douglas for creating "a combination of church and state."

6

DOCUMENTS

VIRGINIA RULES ON
CONDUCT AND RELIGION (1619)

Seventeenth-century England placed numerous restrictions on the conduct of individuals. In addition, the existence of an established church led to many state regulations regarding church attendance and other matters that today are entirely within the sphere of religious freedom. Faced by a hostile wilderness, colonial leaders felt the need of rules to ensure social stability. Virginians, however, were far less concerned with religion than were their peers in New England. The Virginia Rules were designed to enforce social control after near anarchy in the early years had almost led to the colony's extinction. Moreover, the managers of the Virginia Colony hoped that the Rules would attract new settlers by making the colony appear more civilized and less a wilderness outpost. Note that in the absence of ecclesiastical authorities, the Virginia Assembly assumed it had the power to define the duties of clergy. See G. McLaren Brydon, Virginia's Mother Church and the Political Conditions under Which It Grew, 1607–1727 *(Richmond: Virginia Historical Society, 1947).*

Against Idleness, gaming, drunkenness & excesse in apparel, the Assembly hath enacted as followeth:

First in detestation of idlers, be it enacted, that if any man be found to live as an Idler, though a freed man, it shall be lawful for the Incorporation or Plantation to which he belongeth to appoint him a Master to serve for wages till he shewe apparent signes of amendment.

Against gaming at Dice & cards be it ordained by this present Assembly that the winner or winners shall lose all his or their winnings & both winners and loosers shall forfeit ten shillings a man, one ten shillings whereof to goe to the discoverer, & the rest to charitable & pious uses in the Incorporation where the faults are committed.

Against drunkenes be it also decreed, that if any private person be found culpable thereof, for the first time he is to be reprooved privately by the Minister, and second time publiquely, the Third time to lye in boltes 12 houres in the House of the Provost Marshall & to paye his fees, and if he still continue in that vice, to undergo such severe punishment, as the Governor Councell shall think fitt to be inflicted on him. But if any Officer offende in this crime, the first time he shall receive a reproof from the Governour, the second time he shall openly be reproved in the Churche by the minister, & the third time he shall first be committed & then degraded. Provided it be understood, that the Governour hath always power to restore him when he shall in his discretion thinke fitt.

Against excesse of apparell, that every man be assessed in the Churche for all publique contributions, if he be unmarried according to his apparell, if he be married, according to his owne & his wives or either of their apparell.

For Reformation of Swearing, every freeman and Master of a family after thrice admonition shall give 5 shillings to the use of the churche where he dwelleth: and every servant after the like admonition, except his Master discharge the fine, shall be subject to whipping. Provided that the payment of the fine notwithstanding, the said servant shall acknowledge his fault publiquely in the Church.

All persons whatever upon Sabaoth days shall frequente divine service & sermons both forenoon and afternoone; and all suche as beare armes shall bring their pieces, swordes, power, shotte. And Every one that shall transgresse this Law, shall forfeit three shillings a time to the use of the Church, all lawful & necessary impediments excepted. But if a servant in this case shall willfully neglecte his Masters commande he shall suffer bodily punishmente.

All Ministers in the Colony shall once a year, namely in the month of Marche, bring to the Secretary of State a true account of all Christenings, burials & marriages, upon paine, if they faile, to be censured for their negligence by the Governour Councell. Likewise, where there be no ministers, that the commanders of the place doe supply the same duty.

No maide or woman servant, either now resident in the Colonie, or hereafter to come, shall contract herselfe in marriage without either the consente of her parents or her Master or Mistress, or of the magistrate & Minister of the place both together. And whatsoever Minister shall marry or contracte any such persons without some of the foresaid consentes shall be subjecte to the severe censure of the Governour & Counsell.

All ministers shall duely read divine service, and exercise their ministerial function according to the Ecclesiastical Lawes and orders of the church of Englande, and every Sunday in the afternoon shall Catechize suche as are not yet ripe to come to the Communion. And whosoever of them shall be found negligent or faulty in this kinde shall be subject to the censure of the Governour and Councell.

The Ministers and Churchwardens shall seeke to prevent all ungodly disorders, as suspicions of whoredoms, dishonest company keeping with weomen and such like; the committers whereofe if, upon goode admonitions and milde reproofe they will not forbeare the said skandalous offences, they are to be presented and punished accordingly.

If any person after two warnings doe not amende his or her life in point of evident suspicion of Incontinency or of the commission of any other enormous sinnes, that then he or shee shall be presented by the Church-wardens and suspended for a time from the Churche by the minister. In which interim if the same person do not amend and humbly submit him or herselfe to the churche, he is then fully to be excommunicate, and soon after a writt or warrant is to be sente from the Governour for the apprehending of his person & seizing all his goods. Provided alwayes, that all ministers doe meet once a quarter, namely at the feast of St. Michael the Arkangell, of the nativity of our Saviour, of the Annuntiation of the blessed Virgin, and about midsomer, at James Citty or any other place where the Governour shall reside, to determine whom it is fitt to excommunicate, and that they first present their opinion to the Governour ere they proceed to the acte of excommunication.

ROGER WILLIAMS, *THE BLOUDY TENENT OF PERSECUTION* (1644)

Roger Williams, an ordained Puritan minister, was exiled from Massachusetts Bay for his heretical notions of proper church and state relations. In 1636 he fled to Rhode Island, where the Narragansett Indians gave him sanctuary and allowed him to found a new colony (Providence). In 1643–1644 he was in London securing a charter for Providence, when the Puritans, who had recently come to power, convened the Westminster Assembly of Divines to plan England's ecclesiastical future. Still rankled by his expulsion, Williams entered the debate with several pamphlets, of which the lengthy "bloudy tenent" was aimed directly at the views of his arch opponent in the New World, the Puritan divine John Cotton. The work consists primarily of a dense and complex dialogue between Truth and Peace over the proper relations between church and state. The basic argument is summed up in the opening "document," which is the basis for the debate. Williams's arguments are the first in the New World calling for freedom of conscience and a separation between the ecclesiastical and secular authorities. Although these ideas had little impact at the time, they slowly infiltrated American political thought and emerged seemingly full-blown after the Revolution. Significantly, Williams argued for a separation of church and state not to protect the government from undue sectarian influences (which is the modern view of this issue) but rather to protect religion from the state. For example, Williams opposed laws requiring church attendance, on the grounds that he did not want to pray with sinners who were only in church to avoid fines. See Perry Miller, Errand into the Wilderness *(New York: Harper & Row, 1956); and Edwin S. Morgan,* Roger Williams: The Church and the State *(New York: Harcourt, Brace, 1967).*

First, That the blood of so many hundred thousand soules of Protestants and Papists, spilt in the Wars of present and former Ages, for their respective Consciences, is not required nor accepted by Jesus Christ the Prince of Peace.

Secondly, Pregnant Scripturs and Arguments are throughout the Worke proposed against the Doctrine of persecution for cause of Conscience.

Thirdly, Satisfactorie Answers are given to Scriptures, and objections produced by Mr. Calvin, Beza, Mr. Cotton, and the Ministers of the New English Churches and others former and later, tending to prove the Doctrine of persecution for cause of Conscience.

Fourthly, The Doctrine of persecution for cause of Conscience, is proved guilty of all the blood of the Soules crying for vengeance under the Altar.

Fifthly, All Civill States with their Officers of justice in their respective constitutions and administrations are proved essentially Civill, and therefore not Judges, Governours or Defendours of the Spirituall or Christian state and Worship.

Sixthly, It is the will and command of God, that (since the comming of his Sonne the Lord Jesus) a permission of the most Paganish, Jewish, Turkish, or Antichristian consciences and worships, bee granted to all men in all Nations and Countries: and they are onely to bee fought against with that Sword which is only (in Soule matters) able to conquer, to wit, the Sword of Gods Spirit, the Word of God.

Seventhly, The State of the Land of Israel, the Kings and people thereof in Peace & War, is proved figurative and ceremoniall, and no patterne nor president for any Kingdome or civill state in the world to follow.

Eighthly, God requireth not an uniformity of Religion to be inacted and inforced in any civill state; which inforced uniformity (sooner or later) is the greatest occasion of civill Warre, ravishing of conscience, persecution of Christ Jesus in his servants, and of the hypocrisie and destruction of millions of souls.

Ninthly, In holding an inforced uniformity of Religion in a civill state, wee must necessarily disclaime our desires and hopes of the Jewes conversion to Christ.

Tenthly, An inforced uniformity of Religion throughout a Nation or civill state, confounds the Civill and Religious, denies the principles of Christianity and civility, and that Jesus Christ is come in the Flesh.

Eleventhly, The permission of other consciences and worships than a state professeth, only can (according to God) procure a firme and lasting peace, (good assurance being taken according to the wisdome of the civill state for uniformity of civill obedience from all sorts.)

Twelfthly, lastly, true civility and Christianity may both flourish in a state or Kingdome, notwithstanding the permission of divers and contrary consciences, either of Jew or Gentile.

EXCERPTS FROM REVOLUTIONARY-ERA STATE CONSTITUTIONS (1776–1784)

If anyone believes that the Revolution led all of the states to dises-
tablish their churches and extend full religious freedom to all of
their inhabitants, the following excerpts should disabuse them of
that notion. The founding generation took religion very seriously,
and even if they no longer wanted to be taxed for the Church of
England, they still believed government had a major role to play
in fostering religion and in promoting what they saw as the true
faith, Protestant Christianity. Within fifty years nearly all of these
provisions had been discarded, but legal discrimination against
Jews existed in some states until after the Civil War, and even
though the test oath fell into disuse in most states, the Supreme
Court did not declare the oath unconstitutional until 1961. See
Willi Paul Adams, The First American Constitutions: Republican
Ideology and the Making of State Constitutions in the Revolutionary Era *(Chapel Hill: University of North Carolina Press,*
1979); and Donald S. Lutz, Popular Consent and Popular Con-
trol: Whig Political Theory in the Early State Constitutions
(Baton Rouge: Louisiana State University Press, 1980).

Delaware (1776)

Art. 22: Every person who shall be chosen a member of either
house, or appointed to any office or place of trust, before taking
his seat, or entering upon the execution of his office, shall take the
following oath, or affirmation, if conscientiously scrupulous of
taking an oath, to wit:

"I, A B, will bear true allegiance to the Delaware State, submit
to its constitution and laws, and do no act willingly whereby the
freedom thereof may be prejudiced."

And Also make and subscribe the following declaration, to wit:

"I, A B, do profess faith in God the Father, and in Jesus Christ His only Son, and in the Holy Ghost, one God, blessed for evermore; and I do acknowledge the holy scriptures of the Old and New Testament to be given by divine inspiration."

Georgia (1777)

Art. LVI: All persons whatever shall have the free exercise of their religion; provided it be not repugnant to the peace and safety of the State; and shall not, unless by consent, support any teacher or teachers except those of their own profession.

Maryland (1776)

Art. XXXIII: That, as it is the duty of every man to worship God in such manner as he thinks most acceptable to him; all persons, professing the Christian religion, are equally entitled to protection in their religious liberty; where as no person ought by any law to be molested in his person or estate on account of his religious persuasion or profession, or for his religious practice; unless, under colour of religion, any man shall disturb the good order, peace or safety of the State, or shall infringe the laws of morality, or injure others, in their natural, civil, or religious rights; nor ought any person to be compelled to frequent or maintain, or contribute, unless on contract, to maintain any particular place of worship, or any particular ministry; yet the Legislature may, in their discretion, lay a general and equal tax, for the support of the Christian religion; leaving to each individual the power of appointing the payment over of the money, collected from him, to the support of any particular place of worship or minister, or for the benefit of the poor of his own denomination, or the poor in general of any particular county; but the churches, chapels, glebes, and all other property now belonging to the church of England, ought to remain to the church of England forever. And all acts of Assembly, lately passed, for collecting monies for building or repairing particular churches or chapels of ease, shall continue in force, and be executed, unless the Legislature shall, by act, supersede or repeal the same: but no county court shall assess any quantity of tobacco, or sum of money, hereafter, on the application of any vestry-men or church-wardens. . . .

Art. XXXV. That no other test or qualification ought to be required, on admission to any office of trust or profit, than such oath of support and fidelity to this State, and such oath of office, as shall be directed by this convention, or the Legislature of this State, and a declaration of a belief in the Christian religion.

Massachusetts (1780)

Art. II. It is the right as well as the duty of all men in society, publicly and at stated seasons, to worship the Supreme being, the great Creator and Preserver of the universe. And no subject shall be hurt, molested, or restrained, in his person, liberty, or estate, for worshipping God in the manner and season most agreeable to the dictates of his own conscience, or for his religious profession or sentiments, provided he doth not disturb the public peace or obstruct others in their religious worship.

Art. III. As the happiness of a people and the good order and preservation of civil government essentially depend upon piety, religion, and morality, and as these cannot be generally diffused through a community but by the institution of the public worship of God and of public instructions in piety, religion, and morality: Therefore, To promote their happiness and to secure the good order and preservation of their government, the people of this commonwealth have a right to invest their legislature with power to authorize and require, the several towns, parishes, precincts, and other bodies-politic or religious societies to make suitable provision, at their own expense, for the institution of the public worship of God and for the support and maintenance of public

Protestant teachers of piety, religion and morality in all cases where such provision shall not be made voluntarily.

New Hampshire (1784)

V. Every individual has a natural and unalienable right to worship GOD according to the dictates of his own conscience, and reason; and no subject shall be hurt, molested, or restrained in his person, liberty, or estate for worshipping GOD, in the manner and reason most agreeable to the dictates of his own conscience, or for his religious profession, sentiments, or persuasion; provided he doth not disturb the public peace, or disturb others, in their religious worship.

VI. As morality and piety, rightly grounded on evangelical principles, will give the best and greatest security to government, and will lay in the hearts of men the strongest obligations to due subjection; and as the knowledge of these, is most likely to be propagated through a society by the institution of the public worship of the DEITY, and of public instruction in morality and religion; therefore, to promote these important purposes, the people of this state have a right to impower, and do hereby fully impower the legislature to authorize from time to time, the several towns, parishes, bodies-corporate, or religious societies within this state, to make adequate provision at their own expence, for the support and maintenance of public protestant teachers of piety, religion, and morality.

New Jersey (1776)

XVIII. That no person shall ever, within this Colony, be deprived of the inestimable privilege of worshipping Almighty God in a manner agreeable to the dictates of his own conscience; nor, under any pretence whatever, be compelled to attend any place of worship, contrary to his own faith and judgment; nor shall any person, within this Colony, ever be obliged to pay tithes, taxes, or any other rates, for the purpose of building or repairing any church or churches, place or places of worship, or for the maintenance of any minister or ministry, contrary to what he believes to be right, or has deliberately or voluntarily engaged himself to perform.

XIX. There shall be no establishment of any one religious sect in this Province, in preference to another; and that no Protestant inhabitant of this Colony shall be denied the enjoyment of any civil right, merely on account of his religious principles; but that all persons, professing a belief in the faith of any Protestant sect, who shall demean themselves peaceably under the government, as hereby established, shall be capable of being elected into any office of profit or trust, or being a member of either branch of the Legislature, and shall fully and freely enjoy every privilege and immunity, enjoyed by others their fellow subjects.

New York (1777)

XXXVIII. And whereas we are required, by the benevolent principles of rational liberty, not only to expel civil tyranny, but also to guard against that spiritual oppression and intolerance wherewith the bigotry and ambition of weak and wicked priests and princes have scourged mankind, this convention doth further, in the name and by the authority of the good people of this State, ordain, determine, and declare, that the free exercise and enjoyment of religious profession and worship, without discrimination or preference, shall forever hereafter be allowed, within this State, to all mankind: *Provided*, That the liberty of conscience, hereby granted, shall not be so construed as to excuse acts of licentiousness, or justify practices inconsistent with the peace or safety of this State.

XXXIX. And whereas the ministers of the gospel are, by their profession, dedicated to the service of God and the care of souls, and ought not to be diverted from the great duties of their function; therefore, no minister of the gospel, or priest of any denomination whatsoever, shall, at any time hereafter, under any pretence or description whatever, be eligible to, or capable of holding, any civil or military office within this State.

North Carolina (1776)

XIX. That all men have a natural and unalienable right to worship Almighty God according to the dictates of their own consciences.

. . .

XXIII. That no person, who shall deny the being of God or the truth of the Protestant religion, or the divine authority either of the Old or New Testaments, or who shall hold religious principles incompatible with the freedom and safety of the State, shall be capable of holding any office or place of trust or profit in the civil department within this State.

. . .

XXXII. That there shall be no establishment of any one religious church or denomination in this State, in preference to any other; neither shall any person, on any pretence whatsoever, be compelled to attend any place of worship contrary to his own faith or judgment, nor be obliged to pay, for the purchase of any glebe, or the building of any house of worship, or for the maintenance of any minister or ministry, contrary to what he believes right, or has voluntarily and personally engaged to perform; but all persons shall be at liberty to exercise their own mode of worship:—*Provided,* That nothing herein contained shall be construed to exempt preachers of treasonable or seditious discourses, from legal trial and punishment.

Pennsylvania (1776)

Declaration of the Rights of the Inhabitants of the State of Pennsylvania

II. That all men have a natural and unalienable right to worship Almighty God according to the dictates of their own consciences and understanding: And that no man ought or of right can be compelled to attend any religious worship, or erect or support any place of worship, or maintain any ministry, contrary to, or against, his own free will and consent: Nor can any man, who acknowledges the being of a God, be justly deprived or abridged of any civil right as a citizen, on account of his religious sentiments or peculiar mode of religious worship: And that no authority can or ought to be vested in, or assumed by any power whatsoever, that shall in any case interfere with, or in any manner controul, the right of conscience in the free exercise of religious worship.

Plan or Frame of Government

Sect. 10. . . . And each member [of the legislature], before he takes his seat, shall make and subscribe the following declaration, viz:

"I do believe in one God, the creator and governor of the universe, the rewarder of the good and the punisher of the wicked. And I do acknowledge the Scriptures of the Old and New Testament to be given by Divine inspiration."

And no further or other religious test shall ever hereafter be required of any civil officer or magistrate in this State.

South Carolina (1776)

XXXVIII. That all persons and religious societies who acknowledge that there is one God, and a future state of rewards and punishments, and that God is publicly to be worshipped, shall be freely tolerated. The Christian Protestant religion shall be deemed, and is hereby constituted and declared to be, the established religion of this State. That all denominations of Christian Protestants in this State, demeaning themselves peaceably and faithfully, shall enjoy equal religious and civil privileges. To accomplish this desirable purpose without injury to the religious property of those societies of Christians which are by law already incorporated for the purpose of religious worship, and to put it fully into the power of every other society of Christian Protestants, either already formed or hereafter to be formed, to obtain the like incorporation, it is hereby constituted, appointed, and declared that the respective societies of the Church of England that are already formed in this State for the purpose of religious worship shall still continue to incorporate and hold the religious property now in their possession. And that whenever fifteen or more male persons, not under twenty-one years of age, professing the Christian Protestant religion, and agreeing to unite themselves in a society for the purposes of religious worship, they shall, (on complying with the terms hereinafter mentioned,) be, and be constituted, a church, and be esteemed and regarded in law as of the established religion of the State, and on a petition to the legislature shall be entitled to be incorporated and to enjoy equal privileges. That every society of Christians so formed shall give themselves a name or denomination by which they shall be called and known in law, and all that associate with them for the purposes of worship shall be esteemed as belonging to the society so called. But that previous to the establishment and incorporation of the respective societies of every denomination as aforesaid, and in order to entitle them thereto, each society so petitioning shall have agreed to and subscribed in a book the following five articles, without which no agreement or union of men upon pretence of religion shall entitle them to be incorporated and esteemed as a church of the established religion of this State.

1st. That there is one eternal God, and a future state of rewards and punishments.

2nd. That God is publicly to be worshipped.

3rd. That the Christian religion is the true religion.

4th. That the holy scriptures of the Old and New Testaments are of divine inspiration, and are the rule of faith and practice.

5th. That it is lawful and the duty of every man being thereunto called by those that govern, to bear witness to the truth.

And that every inhabitant of this State, when called to make an appeal to God as a witness to truth, shall be permitted to do it in that way which is most agreeable to the dictates of his own conscience. And that the people of this State may forever enjoy the right of electing their own pastors or clergy, and at the same time that the State may have sufficient security for the due discharge of the pastoral office, by those who shall be admitted to be clergymen, no person shall officiate as minister of any established church who shall not have been chosen by a majority of the society to which he shall minister, or by persons appointed by the said majority, to choose and procure a minister for them; nor until the minister so chosen and appointed shall have made and subscribed to the following declaration, over and above the aforesaid five articles, viz: "That he is determined by God's grace out of the holy scriptures, to instruct the people committed to his charge, and to teach nothing as required of necessity to eternal salvation but that which he shall be persuaded may be concluded and proved from the scripture; that he will use both public and private admonitions, as well to the sick as to the whole within his cure, as need shall require and occasion shall be given, and that he will be diligent in prayers, and in reading of the holy scriptures, and in such studies as help to the knowledge of the same; that he will be diligent to frame and fashion his own self and his family according to the doctrine of Christ, and to make both himself and them, as much as in him lieth, wholesome examples and patterns to the flock of Christ; that he will maintain and set forwards, as much as he can, quietness, peace, and love among all people, and especially among those that are or shall be committed to his charge. No person shall disturb or molest any religious assembly; nor shall use any reproachful, reviling, or abusive language against any church, that being the certain way of disturbing the peace, and of hindering the conversion of any to the truth, by engaging them in quarrels and animosities, to the hatred of the professors, and that profession which otherwise they might be brought to assent to. No person whatsoever shall speak anything in their religious assembly irreverently or seditiously of the government of this State. No person shall, by law, be obliged to pay towards the maintenance and support of a religious worship that he does not freely join in, or has not voluntarily engaged to support. But the churches, chapels, parsonages, glebes, and all other property now belonging to any societies of the Church of England, or any other religious societies, shall remain and be secured to them forever. The poor shall be supported, and elections managed in the accustomed manner, until laws shall be provided to adjust those matters in the most equitable way.

Virginia Bill of Rights (1776)

Sec. 16. That religion, or the duty we owe to our Creator, and the manner of discharging it, can be directed only by reason and conviction, not by force or violence; and therefore all men are equally entitled to the free exercise of religion, according to the dictates of conscience; and that it is the mutual duty of all to practice Christian forbearance, love, and charity towards each other.

JAMES MADISON,
"MEMORIAL AND REMONSTRANCE" (1785)

Although Madison was educated at the strongly Presbyterian Princeton College, his wide reading in church history led him to the conviction that church establishments represented a danger both to rational religion and to civil government. "Religion flourishes in greater purity without than with the aid of Government," he concluded. Although Virginia disestablished the Church of England immediately after declaring independence, following the Revolution Patrick Henry came up with the idea of a general tax that would support all Christian churches—a pluralistic establishment. Madison opposed the idea, managed to delay a vote on it in the General Assembly, and then over the summer of 1786 led a campaign against the assessment. The "Memorial and Remonstrance" convinced many people, who voted in a new Assembly that was opposed to the general tax and that eventually passed the Virginia Statute for Religious Freedom (next document). See Robert S. Alley, ed., James Madison on Religious Liberty *(Buffalo, NY: Prometheus Books, 1985); Thomas J. Curry,* The First Freedoms: Church and State in America to the Passage of the First Amendment *(New York: Oxford University Press, 1986); and Robert A. Rutland,* James Madison: The Founding Father *(New York: Macmillan, 1987).*

To the Honorable the General Assembly of the Commonwealth of Virginia: A Memorial and Remonstrance

We the subscribers, citizens of the said Commonwealth, having taken into serious consideration, a Bill printed by order of the last Session of General Assembly, entitled "A Bill establishing a provision for Teachers of the Christian Religion," and conceiving that the same if finally armed with the sanctions of a law, will be a dangerous abuse of power, are bound as faithful members of a free State to remonstrate against it, and to declare the reasons by which we are determined. We remonstrate against the said Bill,

1. Because we hold it for a fundamental and undeniable truth, "that Religion or the duty which we owe to our Creator and the manner of discharging it, can be directed only by reason and conviction, not by force or violence." The Religion then of every man must be left to the conviction and conscience of every man; and it is the right of every man to exercise it as these may dictate. This right is in its nature an unalienable right. It is unalienable, because the opinions of men, depending only on the evidence contemplated by their own minds, cannot follow the dictates of other men: It is unalienable also, because what is here a right towards men, is a

duty towards the Creator. It is the duty of every man to render to the Creator such homage and such only as he believes to be acceptable to him. This duty is precedent, both in order of time and in degree of obligation, to the claims of Civil Society. Before any man can be considered as a member of Civil Society, he must be considered as a subject of the Governour of the Universe: And if a member of Civil Society, who enters into any subordinate Association, must always do it with a reservation of his duty to the General Authority; much more must every man who becomes a member of any particular Civil Society, do it with a saving of his allegiance to the Universal Sovereign. We maintain therefore that in matters of Religion, no man's right is abridged by the institution of Civil Society and that Religion is wholly exempt from its cognizance. True it is, that no other rule exists, by which any question which may divide a Society, can be ultimately determined, but the will of the majority; but it is also true that the majority may trespass on the rights of the minority.

2. Because if Religion be exempt from the authority of the Society at large, still less can it be subject to that of the Legislative Body. The latter are but the creatures and vicegerents of the former. Their jurisdiction is both derivative and limited: it is limited with regard to the co-ordinate departments, more necessarily is it limited with regard to the constituents. The preservation of a free Government requires not merely, that the metes and bounds which separate each department of power be invariably maintained; but more especially that neither of them be suffered to overleap the great Barrier which defends the rights of the people. The Rulers who are guilty of such an encroachment, exceed the commission from which they derive their authority, and are Tyrants. The People who submit to it are governed by laws made neither by themselves nor by an authority derived from them, and are slaves.

3. Because it is proper to take alarm at the first experiment on our liberties. We hold this prudent jealousy to be the first duty of Citizens, and one of the noblest characteristics of the late Revolution.

The free men of America did not wait till usurped power had strengthened itself by exercise, and entangled the question in precedents. They saw all the consequences in the principle, and they avoided the consequences by denying the principle. We revere this lesson too much soon to forget it. Who does not see that the same authority which can establish Christianity, in exclusion of all other Religions, may establish with the same ease any particular sect of Christians, in exclusion of all other Sects? that the same authority which can force a citizen to contribute three pence only of his property for the support of any one establishment, may force him to conform to any other establishment in all cases whatsoever?

4. Because the Bill violates that equality which ought to be the basis of every law, and which is more indispensable, in proportion as the validity or expediency of any law is more liable to be impeached. If "all men are by nature equally free and independent," all men are to be considered as entering into Society on equal conditions; as relinquishing no more, and therefore retaining no less, one than another, of their natural rights. Above all are they to be considered as retaining an "*equal* title to the free exercise of Religion according to the dictates of Conscience." Whilst we assert for ourselves a freedom to embrace, to profess and to observe the Religion which we believe to be of divine origin, we cannot deny an equal freedom to those whose minds have not yet yielded to the evidence which has convinced us. If this freedom be abused, it is an offence against God, not against man: To God, therefore, not to man, must an account of it be rendered. As the Bill violates equality by subjecting some to peculiar burdens, so it violates the same principle, by granting to others peculiar exemptions. Are the Quakers and Menonists the only sects who think a compulsive support of their Religions unnecessary and unwarrantable? Can their piety alone be entrusted with the care of public worship? Ought their Religions to be endowed above all others with extraordinary privileges by which proselytes may be enticed from all others? We think too favorably of the justice and

good sense of these denominations to believe that they either covet pre-eminences over their fellow citizens or that they will be seduced by them from the common opposition to the measure.

5. Because the Bill implies either that the Civil Magistrate is a competent judge of Religious Truth; or that he may employ Religion as an engine of Civil policy. The first is an arrogant pretension falsified by the contradictory opinions of Rulers in all ages, and throughout the world: the second an unhallowed perversion of the means of salvation.

6. Because the establishment proposed by the Bill is not requisite for the support of the Christian Religion. To say that it is, is a contradiction to the Christian Religion itself, for every page of it disavows a dependence on the powers of this world: it is a contradiction to fact; for it is known that this Religion both existed and flourished, not only without the support of human laws, but in spite of every opposition from them, and not only during the period of miraculous aid, but long after it had been left to its own evidence and the ordinary care of Providence. Nay, it is a contradiction in terms; for a Religion not invented by human policy, must have pre-existed and been supported, before it was established by human policy. It is moreover to weaken in those who profess this Religion a pious confidence in its innate excellence and the patronage of its Author; and to foster in those who still reject it, a suspicion that its friends are too conscious of its fallacies to trust its own merits.

7. Because experience witnesseth that ecclesiastical establishments, instead of maintaining the purity and efficacy of Religion, have had a contrary operation. During almost fifteen centuries has the legal establishment of Christianity been on trial. What have been its fruits? More or less in all places, pride and indolence in the Clergy, ignorance and servility in the laity, in both, superstition, bigotry and persecution. Enquire of the Teachers of Christianity for the ages in which it appeared in its greatest lustre; those of every sect, point to the ages prior to its incorporation with Civ-

il policy. Propose a restoration of this primitive State in which its Teachers depended on the voluntary rewards of their flocks, many of them predict its downfall. On which Side ought their testimony to have greatest weight, when for or when against their interest?

8. Because the establishment in question is not necessary for the support of Civil Government. If it be urged as necessary for the support of Civil Government only as it is a means of supporting Religion, and it be not necessary for the latter purpose, it cannot be necessary for the former. If Religion be not within the cognizance of Civil Government how can its legal establishment be necessary to Civil Government? What influence in fact have ecclesiastical establishments had on Civil Society? In some instances they have been seen to erect a spiritual tyranny on the ruins of the Civil authority; in many instances they have been seen upholding the thrones of political tyranny; in no instance have they been seen the guardians of the liberties of the people. Rulers who wished to subvert the public liberty, may have found an established Clergy convenient auxiliaries. A just Government instituted to secure & perpetuate it needs them not. Such a Government will be best supported by protecting every Citizen in the enjoyment of his Religion with the same equal hand which protects his person and his property; by neither invading the equal rights of any Sect, nor suffering any Sect to invade those of another.

9. Because the proposed establishment is a departure from that generous policy, which, offering an Asylum to the persecuted and oppressed of every Nation and Religion, promised a lustre to our country, and an accession to the number of its citizens. What a melancholy mark is the Bill of sudden degeneracy? Instead of holding forth an Asylum to the persecuted, it is itself a signal of persecution. It degrades from the equal rank of Citizen all those whose opinions in Religion do not bend to those of the Legislative authority. Distant as it may be in its present form from the Inquisition, it differs from it only in degree. The one is the first step, the

other the last in the career of intolerance. The magnanimous sufferer under this cruel scourge in foreign Regions, must view the Bill as a Beacon on our Coast, warning him to seek some other haven, where liberty and philanthropy in their due extent, may offer a more certain repose from his Troubles.

10. Because it will have a like tendency to banish our Citizens. The allurements presented by other situations are every day thinning their number. To superadd a fresh motive to emigration by revoking the liberty which they now enjoy, would be the same species of folly which has dishonoured and depopulated flourishing kingdoms.

11. Because it will destroy that moderation and harmony which the forbearance of our laws to intermeddle with Religion has produced among its several sects. Torrents of blood have been spilt in the old world, by vain attempts of the secular arm, to extinguish Religious discord, by proscribing all difference in Religious opinion. Time has at length revealed the true remedy. Every relaxation of narrow and rigorous policy, wherever it has been tried, has been found to assuage the disease. The American Theatre has exhibited proofs that equal and compleat liberty, if it does not wholly eradicate it, sufficiently destroys its malignant influence on the health and prosperity of the State. If with the salutary effects of this system under our own eyes, we begin to contract the bounds of Religious freedom, we know no name that will too severely reproach our folly. At least let warning be taken at the first fruits of the threatened innovation. The very appearance of the Bill has transformed "that Christian forbearance, love and charity," which of late mutually prevailed, into animosities and jealousies, which may not soon be appeased. What mischiefs may not be dreaded, should this enemy to the public quiet be armed with the force of a law?

12. Because the policy of the Bill is adverse to the diffusion of the light of Christianity. The first wish of those who enjoy this precious gift ought to be that it may be imparted to the whole race

of mankind. Compare the number of those who have as yet received it with the number still remaining under the dominion of false Religions; and how small is the former! Does the policy of the Bill tend to lessen the disproportion? No; it at once discourages those who are strangers to the light of revelation from coming into the Region of it; and countenances by example the nations who continue in darkness, in shutting out those who might convey it to them. Instead of Levelling as far as possible, every obstacle to the victorious progress of Truth, the Bill with an ignoble and unchristian timidity would circumscribe it with a wall of defense against the encroachments of error.

13. Because attempts to enforce by legal sanctions, acts obnoxious to so great a proportion of Citizens, tend to enervate the laws in general, and to slacken the bands of Society. If it be difficult to execute any law which is not generally deemed necessary or salutary, what must be the case, where it is deemed invalid and dangerous? And what may be the effect of so striking an example of impotency in the Government, on its general authority?

14. Because a measure of such singular magnitude and delicacy ought not to be imposed, without the clearest evidence that it is called for by a majority of citizens, and no satisfactory method is yet proposed by which the voice of the majority in this case may be determined, or its influence secured. "The people of the respective counties are indeed requested to signify their opinion respecting the adoption of the Bill to the next Session of Assembly." But the representation must be made equal, before the voice of either of the Representatives or of the Counties will be that of the people. Our hope is that neither of the former will, after due consideration, espouse the dangerous principle of the Bill. Should the event disappoint us, it will still leave us in full confidence, that a fair appeal to the latter will reverse the sentence against our liberties.

15. Because finally, "the equal right of every citizen to the free exercise of his Religion according to the dictates of conscience" is

held by the same tenure with all our other rights. If we recur to its origin, it is equally the gift of nature; if we weigh its importance, it cannot be less dear to us; if we consult the "Declaration of those rights which pertain to the good people of Virginia, as the basis and foundation of Government," it is enumerated with equal solemnity, or rather studied emphasis. Either then, we must say, that the Will of the Legislature is the only measure of their authority; and that in the plenitude of this authority, they may sweep away all our fundamental rights; or, that they are bound to leave this particular right untouched and sacred: Either we must say, that they may controul the freedom of the press, may abolish the Trial by jury, may swallow up the Executive and Judiciary Powers of the State; nay that they may despoil us of our very right of suffrage, and erect themselves into an independent and hereditary Assembly or, we must say, that they have no authority to enact into law the Bill under consideration. We the Subscribers say, that the General Assembly of this Commonwealth have no such authority: And that no effort may be omitted on our part against so dangerous an usurpation, we oppose to it, this remonstrance; earnestly praying, as we are in duty bound, that the Supreme Lawgiver of the Universe, by illuminating those to whom it is addressed, may on the one hand, turn their Councils from the very act which would affront his holy prerogative, or violate the trust committed to them: and on the other, guide them into every measure which may be worthy of his blessing, may redound to their own praise, and may establish more firmly the liberties, the prosperity and the happiness of the Commonwealth.

VIRGINIA STATUTE FOR RELIGIOUS FREEDOM (1786)

The move to disestablish the Church of England, which enjoyed official status in parts of New York and all the colonies from Maryland to Georgia, became part of the revolutionary agenda. But dis-

establishment did not automatically lead to religious freedom; several New England states continued their established churches, and as late as 1787 every state but New York and Virginia continued to have religious tests for officeholding. But a trend soon developed that led from disestablishment to tolerance to freedom. The Virginia Bill of Rights of 1776, for example, included an article stating that "all men are equally entitled to the free exercise of religion, according to the dictates of conscience; and that it is the mutual duty of all to practice Christian forbearance, love, and charity towards each other." This did not satisfy Thomas Jefferson, who drafted the following bill in 1777; the legislature did not adopt it, however, until 1786, when Jefferson was out of the country. James Madison, Jefferson's friend and neighbor, guided it through the legislature. Whether or not Jefferson read Roger Williams, there is a direct link between the ideals of the "bloudy tenent" (Roger Williams, The Bloudy Tenent of Persecution *[1644]) and the ideals expressed in the Statute and in the First Amendment. Again one can see the pattern of once-radical notions becoming accepted, mainstream principles. See Merrill D. Peterson and Robert C. Vaughn, eds.,* The Virginia Statute for Religious Freedom: Its Evolution and Consequences in American History *(1988); Thomas J. Curry,* The First Freedoms: Church and State in America to the Passage of the First Amendment *(1986); and William Lee Miller,* The First Liberty: Religion and the American Republic *(1986).*

Whereas Almighty God hath created the mind free; that all attempts to influence it by temporal punishments or burthens, or by civil incapacitations, tend only to beget habits of hypocrisy and meanness, and are a departure from the plan of the Holy author of our religion, who being Lord both of body and mind, yet chose not to propagate it by coercions on either, as was in his Almighty power to do; that the impious presumption of legislators and rulers, civil as well as ecclesiastical, who being themselves but fallible and uninspired men, have assumed dominion over the faith of others, setting up their own opinions and modes of thinking as the only true and infallible, and as such endeavoring to impose them on others, hath established and maintained false religions over the greatest part of the world, and through all time; that to compel a man to furnish contributions of money for the propagation of opinions which he disbelieves, is sinful and tyrannical; that even the forcing him to support this or that teacher of his own religious persuasion, is depriving him of the comfortable liberty of giving his contributions to the particular pastor, whose morals he would make his pattern, and whose powers he feels most persuasive to righteousness, and is withdrawing from the ministry those temporary rewards, which proceeding from an approbation of their personal conduct, are an additional incitement to earnest and unremitting labours for the instruction of mankind; that our civil rights have no dependence on our religious opinions, any more than our opinions in physics or geometry; that therefore the proscribing any citizen as unworthy of the public confidence by laying upon him an incapacity of being called to offices of trust and emolument, unless he profess or renounce this or that religious opinion, is depriving him injuriously of those privileges and advantages to which in common with his fellow-citizens he has a natural right; that it tends only to corrupt the principles of that religion it is meant to encourage, by bribing with a monopoly of worldly honours and emoluments, those who will externally profess and conform to it; that though indeed these are criminal who do not withstand such temptation, yet neither are those innocent who lay the bait in their way; that to suffer the civil magistrate to intrude his powers into the field of opinion, and to restrain the profession or propagation of principles on supposition of their ill tendency, is a dangerous fallacy, which at once destroys all religious liberty, because he being of course judge of that tendency will make his opinions the rule of judgment, and approve or condemn the sentiments of others only as they shall square with or differ from his own; that it is time enough for the rightful purposes of civil government, for its officers to interfere when principles break out into overt acts against peace and good order; and finally, that truth is great and will prevail if left to herself, that she is the proper and sufficient antagonist to error, and has nothing to fear from the conflict, unless by human interposition disarmed of her natural weapons, free argument and debate, errors ceasing to be dangerous when it is permitted freely to contradict them:

Be it enacted by the General Assembly, That no man shall be compelled to frequent or support any religious worship, place, or ministry whatsoever, nor shall be enforced, restrained, molested, or burthened in his body or goods, nor shall otherwise suffer on account of his religious opinions or belief; but that all men shall be free to profess, and by argument to maintain, their opinion in matters of religion, and that the same shall in no wise diminish, enlarge, or affect their civil capacities. And though we well know that this assembly elected by the people for the ordinary purposes of legislation only, have no power to restrain the acts of succeeding assemblies, constituted with powers equal to our own, and that therefore to declare this act to be irrevocable would be of no effect in law; yet we are free to declare, and do declare, that the rights hereby asserted are of the natural rights of mankind, and that if any act shall be hereafter passed to repeal the present, or to narrow its operation, such act will be an infringement of natural right.

Northwest Ordinance (1787)

The Peace of Paris left the newly independent American states in control of a large amount of territory west of the Appalachians. As part of the compromise in adopting the Articles of Confederation, those states whose original charters had given them control of the transmontane area ceded them to the new federal government. The outstanding legislative achievement of the government under the Articles was the Northwest Ordinance, which established the basic rules for governance of the country's western territories and admission of new states for the next 175 years. As part of the government's compact with the settlers of this land, the Ordinance set out certain ideals, including religious freedom. See Peter S. Onuf, Statehood and Union: A History of the Northwest Ordinance *(Bloomington: Indiana University Press, 1987).*

And for extending the fundamental principles of civil and religious liberty, which form the basis whereon these republics, their laws and constitutions are erected; to fix and establish those principles as the basis of all laws, constitutions and governments, which forever hereafter shall be formed in the said territory. . . .

It is hereby ordained and declared . . . that the following articles shall be considered as articles of compact between the original States and the people and the States in said territory, and forever remains unalterable, unless by common consent, to wit:

Article I. No person, demeaning himself in a peaceful and orderly manner, shall ever be molested on account of his mode of worship, or religious sentiments, in the said territory. . . .

Article III. Religion, morality and knowledge, being necessary to good government and the happiness of mankind, schools and the means of education shall forever be encouraged. . . .

ARGUMENT OF COUNSEL IN DEFENSE OF SEAL OF CONFESSION (1813)

A thief, repenting of his sins, had confessed to Father Andrew Kohlmann and asked him to return the stolen goods to their owner, which the priest did. Police demanded that Father Kohlmann identify the thief, but he refused to do so, claiming that information received under the seal of confession remained confidential to all save priest and penitent. Arrested for obstructing justice, Father Kohlmann was tried before the Court of General Sessions in New York City. Counsel on both sides was Protestant. The lawyer who defended Father Kohlmann set out his argument in the broadest possible terms of free exercise. By the early nineteenth century, therefore, at least some people who thought about what religious freedom meant had reached the essentially modern position. See Jay P. Dolan, The American Catholic Experience *(Garden City, NJ: Doubleday, 1985).*

Having thus stripped the cause of embarrassment, and shown, I trust, to the satisfaction of your Honours, that this Court is at perfect liberty, in the judgment that it shall finally pronounce in this cause, to follow the guidance of liberality and wisdom, unfettered by authority; I shall proceed to examine the first proposition which I undertook to maintain, that is, that the 38th Article of the [New York State] Constitution, protects the Reverend Pastor in the exemption which he claims, *independent of every other consideration.*

The whole article is in the words following:

"And whereas we are required by the benevolent principles of rational liberty, not only to expel civil tyranny, but also to guard against that spiritual oppression and intolerance, wherewith the bigotry and ambition of weak and wicked priests and princes have scourged mankind: This convention doth further, in the name and by the authority of the good people of this state, ORDAIN, DETERMINE AND DECLARE, that the free exercise and enjoyment of religious profession and worship, without discrimination or preference, shall forever hereafter be allowed within this state to all mankind. *Provided,* that the liberty of conscience hereby granted, shall not be so construed, as to excuse acts of licentiousness, or justify practices inconsistent with the peace or safety of this State."

Now we cannot easily conceive of more broad and comprehensive terms, than the convention has used. Religious liberty was the great object which they had in view. They felt, that it was the right of every human being, to worship God according to the dictates of his own conscience. They intended to secure, forever, to all mankind, without distinction or preference, the free exercise and enjoyment of religious profession and worship. They employed language commensurate with that object. It is what they have said.

Again, the Catholic religion is an ancient religion. It has existed for eighteen centuries. The sacrament of penance has existed with it. We cannot in legal decorum, suppose the convention to have been ignorant of that fact: nor were they so in truth. The convention was composed of some of the ablest men in this or in any other nation. Their names are known to the court. A few still live, and we revere the memories of those who are no more. They all knew the Catholic faith, and that auricular confession was a part of it. If they had intended any exception would they not have made it? If they had intended that the Catholics should freely enjoy their religion, excepting always, auricular confession, would they not have said so? By every fair rule of construction we are bound to conclude that they would have said so: And as the convention did not make the exception neither ought we to make it.

Again there is no doubt that the convention intended to secure the liberty of conscience. Now, where is the liberty of conscience to the Catholic, if the priest and the penitent, be thus exposed? Has the priest, the liberty of conscience, if he be thus coerced? Has the penitent the liberty of conscience, if he is to be dragged into a court of justice, to answer for what has passed in confession? Have either the privilege of auricular confession? Do they freely enjoy the sacrament of penance? If this be the religious liberty, which the constitution intended to secure, it is as perplexing as the liberty which, in former times, a man had of being tried by the water ordeal, where, if he floated he was guilty—if he sunk he was innocent. . . .

I confess I feel a deep interest in this cause. I am anxious that the decision of the Court should be marked with liberality and wisdom. I consider this a contest between toleration and persecution. A contest involving the rights of conscience. A great constitutional question, which as an American Lawyer, I might, with strict right and perfect propriety have discussed, independent of adjudged cases. To compel the Reverend Pastor to answer, or to be imprisoned, must either force his conscience or lead to persecution. I can conceive of nothing, more barbarous—more cruel—or more unjust than such an alternative. To compel him to answer, against his religious faith or to confine his person, would be the highest violation of right that I have ever witnessed. It would cast a shade upon the jurisprudence of our country. The virtuous and the wise, of all nations, would grieve that America should have so forgotten herself, as to add to the examples of religious despotism!

I cannot express my convictions on this important and delicate subject, better than in the language of that enlightened judge [Lord Mansfield] whose opinion I before quoted. "Conscience is not controllable by human laws, nor amenable to human tribunals. Persecution or attempts to force conscience, will never produce conviction, and are only calculated to make hypocrites, or—Martyrs."

"There is nothing, certainly, more unreasonable, more inconsistent with the rights of human nature, more contrary to the spirit and precepts of the Christian Religion, more iniquitous and unjust, more impolitic than PERSECUTION. It is against natural religion, revealed religion, and sound policy."

Thus have I closed a subject of vast interest to the parties concerned. I could have wished that my argument had been more perfect, and more persuasive. The learned counsel however who is associated with me will more than supply its defects. It only remains for me to make my acknowledgments to the court for the very attentive hearing which it has been pleased to give me, and to express the entire confidence which my reverend client feels, in the wisdom and in the purity of those, to whose judgment he now cheerfully submits himself.

THOMAS KENNEDY SEEKING EQUAL RIGHTS FOR JEWS IN MARYLAND (1818)

Maryland, like many of the other new states, had imposed civil liabilities upon Jews in the sense that they could not hold public office.

*There was certainly more than a note of irony in this, since Mary-
land had been founded as a refuge for persecuted Catholics. The
drive to lift the restriction on Jews can be seen as part of the broader wave of democratic reforms that swept across the country in the
pre–Civil War era. In Maryland as elsewhere, leaders in the fight for
religious equality came from the Protestant majority. Kennedy's
argument, excerpted below, has the ring of modernity about it,
because he suggests that persecution of any one group represents a
danger to all minorities. See Edward Eitches, "Maryland's Jew Bill,"*
American Jewish Historical Quarterly 60: 258–279.

It is with feelings of no ordinary kind, that I now rise to address
this honourable house; the Bill which we are called to decide
upon, is, in my estimation, the most important that has yet come
before us; the most important that will come before us during the
present session.

And, if I am asked why I take so much interest in favour of the
passage of this Bill—to this I would simply answer, because I consider it my DUTY to do so. There are no Jews in the county from
which I come, nor have I the slightest acquaintance with any Jews
in the world. It was not at their request; it was not even known to
any of them, that the subject would be brought forward at this
time.

And if there is any merit in bringing the case of these oppressed
people before this house, that merit does not belong to me; I wish
not to enjoy honours that I do not deserve, nor wear laurels that I
have not earned. The subject was mentioned to me in Baltimore
during the last session, not by a Jew, but by a Gentile gentleman.
My situation was like that of many of the people of Maryland. . . .
[I was faced with] a subject indeed that had never until that time
occupied a moment's reflection in my mind; but the moment it
was mentioned, I was convinced that such distinctions were
wrong and that they ought to be abolished forever.

It is well known to most of the members of this House that I
am not a public speaker. Never before the last session of the Leg-

islature did I ever venture to address a public assembly; yet although I know little of law and less of logic, and although I am master of no language but that which my mother taught me, on this occasion I am not afraid to meet any opponent, let his talents, learning, and eloquence be what they may; and even if my frail vessel should meet with a storm, or suffer shipwreck on the voyage, I see many a friendly hand around me, who will not suffer the unskillful pilot to perish.

There is only one opponent that I fear at this time, and that is PREJUDICE—our prejudices, Mr. Speaker, are dear to us, we all know and feel the force of our political prejudices, but our religious prejudices are still more strong, still more dear; they cling to us through life, and scarcely leave us on the bed of death, and it is not the prejudice of a generation, of an age or a century, that we have now to encounter. No, it is the prejudice which has passed from father to son, for almost eighteen hundred years. . . .

There are very few Jews in the United States; in Maryland there are very few, but if there was only one—to that one, we ought to do justice. I have already observed that I have no acquaintance with any of them, but I have good authority for saying, that those among us are worthy men, and good citizens; and during the late war, when Maryland was invaded, they were found in the ranks by the side of their Christian brethren fighting for those who have hitherto denied them the rights and privileges enjoyed by the veriest wretches.

JOSEPH STORY, "THE RELIGION CLAUSES OF THE FIRST AMENDMENT" (1833)

Next to John Marshall, Joseph Story ranks as the most influential member of the U.S. Supreme Court in the first half of the nineteenth century, and his Commentaries on the Constitution of the United States *(Boston: Hillard, Gray & Co., 1833), from which the following excerpt is taken, have long been considered among the definitive interpretations of early constitutional thought. Yet Story represents an older and now mainly discredited view that government can and should interfere to promote religiosity, and he also assumes that all one has to be concerned about are Christian sects. Although Story is explicit in his prohibitions against government involvement in particular religious affairs, he ignores non-Christian groups for the most part, seeming to assume that whatever would apply to the majoritarian Christian sects would apply to non-Christians as well. See Kent Newmyer,* Supreme Court Justice Joseph Story: Statesman of the Old Republic *(Chapel Hill: University of North Carolina Press, 1985).*

Let us now enter upon the consideration of the amendments, which, it will be found, principally regard subjects properly belonging to a bill of rights.

The first is, "Congress shall make no law respecting an establishment of religion, or prohibiting the free exercise thereof; or abridging the freedom of speech, or of the press; or the right of the people peaceably to assemble, and to petition government for a redress of grievances."

And first, the prohibition of any establishment of religion, and the freedom of religious opinion and worship.

How far any government has a right to interfere in matters touching religion, has been a subject much discussed by writers upon public and political law. The right and the duty of the interference of government, in matters of religion, have been maintained by many distinguished authors, as well as those, who were the warmest advocates of free governments, as those, who were attached to governments of a more arbitrary character. Indeed, the right of a society or government to interfere in matters of religion will hardly be contested by any persons, who believe that piety, religion, and morality are intimately connected with the well being of the state, and indispensable to the administration of civil justice. The promulgation of the great doctrines of religion, the being, and attributes, and providence of one Almighty God; the responsibility to him for all our actions, founded upon moral freedom and accountability; a future state of rewards and punishments; the cultivation of all the personal, social, and benevolent virtues; these never can be a matter of indifference in any well ordered community. It is, indeed, difficult to conceive, how any civilized society can well exist without them. And at all events, it is impossible for those, who believe in the truth of Christianity, as a divine revelation, to doubt, that it is the especial duty of government to foster, and encourage it among all the citizens and subjects. This is a point wholly distinct from that of the right of private judgment in matters of religion, and of the freedom of public worship according to the dictates of one's conscience.

The real difficulty lies in ascertaining the limits, to which government may rightfully go in fostering and encouraging religion. Three cases may easily be supposed. One, where a government affords aid to a particular religion, leaving all persons free to adopt any other; another, where it creates an ecclesiastical establishment for the propagation of the doctrines of a particular sect of that religion, leaving a like freedom to all others; and a third, where it creates such an establishment, and excludes all persons, not belonging to it, either wholly, or in part, from any participation in the public honours, trusts, emoluments, privileges, and immunities of the state. For instance, a government may simply declare, that the Christian religion shall be the religion of the state, and shall be aided, and encouraged in all the varieties of sects belonging to it; or it may declare, that the Catholic or Protestant religion shall be the religion of the state, leaving every man to the free enjoyment of his own religious opinions; or it may establish the doctrines of a particular sect, as of Episcopalians, as the religion of the state, with a like freedom; or it may establish the doctrines of a particular sect, as exclusively the religion of the state, tolerating others to a limited extent, or excluding all, not belonging to it, from all public honours, trusts, emoluments, privileges, and immunities.

Now, there will probably be found few persons in this, or any other Christian country, who would deliberately contend, that it was unreasonable, or unjust to foster and encourage the Christian religion generally, as a matter of sound policy, as well as of revealed truth. In fact, every American colony, from its foundation down to the revolution, with the exception of Rhode Island, (if, indeed, that state be an exception,) did openly, by the whole course of its laws and institutions, support and sustain, in some form, the Christian religion; and almost invariably gave a peculiar sanction to some of its fundamental doctrines. And this has continued to be the case in some of the states down to the present period, without the slightest suspicion, that it was against the principles of public law, or republican liberty. Indeed, in a republic, there would seem to be a peculiar propriety in viewing the Christian religion, as the great basis, on which it must rest for its support and permanence, if it be, what it has ever been deemed by its truest friends to be, the religion of liberty.

Probably at the time of the adoption of the constitution, and of the amendment to it, now under consideration, the general, if not the universal, sentiment in America was, that Christianity ought to receive encouragement from the state, so far as was not incompatible with the private rights of conscience, and the freedom of religious worship. An attempt to level all religions, and to make it a matter of state policy to hold all in utter indifference, would have created universal disapprobation, if not universal indignation.

It yet remains a problem to be solved in human affairs, whether any free government can be permanent, where the public worship of God, and the support of religion, constitute no part of the policy or duty of the state in any assignable shape. The future experience of Christendom, and chiefly of the American states, must settle this problem, as yet new in the history of the world, abundant, as it has been, in experiments in the theory of government.

The real object of the amendment was, not to countenance, much less to advance Mahometanism, or Judaism, or infidelity, by prostrating Christianity; but to exclude all rivalry among Christian sects, and to prevent any national ecclesiastical establishment, which should give to an hierarchy the exclusive patronage of the national government. It thus cut off the means of religious persecution, (the vice and pest of former ages,) and of the subversion of the rights of conscience in matters of religion, which had been trampled upon almost from the days of the Apostles to the present age.

JOHN TYLER ON THE KNOW-NOTHINGS (1854)

The large influx of immigrants beginning in the 1830s, as well as significant social and economic upheavals, led to the rise of nativism, a movement that saw all newcomers and "outsiders" as inferior and to be excluded from the body politic. Those marked as outsiders included Catholics, who were especially targets of a secret nativist organization founded in New York in 1849, known as the Order of the Star-Spangled Banner. Its followers soon began running for office on an anti-immigrant, anti-Catholic platform, and when asked to what party they belonged, they replied that they "knew nothing," or that is, refused to talk about their secret society. The name stuck and applied not only to the members of the order but to all rabid nativists of the time. But although many Protestants did not trust the Catholic Church, some, including Abraham Lincoln and former president John Tyler, despised the Know-Nothing intolerance. See Ray Allan Billington, The Protestant Crusade, 1800–1860 (New York: Rinehart, 1938).

The Catholics seem especially obnoxious to them, whereas that sect seems to me to have been particularly faithful to the Constitution of the country, while their priests have set an example of noninterference in politics which furnishes an example most worthy of imitation on the part of the clergy of the other sects of the North, who have not hesitated to rush into the arena and soil their garments with the dust of bitter strife. The intolerant spirit manifested against the Catholics, as exhibited in the burning of their churches, etc., will, as soon as the thing becomes fairly considered, arouse a strong feeling of dissatisfaction on the part of a large majority of the American people; for if there is one principle of higher import with them than any other, it is the principle of religious freedom.

REYNOLDS V. UNITED STATES (1879)

The Mormon practice of polygamy not only led to popular prejudice against the Mormons but also to the passage of a number of federal laws designed to eradicate the practice. The case of George Reynolds, a secretary to Brigham Young who had been arrested and convicted of violating the Morrill Anti-Polygamy Act, went to the Supreme Court on appeal. Much of Reynolds's appeal centered on technical questions of jury selection and instruction. But Reynolds also claimed that because his multiple marriages were founded in his religious beliefs, he should be found innocent under the Free Exercise Clause. The Court rejected the religious freedom defense. In the deciding opinion excerpted here, Chief Justice Morrison Waite laid down what is still an essential element of First Amendment jurisprudence: the difference between belief and action. See Kimball Young, Isn't One Wife Enough? The Story of Mormon Polygamy *(New York: Holt, 1954); and Edwin Brown Firmage and Richard C. Mangrum,* Zion in the Courts: A Legal History of the Church of Jesus Christ of Latter-Day Saints, 1830–1900 *(Urbana: University of Illinois Press, 1988).*

5. As to the defence of religious belief or duty.

On the trial, the plaintiff in error, the accused, proved that at the time of his alleged second marriage he was, and for many years before had been, a member of the Church of Jesus Christ of Latter-Day Saints, commonly called the Mormon Church, and a believer in its doctrines; that it was an accepted doctrine of that church "that it was the duty of male members of said church, circumstances permitting, to practise polygamy;... that this duty was enjoined by different books which the members of said church believed to be of divine origin, and among others the Holy Bible, and also that the members of the church believed that the practice of polygamy was directly enjoined upon the male members thereof by the Almighty God, in a revelation to Joseph Smith, the founder and prophet of said church; that the failing or refusing to practise polygamy by such male members of said church, when circumstances would admit, would be punished, and that the penalty for such failure and refusal would be damnation in the life to come." He also proved "that he had received permission from the recognized authorities in said church to enter into polygamous marriage; . . . that Daniel H. Wells, one having authority in said church to perform the marriage ceremony, married the said defendant on or about the time the crime is alleged to have been committed, to some woman by the name of Schofield, and that such marriage ceremony was performed under and pursuant to the doctrines of said church."

Upon this proof he asked the court to instruct the jury that if they found from the evidence that he "was married as charged—if he was married—in pursuance of and in conformity with what he believed at the time to be a religious duty, that the verdict must be 'not guilty.'" This request was refused, and the court did charge "that there must have been a criminal intent, but that if the defendant, under the influence of a religious belief that it was right,—under an inspiration, if you please, that it was right,—deliberately married a second time, having a first wife living, the want of consciousness of evil intent—the want of understanding on his part that he was committing a crime—did not excuse him; but the law inexorably in such case implies the criminal intent."

Upon this charge and refusal to charge the question is raised, whether religious belief can be accepted as a justification of an overt act made criminal by the law of the land. The inquiry is not as to the power of Congress to prescribe criminal laws for the Territories, but as to the guilt of one who knowingly violates a law which has been properly enacted, if he entertains a religious belief that the law is wrong.

Congress cannot pass a law for the government of the Territories which shall prohibit the free exercise of religion. The first amendment to the Constitution expressly forbids such legislation. Religious freedom is guaranteed everywhere throughout the United States, so far as congressional interference is concerned. The question to be determined is, whether the law now under consideration comes within this prohibition.

The word "religion" is not defined in the Constitution. We must go elsewhere, therefore, to ascertain its meaning, and nowhere more appropriately, we think, than to the history of the times in the midst of which the provision was adopted. The precise point of the inquiry is, what is the religious freedom which has been guaranteed.

Before the adoption of the Constitution, attempts were made in some of the colonies and States to legislate not only in respect to the establishment of religion, but in respect to its doctrines and precepts as well. The people were taxed, against their will, for the support of religion, and sometimes for the support of particular sects to whose tenets they could not and did not subscribe. Punishments were prescribed for a failure to attend upon public worship, and sometimes for entertaining heretical opinions. The controversy upon this general subject was animated in many of the States, but seemed at last to culminate in Virginia. In 1784, the House of Delegates of that State having under consideration "a bill establishing provision for teachers of the Christian religion," postponed it until the next session, and directed that the bill should be published and distributed, and that the people be requested "to signify their opinion respecting the adoption of such a bill at the next session of assembly."

This brought out a determined opposition. Amongst others, Mr. Madison prepared a "Memorial and Remonstrance," which was widely circulated and signed, and in which he demonstrated "that religion, or the duty we owe the Creator," was not within the cognizance of civil government. At the next session the proposed bill was not only defeated, but another, "for establishing religious freedom," drafted by Mr. Jefferson, was passed. In the preamble of this act religious freedom is defined; and after a recital "that to suffer the civil magistrate to intrude his powers into the field of opinion, and to restrain the profession or propagation of principles on supposition of their ill tendency, is a dangerous fallacy which at once destroys all religious liberty," it is declared "that it is time enough for the rightful purposes of civil government for its officers to interfere when principles break out into overt acts against peace and good order." In these two sentences is found the true distinction between what properly belongs to the church and what to the State.

In a little more than a year after the passage of this statute the convention met which prepared the Constitution of the United States. Of this convention Mr. Jefferson was not a member, he being then absent as minister to France. As soon as he saw the draft of the Constitution proposed for adoption, he, in a letter to a friend, expressed his disappointment at the absence of an express declaration insuring the freedom of religion, but was willing to accept it as it was, trusting that the good sense and honest intentions of the people would bring about the necessary alterations. Five of the States, while adopting the Constitution, proposed amendments. Three—New Hampshire, New York, and Virginia—included in one form or another a declaration of religious freedom in the changes they desired to have made, as did also North Carolina, where the convention at first declined to ratify the Constitution until the proposed amendments were acted upon. Accordingly, at the first session of the first Congress the amendment now under consideration was proposed with others by Mr. Madison. It met the views of the advocates of religious freedom, and was adopted. Mr. Jefferson afterwards, in reply to an address to him by a committee of the Danbury Baptist Association, took occasion to say: "Believing with you that religion is a matter which lies solely between man and his god; that he owes account to none other for his faith or his worship; that the legislative powers of the government reach actions only, and not opinions,—I contemplate with sovereign reverence that act of the whole American people which declared that their legislature should 'make no law respecting an establishment of religion or prohibiting the free exercise thereof,' thus building a wall of separation between church and State. Adhering to this expression of the supreme will of the nation in behalf of the rights of conscience, I shall see with sincere satisfaction the progress of those sentiments which tend to restore man to all his natural rights, convinced he has no natural right in opposition to his social duties." Coming as this does from an acknowledged leader of the advocates of the measure, it may be accepted almost as an authoritative declaration of the scope and effect of the amendment thus secured. Congress was deprived of all legislative power over mere opinion, but was left free to reach actions which were in violation of social duties or subversive of good order.

Polygamy has always been odious among the northern and western nations of Europe, and, until the establishment of the Mormon Church, was almost exclusively a feature of the life of Asiatic and of African people. At common law, the second marriage was always void, and from the earliest history of England polygamy has been treated as an offence against society. . . .

In connection with the case we are now considering, it is a significant fact that on the 8th of December, 1788, after the passage of the act establishing religious freedom, and after the convention of Virginia had recommended as an amendment to the Constitution of the United States the declaration in a bill of rights that "all men have an equal, natural, and unalienable right to the free exercise of religion, according to the dictates of conscience," the legislature of that State substantially enacted the [English] laws, death penalty included, because, as recited in the preamble, "it hath been doubted whether bigamy or polygamy be punishable by the laws of this Commonwealth." From that day to this we think it may safely be said there never has been a time in any State of the Union when polygamy has not been an offence against society, cognizable by the civil courts and punishable with more or less severity. In the face of all this evidence, it is impossible to believe that the constitutional guaranty of religious freedom was intended to prohibit legislation in respect to this most important feature of social life. Marriage, while from its very nature a sacred obligation, is nevertheless, in most civilized nations, a civil contract, and usually regulated by law. Upon it society may be said to be built, and out of its fruits spring social relations and social obligations and duties, with which government is necessarily required to deal. In fact, according as monogamous or polygamous marriages are allowed, do we find the principles on which the government of the people, to a greater or less extent, rests. . . . An exceptional colony of polygamists under an exceptional leadership may sometimes exist for a time without appearing to disturb the social condition of the people who surround it; but there cannot be a doubt that, unless restricted by some form of constitution, it is within the legitimate scope of the power of every civil government to determine whether polygamy or monogamy shall be the law of social life under its dominion. In our opinion, the statute immediately under consideration is within the legislative power of Congress. It is constitutional and valid as prescribing a rule of action for all those residing in the Territories, and in places over which the United States have exclusive control. This being so, the only question which remains is, whether those who make polygamy a part of their religion are excepted from the operation of the statute. If they are, then those who do not make polygamy a part of their religious belief may be found guilty and punished, while those who do, must be acquitted and go free. This would be introducing a new element into criminal law. Laws are made for the government of actions, and while they cannot interfere with mere religious belief and opinions, they may with practices. Suppose one believed that human sacrifices were a necessary part of religious worship, would it be seriously contended that the civil government under which he lived could not interfere to prevent a sacrifice? Or if a wife religiously believed it was her duty to burn herself upon the funeral pile of her dead husband, would it be beyond the power of the civil government to prevent her carrying her belief into practice?

So here, as a law of the organization of society under the exclusive dominion of the United States, it is provided that plural marriages shall not be allowed. Can a man excuse his practices to the contrary because of his religious belief? To permit this would be to make the professed doctrines of religious belief superior to the law of the land, and in effect to permit every citizen to become a law unto himself. Government could exist only in name under such circumstances.

A criminal intent is generally an element of crime, but every man is presumed to intend the necessary and legitimate consequences of what he knowingly does. Here the accused knew he had been once married, and that his first wife was living. He also knew that his second marriage was forbidden by law. When, therefore, he married the second time, he is presumed to have intended to break the law. And the breaking of the law is the crime. Every act necessary to constitute the crime was knowingly done, and the crime was therefore knowingly committed. Ignorance of a fact may sometimes be taken as evidence of a want of criminal intent, but not ignorance of the law. The only defence of the accused in this case is his belief that the law ought not to have been enacted. It matters not that his belief was a part of his professed religion: it was still belief, and belief only.

Upon a careful consideration of the whole case, we are satisfied that no error was committed by the court below.

Judgment affirmed.

ALFRED E. SMITH ON CATHOLICISM AND PATRIOTISM (1927)

The nativism of the Know-Nothings was reborn in the 1920s in the even more vicious form of the Ku Klux Klan, which attacked blacks, Catholics, Jews, and all other "foreigners" as un-American. The hysteria affected people who should have known better. Many Protestants claimed that Catholics took their orders from the Pope and could not be fully loyal Americans. This charge received wide circulation early in 1927, when it appeared certain that the Catholic governor of New York, Alfred Emanuel Smith, would be the 1928 Democratic Party presidential candidate. After Charles Marshall had published an open letter in the Atlantic Monthly *attacking Catholics as disloyal, Smith decided to meet the issue head-on, by writing a similar letter to the same journal. Despite his courageous defense, Smith had little chance in 1928 of defeating Herbert Hoover. In addition to being Catholic, Smith was against prohibition, and he was an urbanite—three strikes against him, in mainstream American public opinion. Making matters worse, the Democrats had to run against Republican prosperity. See Oscar Handlin,* Al Smith and His America *(Boston: Little, Brown, 1958); and Robert K. Murray,* The Politics of Normalcy *(New York: Norton, 1973).*

Dear Sir:

In your open letter to me in the April Atlantic Monthly you "impute" to American Catholics views which, if held by them, would leave open to question the loyalty and devotion to this country and its Constitution of more than twenty million American Catholic citizens. I am grateful to you for defining this issue in the open and for your courteous expression of the satisfaction it will bring to my fellow citizens for me to give "a disclaimer of the convictions" thus imputed. Without mental reservation I can and do make that disclaimer. These convictions are held neither by me nor by any other American Catholic, as far as I know. . . .

Taking your letter as a whole and reducing it to commonplace English, you imply that there is conflict between religious loyalty to the Catholic faith and patriotic loyalty to the United States. Everything that has actually happened to me during my long public career leads me to know that no such thing as that is true. I have taken an oath of office in this State nineteen times. Each time I swore to defend and maintain the Constitution of the United States. All of this represents a period of public service in elective office almost continuous since 1903. I have never known any conflict between my official duties and my religious belief. No such conflict could exist. Certainly the people of this State recognize no such conflict. They have testified to my devotion to public duty by electing me to the highest office within their gift four times. You yourself do me the honor, in addressing me, to refer to "your fidelity to the morality you have advocated in public and private life and to the religion you have revered; your great record of public trusts successfully and honestly discharged." During the years I have discharged these trusts I have been a communicant of the Roman Catholic Church. If there were conflict, I, of all men, could not have escaped it, because I have not been a silent man, but a battler for social and political reform. These battles would in their very nature disclose this conflict if there were any.

But, wishing to meet you on your own ground, I address myself to your definite questions, against which I have thus far made only general statements. I must first call attention to the fact that you often divorce sentences from their context in such a way as to give them something other than their real meaning. I will specify. . . . You quote from the Catholic Encyclopedia that my Church "regards dogmatic intolerance, not alone as her incontestable right, but as her sacred duty." And you say that these words show that Catholics are taught to be politically, socially, and intellectually intolerant of all other people. If you had read the whole of that article in the Catholic Encyclopedia, you would know that the real meaning of these words is that for Catholics alone the Church recognizes no deviation from complete acceptance of its dogma. These words are used in a chapter dealing with that subject only. The very same article in another chapter dealing with toleration toward non-Catholics contains these words: "The intolerant man is avoided as much as possible by every high-minded person. . . . The man who is tolerant in every emergency is alone lovable." The phrase "dogmatic intolerance" does not mean that Catholics are to be dogmatically intolerant of other people, but merely that inside the Catholic Church they are to be intolerant of any variance from the dogma of the Church.

Similar criticism can be made of many of your quotations. But, beyond this, by what right do you ask me to assume responsibility for every statement that may be made in any encyclical letter? As you will find in the *Catholic Encyclopedia (Vol. V, p. 414),* these encyclicals are not articles of our faith. The Syllabus of Pope Pius IX, which you quote on the possible conflict between Church and State, is declared by Cardinal Newman to have "no dogmatic force." You seem to think that Catholics must be all alike in mind and in heart, as though they had been poured into and taken out of the same mould. You have no more right to ask me to defend as part of my faith every statement coming from a prelate than I should have to ask you to accept as an article of your religious faith every statement of an Episcopal bishop, or of your political faith every statement of a President of the United States. So little are these matters of the essence of my faith that I, a devout Catholic since childhood, never heard of them until I read your letter. Nor can you quote from the canons of our faith a syllable that would make us less good citizens than non-Catholics. . . .

Under our system of government the electorate entrusts to its officers of every faith the solemn duty of action according to the dictates of conscience. I may fairly refer once more to my own record to support these truths. No man, cleric or lay, has ever directly or indirectly attempted to exercise Church influence on my administration of any office I have ever held, nor asked me to

show special favor to Catholics or exercise discrimination against
non-Catholics.

It is a well-known fact that I have made all of my appointments
to public office on the basis of merit and have never asked any
man about his religious belief. In the first month of this year there
gathered in the Capitol at Albany the first Governor's cabinet that
ever sat in this State. It was composed, under my appointment, of
two Catholics, thirteen Protestants, and one Jew. The man closest
to me in the administration of the government of the State of New
York is one who bears the title of Assistant to the Governor. He
had been connected with the Governor's office for thirty years, in
subordinate capacities, until I promoted him to the position which
makes him the sharer with me of my every thought and hope and
ambition in the administration of the State. He is a Protestant, a
Republican, and a thirty-second-degree Mason. In my public life
I have exemplified that complete separation of Church from State
which is the faith of American Catholics to-day.

I summarize my creed as an American Catholic. I believe in the
worship of God according to the faith and practice of the Roman
Catholic Church. I recognize no power in the institutions of my
Church to interfere with the operations of the Constitution of the
United States or the enforcement of the law of the land. I believe
in absolute freedom of conscience for all men and in equality of all
churches, all sects, and all beliefs before the law as a matter of
right and not as a matter of favor. I believe in the absolute separation of Church and State and in the strict enforcement of the provisions of the Constitution that Congress shall make no law
respecting an establishment of religion or prohibiting the free
exercise thereof. I believe that no tribunal of any church has any
power to make any decree of any force in the law of the land, other than to establish the status of its own communicants within its
own church. I believe in the support of the public school as one of
the corner stones of American liberty. I believe in the right of
every parent to choose whether his child shall be educated in the

public school or in a religious school supported by those of his own faith. I believe in the principle of noninterference by this country in the internal affairs of other nations and that we should stand steadfastly against any such interference by whomsoever it may be urged. And I believe in the common brotherhood of man under the common fatherhood of God.

In this spirit I join with fellow Americans of all creeds in a fervent prayer that never again in this land will any public servant be challenged because of the faith in which he has tried to walk humbly with his God.

Very truly yours,
Alfred E. Smith

MINERSVILLE SCHOOL DISTRICT v. GOBITIS (1940)

Just as there had been no First Amendment case law on speech prior to the end of World War I, so there was little case law on the First Amendment's religion clauses before World War II. The first concerted exploration of what the religion clauses meant came with a series of challenges against state and local restrictions litigated by the Jehovah's Witnesses. The Witnesses made household solicitations, sold their publications, and held parades, among other things, to proselytize their beliefs. None of these activities was in itself noxious, but all were regulated in one way or another by local ordinances or required permits. The Witnesses could easily have secured the necessary permits, but refused to apply for them, denying that the secular authorities had any power in this area. The Witnesses won their first battle solely on the basis of the Free Exercise Clause, in Cantwell v. Connecticut *(1940), in which a unanimous Court struck down as arbitrary a state law prohibiting solicitation without official approval. The Witnesses also had refused to salute the American flag, claiming that such a salute violated the biblical injunction against worshiping graven images. In*

Gobitis, *the Court upheld this local requirement. With Europe already at war and the United States rearming, patriotism had to be encouraged; balancing community interests against individual rights, the majority found in favor of the community. Only Justice Stone dissented, charging that the required salute violated freedom of speech and of religion. See Leo Pfeffer,* Church, State, and Freedom *(Boston: Beacon Press, 1967 rev. ed.); David Manwaring,* Render unto Caesar: The Flag Salute Controversy *(Chicago: University of Chicago Press, 1962); Irving Dillard, "The Flag Salute Cases," p. 222 in John Garraty, ed.,* Quarrels That Have Shaped the Constitution *(New York: Harper & Row, 1975); and Shawn Francis Peters,* Judging Jehovah's Witnesses *(Lawrence: University Press of Kansas, 2000).*

Justice Frankfurter delivered the opinion of the Court.

A grave responsibility confronts this Court whenever in course of litigation it must reconcile the conflicting claims of liberty and authority. But when the liberty invoked is liberty of conscience, and the authority is authority to safeguard the nation's fellowship, judicial conscience is put to its severest test. Of such a nature is the present controversy.

Lillian Gobitis, aged twelve, and her brother William, aged ten, were expelled from the public schools of Minersville, Pennsylvania, for refusing to salute the national flag as part of a daily school exercise. . . .

We must decide whether the requirement of participation in such a ceremony, exacted from a child who refuses upon sincere religious grounds, infringes without due process of law the liberty guaranteed by the Fourteenth Amendment.

Centuries of strife over the erection of particular dogmas as exclusive or all-comprehending faiths led to the inclusion of a guarantee for religious freedom in the Bill of Rights. The First Amendment, and the Fourteenth through its absorption of the First, sought to guard against repetition of those bitter religious struggles by prohibiting the establishment of a state religion and by securing to every sect the free exercise of its faith. So pervasive is the acceptance of this precious right that its scope is brought into question, as here, only when the conscience of individuals collides with the felt necessities of society.

Certainly the affirmative pursuit of one's convictions about the ultimate mystery of the universe and man's relation to it is placed beyond the reach of law. Government may not interfere with organized or individual expression of belief or disbelief. Propagation of belief—or even of disbelief—in the supernatural is protected, whether in church or chapel, mosque or synagogue, tabernacle or meeting-house. Likewise the Constitution assures generous immunity to the individual from imposition of penalties for offending, in the course of his own religious activities, the religious views of others, be they a minority or those who are dominant in government.

But the manifold character of man's relations may bring his conception of religious duty into conflict with the secular interests of his fellow-men. When does the constitutional guarantee compel exemption from doing what society thinks necessary for the promotion of some great common end, or from a penalty for conduct which appears dangerous to the general good? To state the problem is to recall the truth that no single principle can answer all of life's complexities. The right to freedom of religious belief, however dissident and however obnoxious to the cherished beliefs of others—even of a majority—is itself the denial of an absolute. But to affirm that the freedom to follow conscience has itself no limits in the life of a society would deny that very plurality of principles which, as a matter of history, underlies protection of religious toleration. Our present task, then, as so often the case with courts, is to reconcile two rights in order to prevent either from destroying the other. But, because in safeguarding conscience we are dealing with interests so subtle and so dear, every possible leeway should be given to the claims of religious faith. . . .

The case before us is not concerned with an exertion of legislative power for the promotion of some specific need or interest of secular society—the protection of the family, the promotion of health, the common defense, the raising of public revenues to defray the cost of government. But all these specific activities of government presuppose the existence of an organized political society. The ultimate foundation of a free society is the binding tie of cohesive sentiment. Such a sentiment is fostered by all those agencies of the mind and spirit which may serve to gather up the traditions of a people, transmit them from generation to generation, and thereby create that continuity of a treasured common life which constitutes a civilization. "We live by symbols." The flag is the symbol of our national unity, transcending all internal differences, however large, within the framework of the Constitution. . . .

The precise issue, then, for us to decide is whether the legislatures of the various states and the authorities in a thousand counties and school districts of this country are barred from determining the appropriateness of various means to evoke that unifying sentiment without which there can ultimately be no liberties, civil or religious. To stigmatize legislative judgment in providing for this universal gesture of respect for the symbol of our national life in the setting of the common school as a lawless inroad on that freedom of conscience which the Constitution protects, would amount to no less than the pronouncement of pedagogical and psychological dogma in a field where courts possess no marked and certainly no controlling competence. The influences which help toward a common feeling for the common country are manifold. Some may seem harsh and others no doubt are foolish. Surely, however, the end is legitimate. And the effective means for its attainment are still so uncertain and so unauthenticated by science as to preclude us from putting the widely prevalent belief in flag-saluting beyond the pale of legislative power. It mocks reason and denies our whole history to find in the allowance of a requirement to salute our flag on fitting occasions the seeds of sanction for obeisance to a leader. . . .

The preciousness of the family relation, the authority and independence which give dignity to parenthood, indeed the enjoyment of all freedom, presuppose the kind of ordered society which is summarized by our flag. A society which is dedicated to the preservation of these ultimate values of civilization may in self-protection utilize the educational process for inculcating those almost unconscious feelings which bind men together in a comprehending loyalty, whatever may be their lesser differences and difficulties. That is to say, the process may be utilized so long as men's right to believe as they please, to win others to their way of belief, and their right to assemble in their chosen places of worship for the devotional ceremonies of their faith, are all fully respected.

Judicial review, itself a limitation on popular government, is a fundamental part of our constitutional scheme. But to the legislature no less than to courts is committed the guardianship of deeply-cherished liberties. Where all the effective means of inducing political changes are left free from interference, education in the abandonment of foolish legislation is itself a training in liberty. To fight out the wise use of legislative authority in the forum of public opinion and before legislative assemblies rather than to transfer such a contest to the judicial arena, serves to vindicate the self-confidence of a free people.

Reversed.

Justice Stone, dissenting: . . . The law which is thus sustained is unique in the history of Anglo-American legislation. It does more than suppress freedom of speech and more than prohibit the free exercise of religion, which concededly are forbidden by the First Amendment and are violations of the liberty guaranteed by the Fourteenth. For by this law the state seeks to coerce these children to express a sentiment which, as they interpret it, they do not entertain, and which violates their deepest religious convictions. It is not denied that such compulsion is a prohibited infringement of personal liberty, freedom of speech and religion, guaranteed by the Bill of Rights, except in so far as it may be justified and supported as a proper exercise of the state's power over public education. Since the state, in competition with parents, may through teaching in the public schools indoctrinate the minds of the young, it is said that in aid of its undertaking to inspire loyalty and devotion to constituted authority and the flag which symbolizes it, it may coerce the pupil to make affirmation contrary to his belief and in violation of his religious faith. And, finally, it is said that since the Minersville School Board and others are of the opinion that the country will be better served by conformity than by the observance of religious liberty which the Constitution prescribes, the courts are not free to pass judgment on the Board's choice.

Concededly the constitutional guaranties of personal liberty are not always absolutes. Government has a right to survive and powers conferred upon it are not necessarily set at naught by the express prohibitions of the Bill of Rights. It may make war and raise armies. To that end it may compel citizens to give military service, and subject them to military training despite their religious objections. It may suppress religious practices dangerous to morals, and presumably those also which are inimical to public safety, health and good order. But it is a long step, and one which I am unable to take, to the position that government may, as a supposed educational measure and as a means of disciplining the young, compel public affirmations which violate their religious conscience.

. . . In these cases it was pointed out that where there are competing demands of the interests of government and of liberty under the Constitution, and where the performance of governmental functions is brought into conflict with specific constitutional restrictions, there must, when that is possible, be reasonable accommodation between them so as to preserve the essentials of both and that it is the function of courts to determine whether such accommodation is reasonably possible. In the cases just mentioned the Court was of opinion that there were ways enough to secure the legitimate state end without infringing the asserted immunity, or that the inconvenience caused by the inability to secure that end satisfactorily through other means, did not outweigh freedom of speech or religion. So here, even if we believe that such compulsions will contribute to national unity, there are other ways to teach loyalty and patriotism which are the sources of national unity, than by compelling the pupil to affirm that which he does not believe and by commanding a form of affirmance which violates his religious convictions. Without recourse to such compulsion the state is free to compel attendance at school and require teaching by instruction and study of all in our history and in the structure and organization of our government, including the guaranties of civil liberty which tend to inspire patriotism and love of country. I cannot say that government here is deprived of any interest or function which it is entitled to maintain at the expense of the protection of civil liberties by requiring it to resort to the alternatives which do not coerce an affirmation of belief.

The guaranties of civil liberty are but guaranties of freedom of the human mind and spirit and of reasonable freedom and opportunity to express them. They presuppose the right of the individual to hold such opinions as he will and to give them reasonably free expression, and his freedom, and that of the state as well, to teach and persuade others by the communication of ideas. The very essence of the liberty which they guaranty is the freedom of the individual from compulsion as to what he shall think and what he shall say, at least where the compulsion is to bear false witness to his religion. If these guaranties are to have any meaning they must, I think, be deemed to withhold from the state any authority to compel belief or the expression of it where that expression violates religious convictions, whatever may be the legislative view of the desirability of such compulsion.

History teaches us that there have been but few infringements of personal liberty by the state which have not been justified, as they are here, in the name of righteousness and the public good, and few which have not been directed, as they are now, at politically helpless minorities. The framers were not unaware that under the system which they created most governmental curtailments of personal liberty would have the support of a legislative judgment that the public interest would be better served by its curtailment than by its constitutional protection. I cannot conceive that in prescribing, as limitations upon the powers of government, the freedom of the mind and spirit secured by the explicit guaranties of freedom of speech and religion, they intended or rightly could have left any latitude for a legislative judgment that the compulsory expression of belief which violates religious convictions would better serve the public interest than their protection. The Constitution may well elicit expressions of loyalty to it and to the government which it created, but it does not command such expressions or otherwise give any indication that compulsory expressions of loyalty play any such part in our scheme of government as to override the constitutional protection of freedom of speech and religion. And while such expressions of loyalty, when voluntarily given, may promote national unity, it is quite another matter to say that their compulsory expression by children in violation of their own and their parents' religious convictions can be regarded as playing so important a part in our national unity as to leave school boards free to exact it despite the constitutional guarantee of freedom of religion. The very terms of the Bill of Rights preclude, it seems to me, any reconciliation of such compulsions with the constitutional guaranties by a legislative declaration that they are more important to the public welfare than the Bill of Rights.

. . . We have previously pointed to the importance of a searching judicial inquiry into the legislative judgment in situations where prejudice against discrete and insular minorities may tend to curtail the operation of those political processes ordinarily to be relied on to protect minorities. And until now we have not hesitated similarly to scrutinize legislation restricting the civil liberty of racial and religious minorities although no political process was affected. Here we have such a small minority entertaining in good faith a religious belief, which is such a departure from the usual course of human conduct, that most persons are disposed to regard it with little toleration or concern. In such circumstances careful scrutiny of legislative efforts to secure conformity of belief and opinion by a compulsory affirmation of the desired belief, is especially needful if civil rights are to receive any protection. Tested by this standard, I am not prepared to say that the right of this small and helpless minority, including children having a strong religious conviction, whether they understand its nature or not, to refrain from an expression obnoxious to their religion, is to be overborne by the interest of the state in maintaining discipline in the schools.

The Constitution expresses more than the conviction of the people that democratic processes must be preserved at all costs. It is also an expression of faith and a command that freedom of mind and spirit must be preserved, which government must obey, if it is to adhere to that justice and moderation without which no free government can exist. For this reason it would seem that legislation which operates to repress the religious freedom of small minorities, which is admittedly within the scope of the protection of the Bill of Rights, must at least be subject to the same judicial scrutiny as legislation which we have recently held to infringe the constitutional liberty of religious and racial minorities.

With such scrutiny I cannot say that the inconveniences which may attend some sensible adjustment of school discipline in order that the religious convictions of these children may be spared, presents a problem so momentous or pressing as to outweigh the freedom from compulsory violation of religious faith which has been thought worthy of constitutional protection.

WEST VIRGINIA BOARD OF EDUCATION V. BARNETTE (1943)

Despite their loss in the Gobitis *case, the Witnesses refused to compromise; and in spite of enormous public hostility, they persisted in*

*acting on their religious beliefs. Over the next few years they lost a
series of court cases. In* Cox v. New Hampshire *(1940), a unanimous bench upheld a state regulation requiring parade permits;
and in* Chaplinsky v. New Hampshire *(1942), the Court sustained
the conviction of a Witness who had gotten into a fight after calling a city marshal "a damned fascist." In another Witness case that
year,* Jones v. Opelika, *the Court upheld municipal license fees for
transient merchants or book peddlers; but three of the* Gobitis
*majority—Black, Douglas, and Murphy—now joined with Stone
in dissent. Moreover, many Americans had begun to rethink the
meaning of a mandatory flag salute in light of revelations about
indoctrination methods in Nazi Germany. The climax came in the
second flag salute case, when Justice Jackson, who rarely supported
minority rights, joined the dissenters and wrote one of the most
eloquent opinions of his career. Frankfurter entered an anguished
dissent, objecting especially to Jackson's use of the Holmes clear-
and-present-danger test, and called for increased judicial restraint.
See Leo Pfeffer,* Church, State, and Freedom *(Boston: Beacon
Press, 1967 rev. ed.); David Manwaring,* Render unto Caesar: The
Flag Salute Controversy *(Chicago: University of Chicago Press,
1962); Irving Dillard, "The Flag Salute Cases," p. 222 in John
Garraty, ed.,* Quarrels That Have Shaped the Constitution *(New
York: Harper & Row, 1975); and Shawn Francis Peters,* Judging
Jehovah's Witnesses *(Lawrence: University Press of Kansas, 2000).*

Justice Jackson delivered the opinion of the Court.

Appellees, citizens of the United States and of West Virginia,
brought suit in the United States District Court for themselves
and others similarly situated asking its injunction to restrain
enforcement of these [flag salute] laws and regulations against
Jehovah's Witnesses. The Witnesses are an unincorporated body
teaching that the obligation imposed by law of God is superior to
that of laws enacted by temporal government. Their religious
beliefs include a literal version of Exodus, Chapter 20, verses 4
and 5, which says: "Thou shalt not make unto thee any graven

image, or any likeness of anything that is in heaven above, or that is in the earth beneath, or that is in the water under the earth; thou shalt not bow down thyself to them nor serve them." They consider that the flag is an "image" within this command. For this reason they refuse to salute it.

Children of this faith have been expelled from school and are threatened with exclusion for no other cause. Officials threaten to send them to reformatories maintained for criminally inclined juveniles. Parents of such children have been prosecuted and are threatened with prosecutions for causing delinquency. . . .

There is no doubt that, in connection with the pledges, the flag salute is a form of utterance. Symbolism is a primitive but effective way of communicating ideas. The use of an emblem or flag to symbolize some system, idea, institution, or personality, is a short cut from mind to mind. Causes and nations, political parties, lodges and ecclesiastical groups seek to knit the loyalty of their followings to a flag or banner, a color or design. The State announces rank, function, and authority through crowns and maces, uniforms and black robes; the church speaks through the Cross, the Crucifix, the altar and shrine, and clerical raiment. Symbols of State often convey political ideas just as religious symbols come to convey theological ones. Associated with many of these symbols are appropriate gestures of acceptance or respect: a salute, a bowed or bared head, a bended knee. A person gets from a symbol the meaning he puts into it, and what is one man's comfort and inspiration is another's jest and scorn. . . .

It is also to be noted that the compulsory flag salute and pledge requires affirmation of a belief and an attitude of mind. It is not clear whether the regulation contemplates that pupils forego any contrary convictions of their own and become unwilling converts to the prescribed ceremony or whether it will be acceptable if they simulate assent by words without belief and by a gesture barren of meaning. It is now a commonplace that censorship or suppression of expression of opinion is tolerated by our Constitution only when the expression presents a clear and present danger of action of a kind the State is empowered to prevent and punish. It would seem that involuntary affirmation could be commanded only on even more immediate and urgent grounds than silence. But here the power of compulsion is invoked without any allegation that remaining passive during a flag salute ritual creates a clear and present danger that would justify an effort even to muffle expression. To sustain the compulsory flag salute we are required to say that a Bill of Rights which guards the individual's right to speak his own mind, left it open to public authorities to compel him to utter what is not in his mind.

Whether the First Amendment to the Constitution will permit officials to order observance of ritual of this nature does not depend upon whether as a voluntary exercise we would think it to be good, bad or merely innocuous. Any credo of nationalism is likely to include what some disapprove or to omit what others think essential, and to give off different overtones as it takes on different accents or interpretations. If official power exists to coerce acceptance of any patriotic creed, what it shall contain cannot be decided by courts, but must be largely discretionary with the ordaining authority, whose power to prescribe would no doubt include power to amend. Hence validity of the asserted power to force an American citizen publicly to profess any statement of belief or to engage in any ceremony of assent to one, presents questions of power that must be considered independently of any idea we may have as to the utility of the ceremony in question. . . .

Government of limited power need not be anemic government. Assurance that rights are secure tends to diminish fear and jealousy of strong government, and by making us feel safe to live under it makes for its better support. Without promise of a limiting Bill of Rights it is doubtful if our Constitution could have mustered enough strength to enable its ratification. To enforce those rights today is not to choose weak government over strong government. It is only to adhere as a means of strength to individual freedom of mind in preference to officially disciplined uniformity for which history indicates a disappointing and disastrous end.

The subject now before us exemplifies this principle. Free public education, if faithful to the ideal of secular instruction and political neutrality, will not be partisan or enemy of any class, creed, party, or faction. If it is to impose any ideological discipline, however, each party or denomination must seek to control, or failing that, to weaken the influence of the educational system. Observance of the limitations of the Constitution will not weaken government in the field appropriate for its exercise. . . .

The *Gobitis* opinion reasoned that this is a field "where courts possess no marked and certainly no controlling competence," that it is committed to the legislatures as well as the courts to guard cherished liberties and that it is constitutionally appropriate to "fight out the wise use of legislative authority in the forum of public opinion and before legislative assemblies rather than to transfer such a contest to the judicial arena," since all the "effective means of inducing political changes are left free." . . .

The very purpose of a Bill of Rights was to withdraw certain subjects from the vicissitudes of political controversy, to place them beyond the reach of majorities and officials and to establish them as legal principles to be applied by the courts. One's right to life, liberty, and property, to free speech, a free press, freedom of worship and assembly, and other fundamental rights may not be submitted to vote; they depend on the outcome of no elections.

In weighing arguments of the parties it is important to distinguish between the due process clause of the Fourteenth Amendment as an instrument for transmitting the principles of the First Amendment and those cases in which it is applied for its own sake. The test of legislation which collides with the Fourteenth Amendment, because it also collides with the principles of the First, is much more definite than the test when only the Fourteenth is involved. Much of the vagueness of the due process clause disappears when the specific prohibitions of the First become its standard. The right of a State to regulate, for example, a public utility may well include, so far as the due process test is concerned, power to impose all of the restrictions which a legislature may have a "rational basis" for adopting. But freedoms of speech and of press, of assembly, and of worship may not be infringed on such slender grounds. They are susceptible of restriction only to prevent grave and immediate danger to interests which the State may lawfully protect. It is important to note that while it is the Fourteenth Amendment which bears directly upon the State it is the more specific limiting principles of the First Amendment that finally govern this case.

Nor does our duty to apply the Bill of Rights to assertions of official authority depend upon our possession of marked competence in the field where the invasion of rights occurs. True, the task of translating the majestic generalities of the Bill of Rights, conceived as part of the pattern of liberal government in the eighteenth century, into concrete restraints on officials dealing with the problems of the twentieth century, is one to disturb self-confidence. These principles grew in soil which also produced a philosophy that the individual was the center of society, that his liberty was attainable through mere absence of governmental restraints, and that government should be entrusted with few controls and only the mildest supervision over men's affairs. We must transplant these rights to a soil in which the *laissez-faire* concept or principle of non-interference has withered at least as to economic affairs, and social advancements are increasingly sought through closer integration of society and through expanded and strengthened governmental controls. These changed conditions often deprive precedents of reliability and cast us more than we would choose upon our own judgment. But we act in these matters not by authority of our competence but by force of our commissions. We cannot, because of modest estimates of our competence in such specialties as public education, withhold the judgment that history authenticates as the function of this Court when liberty is infringed. . . .

Lastly, and this is the very heart of the *Gobitis* opinion, it reasons that "National unity is the basis of national security," that the authorities have "the right to select appropriate means for its attainment," and hence reaches the conclusion that such compulsory measures toward "national unity" are constitutional. . . . Upon the verity of this assumption depends our answer in this case.

National unity as an end which officials may foster by persuasion and example is not in question. The problem is whether under our Constitution compulsion as here employed is a permissible means for its achievement.

Struggles to coerce uniformity of sentiment in support of some end thought essential to their time and country have been waged by many good as well as by evil men. Nationalism is a relatively recent phenomenon but at other times and places the ends have been racial or territorial security, support of a dynasty or regime, and particular plans for saving souls. As first and moderate methods to attain unity have failed, those bent on its accomplishment must resort to an ever-increasing severity. As governmental pressure toward unity becomes greater, so strife becomes more bitter as to whose unity it shall be. Probably no deeper division of our people could proceed from any provocation than from finding it necessary to choose what doctrine and whose program public educational officials shall compel youth to unite in embracing. Ultimate futility of such attempts to compel coherence is the lesson of every such effort from the Roman drive to stamp out Christianity as a disturber of its pagan unity, the Inquisition as a means to religious and dynastic unity, the Siberian exiles as a means to Russian unity, down to the fast failing efforts of our present totalitarian enemies. Those who begin coercive elimination of dissent soon find themselves exterminating dissenters. Compulsory unification of opinion achieves only the unanimity of the graveyard. It seems trite but necessary to say that the First

Amendment to our Constitution was designed to avoid these ends by avoiding these beginnings. There is no mysticism in the American concept of the State or of the nature or origin of its authority. We set up government by consent of the governed, and the Bill of Rights denies those in power any legal opportunity to coerce that consent. Authority here is to be controlled by public opinion, not public opinion by authority.

The case is made difficult not because the principles of its decision are obscure but because the flag involved is our own. Nevertheless, we apply the limitations of the Constitution with no fear that freedom to be intellectually and spiritually diverse or even contrary will disintegrate the social organization. To believe that patriotism will not flourish if patriotic ceremonies are voluntary and spontaneous instead of a compulsory routine is to make an unflattering estimate of the appeal of our institutions to free minds. We can have intellectual individualism and the rich cultural diversities that we owe to exceptional minds only at the price of occasional eccentricity and abnormal attitudes. When they are so harmless to others or to the State as those we deal with here, the price is not too great. But freedom to differ is not limited to things that do not matter much. That would be a mere shadow of freedom. The test of its substance is the right to differ as to things that touch the heart of the existing order.

If there is any fixed star in our constitutional constellation, it is that no official, high or petty, can prescribe what shall be orthodox in politics, nationalism, religion, or other matters of opinion or force citizens to confess by word or act their faith therein. If there are any circumstances which permit an exception, they do not now occur to us.

We think the action of the local authorities in compelling the flag salute and pledge transcends constitutional limitations on their power and invades the sphere of intellect and spirit which it is the purpose of the First Amendment to our Constitution to reserve from all official control.

The decision of this Court in *Minersville School District v. Gobitis* and the holdings of those few per curiam decisions which preceded and foreshadowed it are overruled, and the judgment enjoining enforcement of the West Virginia Regulation is Affirmed.

Justice Frankfurter, dissenting:

One who belongs to the most vilified and persecuted minority in history is not likely to be insensible to the freedoms guaranteed by our Constitution. Were my purely personal attitude relevant I should wholeheartedly associate myself with the general libertarian views in the Court's opinion, representing as they do the thought and action of a lifetime. But as judges we are neither Jew nor Gentile, neither Catholic nor agnostic. We owe equal attachment to the Constitution and are equally bound by our judicial obligations whether we derive our citizenship from the earliest or the latest immigrants to these shores. As a member of this Court I am not justified in writing my private notions of policy into the Constitution, no matter how deeply I may cherish them or how mischievous I may deem their disregard. The duty of a judge who must decide which of two claims before the Court shall prevail, that of a State to enact and enforce laws within its general competence or that of an individual to refuse obedience because of the demands of his conscience, is not that of the ordinary person. It can never be emphasized too much that one's own opinion about the wisdom or evil of a law should be excluded altogether when one is doing one's duty on the bench. The only opinion of our own even looking in that direction that is material is our opinion whether legislators could in reason have enacted such a law. In the light of all the circumstances, including the history of this question in this Court, it would require more daring than I possess to deny that reasonable legislators could have taken the action which is before us for review. Most unwillingly, therefore, I must differ from my brethren with regard to legislation like this. I cannot bring my mind to believe that the "liberty" secured by the Due

Process Clause gives this Court authority to deny to the State of West Virginia the attainment of that which we all recognize as a legitimate legislative end, namely, the promotion of good citizenship, by employment of the means here chosen. . . .

Practically we are passing upon the political power of each of the forty-eight states. Moreover, since the First Amendment has been read into the Fourteenth, our problem is precisely the same as it would be if we had before us an Act of Congress for the District of Columbia. To suggest that we are here concerned with the heedless action of some village tyrants is to distort the augustness of the constitutional issue and the reach of the consequences of our decision.

Under our constitutional system the legislature is charged solely with civil concerns of society. If the avowed or intrinsic legislative purpose is either to promote or to discourage some religious community or creed, it is clearly within the constitutional restrictions imposed on legislatures and cannot stand. But it by no means follows that legislative power is wanting whenever a general non-discriminatory civil regulation in fact touches conscientious scruples or religious beliefs of an individual or a group. Regard for such scruples or beliefs undoubtedly presents one of the most reasonable claims for the exertion of legislative accommodation. It is, of course, beyond our power to rewrite the State's requirement, by providing exemptions for those who do not wish to participate in the flag salute or by making some other accommodations to meet their scruples. That wisdom might suggest the making of such accommodations and that school administration would not find it too difficult to make them and yet maintain the ceremony for those not refusing to conform, is outside our province to suggest. Tact, respect, and generosity toward variant views will always commend themselves to those charged with the duties of legislation so as to achieve a maximum of good will and to require a minimum of unwilling submission to a general law. But the real question is, who is to make such accommodations, the courts or the legislature?

EVERSON V. BOARD OF EDUCATION (1947)

A New Jersey law authorized local school districts to arrange for transportation of pupils to and from schools, including the transportation of children attending private and parochial schools. In one district, the board voted to reimburse the parents of parochial school students for the expenses of transporting them to school. A local taxpayer challenged the payments as a violation of the First Amendment's ban on an establishment of religion. Justice Black's opinion for the narrow five-man majority is noteworthy because even though he lauded the Jeffersonian notion of a "wall of separation" and seemed to indicate compelling reasons against any form of aid to parochial schools, he nonetheless upheld the statute. Although Catholic groups applauded the decision, Protestants and civil libertarians condemned it. The conclusion reached by the Court in this first instance of its dealing with the Establishment Clause has not withstood the test of time; but the arguments Black marshaled in support of a wall of separation have often been quoted by subsequent courts. See Richard E. Morgan, The Supreme Court and Religion *(New York: Free Press, 1972); Frank J. Sorauf,* The Wall of Separation *(Princeton, NJ: Princeton University Press, 1976); Jesse Choper, "The Establishment Clause and Aid to Parochial Schools,"* California Law Review 56: 260 (1968); and *John T. Noonan, Jr.,* The Lustre of Our Country *(Berkeley: University of California Press, 1998).*

Justice Black delivered the opinion of the Court.

The only contention here is that the state statute and the resolution, insofar as they authorized reimbursement to parents of children attending parochial schools, violate the Federal Constitution in two respects, which to some extent overlap. *First.* They authorize the State to take by taxation the private property of some and bestow it upon others, to be used for their own private purposes, (in violation of the due process clause.) *Second.* The statute and the resolution forced inhabitants to pay taxes to help support and maintain schools which are dedicated to, and which regularly teach, the Catholic Faith. This is alleged to be a use of state power to support church schools contrary to the prohibition of the First Amendment which the Fourteenth Amendment made applicable to the states.

First. It is much too late to argue that legislation intended to facilitate the opportunity of children to get a secular education serves no public purpose. . . .

The same thing is no less true of legislation to reimburse needy parents, or all parents, for payment of the fares of their children so that they can ride in public busses to and from schools rather than run the risk of traffic and other hazards incident to walking or "hitchhiking." . . .

Second. The New Jersey statute is challenged as a "law respecting an establishment of religion." [Whether this law] is one respecting an "establishment of religion" requires an understanding of the meaning of that language, particularly with respect to the imposition of taxes. . . .

Justice Black then examined at length the historical antecedents of the Establishment Clause.

The "establishment of religion" clause of the First Amendment means at least this: Neither a state nor the Federal Government can set up a church. Neither can pass laws which aid one religion, aid all religions, or prefer one religion over another. Neither can force nor influence a person to go to or to remain away from church against his will or force him to profess a belief or disbelief in any religion. No person can be punished for entertaining or professing religious beliefs or disbeliefs, for church attendance or non-attendance. No tax in any amount, large or small, can be levied to support any religious activities or institutions, whatever they may be called, or whatever form they may adopt to teach or practice religion. Neither a state nor the Federal Government can, openly or secretly, participate in the affairs of any religious organizations or groups and vice versa. In the words of Jefferson, the clause against establishment of religion by law was intended to erect "a wall of separation between church and State."

We must [sustain the New Jersey law] if it is within the State's constitutional power even though it approaches the verge of that power. New Jersey cannot consistently with the "establishment of religion" clause of the First Amendment contribute tax-raised funds to the support of an institution which teaches the tenets and faith of any church. On the other hand, other language of the amendment commands that New Jersey cannot hamper its citizens in the free exercise of their own religion. Consequently, it cannot exclude individual Catholics, Lutherans, Mohammedans, Baptists, Jews, Methodists, Non-believers, Presbyterians, or the members of any other faith, *because of their faith, or lack of it,* from receiving the benefits of public welfare legislation. While we do not mean to intimate that a state could not provide transportation only to children attending public schools, we must be careful, in protecting the citizens of New Jersey against state-established churches, to be sure that we do not inadvertently prohibit New Jersey from extending its general state law benefits to all its citizens without regard to their religious belief.

Measured by these standards, we cannot say that the First Amendment prohibits New Jersey from spending tax-raised funds to pay the bus fares of parochial school pupils as a part of a general program under which it pays the fares of pupils attending public and other schools. It is undoubtedly true that children are helped to get to church schools. There is even a possibility that some of the children might not be sent to the church schools if the parents were compelled to pay their children's bus fares out of their own pockets when transportation to a public school would have been paid for by the State. . . . The [First] Amendment requires the state to be a neutral in its relations with groups of religious believers and non-believers; it does not require the state to be their adversary. State power is no more to be used so as to handicap religions than it is to favor them.

This Court has said that parents may, in the discharge of their duty under state compulsory education laws, send their children to a religious rather than a public school if the school meets the secular educational requirements which the state has power to impose. See *Pierce v. Society of Sisters.* ... It appears that these parochial schools meet New Jersey's requirements. The State contributes no money to the schools. It does not support them. Its legislation, as applied, does no more than provide a general program to help parents get their children, regardless of their religion, safely and expeditiously to and from accredited schools.

The First Amendment has erected a wall between church and state. That wall must be kept high and impregnable. We could not approve the slightest breach. New Jersey has not breached it here.

Affirmed.

Justice Jackson joined by Justice Frankfurter, dissenting:

The Court's opinion marshals every argument in favor of state aid and puts the case in its most favorable light, but much of its reasoning confirms my conclusions that there are no good grounds upon which to support the present legislation. In fact, the undertones of the opinion, advocating complete and uncompromising separation of Church from State, seem utterly discordant with its conclusion yielding support to their commingling in educational matters. The case which irresistibly comes to mind as the most fitting precedent is that of Julia who, according to Byron's reports, "whispering 'I will ne'er consent,'—consented."

ZORACH V. CLAUSON (1952)

In McCollum v. Board of Education *(1948), the Court struck down the released-time program in which priests, ministers, and rabbis came into the public schools one hour a week to provide religious instruction. The public outcry against that decision, as well as* Everson v. Board of Education *(see above), led the Court to back off from the strict wall-of-separation interpretation of the Estab-*

lishment Clause that Justice Black had laid out in the two cases. Here we have the Court's first "accommodationist" decision, in which the Court allowed schoolchildren to be released one hour a week for religious instruction, provided the instruction took place off the school grounds. Although future decisions by the Court were guided by McCollum, *the decision in* Zorach *has never been overruled, and off-the-premises released-time programs continue to operate in many communities around the country. See Samuel Alito, "The 'Released Time' Cases Revisited: A Study of Group Decisionmaking by the Supreme Court,"* Yale Law Journal *83: 1202 (1974); and George Reed, "Church-State and the* Zorach *Case,"* Notre Dame Lawyer *27: 529 (1952).*

Justice Douglas delivered the opinion of the Court.

New York City has a program which permits its public schools to release students during the school day so that they may leave the school buildings and school grounds and go to religious centers for religious instruction or devotional exercises. A student is released on written request of his parents. Those not released stay in the classrooms. The churches make weekly reports to the schools, sending a list of children who have been released from public school but who have not reported for religious instruction.

This "released time" program involves neither religious instruction in public school classrooms nor the expenditure of public funds. All costs, including the application blanks, are paid by the religious organizations. The case is therefore unlike *McCollum v. Board of Education,* 333 U.S. 203, which involved a "released time" program from Illinois. In that case the classrooms were turned over to religious instructors. We accordingly held that the program violated the First Amendment which (by reason of the Fourteenth Amendment) prohibits the states from establishing religion or prohibiting its free exercise.

Appellants, who are taxpayers and residents of New York City and whose children attend its public schools, challenge the present law, contending it is in essence not different from the one involved in the *McCollum* case. Their argument, stated elaborately in various ways, reduces itself to this: the weight and influence of the school is put behind a program for religious instruction; public school teachers police it, keeping tab on students who are released; the classroom activities come to a halt while the students who are released for religious instruction are on leave; the school is a crutch on which the churches are leaning for support in their religious training; without the cooperation of the schools this "released time" program, like the one in the *McCollum* case, would be futile and ineffective. . . . Our problem reduces itself to whether New York by this system has either prohibited the "free exercise" of religion or has made a law "respecting an establishment of religion" within the meaning of the First Amendment.

It takes obtuse reasoning to inject any issue of the "free exercise" of religion into the present case. No one is forced to go to the religious classroom and no religious exercise or instruction is brought to the classrooms of the public schools. A student need not take religious instruction. He is left to his own desires as to the manner or time of his religious devotions, if any.

There is a suggestion that the system involves the use of coercion to get public school students into religious classrooms. There is no evidence in the record before us that supports that conclusion. The present record indeed tells us that the school authorities are neutral in this regard and do no more than release students whose parents so request. If in fact coercion were used, if it were established that any one or more teachers were using their office to persuade or force students to take the religious instruction, a wholly different case would be presented. Hence we put aside that claim of coercion both as respects the "free exercise" of religion and "an establishment of religion" within the meaning of the First Amendment.

Moreover, apart from that claim of coercion, we do not see how New York by this type of "released time" program has made a law respecting an establishment of religion within the meaning of the First Amendment. There is much talk of the separation of Church and State in the history of the Bill of Rights and in the decisions clustering around the First Amendment. There cannot be the slightest doubt that the First Amendment reflects the philosophy that Church and State should be separated. And so far as interference with the "free exercise" of religion and an "establishment" of religion are concerned, the separation must be complete and unequivocal. The First Amendment within the scope of its coverage permits no exception; the prohibition is absolute. The First Amendment, however, does not say that in every and all respects there shall be a separation of Church and State. Rather, it studiously defines the manner, the specific ways, in which there shall be no concern or union or dependency one on the other. That is the common sense of the matter. Otherwise the state and religion would be aliens to each other—hostile, suspicious, and even unfriendly. Churches could not be required to pay even property taxes. Municipalities would not be permitted to render police or fire protection to religious groups. Policemen who helped parishioners into their places of worship would violate the Constitution. Prayers in our legislative halls; the appeals to the Almighty in the messages of the Chief Executive; the proclamations making Thanksgiving Day a holiday; "so help me God" in our courtroom oaths—these and all other references to the Almighty that run through our laws, our public rituals, our ceremonies would be flouting the First Amendment. A fastidious atheist or agnostic could even object to the supplication with which the Court opens each session: "God save the United States and this Honorable Court."

We would have to press the concept of separation of Church and State to these extremes to condemn the present law on constitutional grounds. The nullification of this law would have wide and profound effects. A Catholic student applies to his teacher for permission to leave the school during hours on a Holy Day of Obligation to attend a mass. A Jewish student asks his teacher for permission to be excused for Yom Kippur. A Protestant wants the afternoon off for a family baptismal ceremony. In each case the teacher requires parental consent in writing. In each case the teacher, in order to make sure the student is not a truant, goes further and requires a report from the priest, the rabbi, or the minister. The teacher in other words cooperates in a religious program to the extent of making it possible for her students to participate in it. Whether she does it occasionally for a few students, regularly for one, or pursuant to a systematized program designed to further the religious needs of all the students does not alter the character of the act.

We are a religious people whose institutions presuppose a Supreme Being. We guarantee the freedom to worship as one chooses. We make room for as wide a variety of beliefs and creeds as the spiritual needs of man deem necessary. We sponsor an attitude on the part of government that shows no partiality to any one group and that lets each flourish according to the zeal of its adherents and the appeal of its dogma. When the state encourages religious instruction or cooperates with religious authorities by adjusting the schedule of public events to sectarian needs, it follows the best of our traditions. For it then respects the religious nature of our people and accommodates the public service to their spiritual needs. To hold that it may not would be to find in the Constitution a requirement that the government show a callous indifference to religious groups. That would be preferring those who believe in no religion over those who do believe. Government may not finance religious groups nor undertake religious instruction nor blend secular and sectarian education nor use secular institutions to force one or some religion on any person. But we find no constitutional requirement which makes it necessary for government to be hostile to religion and to throw its weight against efforts to widen the effective scope of religious influence. The government must be neutral when it comes to competition between sects. It may not thrust any sect on any person. It may not make a religious observance compulsory. It may not coerce anyone to attend church, to observe a religious holiday, or to take religious instruction. But it can close its doors or suspend its operations as to those who want to repair to their religious sanctuary for worship or instruction. No more than that is undertaken here.

This program may be unwise and improvident from an educational or a community viewpoint. That appeal is made to us on a theory, previously advanced, that each case must be decided on the basis of "our own prepossessions." Our individual preferences, however, are not the constitutional standard. The constitutional standard is the separation of Church and State. The problem, like many problems in constitutional law, is one of degree.

In the *McCollum* case the classrooms were used for religious instruction and the force of the public school was used to promote that instruction. Here, as we have said, the public schools do no more than accommodate their schedules to a program of outside religious instruction. We follow the *McCollum* case. But we cannot expand it to cover the present released time program unless separation of Church and State means that public institutions can make no adjustments of their schedules to accommodate the religious needs of the people. We cannot read into the Bill of Rights such a philosophy of hostility to religion.

Affirmed.

Dissents by Justices Black, Frankfurter, and Jackson.

JOHN F. KENNEDY ON
CHURCH AND STATE (1960)

The belief that Catholics acted on direct orders from the Vatican persisted well after the decline of the Klan. John Kennedy, the first Catholic to receive a major party's nomination for the U.S. presidency after the Smith defeat of 1928, found that this popular suspicion dogged his campaign. Finally, he decided to face it head-on: he spoke to a meeting of Southern Baptist ministers about his beliefs as a Catholic and his duties as an American citizen. It is widely believed that this talk, which received national attention, did much

to defuse the religious issue in the election. See Theodore H. White,
The Making of the President 1960 *(New York: Atheneum, 1961).*

I am grateful for your generous invitation to state my views.

While the so-called religious issue is necessarily and properly the chief topic here tonight, I want to emphasize from the outset that I believe that we have far more critical issues in the 1960 election: the spread of Communist influence, until it now festers only ninety miles off the coast of Florida—the humiliating treatment of our President and Vice-President by those who no longer respect our power—the hungry children I saw in West Virginia, the old people who cannot pay their doctor's bills, the families forced to give up their farms—an America with too many slums, with too few schools, and too late to the moon and outer space.

These are the real issues which should decide this campaign. And they are not religious issues—for war and hunger and ignorance and despair know no religious barrier.

But because I am a Catholic, and no Catholic has ever been elected President, the real issues in this campaign have been obscured—perhaps deliberately in some quarters less responsible than this. So it is apparently necessary for me to state once again—not what kind of church I believe in, for that should be important only to me, but what kind of America I believe in.

I believe in an America where the separation of church and state is absolute—where no Catholic prelate would tell the President (should he be a Catholic) how to act and no Protestant minister would tell his parishioners for whom to vote—where no church or church school is granted any public funds or political preference—and where no man is denied public office merely because his religion differs from the President who might appoint him or the people who might elect him.

I believe in an America that is officially neither Catholic, Protestant nor Jewish—where no public official either requests or accepts instructions on public policy from the Pope, the National Council of Churches or any other ecclesiastical source—where no religious body seeks to impose its will directly or indirectly upon the general populace or the public acts of its officials—and where religious liberty is so indivisible that an act against one church is treated as an act against all.

For while this year it may be a Catholic against whom the finger of suspicion is pointed, in other years it has been, and may someday be again, a Jew—or a Quaker—or a Unitarian—or a Baptist. It was Virginia's harassment of Baptist preachers, for example, that led to Jefferson's statute of religious freedom. Today, I may be the victim—but tomorrow it may be you—until the whole fabric of our harmonious society is ripped apart at a time of great national peril.

Finally, I believe in an America where religious intolerance will someday end—where all men and all churches are treated as equal—where every man has the same right to attend or not attend the church of his choice—where there is no Catholic vote, no anti-Catholic vote, no bloc voting of any kind—and where Catholics, Protestants and Jews, both the lay and the pastoral level, will refrain from those attitudes of disdain and division which have so often marred their works in the past, and promote instead the American ideal of brotherhood.

That is the kind of America in which I believe. And it represents the kind of Presidency in which I believe—a great office that must be neither humbled by making it the instrument of any religious group, nor tarnished by arbitrarily withholding it, its occupancy, from the members of any religious group. I believe in a President whose views on religion are his own private affair, neither imposed upon him by the nation or imposed by the nation upon him as a condition to holding that office.

I would not look with favor upon a President working to subvert the First Amendment's guarantees of religious liberty (nor would our system of checks and balances permit him to do so). And neither do I look with favor upon those who would work to subvert Article VI of the Constitution by requiring a religious test—even by indirection—for if they disagree with that safe-guard, they should be openly working to repeal it.

I want a Chief Executive whose public acts are responsible to all and obligated to none—who can attend any ceremony, service or dinner his office may appropriately require him to fulfill—and whose fulfillment of his Presidential office is not limited or conditioned by any religious oath, ritual or obligation.

This is the kind of America I believe in—and this is the kind of America I fought for in the South Pacific and the kind my brother died for in Europe. No one suggested then that we might have a "divided loyalty," that we did "not believe in liberty" or that we belonged to a disloyal group that threatened "the freedoms for which our forefathers died."

And in fact this is the kind of America for which our forefathers did die when they fled here to escape religious test oaths, that denied office to members of less favored churches, when they fought for the Constitution, the Bill of Rights, the Virginia Statute of Religious Freedom—and when they fought at the shrine I visited today—the Alamo. For side by side with Bowie and Crockett died Fuentes and McCafferty and Bailey and Bedillio and Carey—but no one knows whether they were Catholics or not. For there was no religious test there.

I ask you tonight to follow in that tradition, to judge me on the basis of fourteen years in the Congress—on my declared stands against an ambassador to the Vatican, against unconstitutional aid to parochial schools, and against any boycott of the public schools (which I attended myself)—instead of judging me on the basis of these pamphlets and publications we have all seen that carefully select quotations out of context from the statements of Catholic Church leaders, usually in other countries, frequently in other centuries, and rarely relevant to any situation here—and always omitting, of course, that statement of the American bishops in 1948 which strongly endorsed church-state separation.

I do not consider these other quotations binding upon my public acts—why should you? But let me say, with respect to other countries, that I am wholly opposed to the state being used by any religious group, Catholic or Protestant, to compel, prohibit or persecute the free exercise of any other religion. And that goes for any persecution at any time, by anyone, in any country.

And I hope you and I condemn with equal fervor those nations which deny their Presidency to Protestants and those which deny it to Catholics. And rather than cite the misdeeds of those who differ, I would also cite the record of the Catholic Church in such nations as France and Ireland—and the independence of such statesmen as de Gaulle and Adenauer.

But let me stress again that these are my views—for, contrary to common newspaper usage, I am not the Catholic candidate for President. I am the Democratic Party candidate for President, who happens also to be a Catholic.

I do not speak for my church on public matters—and the church does not speak for me.

Whatever issue may come before me as President, if I should be elected—on birth control, divorce, censorship, gambling, or any other subject—I will make my decision in accordance with these views, in accordance with what my conscience tells me to be in the national interest, and without regard to outside religious pressure or dictate. And no power or threat of punishment could cause me to decide otherwise.

But if the time should ever come—and I do not concede any conflict to be remotely possible—when my office would require me to either violate my conscience, or violate the national interest, then I would resign the office, and I hope any other conscientious public servant would do likewise.

But I do not intend to apologize for these views to my critics of either Catholic or Protestant faith, nor do I intend to disavow either my views or my church in order to win this election. If I should lose on the real issues, I shall return to my seat in the Senate, satisfied that I tried my best and was fairly judged.

But if this election is decided on the basis that 40,000,000 Americans lost their chance of being President on the day they were baptized, then it is the whole nation that will be the loser in the eyes of Catholics and non-Catholics around the world, in the eyes of history, and in the eyes of our own people.

But if, on the other hand, I should win this election, I shall devote every effort of mind and spirit to fulfilling the oath of the Presidency—practically identical, I might add, with the oath I have taken for fourteen years in the Congress. For, without reservation, I can, and I quote, "solemnly swear that I will faithfully execute the office of President of the United States and will to the best of my ability preserve, protect and defend the Constitution, so help me God."

ENGEL V. VITALE (1962)

New York public schools opened each school day with a prayer, a "nonsectarian" prayer composed by the Board of Regents. Other states and localities used other invocations, such as the Lord's Prayer, or in some cases borrowed from sectarian services. In Engel, the Court ruled that any mandatory prayer violated the First Amendment's ban on an establishment of religion. The decision created a huge uproar, because many Americans had become used to beginning school days and public functions with a prayer. Many people, and nearly all the mainstream religious groups, accepted Justice Black's argument that a prescribed prayer violated the Establishment Clause, but many fundamentalist sects did not. They claimed that there had always been a national commitment to prayer. Now the Court had banned God from the schools and they intended to use all possible means to get around the ruling. See Frank J. Sorauf, The Wall of Separation: The Constitutional Politics of Church and State *(Princeton, NJ: Princeton University Press, 1976); John H. Laubach,* School Prayers: Congress, the Courts, and the Public *(Washington, DC: Public Affairs Press,*

1969); and Kenneth M. Dolbeare and Phillip E. Hammond, The School Prayer Decisions: From Court Policy to Local Practice *(Chicago: University of Chicago Press, 1971).*

Justice Black delivered the opinion of the Court.

The respondent Board of Education of Union Free School District No. 9, New Hyde Park, New York, acting in its official capacity under state law, directed the School District's principal to cause the following prayer to be said aloud by each class in the presence of a teacher at the beginning of each school day:

"Almighty God, we acknowledge our dependence upon Thee, and we beg Thy blessings upon us, our parents, our teachers and our Country."

This daily procedure was adopted on the recommendation of the State Board of Regents, a governmental agency created by the State Constitution to which the New York Legislature has granted broad supervisory, executive, and legislative powers over the State's public school system. These state officials composed the prayer which they recommended and published as a part of their "Statement on Moral and Spiritual Training in the Schools," saying: "We believe that this Statement will be subscribed to by all men and women of good will, and we call upon all of them to aid in giving life to our program. . . ."

We think that by using its public school system to encourage recitation of the Regents' prayer, the State of New York has adopted a practice wholly inconsistent with the Establishment Clause. There can, of course, be no doubt that New York's program of daily classroom invocation of God's blessings as prescribed in the Regents' prayer is a religious activity. It is a solemn avowal of divine faith and supplication for the blessings of the Almighty. The nature of such a prayer has always been religious, none of the respondents has denied this and the trial court expressly so found. . . .

The petitioners contend among other things that the state laws requiring or permitting use of the Regents' prayer must be struck down as a violation of the Establishment Clause because that prayer was composed by governmental officials as a part of a governmental program to further religious beliefs. For this reason, petitioners argue, the State's use of the Regents' prayer in its public school system breaches the constitutional wall of separation between Church and State. We agree with that contention since we think that the constitutional prohibition against laws respecting an establishment of religion must at least mean that in this country it is no part of the business of government to compose official prayers for any group of the American people to recite as a part of a religious program carried on by government.

It is a matter of history that this very practice of establishing governmentally composed prayers for religious services was one of the reasons which caused many of our early colonists to leave England and seek religious freedom in America. The Book of Common Prayer, which was created under governmental direction and which was approved by Acts of Parliament in 1548 and 1549, set out in minute detail the accepted form and content of prayer and other religious ceremonies to be used in the established, tax-supported Church of England. . . .

It is an unfortunate fact of history that when some of the very groups which had most strenuously opposed the established Church of England found themselves sufficiently in control of colonial governments in this country to write their own prayers into law, they passed laws making their own religion the official religion of their respective colonies. Indeed, as late as the time of the Revolutionary War, there were established churches in at least eight of the thirteen former colonies and established religions in at least four of the other five. But the successful Revolution against English political domination was shortly followed by intense opposition to the practice of establishing religion by law. This opposition crystallized rapidly into an effective political force in Virginia where the minority religious groups such as Presbyterians, Lutherans, Quakers and Baptists had gained such strength that the adherents to the established Episcopal Church were actually a minority themselves. In 1785–1786, those opposed to the established Church, led by James Madison and Thomas Jefferson, who, though themselves not members of any of these dissenting religious groups, opposed all religious establishments by law on grounds of principle, obtained the enactment of the famous "Virginia Bill for Religious Liberty" by which all religious groups were placed on an equal footing so far as the State was concerned. Similar though less far-reaching legislation was being considered and passed in other States. . . .

The First Amendment was added to the Constitution to stand as a guarantee that neither the power nor the prestige of the Federal Government would be used to control, support or influence the kinds of prayer the American people can say—that the people's religions must not be subjected to the pressures of government for change each time a new political administration is elected to office. Under that Amendment's prohibition against governmental establishment of religion, as reinforced by the provisions of the Fourteenth Amendment, government in this country, be it state or federal, is without power to prescribe by law any particular form of prayer which is to be used as an official prayer in carrying on any program of governmentally sponsored religious activity.

There can be no doubt that New York's state prayer program officially establishes the religious beliefs embodied in the Regents' prayer. The respondents' argument to the contrary, which is largely based upon the contention that the Regents' prayer is "nondenominational" and the fact that the program, as modified and approved by state courts, does not require all pupils to recite the prayer but permits those who wish to do so to remain silent or be excused from the room, ignores the essential nature of the program's constitutional defects. Neither the fact that the prayer may be denominationally neutral nor the fact that its observance on the part of the students is voluntary can serve to free it from the limi-

tations of the Establishment Clause, as it might from the Free
Exercise Clause, of the First Amendment, both of which are oper-
ative against the States by virtue of the Fourteenth Amendment.
Although these two clauses may in certain instances overlap, they
forbid two quite different kinds of governmental encroachment
upon religious freedom. The Establishment Clause, unlike the
Free Exercise Clause, does not depend upon any showing of
direct governmental compulsion and is violated by the enactment
of laws which establish an official religion whether those laws
operate directly to coerce nonobserving individuals or not. This is
not to say, of course, that laws officially prescribing a particular
form of religious worship do not involve coercion of such individuals. When the power, prestige and financial support of government is placed behind a particular religious belief, the indirect
coercive pressure upon religious minorities to conform to the prevailing officially approved religion is plain. But the purposes
underlying the Establishment Clause go much further than that.
Its first and most immediate purpose rested on the belief that a
union of government and religion tends to destroy government
and to degrade religion. The history of governmentally established religion, both in England and in this country, showed that
whenever government had allied itself with one particular form of
religion, the inevitable result had been that it had incurred the
hatred, disrespect and even contempt of those who held contrary
beliefs. That same history showed that many people had lost their
respect for any religion that had relied upon the support of government to spread its faith. The Establishment Clause thus stands
as an expression of principle on the part of the Founders of our
Constitution that religion is too personal, too sacred, too holy, to
permit its "unhallowed perversion" by a civil magistrate.

Another purpose of the Establishment Clause rested upon an
awareness of the historical fact that governmentally established
religions and religious persecutions go hand in hand. The
Founders knew that only a few years after the Book of Common

Prayer became the only accepted form of religious services in the established Church of England, an Act of Uniformity was passed to compel all Englishmen to attend those services and to make it a criminal offense to conduct or attend religious gatherings of any other kind—a law which was consistently flouted by dissenting religious groups in England and which contributed to widespread persecutions of people like John Bunyan who persisted in holding "unlawful [religious] meetings . . . to the great disturbance and distraction of the good subjects of this kingdom. . . ." And they knew that similar persecutions had received the sanction of law in several of the colonies in this country soon after the establishment of official religions in those colonies. It was in large part to get completely away from this sort of systematic religious persecution that the Founders brought into being our Nation, our Constitution, and our Bill of Rights with its prohibition against any governmental establishment of religion. The New York laws officially prescribing the Regents' prayer are inconsistent both with the purposes of the Establishment Clause and with the Establishment Clause itself.

It has been argued that to apply the Constitution in such a way as to prohibit state laws respecting an establishment of religious services in public schools is to indicate a hostility toward religion or toward prayer. Nothing, of course, could be more wrong. The history of man is inseparable from the history of religion. And perhaps it is not too much to say that since the beginning of that history many people have devoutly believed that more things are wrought by prayer than this world dreams of. It was doubtless largely due to men who believed this that there grew up a sentiment that caused men to leave the crosscurrents of officially established state religions and religious persecution in Europe and come to this country filled with the hope that they could find a place in which they could pray when they pleased to the God of their faith in the language they chose. And there were men of this same faith in the power of prayer who led the fight for adoption of our Constitution and also for our Bill of Rights with the very guarantees of religious freedom that forbid the sort of governmental activity which New York has attempted here. These men knew that the First Amendment, which tried to put an end to governmental control of religion and of prayer, was not written to destroy either. They knew rather that it was written to quiet well-justified fears which nearly all of them felt arising out of an awareness that governments of the past had shackled men's tongues to make them speak only the religious thoughts that government wanted them to speak and to pray only to the God that government wanted them to pray to. It is neither sacrilegious nor antireligious to say that each separate government in this country should stay out of the business of writing or sanctioning official prayers and leave that purely religious function to the people themselves and to those the people choose to look to for religious guidance. . . .

The judgment of the Court of Appeals of New York is reversed and the cause remanded for further proceedings not inconsistent with this opinion.

Reversed and remanded.

SHERBERT V. VERNER (1963)

For nearly thirty years this case anchored the doctrine that governmental practices that burden the free exercise of religion may be enforced only if necessary to achieve a compelling governmental interest. Adele Sherbert, a Seventh-day Adventist, lost her job when she refused to work on Saturdays. Since she lived in a mill town, there was no other work for her at that time that would have allowed her to have Saturdays off. South Carolina refused her unemployment compensation, and she appealed. The case has been the cause of a great deal of scholarly debate and literature, because it shows off, as few cases do, an inner tension between the two religion clauses. By allowing Ms. Sherbert her free exercise, the state had to, in effect, give a preference (establishment) to her religion that it did not provide to others. It is unclear after Oregon v. Smith *(1990) just how much of* Sherbert *remains in effect. See Stephen Pepper, "Taking the Free Exercise Clause Seriously,"* Brigham Young University Law Review *(1986) 299; and Marc Galanter, "Religious Freedom in the United States: A Turning Point?"* Wisconsin Law Review *(1966) 217.*

Justice Brennan delivered the opinion of the Court.

Appellant, a member of the Seventh-day Adventist Church, was discharged by her South Carolina employer because she would not work on Saturday, the Sabbath Day of her faith. When she was unable to obtain other employment because from conscientious scruples she would not take Saturday work, she filed a claim for unemployment compensation benefits under the South Carolina Unemployment Compensation Act. That law provides that, to be eligible for benefits, a claimant must be "able to work and . . . available for work"; and, further, that a claimant is ineligible for benefits "if . . . he has failed, without good cause . . . to accept available suitable work when offered him by the employment office or the employer. . . ." The Employment Security Commission, in administrative proceedings under the statute, found that appellant's restriction upon her availability for Saturday work brought her within the provision disqualifying for benefits insured workers who fail, without good cause, to accept "suitable work when offered . . . by the employment office or the employer. . . ."

The door of the Free Exercise Clause stands tightly closed against any governmental regulation of religious *beliefs* as such. Government may neither compel affirmation of a repugnant belief; nor penalize or discriminate against individuals or groups because they hold religious views abhorrent to the authorities; nor employ the taxing power to inhibit the dissemination of particular religious views. On the other hand, the Court has rejected challenges under the Free Exercise Clause to governmental regulation of certain overt acts prompted by religious beliefs or principles, for "even when the action is in accord with one's religious convictions, it is not totally free from legislative restrictions." The conduct or actions so regulated have invariably posed some substantial threat to public safety, peace or order.

Plainly enough, appellant's conscientious objection to Saturday work constitutes no conduct prompted by religious principles of a kind within the reach of state legislation. If, therefore, the decision of the South Carolina Supreme Court is to withstand appellant's constitutional challenge, it must be either because her disqualification as a beneficiary represents no infringement by the State of her constitutional rights of free exercise, or because any incidental burden on the free exercise of appellant's religion may be justified by a "compelling state interest in the regulation of a subject within the State's constitutional power to regulate. . . ."

We turn first to the question whether the disqualification for benefits imposes any burden on the free exercise of appellant's religion. We think it is clear that it does. In a sense the consequences of such a disqualification to religious principles and practices may be only an indirect result of welfare legislation within the State's general competence to enact; it is true that no criminal sanctions directly compel appellant to work a six-day week. But this is only the beginning, not the end, of our inquiry. For "if the purpose or effect of a law is to impede the observance of one or all religions or is to discriminate invidiously between religions, that law is constitutionally invalid even though the burden may be characterized as being only indirect." Here not only is it apparent that appellant's declared ineligibility for benefits derives solely from the practice of her religion, but the pressure upon her to forego that practice is unmistakable. The ruling forces her to choose between following the precepts of her religion and forfeiting benefits, on the one hand, and abandoning one of the precepts of her religion in order to accept work, on the other hand. Governmental imposition of such a choice puts the same kind of burden upon the free exercise of religion as would a fine imposed against appellant for her Saturday worship.

Nor may the South Carolina court's construction of the statute be saved from constitutional infirmity on the ground that unemployment compensation benefits are not appellant's "right" but merely a "privilege." It is too late in the day to doubt that the liberties of religion and expression may be infringed by the denial of or placing of conditions upon a benefit or privilege. . . .

Significantly South Carolina expressly saves the Sunday worshipper from having to make the kind of choice which we here hold infringes the Sabbatarian's religious liberty. When in times of "national emergency" the textile plants are authorized by the State Commissioner of Labor to operate on Sunday, "no employee shall be required to work on Sunday . . . who is conscientiously opposed to Sunday work; and if any employee should refuse to work on Sunday on account of conscientious . . . objections he or she shall not jeopardize his or her seniority by such refusal or be discriminated against in any other manner." No question of the disqualification of a Sunday worshipper for benefits is likely to arise, since we cannot suppose that an employer will discharge him in violation of this statute. The unconstitutionality of the disqualification of the Sabbatarian is thus compounded by the religious discrimination which South Carolina's general statutory scheme necessarily effects.

We must next consider whether some compelling state interest enforced in the eligibility provisions of the South Carolina statute justifies the substantial infringement of appellant's First Amendment right. It is basic that no showing merely of a rational relationship to some colorable state interest would suffice; in this highly sensitive constitutional area, "only the gravest abuses, endangering paramount interests, give occasion for permissible limitation." No such abuse or danger has been advanced in the present case. . . .

In holding as we do, plainly we are not fostering the "establishment" of the Seventh-day Adventist religion in South Carolina, for the extension of unemployment benefits to Sabbatarians in common with Sunday worshippers reflects nothing more than the governmental obligation of neutrality in the face of religious differences, and does not represent that involvement of religious with secular institutions which it is the object of the Establishment Clause to forestall. Nor does the recognition of the appellant's right to unemployment benefits under the state statute serve to abridge any other person's religious liberties. Nor do we, by our decision today, declare the existence of a constitutional right to unemployment benefits on the part of all persons whose religious convictions are the cause of their unemployment. This is not a case in which an employee's religious convictions serve to make him a nonproductive member of society. Finally, nothing we say today constrains the States to adopt any particular form or scheme of unemployment compensation. Our holding today is only that South Carolina may not constitutionally apply the eligibility provisions so as to constrain a worker to abandon his religious convictions respecting the day of rest. This holding but reaffirms a principle that we announced a decade and a half ago, namely that no State may "exclude individual Catholics, Lutherans, Mohammedans, Baptists, Jews, Methodists, Non-believers, Presbyterians, or the members of any other faith, *because of their faith, or lack of it,* from receiving the benefits of public welfare legislation."

In view of the result we have reached under the First and Fourteenth Amendments' guarantee of free exercise of religion, we have no occasion to consider appellant's claim that the denial of benefits also deprived her of the equal protection of the laws in violation of the Fourteenth Amendment. The judgment of the South Carolina Supreme Court is reversed and the case is remanded for further proceedings not inconsistent with this opinion.

It is so ordered.

Justice Stewart concurring in the result.

Although fully agreeing with the result which the Court reaches in this case, I cannot join the Court's opinion. This case presents a double-barreled dilemma, which in all candor I think the Court's opinion has not succeeded in papering over. The dilemma ought to be resolved. . . .

My views as to the correctness of the Court's decisions in [previous religion] cases is besides the point here. The point is that the decisions are on the books. And the result is that there are many situations where legitimate claims under the Free Exercise Clause will run into head-on collision with the Court's insensitive and sterile construction of the Establishment Clause. The controversy now before us is clearly such a case.

Because the appellant refuses to accept available jobs which would require her to work on Saturdays, South Carolina has declined to pay unemployment compensation benefits to her. Her refusal to work on Saturdays is based on the tenets of her religious faith. The Court says that South Carolina cannot under these circumstances declare her to be not "available for work" within the meaning of its statute because to do so would violate her constitutional right to the free exercise of her religion.

Yet what this Court has said about the Establishment Clause must inevitably lead to a diametrically opposite result. If the appellant's refusal to work on Saturdays were based on indolence, or on a compulsive desire to watch the Saturday television programs, no one would say that South Carolina could not hold that she was not "available for work" within the meaning of its statute. That being so, the Establishment Clause as construed by this Court not only *permits* but affirmatively *requires* South Carolina equally to deny the appellant's claim for unemployment compensation when her refusal to work on Saturdays is based upon her religious creed. For, as said in *Everson,* the Establishment Clause bespeaks "a government . . . stripped of all power . . . to support, or otherwise to assist any or all religions . . . ," and no State "can pass laws which aid one religion. . . ." In Mr. Justice Rutledge's words, adopted by the Court today in *Schempp,* the Establishment Clause forbids "every form of public aid or support for religion."

To require South Carolina to so administer its laws as to pay public money to the appellant under the circumstances of this case is thus clearly to require the State to violate the Establishment Clause as construed by this Court. This poses no problem for me, because I think the Court's mechanistic concept of the Establishment Clause is historically unsound and constitutionally wrong. I think the process of constitutional decision in the area of the relationships between government and religion demands considerably more than the invocation of broad-brushed rhetoric of the kind I have quoted. And I think that the guarantee of religious liberty embodied in the Free Exercise Clause affirmatively requires government to create an atmosphere of hospitality and accommodation to individual belief or disbelief. In short, I think our Constitution commands the positive protection by government of religious freedom—not only for a minority, however small—not only for the majority, however large—but for each of us.

South Carolina would deny unemployment benefits to a mother unavailable for work on Saturdays because she was unable to get a babysitter. Thus, we do not have before us a situation where a State provides unemployment compensation generally, and singles out for disqualification only those persons who are unavailable for work on religious grounds. This is not, in short, a scheme which operates so as to discriminate against religion as such. But the Court nevertheless holds that the State must prefer a religious over a secular ground for being unavailable for work—that state financial support of the appellant's religion is constitutionally required to carry out "the governmental obligation of neutrality in the face of religious differences. . . ."

Yet in cases decided under the Establishment Clause the Court has decreed otherwise. It has decreed that government must blind itself to the differing religious beliefs and traditions of the people. With all respect, I think it is the Court's duty to face up to the dilemma posed by the conflict between the Free Exercise Clause of the Constitution and the Establishment Clause as interpreted by the Court. It is a duty, I submit, which we owe to the people, the States, and the Nation, and a duty which we owe to ourselves. For so long as the resounding but fallacious fundamentalist rhetoric of some of our Establishment Clause opinions remains on our books, to be disregarded at will as in the present case, or to be undiscriminatingly invoked as in the *Schempp* case, so long will the possibility of consistent and perceptive decision in this most difficult and delicate area of constitutional law be impeded and impaired. And so long, I fear, will the guarantee of true religious freedom in our pluralistic society be uncertain and insecure.

Justice Harlan, with whom Justice White joins, dissenting.

Today's decision is disturbing both in its rejection of existing precedent and in its implications for the future.... What the Court is holding is that if the State chooses to condition unemployment compensation on the applicant's availability for work, it is constitutionally compelled to *carve out an exception*—and to provide benefits—for those whose unavailability is due to their religious convictions. Such a holding has particular significance in two respects.

First, despite the Court's protestations to the contrary, the decision necessarily overrules *Braunfeld v. Brown,* which held that it did not offend the "Free Exercise" Clause of the Constitution for a State to forbid a Sabbatarian to do business on Sunday. The secular purpose of the statute before us today is even clearer than that involved in *Braunfeld.* And just as in *Braunfeld*—where exceptions to the Sunday closing laws for Sabbatarians would have been inconsistent with the purpose to achieve a uniform day of rest and would have required case-by-case inquiry into religious beliefs— so here, an exception to the rules of eligibility based on religious convictions would necessitate judicial examination of those convictions and would be at odds with the limited purpose of the statute to smooth out the economy during periods of industrial instability.

Second, the implications of the present decision are far more troublesome than its apparently narrow dimensions would indicate at first glance. The meaning of today's holding, as already noted, is that the State must furnish unemployment benefits to one who is unavailable for work if the unavailability stems from the exercise of religious convictions. The State, in other words, must *single out* for financial assistance those whose behavior is religiously motivated, even though it denies such assistance to others whose identical behavior (in this case, inability to work on Saturdays) is not religiously motivated.

It has been suggested that such singling out of religious conduct for special treatment may violate the constitutional limitations on state action. My own view, however, is that at least under the circumstances of this case it would be a permissible accommodation of religion for the State, if it *chose* to do so, to create an exception to its eligibility requirements for persons like the appellant. The constitutional obligation of "neutrality" is not so narrow a channel that the slightest deviation from an absolutely straight course leads to condemnation. There are too many instances in which no such course can be charted, too many areas in which the pervasive activities of the State justify some special provision for religion to prevent it from being submerged by an all-embracing secularism. The State violates its obligation of neutrality when, for example, it mandates a daily religious exercise in its public schools, with all the attendant pressures on the school children that such an exercise entails. But there is, I believe, enough flexibility in the Constitution to permit a legislative judgment accommodating an unemployment compensation law to the exercise of religious beliefs such as appellant's.

For very much the same reasons, however, I cannot subscribe to the conclusion that the State is constitutionally *compelled* to carve out an exception to its general rule of eligibility in the present case. Those situations in which the Constitution may require special treatment on account of religion are, in my view, few and far between, and this view is amply supported by the course of constitutional litigation in this area. Such compulsion in the present case is particularly inappropriate in light of the indirect, remote, and insubstantial effect of the decision below on the exercise of appellant's religion and in light of the direct financial assistance to religion that today's decision requires. For these reasons I respectfully dissent from the opinion and judgment of the Court.

EPPERSON V. ARKANSAS (1968)

In the famous "Monkey Trial" of 1927, John Scopes had been convicted in Dayton, Tennessee, of violating the state's ban on teaching evolution in his biology class. Scopes's conviction had been thrown out by the Tennessee Supreme Court on a technicality, thus preventing a challenge to the antievolution law from going on to the United States Supreme Court. As a result, the constitutionality of anti-evolution statutes in Tennessee and other states had never been tested. Forty years after the Scopes trial, a schoolteacher in Arkansas sought a declaratory judgment on the constitutionality of that state's law, which prohibited the teaching in state-supported schools of "the theory or doctrine that mankind is ascended or descended from a lower order of animals." She claimed she could not teach her biology course from the assigned syllabus without running afoul of the law. The state's high court evaded the issue, but a unanimous Supreme Court, speaking through Justice Fortas, faced the establishment issue squarely. The decision, however, did not end efforts to ban evolution from the schools. See Richard E. Morgan, The Supreme Court and Religion *(New York: Free Press, 1972); Frank J. Sorauf,* The Wall of Separation: The Constitutional Politics of Church and State *(Princeton, NJ: Princeton University Press, 1976); and C. R. Ledbetter, Jr., "The Antievolution Law: Church and State in Arkansas,"* Arkansas Historical Quarterly *38: 299 (1979).*

Justice Fortas delivered the opinion of the Court.

The Arkansas law makes it unlawful for a teacher in any state-supported school or university "to teach the theory or doctrine that mankind ascended or descended from a lower order of animals," or "to adopt or use in any such institution a textbook that teaches" this theory. Violation is a misdemeanor and subjects the violator to dismissal from his position. . . .

Only Arkansas and Mississippi have such "antievolution" or "monkey" laws on their books. There is no record of any prosecutions in Arkansas under its statute. It is possible that the statute is presently more of a curiosity than a vital facet of life in these States. Nevertheless, the present case was brought, the appeal as of right is properly here, and it is our duty to decide the issues presented.

At the outset, it is urged upon us that the challenged statute is vague and uncertain and therefore within the condemnation of the Due Process Clause of the Fourteenth Amendment. The contention that the Act is vague and uncertain is supported by language in the brief opinion of Arkansas' Supreme Court. That court, perhaps reflecting the discomfort which the statute's quixotic prohibition necessarily engenders in the modern mind, stated that it "expresses no opinion" as to whether the Act prohibits "explanation" of the theory of evolution or merely forbids "teaching that the theory is true." Regardless of this uncertainty, the court held that the statute is constitutional.

On the other hand, counsel for the State, in oral argument in this Court, candidly stated that, despite the State Supreme Court's equivocation, Arkansas would interpret the statute "to mean that to make a student aware of the theory . . . just to teach that there was such a theory" would be grounds for dismissal and for prosecution under the statute; and he said "that the Supreme Court of Arkansas' opinion should be interpreted in that manner." He said: "If Mrs. Epperson would tell her students that 'Here is Darwin's theory, that man ascended or descended from a lower form of being,' then I think she would be under this statute liable for prosecution."

In any event, we do not rest our decision upon the asserted vagueness of the statute. On either interpretation of its language, Arkansas' statute cannot stand. It is of no moment whether the law is deemed to prohibit mention of Darwin's theory, or to forbid any or all of the infinite varieties of communication embraced within the term "teaching." Under either interpretation, the law must be stricken because of its conflict with the constitutional prohibition of state laws respecting an establishment of religion or prohibiting the free exercise thereof. The overriding facet is that Arkansas' law selects from the body of knowledge a particular segment which it proscribes for the sole reason that it is deemed to conflict with a particular religious doctrine; that is, with a particular interpretation of the Book of Genesis by a particular religious group.

The antecedents of today's decision are many and unmistakable. They are rooted in the foundation soil of our Nation. They are fundamental to freedom.

Government in our democracy, state and national, must be neutral in matters of religious theory, doctrine, and practice. It may not be hostile to any religion or to the advocacy of no-religion; and it may not aid, foster, or promote one religion or religious theory against another or even against the militant opposite. The First Amendment mandates governmental neutrality between religion and religion, and between religion and nonreligion. . . .

The earliest cases in this Court on the subject of the impact of constitutional guarantees upon the classroom were decided before the Court expressly applied the specific prohibitions of the First Amendment to the States. But as early as 1923, the Court did not hesitate to condemn under the Due Process Clause "arbitrary" restrictions upon the freedom of teachers to teach and of students to learn. In that year, the Court, in an opinion by Justice McReynolds, held unconstitutional an Act of the State of Nebraska making it a crime to teach any subject in any language other than English to pupils who had not passed the eighth grade. The state's purpose in enacting the law was to promote civic cohesiveness by encouraging the learning of English and to combat the "baneful effect" of permitting foreigners to rear and educate their children in the language of the parents' native land. The Court recognized these purposes, and it acknowledged the State's power to prescribe the school curriculum, but it held that these were not adequate to support the restriction upon the liberty of teacher and pupil. The challenged statute it held, unconstitutionally interfered with the right of the individual, guaranteed by the Due Process Clause, to engage in any of the common occupations of life and to acquire useful knowledge.

For purposes of the present case, we need not reenter the difficult terrain which the Court, in 1923, traversed without apparent misgivings. We need not take advantage of the broad premise which the Court's decision in Meyer furnishes, nor need we explore the implications of that decision in terms of the justiciability of the multitude of controversies that beset our campuses today. Today's problem is capable of resolution in the narrower terms of the First Amendment's prohibition of laws respecting an establishment of religion or prohibiting the free exercise thereof. There is and can be no doubt that the First Amendment does not permit the State to require that teaching and learning must be tailored to the principles or prohibitions of any religious sect or dogma. . . .

In the present case, there can be no doubt that Arkansas has sought to prevent its teachers from discussion of the theory of evolution because it is contrary to the belief of some that the Book of Genesis must be the exclusive source of doctrine as to the origin of man. No suggestion has been made that Arkansas' law may be justified by considerations of state policy other than the religious views of some of its citizens. It is clear that fundamentalist sectarian conviction was and is the law's reason for existence. . . .

Arkansas' law cannot be defended as an act of religious neutrality. Arkansas did not seek to excise from the curricula of its schools and universities all discussion of the origin of man. The law's effort was confined to an attempt to blot out a particular theory because of its supposed conflict with the Biblical account, literally read. Plainly, the law is contrary to the mandate of the First, and in violation of the Fourteenth, Amendments to the Constitution.

The judgment of the Supreme Court of Arkansas is reversed.

LEMON V. KURTZMAN (1971)

The enormous educational aid programs initiated by the Johnson administration led to corresponding increases in funding by the states, as well as a demand by parochial schools that they be allowed to share in the aid programs, since they carried the burden of educating a large number of children. The Court had been dealing with the problem of aid to parochial schools since 1947, and during the Warren years had developed a two-pronged test of whether legislative aid violated the Establishment Clause: The activity must have a secular legislative purpose and must neither advance nor hinder religion. In this case, the Burger Court added a third prong: The aid must avoid excessive governmental entanglement with religion. The Lemon *test has been the standard criterion by which state aid programs have been judged ever since. In recent years, however, the exact meaning of the test has become somewhat clouded. In a number of cases, both the majority and the minority have invoked* Lemon *to justify their support for or opposition to specific aid programs. See Leonard W. Levy,* The Establishment Clause: Religion and the First Amendment *(2d ed., rev., Chapel Hill: University of North Carolina Press, 1994); Leo Pfeffer, "Freedom and/or Separation . . . ,"* Minnesota Law Review *64: 561 (1980); Jesse Choper, "The Religion Clauses of the First Amendment . . . ,"* University of Pittsburgh Law Review *41: 673 (1980); and K. Ripple, "The Entanglement Test of the Religion Clauses—A Ten Year Assessment,"* UCLA Law Review *27: 1195 (1980).*

Chief Justice Burger delivered the opinion of the Court.

These two appeals raise questions as to Pennsylvania and Rhode Island statutes providing state aid to church-related elementary and secondary schools. Both statutes are challenged as violative of the Establishment and Free Exercise Clauses of the First Amendment and the Due Process Clause of the Fourteenth Amendment.

Pennsylvania has adopted a statutory program that provides financial support to nonpublic elementary and secondary schools by way of reimbursement for the cost of teachers' salaries, textbooks, and instructional materials in specified secular subjects. Rhode Island has adopted a statute under which the State pays directly to teachers in nonpublic elementary schools a supplement of 15 percent of their annual salary. Under each statute state aid has been given to church-related educational institutions. We hold that both statutes are unconstitutional. . . .

In *Everson v. Board of Education . . .* (1947), this Court upheld a state statute that reimbursed the parents of parochial school children for bus transportation expenses. There Mr. Justice Black, writing for the majority, suggested that the decision carried to "the verge" of forbidden territory under the Religion Clauses. . . . Candor compels acknowledgment, moreover, that we can only dimly perceive the lines of demarcation in this extraordinarily sensitive area of constitutional law.

The language of the Religion Clauses of the First Amendment is at best opaque, particularly when compared with other portions of the Amendment. Its authors did not simply prohibit the establishment of a state church or a state religion, an area history shows they regarded as very important and fraught with great dangers. Instead they commanded that there should be "no law *respecting* an establishment of religion." A law may be one "respecting" the forbidden objective while falling short of its total realization. A law "respecting" the proscribed result, that is, the establishment of religion, is not always easily identifiable as one violative of the Clause. A given law might not *establish* a state religion but nevertheless be one "respecting" that end in the sense of being a step that could lead to such establishment and hence offend the First Amendment.

In the absence of precisely stated constitutional prohibitions, we must draw lines with reference to the three main evils against which the Establishment Clause was intended to afford protection: "sponsorship, financial support, and active involvement of the sovereign in religious activity." . . .

Every analysis in this area must begin with consideration of the cumulative criteria developed by the Court over many years. Three such tests may be gleaned from our cases. First, the statute must have a secular legislative purpose; second, its principal or primary effect must be one that neither advances nor inhibits religion; . . . finally, the statute must not foster "an excessive government entanglement with religion." . . .

Inquiry into the legislative purposes of the Pennsylvania and Rhode Island statutes affords no basis for a conclusion that the legislative intent was to advance religion. On the contrary, the statutes themselves clearly state that they are intended to enhance the quality of the secular education in all schools covered by the compulsory attendance laws. There is no reason to believe the legislatures meant anything else. . . .

The two legislatures, however, have also recognized that church-related elementary and secondary schools have a significant religious mission and that a substantial portion of their activities is religiously oriented. They have therefore sought to create statutory restrictions designed to guarantee the separation between secular and religious educational functions and to ensure that State financial aid supports only the former. All these provisions are precautions taken in candid recognition that these programs approached, even if they did not intrude upon, the forbidden areas under the Religion Clauses. We need not decide whether these legislative precautions restrict the principal or primary effect of the programs to the point where they do not offend the Religion Clauses, for we conclude that the cumulative impact of the entire relationship arising under the statutes in each State involves excessive entanglement between government and religion.

In *Walz v. Tax Commission* [1970], the Court upheld state tax exemptions for real property owned by religious organizations and used for religious worship. That holding, however, tended to confine rather than enlarge the area of permissible state involvement with religious institutions by calling for close scrutiny of the degree of entanglement involved in the relationship. The objective is to prevent, as far as possible, the intrusion of either into the precincts of the other.

Our prior holdings do not call for total separation between church and state; total separation is not possible in an absolute sense. Some relationship between government and religious organizations is inevitable. . . . Judicial caveats against entanglement must recognize that the line of separation, far from being a "wall," is a blurred, indistinct, and variable barrier depending on all the circumstances of a particular relationship.

This is not to suggest, however, that we are to engage in a legalistic minuet in which precise rules and forms must govern. A true minuet is a matter of pure form and style, the observance of which is itself the substantive end. Here we examine the form of the relationship for the light that it casts on the substance.

In order to determine whether the government entanglement with religion is excessive, we must examine the character and purposes of the institutions that are benefited, the nature of the aid that the State provides, and the resulting relationship between the government and the religious authority. Mr. Justice Harlan, in a separate opinion in *Walz*, . . . echoed the classic warning as to "programs, whose very nature is apt to entangle the state in details of administration." . . . Here we find that both statutes foster an impermissible degree of entanglement. . . .

We need not and do not assume that teachers in parochial schools will be guilty of bad faith or any conscious design to evade the limitations imposed by the statute and the First Amendment. We simply recognize that a dedicated religious person, teaching in a school affiliated with his or her faith and operated to inculcate its tenets, will inevitably experience great difficulty in remaining religiously neutral. Doctrines and faith are not inculcated or advanced by neutrals. With the best of intentions such a teacher would find it hard to make a total separation between secular teaching and religious doctrine. What would appear to some to be essential to good citizenship might well for others border on or constitute instruction in religion. Further difficulties are inherent in the combination of religious discipline and the possibility of disagreement between teacher and religious authorities over the meaning of the statutory restrictions.

We do not assume, however, that parochial school teachers will be unsuccessful in their attempts to segregate their religious beliefs from their secular educational responsibilities. But the potential for impermissible fostering of religion is present. . . .

A comprehensive, discriminating, and continuing state surveillance will inevitably be required to ensure that these restrictions are obeyed and the First Amendment otherwise respected. Unlike a book, a teacher cannot be inspected once so as to determine the extent and intent of his or her personal beliefs and subjective acceptance of the limitations imposed by the First Amendment. These prophylactic contacts will involve excessive and enduring entanglement between state and church. . . .

The very restrictions and surveillance necessary to ensure that teachers play a strictly nonideological role give rise to entanglements between church and state. The Pennsylvania statute, like that of Rhode Island, fosters this kind of relationship. Reimbursement is not only limited to courses offered in the public schools and materials approved by state officials, but the statute excludes "any subject matter expressing religious teaching, or the morals or forms of worship of any sect." In addition, schools seeking reimbursement must maintain accounting procedures that require the State to establish the cost of the secular as distinguished from the religious instruction.

The Pennsylvania statute, moreover, has the further defect of providing state financial aid directly to the church-related schools. . . . The history of government grants of a continuing cash subsidy indicates that such programs have almost always been accompanied by varying measures of control and surveillance. The government cash grants before us now provide no basis for predicting that comprehensive measures of surveillance and controls will not follow. In particular the government's post-audit power to inspect and evaluate a church-related school's financial records and to determine which expenditures are religious and which are secular creates an intimate and continuing relationship between church and state.

A broader base of entanglement of yet a different character is presented by the divisive political potential of these state programs. In a community where such a large number of pupils are served by church-related schools, it can be assumed that state assistance will entail considerable political activity. Partisans of parochial schools, understandably concerned with rising costs and sincerely dedicated to both the religious and secular educational missions of their schools, will inevitably champion this cause and promote political action to achieve their goals. Those who oppose state aid, whether for constitutional, religious, or fiscal reasons, will inevitably respond and employ all of the usual political campaign techniques to prevail. Candidates will be forced to declare and voters to choose. It would be unrealistic to ignore the fact that many people confronted with issues of this kind will find their votes aligned with their faith. . . .

Finally, nothing we have said can be construed to disparage the role of church-related elementary and secondary schools in our national life. Their contribution has been and is enormous. Nor do we ignore their economic plight in a period of rising costs and expanding need. Taxpayers generally have been spared vast sums by the maintenance of these educational institutions by religious organizations, largely by the gifts of faithful adherents.

The merit and benefits of these schools, however are not the issue before us in these cases. The sole question is whether state aid to these schools can be squared with the dictates of the Religion Clauses. Under our system the choice has been made that government is to be entirely excluded from the area of religious instruction and churches excluded from the affairs of government. The Constitution decrees that religion must be a private matter for the individual, the family, and the institutions of private choice, and that while some involvement and entanglement are inevitable, lines must be drawn. The judgment of the Pennsylvania District Court is reversed, and the case is remanded for further proceedings consistent with this opinion.

WISCONSIN V. YODER (1972)

Wisconsin law required all children between the ages of 7 and 16 to attend school, but the Old Order Amish objected to having their children go past the eighth grade (age 14), lest worldly influences corrupt them. The school board took three sets of parents to court. The local court, although sympathetic, found them guilty and imposed the minimal $5 fine. But the Wisconsin Supreme Court reversed this decision, noting that the exemption of the Amish would not pose a serious threat to the economic vitality of the public school system. In the Supreme Court Chief Justice Burger wrote a sweeping decision reaffirming Sherbert v. Verner *(above). Only Justice Douglas dissented, on the grounds that education was a right of children, not parents, and that it should be up to the children to make the decision of whether to continue. See Albert N. Keim, ed.,* Compulsory Education and the Amish: The Right Not To Be Modern *(Boston: Beacon Press, 1975).*

Chief Justice Burger delivered the opinion of the Court.

On complaint of the school district administrator for the public schools, respondents were charged, tried, and convicted of violating the compulsory-attendance law in Green County Court and were fined the sum of $5 each. Respondents defended on the ground that the application of the compulsory-attendance law violated their rights under the First and Fourteenth Amendments. The trial testimony showed that respondents believed, in accordance with the tenets of Old Order Amish communities generally, that their children's attendance at high school, public or private, was contrary to the Amish religion and way of life. They believed that by sending their children to high school, they would not only expose themselves to the danger of the censure of the church community, but, as found by the county court, also endanger their own salvation and that of their children. The State stipulated that respondents' religious beliefs were sincere. . . .

Old Order Amish communities today are characterized by a fundamental belief that salvation requires life in a church community separate and apart from the world and worldly influence. This concept of life aloof from the world and its values is central to their faith. A related feature of Old Order Amish communities is their devotion to a life in harmony with nature and the soil, as exemplified by the simple life of the early Christian era that continued in America during much of our early national life. Amish beliefs require members of the community to make their living by farming or closely related activities. Broadly speaking, the Old Order Amish religion pervades and determines the entire mode of life of its adherents. Their conduct is regulated in great detail by the *Ordnung,* or rules, of the church community. . . .

Amish objection to formal education beyond the eighth grade is firmly grounded in these central religious concepts. They object to the high school, and higher education generally, because the values they teach are in marked variance with Amish values and the Amish way of life; they view secondary school education as an impermissible exposure of their children to a "worldly" influence in conflict with their beliefs. The high school tends to emphasize intellectual and scientific accomplishments, self-distinction, competitiveness, worldly success, and social life with other students.

Amish society emphasizes informal learning-through-doing; a life of "goodness," rather than a life of intellect; wisdom, rather than technical knowledge; community welfare, rather than competition; and separation from, rather than integration with, contemporary worldly society. . . .

There is no doubt as to the power of a State, having a high responsibility for education of its citizens, to impose reasonable regulations for the control and duration of basic education. Providing public schools ranks at the very apex of the function of a State. Yet even this paramount responsibility was made to yield to the right of parents to provide an equivalent education in a privately operated system. . . . The values of parental direction of the religious upbringing and education of their children in their early and formative years have a high place in our society. Thus, a State's interest in universal education, however highly we rank it, is not totally free from a balancing process when it impinges on fundamental rights and interests, such as those specifically protected by the Free Exercise Clause of the First Amendment, and the traditional interest of parents with respect to the religious upbringing of their children.

It follows that in order for Wisconsin to compel school attendance beyond the eighth grade against a claim that such attendance interferes with the practice of a legitimate religious belief, it must appear either that the State does not deny the free exercise of religious belief by its requirement, or that there is a state interest of sufficient magnitude to override the interest claiming protection under the Free Exercise Clause. Long before there was general acknowledgment of the need for universal formal education, the Religion Clauses had specifically and firmly fixed the right to free exercise of religious beliefs, and buttressing this fundamental right was an equally firm, even if less explicit, prohibition against the establishment of any religion by government. The values underlying these two provisions relating to religion have been zealously protected, sometimes even at the expense of other interests of

admittedly high social importance. . . . The essence of all that has
been said and written on the subject is that only those interests of
the highest order and those not otherwise served can overbalance
legitimate claims to the free exercise of religion. We can accept it
as settled, therefore, that, however strong the State's interest in
universal compulsory education, it is by no means absolute to the
exclusion or subordination of all other interests.

We come then to the quality of the claims of the respondents
concerning the alleged encroachment of Wisconsin's compulsory
school-attendance statute on their rights and the rights of their
children to the free exercise of the religious beliefs they and their
forebears have adhered to for almost three centuries. In evaluating
those claims we must be careful to determine whether the Amish
religious faith and their mode of life are, as they claim, inseparable
and interdependent. A way of life, however virtuous and
admirable, may not be interposed as a barrier to reasonable state
regulation of education if it is based on purely secular considerations; to have the protection of the Religion Clauses, the claims
must be rooted in religious belief. Although a determination of
what is a "religious" belief or practice entitled to constitutional
protection may present a most delicate question, the very concept
of ordered liberty precludes allowing every person to make his
own standards on matters of conduct in which society as a whole
has important interests. Thus, if the Amish asserted their claims
because of their subjective evaluation and rejection of the contemporary secular values accepted by the majority, much as Thoreau
rejected the social values of his time and isolated himself at
Walden Pond, their claims would not rest on a religious basis.
Thoreau's choice was philosophical and personal rather than religious, and such belief does not rise to the demands of the Religion
Clauses.

Giving no weight to such secular considerations, however, we
see that the record in this case abundantly supports the claim that
the traditional way of life of the Amish is not merely a matter of

personal preference, but one of deep religious conviction, shared by an organized group, and intimately related to daily living. That the Old Order Amish daily life and religious practice stem from their faith is shown by the fact that it is in response to their literal interpretation of the Biblical injunction from the Epistle of Paul to the Romans, "be not conformed to this world . . . ." This command is fundamental to the Amish faith. Moreover, for the Old Order Amish, religion is not simply a matter of theocratic belief. As the expert witnesses explained, the Old Order Amish religion pervades and determines virtually their entire way of life, regulating it with the detail of the Talmudic diet through the strictly enforced rules of the church community. . . .

As the society around the Amish has become more populous, urban, industrialized, and complex, particularly in this century, government regulation of human affairs has correspondingly become more detailed and pervasive. The Amish mode of life has thus come into conflict increasingly with requirements of contemporary society exerting a hydraulic insistence on conformity to majoritarian standards. So long as compulsory education laws were confined to eight grades of elementary basic education imparted in a nearby rural schoolhouse, with a large proportion of students of the Amish faith, the Old Order Amish had little basis to fear that school attendance would expose their children to the worldly influence they reject. But modern compulsory secondary education in rural areas is now largely carried on in a consolidated school, often remote from the student's home and alien to his daily home life. As the record so strongly shows, the values and programs of the modern secondary school are in sharp conflict with the fundamental mode of life mandated by the Amish religion; modern laws requiring compulsory secondary education have accordingly engendered great concern and conflict. The conclusion is inescapable that secondary schooling, by exposing Amish children to worldly influences in terms of attitudes, goals, and values contrary to beliefs, and by substantially interfering with the religious development of the Amish child and his integration into the way of life of the Amish faith community at the crucial adolescent stage of development, contravenes the basic religious tenets and practice of the Amish faith, both as to the parent and the child.

In sum, the unchallenged testimony of acknowledged experts in education and religious history, almost 300 years of consistent practice, and strong evidence of a sustained faith pervading and regulating respondents' entire mode of life support the claim that enforcement of the State's requirement of compulsory formal education after the eighth grade would gravely endanger if not destroy the free exercise of respondents' religious beliefs.

Neither the findings of the trial court nor the Amish claims as to the nature of their faith are challenged in this Court by the State of Wisconsin. Its position is that the State's interest in universal compulsory formal secondary education to age 16 is so great that it is paramount to the undisputed claims of respondents that their mode of preparing their youth for Amish life, after the traditional elementary education, is an essential part of their religious belief and practice. Nor does the State undertake to meet the claim that the Amish mode of life and education is inseparable from and a part of the basic tenets of their religion—indeed, as much a part of their religious belief and practices as baptism, the confessional, or a sabbath may be for others. . . .

We turn to the State's broader contention that its interest in its system of compulsory education is so compelling that even the established religious practices of the Amish must give way. Where fundamental claims of religious freedom are at stake, however, we cannot accept such a sweeping claim; despite its admitted validity in the generality of cases, we must searchingly examine the interests that the State seeks to promote by its requirement for compulsory education to age 16, and the impediment to those objectives that would flow from recognizing the claimed Amish exemption.

The State advances two primary arguments in support of its system of compulsory education. It notes, as Thomas Jefferson pointed out early in our history, that some degree of education is necessary to prepare citizens to participate effectively and intelligently in our open political system if we are to preserve freedom and independence. Further, education prepares individuals to be self-reliant and self-sufficient participants in society. We accept these propositions.

However, the evidence adduced by the Amish in this case is persuasively to the effect that an additional one or two years of formal high school for Amish children in place of their long-established program of informal vocational education would do little to serve those interests. Respondents' experts testified at trial, without challenge, that the value of all education must be assessed in terms of its capacity to prepare the child for life. It is one thing to say that compulsory education for a year or two beyond the eighth grade may be necessary when its goal is the preparation of the child for life in modern society as the majority live, but it is quite another if the goal of education be viewed as the preparation of the child for life in the separated agrarian community that is the keystone of the Amish faith.

It is neither fair nor correct to suggest that the Amish are opposed to education beyond the eighth grade level. What this record shows is that they are opposed to conventional formal education of the type provided by a certified high school because it comes at the child's crucial adolescent period of religious development. . . .

There is nothing in this record to suggest that the Amish qualities of reliability, self-reliance, and dedication to work would fail to find ready markets in today's society. Absent some contrary evidence supporting the State's position, we are unwilling to assume that persons possessing such valuable vocational skills and habits are doomed to become burdens on society should they determine to leave the Amish faith, nor is there any basis in the record to warrant a finding that an additional one or two years of formal school education beyond the eighth grade would serve to eliminate any such problem that might exist. . . .

Finally, the State argues that a decision exempting Amish children from the State's requirement fails to recognize the substantive right of the Amish child to a secondary education, and fails to give due regard to the power of the State as *parens patriae* to extend the benefit of secondary education to children regardless of the wishes of their parents. . . .

Contrary to the suggestion of the dissenting opinion of Mr. Justice Douglas, our holding today in no degree depends on the assertion of the religious interest of the child as contrasted with that of the parents. It is the parents who are subject to prosecution here for failing to cause their children to attend school, and it is their right of free exercise, not that of their children, that must determine Wisconsin's power to impose criminal penalties on the parent. The dissent argues that a child who expresses a desire to attend public high school in conflict with the wishes of his parents should not be prevented from doing so. There is no reason for the Court to consider that point since it is not an issue in the case. The children are not parties to this litigation. The State has at no point tried this case on the theory that respondents were preventing their children from attending school against their expressed desires, and indeed the record is to the contrary. The State's position from the outset has been that it is empowered to apply its compulsory-attendance law to Amish parents in the same manner as to other parents—that is, without regard to the wishes of the child. That is the claim we reject today.

In the face of our consistent emphasis on the central values underlying the Religion Clauses in our constitutional scheme of government, we cannot accept a *parens patriae* claim of such all-encompassing scope and with such sweeping potential for broad and unforeseeable application as that urged by the State.

For the reasons stated we hold that the First and Fourteenth Amendments prevent the State from compelling respondents to cause their children to attend formal high school to age 16. Our disposition of this case, however, in no way alters our recognition of the obvious fact that courts are not school boards or legislatures, and are ill-equipped to determine the "necessity" of discrete aspects of a State's program of compulsory education. This should suggest that courts must move with great circumspection in performing the sensitive and delicate task of weighing a State's legitimate social concern when faced with religious claims for exemption from generally applicable educational requirements. It cannot be overemphasized that we are not dealing with a way of life and mode of education by a group claiming to have recently discovered some "progressive" or more enlightened process for rearing children for modern life.

Aided by a history of three centuries as an identifiable religious sect and a long history as a successful and self-sufficient segment of American society, the Amish in this case have convincingly demonstrated the sincerity of their religious beliefs, the interrelationship of belief with their mode of life, the vital role that belief and daily conduct play in the continued survival of Old Order Amish communities and their religious organization, and the hazards presented by the State's enforcement of a statute generally valid as to others. Beyond this, they have carried the even more difficult burden of demonstrating the adequacy of their alternative mode of continuing informal vocational education in terms of precisely those overall interests that the State advances in support of its program of compulsory high school education. In light of this convincing showing, one that probably few other religious groups or sects could make, and weighing the minimal difference between what the State would require and what the Amish already accept, it was incumbent on the State to show with more particularity how its admittedly strong interest in compulsory education would be adversely affected by granting an exemption to the Amish.

Affirmed.

Justice Douglas dissenting in part.

I agree with the Court that the religious scruples of the Amish are opposed to the education of their children beyond the grade schools, yet I disagree with the Court's conclusion that the matter is within the dispensation of parents alone. The Court's analysis assumes that the only interests at stake in the case are those of the Amish parents on the one hand, and those of the State on the other. The difficulty with this approach is that, despite the Court's claim, the parents are seeking to vindicate not only their own free exercise claims, but also those of their high-school-age children.

It is argued that the right of the Amish children to religious freedom is not presented by the facts of the case, as the issue before the Court involves only the Amish parents' religious freedom to defy a state criminal statute imposing upon them an affirmative duty to cause their children to attend high school.

First, respondents' motion to dismiss in the trial court expressly asserts, not only the religious liberty of the adults, but also that of the children, as a defense to the prosecutions. It is, of course, beyond question that the parents have standing as defendants in a criminal prosecution to assert the religious interests of their children as a defense. Although the lower courts and a majority of this Court assume an identity of interest between parent and child, it is clear that they have treated the religious interest of the child as a factor in the analysis.

Second, it is essential to reach the question to decide the case, not only because the question was squarely raised in the motion to dismiss, but also because no analysis of religious-liberty claims can take place in a vacuum. If the parents in this case are allowed a religious exemption, the inevitable effect is to impose the parents' notions of religious duty upon their children. Where the child is mature enough to express potentially conflicting desires, it would be an invasion of the child's rights to permit such an imposition without canvassing his views. As the child has no other effective forum, it is in this litigation that his rights should be considered. And, if an Amish child desires to attend high school, and is mature enough to have that desire respected, the State may well be able to override the parents' religiously motivated objections.

Religion is an individual experience. It is not necessary, nor even appropriate, for every Amish child to express his views on the subject in a prosecution of a single adult. Crucial, however, are the views of the child whose parent is the subject of the suit. Frieda Yoder has in fact testified that her own religious views are opposed to high-school education. I therefore join the judgment of the Court as to respondent Jonas Yoder. But Frieda Yoder's views may not be those of Vernon Yutzy or Barbara Miller. I must dissent, therefore, as to respondents Adin Yutzy and Wallace Miller as their motion to dismiss also raised the question of their children's religious liberty.

This issue has never been squarely presented before today. Our opinions are full of talk about the power of the parents over the child's education. And we have in the past analyzed similar conflicts between parent and State with little regard for the views of the child. Recent cases, however, have clearly held that the children themselves have constitutionally protectible interests.

These children are "persons" within the meaning of the Bill of Rights. We have so held over and over again. . . . On this important and vital matter of education, I think the children should be entitled to be heard. While the parents, absent dissent, normally speak for the entire family, the education of the child is a matter on which the child will often have decided views. He may want to be a pianist or an astronaut or an oceanographer. To do so he will have to break from the Amish tradition.

It is the future of the student, not the future of the parents, that is imperiled by today's decision. If a parent keeps his child out of school beyond the grade school, then the child will be forever barred from entry into the new and amazing world of diversity that we have today. The child may decide that that is the preferred course, or he may rebel. It is the student's judgment, not his parents', that is essential if we are to give full meaning to what we have said about the Bill of Rights and of the right of students to be masters of their own destiny. If he is harnessed to the Amish way of life by those in authority over him and if his education is truncated, his entire life may be stunted and deformed. The child, therefore, should be given an opportunity to be heard before the State gives the exemption which we honor today.

WALLACE v. JAFFREE (1985)

Following Engel v. Vitale *and* Abington School District v. Schempp *(1963), people who wanted prayer and Bible reading in schools mounted a number of campaigns to overturn the Court's rulings. The revival of a strong fundamentalist Christian movement in the 1980s led to repeated efforts to introduce a variety of religious activities into the public school system. In 1980, the Court struck down a Kentucky statute requiring the posting of the Ten Commandments in all public school classrooms. The per curiam opinion in* Stone v. Graham *characterized the law as plainly religious. The decision led President Reagan and others to call once again for an amendment to permit prayer in school. In Alabama the legislature tried to get around the* Engel *rule with a series of laws. The first, passed in 1978, simply provided for a one-minute period of silent meditation; a 1981 amendment authorized "meditation or voluntary prayer." In 1982, however, the legislature directed teachers to lead "willing students" in a prescribed prayer. The decision dealt primarily with the 1981 law, which was obviously religious in intent, and left to a future decision the question of whether silence that could be devoted to prayer was constitutional. See Norman Redlich, "Separation of Church and State: The Burger Court's Tortuous Journey,"* Notre Dame Law Review *60:*

1094 (1985); Leonard W. Levy, The Establishment Clause: Religion and the First Amendment *(Chapel Hill: Unversity of North Carolina Press, 1994); and Michael W. McConnell, "Accommodation of Religion,"* Supreme Court Review *1985: 1 (1986).*

Justice Stevens delivered the opinion of the Court.

The narrow question for decision is whether §16-1-20.1, which authorizes a period of silence for "meditation or voluntary prayer," is a law respecting the establishment of religion within the meaning of the First Amendment.

I. Appellee Ishmael Jaffree is a resident of Mobile County, Alabama. On May 28, 1982, he filed a complaint on behalf of three of his minor children; two of them were second-grade students and the third was then in kindergarten. [The complaint alleged] that two of the children had been subjected to various acts of religious indoctrination "from the beginning of the school year in September, 1981"; that the defendant teachers had "on a daily basis" led their classes in saying certain prayers in unison; that the minor children were exposed to ostracism from their peer group class members if they did not participate; and that Ishmael Jaffree had repeatedly but unsuccessfully requested that the devotional services be stopped.

On August 2, 1982, the District Court held an evidentiary hearing on appellees' motion for a preliminary injunction. At that hearing, State Senator Donald G. Holmes testified that he was the "prime sponsor" of the bill that was enhanced in 1981 as §16-1-20.1. He explained that the bill was an " effort to return voluntary prayer to our public schools . . . a beginning and a step in the right direction." Apart from the purpose to return voluntary prayer to public school, Senator Holmes unequivocally testified that he had "no other purpose in mind." . . .

II. Our unanimous affirmance of the Court of Appeals' judgment . . . makes it unnecessary to comment at length on the District Court's remarkable conclusion that the Federal Constitution imposes no obstacle to Alabama's establishment of a state religion.

Before analyzing the precise issue that is presented to us, it is nevertheless appropriate to recall how firmly embedded in our constitutional jurisprudence is the proposition that the several States have no greater power to restrain the individual freedoms protected by the First Amendment than does the Congress of the United States.

As is plain from its text, the First Amendment was adopted to curtail the power of Congress to interfere with the individual's freedom to believe, to worship, and to express himself in accordance with the dictates of his own conscience. Until the Fourteenth Amendment was added to the Constitution, the First Amendment's restraints on the exercise of federal power simply did not apply to the States. But when the Constitution was amended to prohibit any State from depriving any person of liberty without due process of law, that Amendment imposed the same substantive limitations on the States' power to legislate that the First Amendment had always imposed on the Congress' power. This Court has confirmed and endorsed this elementary proposition of law time and time again.

Just as the right to speak and the right to refrain from speaking are complementary components of a broader concept of individual freedom of mind, so also the individual's freedom to choose his own creed is the counterpart of his right to refrain from accepting the creed established by the majority. At one time it was thought that this right merely proscribed the preference of one Christian sect over another, but would not require equal respect for the conscience of the infidel, the atheist, or the adherent of a non-Christian faith such as Mohammedism or Judaism. But when the underlying principle has been examined in the crucible of litigation, the Court has unambiguously concluded that the individual freedom of conscience protected by the First Amendment embraces the right to select any religious faith or not at all. This conclusion derives support not only from the interest in respecting the individual's freedom of conscience, but also from the conviction that religious beliefs worthy of respect are the product of free and voluntary choice by the faithful, and from recognition of the fact that the political interest in forestalling intolerance extends beyond intolerance among Christian sects or even intolerance among "religions"—to encompass intolerance of the disbeliever and the uncertain. The State of Alabama, no less than the Congress of the United States, must respect that basic truth.

III. It is the first of [the *Lemon*] criteria that is most plainly implicated by this case. As the District Court correctly recognized, no consideration of the second or third criteria is necessary if a statute does not have a clearly secular purpose. . . . The First Amendment requires that a statute must be invalidated if it is entirely motivated by a purpose to advance religion.

In applying the purpose thesis, it is appropriate to ask "whether government's actual purpose is to endorse or disapprove of religion." . . . In this case, the answer to that question is dispositive. For the record not only provides us with an unambiguous affirmative answer, but it also reveals that the enactment of §16-1-20.1 was not motivated by any clearly secular purpose—indeed, the statue had no secular purpose.

IV. The sponsor of the bill that became §16-1-20.1, Senator Donald Holmes, inserted into the legislative record—apparently without dissent—a statement indicating that the legislation was an "effort to return voluntary prayer" to the public schools. Later Senator Holmes confirmed this purpose before the District Court. In response to the question whether he had any purpose for the legislation other than returning voluntary prayer to public schools, he stated, "No, I had no other purpose in mind." The State did not present evidence of any secular purpose. . . .

The Legislature enacted §16-1-20.1 . . . for the sole purpose of expressing the State's endorsement of prayer activities for one minute at the beginning of each school day. The addition of "or voluntary prayer" indicates that the State intended to characterize prayer as a favored practice. Such an endorsement is not consistent with the established principle that the Government must pursue a course of complete neutrality toward religion.

The importance of that principle does not permit us to treat this as an inconsequential case involving nothing more than a few words of symbolic speech on behalf of the political majority. For whenever the State itself speaks on a religious subject, one of the questions that we must ask is "whether the Government intends to convey a message of endorsement or disapproval of religion." The well-supported concurrent findings of the District Court and the Court of Appeals—that §16-1-20.1 . . . was intended to convey a message of State approval of prayer activities in the public schools—make it unnecessary, and indeed inappropriate, to evaluate the practical significance of the addition of the words "or voluntary prayer" to the statute. Keeping in mind, as we must, "both the fundamental place held by the Establishment Clause in our constitutional scheme and the myriad, subtle ways in which Establishment Clause values can be eroded," . . . we conclude that §16-1-20.1 violates the First Amendment.

The judgment of the Court of Appeals is affirmed.

EDWARDS V. AGUILLARD (1987)

The growth of a powerful conservative religious and social movement in the 1980s led to a number of legislative attempts to undo what militant religious leaders viewed as the dreadful mistakes of the Court. In Wallace v. Jaffree *the Alabama legislature tried to overturn the ban on state-sponsored school prayer. In* Edwards v. Aguillard *Louisiana resumed the fundamentalist fight against evolution, mandating that if a school taught "evolution science," then it had to give equal time to so-called creation science. Most reputable scientists dismissed "creation science" as a blind for teaching the creation as told in Genesis; science, in contrast, is a system built on doubt and questioning, not on blind faith. The majority dismissed the law as a ploy, although newly named Chief Justice William*

Rehnquist, joined by Justice Scalia, continued his pattern of defer-
ring to the legislative will and of calling for a greater accommoda-
tion of religion with the state. See Michael McConnell, "The Origins
and Historical Understanding of Free Exercise of Religion," Har-
vard Law Review *103: 1409 (1990); Derek Davis,* Original Intent:
Chief Justice Rehnquist and the Course of Church/State Relations
(Buffalo, NY: Prometheus Books, 1991); Gregg Ivers, Lowering the
Wall: Religion and the Supreme Court in the 1980s *(New York:*
Anti-Defamation League, 1991); and Edward J. Larson, Summer
for the Gods *(New York: Basic Books, 1997).*

Justice Brennan delivered the opinion of the Court.

The Creationism Act forbids the teaching of the theory of evolution in public schools unless accompanied by instruction in
"creation science." No school is required to teach evolution or
creation science. If either is taught, however, the other must also
be taught. The theories of evolution and creation science are statu-
torily defined as "the scientific evidences for [creation or evolu-
tion] and inferences from those scientific evidences."

Appellees, who include parents of children attending Louisiana
public schools, Louisiana teachers, and religious leaders, challenged the constitutionality of the Act in District court, seeking an
injunction and declaratory relief. Appellants, Louisiana officials
charged with implementing the Act, defended on the ground that
the purpose of the Act is to protect a legitimate secular interest,
namely, academic freedom. . . .

The Establishment Clause forbids the enactment of any law
"respecting an establishment of religion." The Court has applied a
three-pronged test to determine whether legislation comports with
the Establishment Clause. First, the legislature must have adopted
the law with a secular purpose. Second, the statute's principal or
primary effect must be one that neither advances nor prohibits religion. Third, the statute must not result in an excessive entanglement of government with religion. State action violates the Establishment Clause if it fails to satisfy any of these prongs. . . .

The Court has been particularly vigilant in monitoring compliance with the Establishment Clause in elementary and secondary schools. . . . Students in such institutions are impressionable and their attendance is involuntary. . . . Furthermore, "the public school is at once the symbol of our democracy and the most pervasive means for promoting our common destiny. In no activity of the State is it more vital to keep out divisive forces than in its schools. . . ."

Consequently, the Court has been required often to invalidate statutes which advance religion in public elementary and secondary schools. . . .

Therefore, in employing the three-pronged *Lemon* test, we must do so mindful of the particular concerns that arise in the context of public elementary and secondary schools. We now turn to the evolution of the Act under the *Lemon* test. . . .

"The purpose prong of the *Lemon* test asks whether government's actual purpose is to endorse or disapprove of religion." A governmental intention to promote religion is clear when the State enacts a law to serve a religious purpose. . . . If the law was enacted for the purpose of endorsing religion, "no consideration of the second or third criteria is necessary." In this case, the petitioners have identified no clear secular purpose for the Louisiana Act.

True, the Act's stated purpose is to protect academic freedom. . . . However, even if "academic freedom" is read to mean "teaching all of the evidence" with respect to the origin of human beings, the Act does not further this purpose. The goal of providing a more comprehensive science curriculum is not furthered either by outlawing the teaching of evolution or by requiring the teaching of creation science.

While the Court is normally deferential to a State's articulation of a secular purpose, it is required that the statement of such purpose be sincere and not a sham. . . .

It is clear from the legislative history that the purpose of the legislative sponsor, Senator Bill Keith, was to narrow the science curriculum. During the legislative hearings, Senator Keith stated: "My preference would be that neither [creationism nor evolution] be taught." . . . It is clear that requiring schools to teach creation science with evolution does not advance academic freedom. . . . As the president of the Louisianan Science Teachers Association testified, "any scientific concept that's based on established fact can be included in our curriculum already, and no legislation allowing this is necessary." The Act provides Louisiana schoolteachers with no new authority. Thus the stated purpose is not furthered by it.

If the Louisiana legislature's purpose was solely to maximize the comprehensiveness and effectiveness of science instruction, it would have encouraged the teaching of all scientific theories about the origins of humankind. But under the Act's requirements, teachers who were once free to teach any and all facets of this subject are now unable to do so. Moreover, the Act fails even to ensure that creation science will be taught, but instead requires the teaching of this theory only when the theory of evolution is taught. . . . Thus the Act does not serve to protect academic freedom, but has the distinctly different purpose of discrediting "evolution by counterbalancing its teaching at every turn with teaching of creation science. . . ."

The preeminent purpose of the Louisiana legislature was clearly to advance the religious viewpoint that a supernatural being created humankind. . . . Furthermore, it is not happenstance that the legislature required the teaching of a theory that coincided with this religious view. The legislative history documents that the Act's primary purpose was to change the science curriculum of public schools in order to provide persuasive advantage to a particular religious doctrine that rejects the factual basis of evolution in its entirety. . . .

The Creationism Act is designed *either* to promote the theory of creation science which embodies a particular religious tenet by requiring that creation science be taught whenever evolution is taught or to prohibit the teaching of a scientific theory disfavored by certain religious sects by forbidding the teaching of evolution when creation science is not also taught. The Establishment Clause, however, forbids *alike* the preference of a religious doctrine or the prohibition of theory which is deemed antagonistic to a particular dogma. Because the primary purpose of the Creationism Act is to advance a particular religious belief, the Act endorses religion in violation of the First Amendment.

We do not imply that a legislature could never require that scientific critiques of prevailing scientific theories be taught.... Teaching a variety of scientific theories about the origins of humankind to schoolchildren might be validly done with the clear secular intent of enhancing the effectiveness of science instruction. But because the primary purpose of the Creationism Act is to endorse a particular religious doctrine, the Act furthers religion in violation of the Establishment Clause.

The judgment of the Court of Appeals therefore is Affirmed.

Justice Powell, with whom Justice O'Connor joins, concurring.

I write separately to note certain aspects of the legislative history, and to emphasize that nothing in the Court's opinion diminishes the traditionally broad discretion accorded state and local school officials in the selection of the public school curriculum....

When, as here, "both courts below are unable to discern an arguably valid secular purpose, the Court normally should hesitate to find one." My examination of the language and the legislative history of the Balanced Treatment Act confirms that the intent of the Louisiana legislature was to promote a particular religious belief....

Here, it is clear that religious belief is the Balanced Treatment Act's "reason for existence." The tenets of creation-science parallel the Genesis story of creation, and this is a religious belief. "No legislative recitation of a supposed secular purpose can blind us to that fact...."

The legislature acted with the unconstitutional purpose of

structuring the public school curriculum to make it compatible with a particular religious belief: the "divine creation of man." . . .

Whatever the academic merit of particular subjects or theories, the Establishment Clause limits the discretion of state officials to pick and choose among them for the purpose of promoting a particular religious belief. The language of the statute and its legislative history convince me that the Louisiana legislature exercised its discretion for this purpose in the case.

A decision respecting the subject matter to be taught in public schools does not violate the Establishment Clause simply because the material to be taught "'happens to consider or harmonize with the tenets of some or all religions.'"

As matter of history, school children can and should properly be informed of all aspects of this Nation's religious heritage. I would see no constitutional problem if school children were taught the nature of the Founding Fathers' religious beliefs and how these beliefs affected the attitudes of the times and the structure of our government. Courses in comparative religion of course are customary and constitutionally appropriate. In fact, since religion permeates our history, a familiarity with the nature of religious beliefs is necessary to understand many historical as well as contemporary events. In addition, it is worth noting that the Establishment Clause does not prohibit *per se* the educational use of religious documents in public school education. . . . The Establishment Clause is properly understood to prohibit the use of the Bible and other religious documents in public school education only when the purpose of the use is to advance a particular religious belief.

Justice Scalia, with whom the Chief Justice joins, dissenting.

Even if I agreed with the questionable premise that legislation can be invalidated under the Establishment Clause on the basis of its motivation alone, without regard to its effects, I would still find no justification for today's decision. The Louisiana legislators who passed the "Balanced Treatment for Creation-Science and

Evolution-Science Act," each of whom had sworn to support the Constitution, were well aware of the potential Establishment Clause problems and considered that aspect of the legislation with great care. After seven hearings and several months of study, resulting in substantial revision of the original proposal, they approved the Act overwhelmingly and specifically articulated the secular purpose they meant it to serve. Although the record contains abundant evidence of the sincerity of that purpose (the only issue pertinent to this case), the Court today holds, essentially on the basis of "its visceral knowledge regarding what *must* have motivated the legislators," that the members of the Louisiana Legislature knowingly violated their oaths and then lied about it. I dissent. . . .

We have relatively little information upon which to judge the motives of those who supported the Act. About the only direct evidence is the statute itself and transcripts of the seven committee hearings at which it was considered. Unfortunately, several of those hearings were sparsely attended, and the legislators who were present revealed little about their motives. We have no committee reports, no floor debates, no remarks inserted into the legislative history, no statement from the Governor, and no post-enactment statements or testimony from the bill's sponsor or any other legislators. Nevertheless, there is ample evidence that the majority is wrong in holding that the Balanced Treatment Act is without secular purpose. . . .

Our task is not to judge the debate about teaching the origins of life, but to ascertain what the members of the Louisiana Legislature believed. The vast majority of them voted to approve a bill which explicitly stated a secular purpose; what is crucial is not their wisdom in believing that purpose would be achieved by the bill, but their *sincerity* in believing it would be. . . .

Striking down a law approved by the democratically elected representatives of the people is no minor matter. "The cardinal principle of statutory construction is to save and not to destroy.

We have repeatedly held that as between two possible interpretations of a statute, by one of which it would be unconstitutional and by the other valid, our plain duty is to adopt that which will save the act." So, too, it seems to me, with discerning statutory purpose. Even if the legislative history were silent or ambiguous about the existence of a secular purpose—and here it is not—the statute should survive *Lemon*'s purpose test. But even more validation than mere legislative history is present here. The Louisiana Legislature explicitly set forth its secular purpose ("protecting academic freedom") in the very text of the Act.

The legislative history gives ample evidence of the sincerity of the Balanced Treatment Act's articulated purpose. Witness after witness urged the legislators to support the Act so that students would not be "indoctrinated" but would instead be free to decide for themselves, based upon a fair presentation of the scientific evidence, about the origin of life. . . .

It is undoubtedly true that what prompted the Legislature to direct its attention to the misrepresentation of evolution in the schools (rather than the inaccurate presentation of other topics) was its awareness of the tension between evolution and the religious beliefs of many children. But even appellees concede that a valid secular purpose is not rendered impermissible simply because its pursuit is promoted by concern for religious sensitivities. . . .

In sum, even if one concedes, for the sake of argument, that a majority of the Louisiana Legislature voted for the Balanced Treatment Act partly in order to foster (rather than merely eliminate discrimination against) Christian fundamentalist beliefs, our cases establish that that alone would not suffice to invalidate the Act, so long as there was a genuine secular purpose as well. We have, moreover, no adequate basis for disbelieving the secular purpose set forth in the Act itself, or for concluding that it is a sham enacted to conceal the legislators' violation of their oaths of office. . . .

I have to this point assumed the validity of the *Lemon* "purpose" test. . . . In the past we have attempted to justify our embarrassing Establishment Clause jurisprudence on the ground that it "sacrifices clarity and predictability for flexibility." . . . I think it is time that we sacrifice some "flexibility" for "clarity and predictability." Abandoning *Lemon's* purpose test—a test which exacerbates the tension between the Free Exercise and Establishment Clauses, has no basis in the language or history of the amendment, and, as today's decision shows, has wonderfully flexible consequences—would be a good place to start.

EMPLOYMENT DIVISION, OREGON DEPARTMENT OF HUMAN RESOURCES V. SMITH (1990)

Beginning with Sherbert v. Verner *in 1963 (see above), the Court consistently held that under the protection afforded free exercise of religion by the First Amendment, states had to make reasonable accommodations to the religious practices of their citizens. In most instances the laws involved were general in their application, such as induction into military service or compulsory school attendance. These laws were also civil in nature. The case profiled here originated when Alfred Smith and Galen Black were fired from their jobs because they had participated in a peyote ceremony of the Native American Church, and were then turned down for unemployment insurance. They appealed the decision based on* Sherbert's *rule that unemployment insurance could not be conditioned on a person's religiously required conduct. The difference was that in the cases following* Sherbert, *none of the religious activity had been in conflict with criminal laws. But in Oregon the ingestion of peyote, even for religious purposes, was illegal. The response to this case, in which the Court held that religious activity could not trump general criminal laws, led to the passage of the Religious Freedom Restoration Act. See Michael McConnell, "Free Exercise Revisionism and the Smith Decision,"* University of Chicago Law

Review *57: 1109 (1990); Garrett Epps,* To an Unknown God: Religious Freedom on Trial *(New York: St. Martin's Press, 2001); and Carolyn N. Long,* Religious Freedom and Indian Rights: The Case of *Oregon v. Smith (Lawrence: University Press of Kansas, 2000).*

Justice Scalia delivered the opinion of the Court.

Oregon law prohibits the knowing or intentional possession of a "controlled substance" unless the substance has been prescribed by a medical practitioner. The law defines "controlled substance" as [including] the drug peyote, a hallucinogen derived from the plant *Lophophorawilliamsii Lemaire.*

Respondents Alfred Smith and Galen Black were fired from their jobs with a private drug rehabilitation organization because they ingested peyote for sacramental purposes at a ceremony of the Native American Church, of which both are members. When respondents applied to petitioner Employment Division for unemployment compensation, they were determined to be ineligible for benefits because they had been discharged for work-related "misconduct."

[Respondents' claim for relief rests on] our decisions in *Sherbert v. Verner, Thomas v. Review Board, Indiana Employment Security Div.* (1981), . . . and *Hobbie v. Unemployment Appeals Commission of Florida,* in which we held that a State could not condition the availability of unemployment insurance on an individual's willingness to forgo conduct required by his religion. . . . However, the conduct at issue in those cases was not prohibited by law.

The free exercise of religion means, first and foremost, the right to believe and profess whatever religious doctrine one desires. Thus, the First Amendment obviously excludes all "governmental regulation of religious *beliefs* as such."

But the "exercise of religion" often involves not only belief and profession but the performance of (or abstention from) physical acts: assembling with others for a worship service, participating in the sacramental use of bread and wine, proselytizing, abstaining from certain foods or certain modes of transportation. It would be true, we think (though no case of ours has involved the point), that a state would be "prohibiting the free exercise [of religion]" if it sought to ban such acts or abstentions only when they are engaged in for religious reasons, or only because of the religious belief that they display. It would doubtless be unconstitutional, for example, to ban the casting of statues that are to be used for worship purposes, or to prohibit bowing down before a golden calf.

We have never held that an individual's religious beliefs excuse him from compliance with an otherwise valid law prohibiting conduct that the State is free to regulate. On the contrary, the record of more than a century of our free exercise jurisprudence contradicts that proposition. As described succinctly by Justice Frankfurter in *Minersville School Dist. Bd. of Educ. v. Gobitis:* "Conscientious scruples have not, in the course of the long struggle for religious toleration, relieved the individual from obedience to a general law not aimed at the promotion or restriction of religious beliefs. The mere possession of religious convictions which contradict the relevant concerns of a political society does not relieve the citizen from the discharge of political responsibilities." We first had occasion to assert that principle in *Reynolds v. United States,* where we rejected the claim that criminal laws against polygamy could not be constitutionally applied to those whose religion commanded the practice. "Laws," we said, "are made for the government of actions, and while they cannot interfere with mere religious belief and opinions, they may with practices. . . . Can a man excuse his practices to the contrary because of his religious belief? To permit this would be to make the professed doctrines of religious belief superior to the law of the land, and in effect to permit every citizen to become a law unto himself."

Our most recent decision involving a neutral, generally applicable regulatory law that compelled activity forbidden by an individual's religion was *United States v. Lee.* There, an Amish employer, on behalf of himself and his employees, sought exemption from collection and payment of Social Security taxes on the ground that the Amish faith prohibited participation in governmental support programs. We rejected the claim that an exemption was constitutionally required. There would be no way, we observed, to distinguish the Amish believer's objection to Social Security taxes from the religious objections that others might have to the collection or use of other taxes. . . .

Respondents argue that even though exemption from generally applicable criminal laws need not automatically be extended to religiously motivated actors, at least the claim for a religious exemption must be evaluated under the balancing test set forth in *Sherbert v. Verner.* Under the *Sherbert* test, governmental actions that substantially burden a religious practice must be justified by a compelling governmental interest. . . . In recent years we have abstained from applying the *Sherbert* test (outside the unemployment compensation field) at all.

Even if we were inclined to breathe into *Sherbert* some life beyond the unemployment compensation field, we would not apply it to require exemptions from a generally applicable criminal law.

[It is not] possible to limit the impact of respondents' proposal by requiring a "compelling state interest" only when the conduct prohibited is "central" to the individual's religion. It is no more appropriate for judges to determine the "centrality" of religious beliefs before applying a "compelling interest" test in the free exercise field, than it would be for them to determine the "importance" of ideas before applying the "compelling interest" test in the free speech field. . . . As we affirmed only last Term, "[i]t is not within the judicial ken to question the centrality of particular beliefs or practices to a faith, or the validity of particular litigants' interpretation of those creeds."

Because respondents' ingestion of peyote was prohibited under Oregon law, and because that prohibition is constitutional, Oregon may, consistent with the Free Exercise Clause, deny respondents unemployment compensation when their dismissal results from use of the drug. The decision of the Oregon Supreme Court is accordingly reversed.

Justice O'Connor, with whom Justice Brennan, Justice Marshall, and Justice Blackmun join, concurring in the judgments.

. . . Respondents invoke our traditional compelling interest test to argue that the Free Exercise Clause requires the State to grant them a limited exemption from its general criminal prohibition against the possession of peyote. The Court today, however, denies them even the opportunity to make that argument, concluding that "the sounder approach, and the approach in accord with the vast majority of our precedents, is to hold the [compelling interest] test inapplicable to" challenges to general criminal prohibitions.

In my view, however, the essence of a free exercise claim is relief from a burden imposed by government on religious practices or beliefs, whether the burden is imposed directly through laws that prohibit or compel specific religious practices, or indirectly through laws that, in effect, make abandonment of one's own religion or conformity to the religious beliefs of others the price of an equal place in the civil community. . . .

A State that makes criminal an individual's religiously motivated conduct burdens that individual's free exercise of religion in the severest manner possible, for it "results in the choice to the individual of either abandoning his religious principle or facing criminal prosecution."

Given the range of conduct that a State might legitimately make criminal, we cannot assume, merely because a law carries criminal sanctions and is generally applicable, that the First Amendment *never* requires the State to grant a limited exemption for religiously motivated conduct.

Moreover, we have not "rejected" or "declined to apply" the compelling interest test in our recent cases. Recent cases have instead affirmed that test as a fundamental part of our First Amendment doctrine. . . .

There is no dispute that Oregon's criminal prohibition of peyote places a severe burden on the ability of respondents to freely exercise their religion. Peyote is a sacrament of the Native American Church and is regarded as vital to respondents' ability to practice their religion. . . . Under Oregon law, as construed by that State's highest court, members of the Native American Church must choose between carrying out the ritual embodying their religious beliefs and avoidance of criminal prosecution. That choice is, in my view, more than sufficient to trigger First Amendment scrutiny. . . .

Thus, the critical question in this case is whether exempting respondents from the State's general criminal prohibition "will unduly interfere with fulfillment of the governmental interest." . . .

I believe that granting a selective exemption in this case would seriously impair Oregon's compelling interest in prohibiting possession of peyote by its citizens. Under such circumstances, the Free Exercise Clause does not require the State to accommodate respondents' religiously motivated conduct. . . .

Justice Blackmun, with whom Justice Brennan and Justice Marshall join, dissenting.

In weighing respondents' clear interest in the free exercise of their religion against Oregon's asserted interest in enforcing its drug laws, it is important to articulate in precise terms the state interest involved. It is not the State's broad interest in fighting the critical "war on drugs" that must be weighed against respondents' claim, but the State's narrow interest in refusing to make an exception for the religious, ceremonial use of peyote. . . .

The State's interest in enforcing its prohibition in order to be sufficiently compelling to outweigh a free exercise claim, cannot be merely abstract or symbolic. The State cannot plausibly assert that unbending application of a criminal prohibition is essential to fulfill any compelling interest, if it does not, in fact, attempt to enforce that prohibition. . . . Oregon has never sought to prosecute respondents, and does not claim that it has made significant enforcement efforts against other religious users of peyote. The State's asserted interest thus amounts only to the symbolic preservation of an unenforced prohibition. But a government interest in "symbolism, even symbolism for so worthy a cause as the abolition of unlawful drugs," cannot suffice to abrogate the constitutional rights of individuals.

Similarly, this Court's prior decisions have not allowed a government to rely on mere speculation about potential harms, but have demanded evidentiary support for a refusal to allow a religious exception. . . .

The State of Oregon cannot, consistently with the Free Exercise Clause, deny respondents unemployment benefits.

I dissent.

LEE V. WEISMAN (1992)

The appointment of conservative justices by Presidents Reagan and George Bush led many to hope that the liberal activist decisions of the Warren and Burger eras could be reversed. In this instance, conservatives hoped that the Court would abandon the proscription against school prayer first enunciated in Engel v. Vitale. *In Providence, Rhode Island, the Weisman family had complained when at a middle school graduation of one of their children there had been an official prayer. When another child, Deborah Weisman, was scheduled to graduate, the school invited a rabbi to deliver the prayers, and had furnished him with a list of guidelines in order to make the prayers as nonsectarian and inoffensive as possible. Deborah raised a challenge on the grounds that prayer at any school function involving a captive audience violated the Establishment Clause. Once again, the centrists on the Court dominated. See Jesse H. Choper, "The Unpredictability of the Supreme Court's Doctrine in Establishment Clause Cases,"* Wayne Law Review *43: 1439 (1997); and George W. Dent, Jr., "Of*

God and Caesar: The Free Exercise Rights of Public School Students," Case Western Reserve Law Review *43: 707 (1993).*
 Justice Kennedy delivered the opinion of the Court.

These dominant facts mark and control the confines of our decision: State officials direct the performance of a formal religious exercise at promotional and graduation ceremonies for secondary schools. Even for those students who object to the religious exercise, their attendance and participation in the state-sponsored religious activity are in a fair and real sense obligatory, though the school district does not require attendance as a condition for receipt of the diploma. . . . The controlling precedents as they relate to prayer and religious exercise in primary and secondary public schools compel the holding here that the policy of the city of Providence is an unconstitutional one. We can decide the case without reconsidering the general constitutional framework by which public schools' efforts to accommodate religion are measured. Thus we do not accept the invitation of petitioners and amicus the United States to reconsider our decision in *Lemon v. Kurtzman.* The government involvement with religious activity in this case is pervasive, to the point of creating a state-sponsored and state-directed religious exercise in a public school. Conducting this formal religious observance conflicts with settled rules pertaining to prayer exercises for students, and that suffices to determine the question before us.

Petitioners argue, and we find nothing in the case to refute it, that the directions for the content of the prayers were a good-faith attempt by the school to ensure that the sectarianism which is so often the flashpoint for religious animosity be removed from the graduation ceremony. . . . The question is not the good faith of the school in attempting to make the prayer acceptable to most persons, but the legitimacy of its undertaking that enterprise at all when the object is to produce a prayer to be used in a formal religious exercise which students, for all practical purposes, are obliged to attend. We are asked to recognize the existence of a practice of nonsectarian prayer, prayer within the embrace of what is known as the Judeo-Christian tradition, prayer which is more acceptable than one which, for example, makes explicit references to the God of Israel, or to Jesus Christ, or to a patron saint.... But though the First Amendment does not allow the government to stifle prayers which aspire to [a civic religion], neither does it permit the government to undertake that task for itself.

The First Amendment's Religion Clauses mean that religious beliefs and religious expression are too precious to be either proscribed or prescribed by the State. The design of the Constitution is that preservation and transmission of religious beliefs and worship is a responsibility and a choice committed to the private sphere, which itself is promised freedom to pursue that mission.... The suggestion that government may establish an official or civic religion as a means of avoiding the establishment of a religion with more specific creeds strikes us as a contradiction that cannot be accepted.

The degree of school involvement here made it clear that the graduation prayers bore the imprint of the State and thus put school-age children who objected in an untenable position.... The lessons of the First Amendment are as urgent in the modern world as in the 18th century when it was written. One timeless lesson is that if citizens are subjected to state-sponsored religious exercises, the State disavows its own duty to guard and respect that sphere of inviolable conscience and belief which is the mark of a free people. To compromise that principle today would be to deny our own tradition and forfeit our standing to urge others to secure the protections of that tradition for themselves. As we have observed before, there are heightened concerns with protecting freedom of conscience from subtle coercive pressure in the elementary and secondary public schools. Our decisions in *Engel* and *Abington* recognize, among other things, that prayer exercises in public schools carry a particular risk of indirect coercion.

The concern may not be limited to the context of schools, but it is most pronounced there. What to most believers may seem nothing more than a reasonable request that the nonbeliever respect their religious practices, in a school context may appear to the nonbeliever or dissenter to be an attempt to employ the machinery of the State to enforce a religious orthodoxy.

We need not look beyond the circumstances of this case to see the phenomenon at work. The undeniable fact is that the school district's supervision and control of a high school graduation ceremony places public pressure, as well as peer pressure, on attending students to stand as a group or, at least, maintain respectful silence during the invocation and benediction. This pressure, though subtle and indirect, can be as real as any overt compulsion. Of course, in our culture standing or remaining silent can signify adherence to a view or simple respect for the views of others. And no doubt some persons who have no desire to join a prayer have little objection to standing as a sign of respect for those who do. But for the dissenter of high school age, who has a reasonable perception that she is being forced by the State to pray in a manner her conscience will not allow, the injury is no less real. There can be no doubt that for many, if not most, of the students at the graduation, the act of standing or remaining silent was an expression of participation in the rabbi's prayer. That was the very point of the religious exercise. It is of little comfort to a dissenter, then, to be told that for her the act of standing or remaining in silence signifies mere respect, rather than participation. What matters is that, given our social conventions, a reasonable dissenter in this milieu could believe that the group exercise signified her own participation or approval of it.

Finding no violation under these circumstances would place objectors in the dilemma of participating, with all that implies, or protesting. We do not address whether that choice is acceptable if the affected citizens are mature adults, but we think the State may not, consistent with the Establishment Clause, place primary and secondary school children in this position. Research in psychology supports the common assumption that adolescents are often susceptible to pressure from their peers towards conformity, and that the influence is strongest in matters of social convention. To recognize that the choice imposed by the State constitutes an unacceptable constraint only acknowledges that the government may no more use social pressure to enforce orthodoxy than it may use more direct means.

The injury caused by the government's action, and the reason why Daniel and Deborah Weisman object to it, is that the State, in a school setting, in effect required participation in a religious exercise. It is, we concede, a brief exercise during which the individual can concentrate on joining its message, meditate on her own religion, or let her mind wander. But the embarrassment and the intrusion of the religious exercise cannot be refuted by arguing that these prayers, and similar ones to be said in the future, are of a *de minimis* character. To do so would be an affront to the rabbi who offered them and to all those for whom the prayers were an essential and profound recognition of divine authority. And for the same reason, we think that the intrusion is greater than the two minutes or so of time consumed for prayers like these. Assuming, as we must, that the prayers were offensive to the student and the parent who now object, the intrusion was both real and, in the context of a secondary school, a violation of the objectors' rights. That the intrusion was in the course of promulgating religion that sought to be civic or nonsectarian rather than pertaining to one sect does not lessen the offense or isolation to the objectors. At best it narrows their number, at worst increases their sense of isolation and affront.

There was a stipulation in the District Court that attendance at graduation and promotional ceremonies is voluntary. Petitioners and the United States, as amicus, made this a center point of the case, arguing that the option of not attending the graduation excuses any inducement or coercion in the ceremony itself. The argument lacks all persuasion. Law reaches past formalism. And to say a teenage student has a real choice not to attend her high school graduation is formalistic in the extreme. True, Deborah could elect not to attend commencement without renouncing her diploma; but we shall not allow the case to turn on this point. Everyone knows that in our society and in our culture high school graduation is one of life's most significant occasions. A school rule which excuses attendance is beside the point. Attendance may not be required by official decree, yet it is apparent that a student is not free to absent herself from the graduation exercise in any real sense of the term "voluntary," for absence would require forfeiture of those intangible benefits which have motivated the student through youth and all her high school years. Graduation is a time for family and those closest to the student to celebrate success and express mutual wishes of gratitude and respect, all to the end of impressing upon the young person the role that it is his or her right and duty to assume in the community and all of its diverse parts.

The Government's argument gives insufficient recognition to the real conflict of conscience faced by the young student. The essence of the Government's position is that with regard to a civic, social occasion of this importance it is the objector, not the majority, who must take unilateral and private action to avoid compromising religious scruples, hereby electing to miss the graduation exercise. This turns conventional First Amendment analysis on its head. It is a tenet of the First Amendment that the State cannot require one of its citizens to forfeit his or her rights and benefits as the price of resisting conformance to state-sponsored religious practice. To say that a student must remain apart from the ceremony at the opening invocation and closing benediction is to risk compelling conformity in an environment analogous to the classroom setting, where we have said the risk of compulsion is especially high. Just as in *Engel* and *Schempp,* where we found that provisions within the challenged legislation permitting a student to be voluntarily excused from attendance or participation in the daily prayers did not shield those practices from invalidation, the fact that attendance at the graduation ceremonies is voluntary in a legal sense does not save the religious exercise. . . .

We do not hold that every state action implicating religion is invalid if one or a few citizens find it offensive. People may take offense at all manner of religious as well as nonreligious messages, but offense alone does not in every case show a violation. We know too that sometimes to endure social isolation or even anger may be the price of conscience or nonconformity. But, by any reading of our cases, the conformity required of the student in this case was too high an exaction to withstand the test of the Establishment Clause. The prayer exercises in this case are especially improper because the State has in every practical sense compelled attendance and participation in an explicit religious exercise at an event of singular importance to every student, one the objecting student had no real alternative to avoid. Our jurisprudence in this area is of necessity one of line-drawing, of determining at what point a dissenter's rights of religious freedom are infringed by the State. . . .

The sole question presented is whether a religious exercise may be conducted at a graduation ceremony in circumstances where, as we have found, young graduates who object are induced to conform. No holding by this Court suggests that a school can persuade or compel a student to participate in a religious exercise. That is being done here, and it is forbidden by the Establishment Clause of the First Amendment.

Justice Blackmun, with whom Justice Stevens and Justice O'Connor join, concurring.

I join the Court's opinion today because I find nothing in it inconsistent with the essential precepts of the Establishment Clause developed in our precedents. The Court holds that the graduation prayer is unconstitutional because the State "in effect required participation in a religious exercise." Although our precedents make clear that proof of government coercion is not necessary to prove an Establishment Clause violation, it is sufficient. Government pressure to participate in a religious activity is an obvious indication that the government is endorsing or promoting religion.

But it is not enough that the government restrain from compelling religious practices: It must not engage in them either. The Court repeatedly has recognized that a violation of the Establishment Clause is not predicated on coercion. The Establishment Clause proscribes public schools from "conveying or attempting to convey a message that religion or a particular religious belief is favored or preferred," even if the schools do not actually "impose pressure upon a student to participate in a religious activity." There is no doubt that attempts to aid religion through government coercion jeopardize freedom of conscience. Even subtle pressure diminishes the right of each individual to choose voluntarily what to believe. . . . Our decisions have gone beyond prohibiting coercion, however, because the Court has recognized that "the fullest possible scope of religious liberty" entails more than freedom from coercion. The Establishment Clause protects religious liberty on a grand scale; it is a social compact that guarantees for generations a democracy and a strong religious community— both essential to safeguarding religious liberty. For the reasons we have stated, the judgment of the Court of Appeals is Affirmed.

Justice Souter, with whom Justice Stevens and Justice O'Connor joined, concurred separately, exploring the larger implications of coercion in the school context.

Justice Scalia, with whom the Chief Justice, Justice White, and Justice Thomas join, dissenting.

In holding that the Establishment Clause prohibits invocations and benedictions at public school graduation ceremonies, the Court—with nary a mention that it is doing so—lays waste a tradition that is as old as public school graduation ceremonies themselves, and that is a component of an even more longstanding

American tradition of nonsectarian prayer to God at public celebrations generally. As its instrument of destruction, the bulldozer of its social engineering, the Court invents a boundless, and boundlessly manipulable, test of psychological coercion, which promises to do for the Establishment Clause what the Durham rule did for the insanity defense. Today's opinion shows more forcefully than volumes of argumentation why our Nation's protection, that fortress which is our Constitution, cannot possibly rest upon the changeable philosophical predilections of the Justices of this Court, but must have deep foundations in the historic practices of our people.

From our Nation's origin, prayer has been a prominent part of governmental ceremonies and proclamations. The Declaration of Independence, the document marking our birth as a separate people, "appealed to the Supreme Judge of the world for the rectitude of our intentions" and avowed "a firm reliance on the protection of divine Providence." In his first inaugural address, after swearing his oath of office on a Bible, George Washington deliberately made a prayer a part of his first official act as President. . . . Such supplications have been a characteristic feature of inaugural addresses ever since. . . .

The Court's notion that a student who simply sits in "respectful silence" during the invocation and benediction (when all others are standing) has somehow joined—or would somehow be perceived as having joined—in the prayers is nothing short of ludicrous. We indeed live in a vulgar age. But surely "our social conventions," have not coarsened to the point that anyone who does not stand on his chair and shout obscenities can reasonably be deemed to have assented to everything said in his presence. . . . But let us assume the very worst, that the nonparticipating graduate is "subtly coerced" . . . to stand! Even that does not remotely establish a "participation" (or an "appearance of participation") in a religious exercise. . . .

The deeper flaw in the Court's opinion does not lie in its wrong answer to the question whether there was state-induced "peer-pressure" coercion; it lies, rather, in the Court's making violation of the Establishment Clause hinge on such a precious question. The coercion that was a hallmark of historical establishments of religion was coercion of religious orthodoxy and of financial support by force of law and threat of penalty. Typically, attendance at the state church was required; only clergy of the official church could lawfully perform sacraments; and dissenters, if tolerated, faced an array of civil disabilities. . . . Thus, while I have no quarrel with the Court's general proposition that the Establishment Clause "guarantees that government may not coerce anyone to support or participate in religion or its exercise," I see no warrant for expanding the concept of coercion beyond acts backed by threat of penalty—a brand of coercion that, happily, is readily discernible to those of us who have made a career of reading the disciples of Blackstone rather than of Freud. The Framers were indeed opposed to coercion of religious worship by the National Government; but, as their own sponsorship of nonsectarian prayer in public events demonstrates, they understood that "speech is not coercive; the listener may do as he likes." . . .

Our Religion Clause jurisprudence has become bedeviled (so to speak) by reliance on formulaic abstractions that are not derived from, but positively conflict with, our long-accepted constitutional traditions. Foremost among these has been the so-called *Lemon* test. The Court today demonstrates the irrelevance of *Lemon* by essentially ignoring it, and the interment of that case may be the one happy byproduct of the Court's otherwise lamentable decision. Unfortunately, however, the Court has replaced *Lemon* with its psycho-coercion test, which suffers the double disability of having no roots whatever in our people's historic practice, and being as infinitely expandable as the reasons for psychotherapy itself.

Another happy aspect of the case is that it is only a jurisprudential disaster and not a practical one. Given the odd basis for
the Court's decision, invocations and benedictions will be able to
be given at public school graduations next June, as they have for
the past century and a half, so long as school authorities make
clear that anyone who abstains from screaming in protest does
not necessarily participate in the prayers. All that is seemingly
needed is an announcement, or perhaps a written insertion at the
beginning of the graduation program, to the effect that, while all
are asked to rise for the invocation and benediction, none is compelled to join in them, nor will be assumed, by rising, to have
done so. That obvious fact recited, the graduates and their parents may proceed to thank God, as Americans have always done,
for the blessings He has generously bestowed on them and on
their country. . . .

RELIGIOUS FREEDOM RESTORATION ACT (1993)

After the Court denied a rehearing in Oregon v. Smith, *a broad
coalition of religious groups began working for legislation to force
the Court to return to the broader view of free exercise contained
in* Sherbert v. Verner *and* Wisconsin v. Yoder. *The coalition
attracted broad bipartisan support, but the effort almost bogged
down in details as conservatives wanted provisions that liberals
found crossed the line between church and state, such as restrictions
on abortion. In the end, broad and in large measure vague language was adopted. A popular law, the Religious Freedom
Restoration Act (RFRA) purported to bind government at all levels—federal, state, and local—as well as all branches of government—executive, legislative, and judicial. But where did Congress
get the authority to pass RFRA? A legislature can always override
a court's interpretation of a statute by repassing it with more
explicit language; but what provision of the Constitution allowed
Congress to override the high court's interpretation of the First*

Amendment? Unlike the Reconstruction Amendments with their enforcement clauses, the first eight amendments bind Congress and do not give them any enforcement authority. Because the RFRA presented a clear challenge to the Court's authority, no one doubted that a test case would soon be heard. See Douglas Laycock, "The Religious Freedom Restoration Act," Brigham Young University Law Review *(1993) 221; Scott Idleman, "The Religious Freedom Restoration Act: Pushing the Limits of Legislative Power,"* Texas Law Review *73: 247 (1994); and Christopher L. Eisgruber and Lawrence G. Sager, "Why the Religious Freedom Restoration Act Is Unconstitutional,"* N.Y.U. Law Review *69: 437 (1994).*

§2000bb. Congressional findings and declaration of purposes

(b) Findings

a. the framers of the Constitution, recognizing free exercise of religion as an unalienable right, secured its protection in the First Amendment to the Constitution;

b. laws "neutral" toward religion may burden religious exercise as surely as laws intended to interfere with religious exercise;

c. governments should not substantially burden religious exercise without compelling justification;

d. in *Employment Division v. Smith,* 494 U.S. 872 (1990), the Supreme Court virtually eliminated the requirement that the government justify burdens on religious exercise imposed by laws neutral toward religion; and

e. the compelling interest test as set forth in prior Federal court rulings is a workable test for striking sensible balances between religious liberty and competing prior governmental interests.

(c) Purposes

a. to restore the compelling interest test as set forth in *Sherbert v. Verner,* 374 U.S. 398 (1963), and *Wisconsin v. Yoder,* 406 U.S. 205 (1972), and to guarantee its application in all cases where free exercise of religion is substantially burdened; and

b. to provide a claim or defense to persons whose religious exercise is substantially burdened by government.

§2000bb-1. Free exercise of religion protected

(b) In General

Government shall not substantially burden a person's exercise of religion even if the burden results from a rule of general applicability, except as provided in subsection (b) of this section.

(c) Exception

Government may substantially burden a person's exercise of religion only if it demonstrates that application of the burden to the person—

a. is in furtherance of a compelling governmental interest; and

b. is the least restrictive means of furthering that compelling governmental interest.

(d) Judicial relief

A person whose religious exercise has been burdened in violation of this section may assert that violation as a claim or defense in a judicial proceeding and obtain appropriate relief against a government. Standing to assert a claim or defense under this section shall be governed by the general rules of standing under Article III of the Constitution.

§2000bb-2. Definitions

As used in this chapter—

(b) the term "government" includes a branch, department, agency, instrumentality, and official (or other person acting under color of law) of the United States, a State, or a subdivision of a State;

(c) the term "State" includes the District of Columbia, the Commonwealth of Puerto Rico, and each territory and possession of the United States;

(d) the term "demonstrates" means meets the burdens of going forward with the evidence and of persuasion; and

(e) the term "exercise of religion" means the exercise of religion under the First Amendment to the Constitution.

§2000bb-3. Applicability

(a) In General

This chapter applies to all Federal and State law, and the implementation of that law, whether statutory or otherwise, and whether adopted before or after November 16, 1993.

(b) Rule of construction

Federal statutory law adopted after November 16, 1993 is subject to this chapter unless such law explicitly excludes such application by reference to this chapter.

(c) Religious belief unaffected

Nothing in this chapter shall be construed to authorize any government to burden any religious belief.

§2000bb-4. Establishment clause unaffected

Nothing in this chapter shall be construed to affect, interpret, or in any way address that portion of the First Amendment prohibiting laws respecting the establishment of religion (referred to in this section as the "Establishment Clause"). Granting government funding, benefits, or exemption, to the extent permissible under the Establishment Clause, shall not constitute a violation of this chapter. As used in this section, the term "granting," used with respect to government funding, benefits, or exemptions, does not include the denial of government funding, benefits, or exemption.

ROSENBERGER V. RECTOR AND VISITORS OF THE UNIVERSITY OF VIRGINIA (1995)

Wide Awake Publications, a student-sponsored Christian evangelical magazine, sought funding from the University of Virginia, claiming that as a student organization it should not be denied funds simply because it focused on religious rather than secular matters. The university declined, arguing that to support a seemingly proselytizing club would violate the Establishment Clause. The university's case had a number of weak spots, including the fact that it routinely funded other clearly religious groups, such as the Jewish Hillel Society and a Muslim student organization. By a

5–4 vote, the Court held that the university could not discriminate against Wide Awake. Justice Kennedy's opinion is a mixture of speech and establishment jurisprudence, since denying funds to a student publication because of the content violated the Speech Clause. The dissenters, led by Justice Souter, denied this interpretation, and rallied once again to the notion of a wall of separation. See Casey M. Nault, "Bridging the Separation of Church and State: How Rosenberger Threatens Religious Liberty," Southern California Law Review *70: 1049 (1997); Kent Greenawalt, "Viewpoints from Olympus,"* Columbia Law Review *96: 697 (1996); and A. Louise Oliver, "Tearing Down the Wall . . . ,"* Harvard Journal of Law and Public Policy *19: 587 (1996).*

Justice Kennedy delivered the opinion of the Court.

The University of Virginia, an instrumentality of the Commonwealth for which it is named and thus bound by the First and Fourteenth Amendments, authorizes the payment of outside contractors for the printing costs of a variety of student publications. It withheld any authorization for payments on behalf of petitioners for the sole reason that their student paper "primarily promotes or manifests a particular belief in or about a deity or an ultimate reality." That the paper did promote or manifest views within the defined exclusion seems plain enough. The challenge is to the University's regulation and its denial of authorization, the case raising issues under the Speech and Establishment Clauses of the First Amendment.

The public corporation we refer to as the "University" is denominated by state law as "the Rector and Visitors of the University of Virginia," and it is responsible for governing the school. Founded by Thomas Jefferson in 1819, and ranked by him, together with the authorship of the Declaration of Independence and of the Virginia Act for Religious Freedom, as one of his proudest achievements, the University is among the Nation's oldest and most respected seats of higher learning. It has more than 11,000 undergraduate students, and 6,000 graduate and professional students. An understanding of the case requires a somewhat detailed description of the program the University created to support extracurricular student activities on its campus.

Before a student group is eligible to submit bills from its outside contractors for payment by the fund described below, it must become a "Contracted Independent Organization" (CIO). CIO status is available to any group the majority of whose members are students, whose managing officers are full-time students, and that complies with certain procedural requirements. . . .

All CIOs may exist and operate at the University, but some are also entitled to apply for funds from the Student Activities Fund (SAF). . . . The SAF receives its money from a mandatory fee of $14 per semester assessed to each full-time student. The Student Council, elected by the students, has the initial authority to disburse the funds, but its actions are subject to review by a faculty body chaired by a designee of the Vice President for Student Affairs.

Some, but not all, CIOs may submit disbursement requests to the SAF. The Guidelines recognize 11 categories of student groups that may seek payment to third-party contractors because they "are related to the educational purpose of the University of Virginia." One of these is "student news, information, opinion, entertainment, or academic communications media groups." The Guidelines also specify, however, that the costs of certain activities of CIOs that are otherwise eligible for funding will not be reimbursed by the SAF. The student activities which are excluded from SAF support are religious activities, philanthropic contributions and activities, political activities, activities that would jeopardize the University's tax exempt status, those which involve payment of honoraria or similar fees, or social entertainment or related expenses. The prohibition on "political activities" is defined so that it is limited to electioneering and lobbying. The Guidelines provide that "these restrictions on funding political activities are not intended to preclude funding of any otherwise eligible student organization which . . . espouses particular positions or ideological viewpoints, including those that may be unpopular or are not generally accepted." A "religious activity," by contrast, is defined as any activity that "primarily promotes or manifests a particular belief in or about a deity or an ultimate reality." . . .

Petitioners' organization, Wide Awake Publications (WAP), qualified as a CIO. Formed by petitioner Ronald Rosenberger and other undergraduates in 1990, WAP was established "to publish a magazine of philosophical and religious expression," "to facilitate discussion which fosters an atmosphere of sensitivity to and tolerance of Christian viewpoints," and "to provide a unifying focus for Christians of multicultural backgrounds." WAP publishes *Wide Awake: A Christian Perspective at the University of Virginia.* The paper's Christian viewpoint was evident from the first issue, in which its editors wrote that the journal "offers a Christian perspective on both personal and community issues, especially those relevant to college students at the University of Virginia." The editors committed the paper to a two-fold mission: "to challenge Christians to live, in word and deed, according to the faith they proclaim and to encourage students to consider what a personal relationship with Jesus Christ means." The first issue had articles about racism, crisis pregnancy, stress, prayer, C. S. Lewis' ideas about evil and free will, and reviews of religious music. In the next two issues, *Wide Awake* featured stories about homosexuality, Christian missionary work, and eating disorders, as well as music reviews and interviews with University professors. Each page of *Wide Awake,* and the end of each article or review, is marked by a cross. The advertisements carried in *Wide Awake* also reveal the Christian perspective of the journal. For the most part, the advertisers are churches, centers for Christian study, or Christian bookstores. By June 1992, WAP had distributed about 5,000 copies of *Wide Awake* to University students, free of charge.

WAP had acquired CIO status soon after it was organized. This is an important consideration in this case, for had it been a "religious organization," WAP would not have been accorded CIO status. As defined by the Guidelines, a "religious organization" is "an organization whose purpose is to practice a devotion to an acknowledged ultimate reality or deity." At no stage in this controversy has the University contended that WAP is such an organization.

A few months after being given CIO status, WAP requested the SAF to pay its printer $5,862 for the costs of printing its newspaper. The Appropriations Committee of the Student Council denied WAP's request on the ground that *Wide Awake* was a "religious activity" within the meaning of the Guidelines, i.e., that the newspaper "promoted or manifested a particular belief in or about a deity or an ultimate reality." It made its determination after examining the first issue. WAP appealed the denial to the full Student Council, contending that WAP met all the applicable Guidelines and that denial of SAF support on the basis of the magazine's religious perspective violated the Constitution. The appeal was denied without further comment, and WAP appealed to the next level, the Student Activities Committee. In a letter signed by the Dean of Students, the committee sustained the denial of funding. . . .

It is axiomatic that the government may not regulate speech based on its substantive content or the message it conveys. Other principles follow from this precept. In the realm of private speech or expression, government regulation may not favor one speaker over another. Discrimination against speech because of its message is presumed to be unconstitutional. These rules informed our determination that the government offends the First Amendment when it imposes financial burdens on certain speakers based on the content of their expression. When the government targets not subject matter but particular views taken by speakers on a subject, the violation of the First Amendment is all the more blatant. Viewpoint discrimination is thus an egregious form of content discrimination. The government must abstain from regulating speech when the specific motivating ideology or the opinion or perspective of the speaker is the rationale for the restriction. . . .

The University does acknowledge (as it must in light of our precedents) that "ideologically driven attempts to suppress a particular point of view are presumptively unconstitutional in funding, as in other contexts," but insists that this case does not present that issue because the Guidelines draw lines based on content, not viewpoint. As we have noted, discrimination against one set of views or ideas is but a subset or particular instance of the more general phenomenon of content discrimination. And, it must be acknowledged, the distinction is not a precise one. It is, in a sense, something of an understatement to speak of religious thought and discussion as just a viewpoint, as distinct from a comprehensive body of thought. The nature of our origins and destiny and their dependence upon the existence of a divine being have been subjects of philosophic inquiry throughout human history. We conclude, nonetheless, that here, as in *Lamb's Chapel,* viewpoint discrimination is the proper way to interpret the University's objections to *Wide Awake.* By the very terms of the SAF prohibition, the University does not exclude religion as a subject matter but selects for disfavored treatment those student journalistic efforts with religious editorial viewpoints. Religion may be a vast area of inquiry, but it also provides, as it did here, a specific premise, a perspective, a standpoint from which a variety of subjects may be discussed and considered. The prohibited perspective, not the general subject matter, resulted in the refusal to make third-party payments, for the subjects discussed were otherwise within the approved category of publications. . . .

The University tries to escape the consequences of our [prior precedents] by urging that this case involves the provision of funds rather than access to facilities. The University begins with the unremarkable proposition that the State must have substantial discretion in determining how to allocate scarce resources to accomplish its educational mission. Citing our decisions, the University argues that content-based funding decisions are both inevitable and lawful. . . .

It does not follow, however, . . . that viewpoint-based restrictions are proper when the University does not itself speak or subsidize transmittal of a message it favors but instead expends funds to encourage a diversity of views from private speakers. A holding that the University may not discriminate based on the viewpoint of private persons whose speech it facilitates does not restrict the University's own speech, which is controlled by different principles. . . .

Vital First Amendment speech principles are at stake here. The first danger to liberty lies in granting the State the power to examine publications to determine whether or not they are based on some ultimate idea and if so for the State to classify them. The second, and corollary, danger is to speech from the chilling of individual thought and expression. That danger is especially real in the University setting, where the State acts against a background and tradition of thought and experiment that is at the center of our intellectual and philosophic tradition. . . . For the University, by regulation, to cast disapproval on particular viewpoints of its students risks the suppression of free speech and creative inquiry in one of the vital centers for the nation's intellectual life, its college and university campuses. . . .

The prohibition on funding on behalf of publications that "primarily promote or manifest a particular belief in or about a deity or an ultimate reality," in its ordinary and commonsense meaning, has a vast potential reach. The term "promote" as used here would comprehend any writing advocating a philosophic position that rests upon a belief in a deity or ultimate reality. And the term "manifests" would bring within the scope of the prohibition any writing that is explicable as resting upon a premise which presupposes the existence of a deity or ultimate reality. . . .

Based on the principles we have discussed, we hold that the regulation invoked to deny SAF support, both in its terms and in its application to these petitioners, is a denial of their right of free speech guaranteed by the First Amendment. It remains to be considered whether the violation following from the University's action is excused by the necessity of complying with the Constitution's prohibition against state establishment of religion. We turn to that question.

... A central lesson of our decisions is that a significant factor in upholding governmental programs in the face of Establishment Clause attack is their neutrality towards religion. We have decided a series of cases addressing the receipt of government benefits where religion or religious views are implicated in some degree.... We have held that the guarantee of neutrality is respected, not offended, when the government, following neutral criteria and evenhanded policies, extends benefits to recipients whose ideologies and viewpoints, including religious ones, are broad and diverse. More than once have we rejected the position that the Establishment Clause even justifies, much less requires, a refusal to extend free speech rights to religious speakers who participate in broad-reaching government programs neutral in design.

The governmental program here is neutral toward religion. There is no suggestion that the University created it to advance religion or adopted some ingenious device with the purpose of aiding a religious cause. The object of the SAF is to open a forum for speech and to support various student enterprises, including the publication of newspapers, in recognition of the diversity and creativity of student life. The University's SAF Guidelines have a separate classification for, and do not make third-party payments on behalf of, "religious organizations," which are those "whose purpose is to practice a devotion to an acknowledged ultimate reality or deity." The category of support here is for "student news, information, opinion, entertainment, or academic communications media groups," of which Wide Awake was 1 of 15 in the 1990 school year. WAP did not seek a subsidy because of its Christian editorial viewpoint; it sought funding as a student journal, which it was.

The neutrality of the program distinguishes the student fees from a tax levied for the direct support of a church or group of churches. A tax of that sort, of course, would run contrary to Establishment Clause concerns dating from the earliest days of the Republic. The apprehensions of our predecessors involved the levying of taxes upon the public for the sole and exclusive purpose of establishing and supporting specific sects. The exaction here, by contrast, is a student activity fee designed to reflect the reality that student life in its many dimensions includes the necessity of wide-ranging speech and inquiry and that student expression is an integral part of the University's educational mission. The fee is mandatory, and we do not have before us the question whether an objecting student has the First Amendment right to demand a pro rata return to the extent the fee is expended for speech to which he or she does not subscribe. We must treat it, then, as an exaction upon the students. But the $14 paid each semester by the students is not a general tax designed to raise revenue for the University. The SAF cannot be used for unlimited purposes, much less the illegitimate purpose of supporting one religion. Much like the arrangement in *Widmar,* the money goes to a special fund from which any group of students with CIO status can draw for purposes consistent with the University's educational mission; and to the extent the student is interested in speech, withdrawal is permitted to cover the whole spectrum of speech, whether it manifests a religious view, an antireligious view, or neither. Our decision, then, cannot be read as addressing an expenditure from a general tax fund. Here, the disbursements from the fund go to private contractors for the cost of printing that which is protected under the Speech Clause of the First Amendment. This is a far cry from a general public assessment designed and effected to provide financial support for a church. . . .

It does not violate the Establishment Clause for a public university to grant access to its facilities on a religion-neutral basis to a wide spectrum of student groups, including groups which use meeting rooms for sectarian activities, accompanied by some devotional exercises. This is so even where the upkeep, maintenance, and repair of the facilities attributed to those uses is paid from a student activities fund to which students are required to contribute. The government usually acts by spending money. . . .

By paying outside printers, the University in fact attains a further degree of separation from the student publication, for it avoids the duties of supervision, escapes the costs of upkeep, repair, and replacement attributable to student use, and has a clear record of costs. . . .

To obey the Establishment Clause, it was not necessary for the University to deny eligibility to student publications because of their viewpoint. The neutrality commanded of the State by the separate Clauses of the First Amendment was compromised by the University's course of action. The viewpoint discrimination inherent in the University's regulation required public officials to scan and interpret student publications to discern their underlying philosophic assumptions respecting religious theory and belief. That course of action was a denial of the right of free speech and would risk fostering a pervasive bias or hostility to religion, which could undermine the very neutrality the Establishment Clause requires. There is no Establishment Clause violation in the University's honoring its duties under the Free Speech Clause.

The judgment of the Court of Appeals must be, and is, reversed.

It is so ordered.

Justice Souter, with whom Justice Stevens, Justice Ginsburg and Justice Breyer join, dissenting.

The Court today, for the first time, approves direct funding of core religious activities by an arm of the State. It does so, however, only after erroneous treatment of some familiar principles of law implementing the First Amendment's Establishment and Speech Clauses, and by viewing the very funds in question as beyond the reach of the Establishment Clause's funding restrictions as such. Because there is no warrant for distinguishing among public funding sources for purposes of applying the First Amendment's prohibition of religious establishment, I would hold that the University's refusal to support petitioners' religious activities is compelled by the Establishment Clause. I would therefore affirm.

The central question in this case is whether a grant from the Student Activities Fund to pay *Wide Awake*'s printing expenses would violate the Establishment Clause. Although the Court does not dwell on the details of *Wide Awake*'s message, it recognizes something sufficiently religious in the publication to demand Establishment Clause scrutiny. Although the Court places great stress on the eligibility of secular as well as religious activities for grants from the Student Activities Fund, it recognizes that such evenhanded availability is not by itself enough to satisfy constitutional requirements for any aid scheme that results in a benefit to religion. Something more is necessary to justify any religious aid. Some members of the Court, at least, may think the funding permissible on a view that it is indirect, since the money goes to *Wide Awake*'s printer, not through *Wide Awake*'s own checking account. The Court's principal reliance, however, is on an argument that providing religion with economically valuable services is permissible on the theory that services are economically indistinguishable from religious access to governmental speech forums, which sometimes is permissible. But this reasoning would commit the Court to approving direct religious aid beyond anything justifiable for the sake of access to speaking forums. The Court implicitly recognizes this in its further attempt to circumvent the clear bar to direct governmental aid to religion. Different members of the Court seek to avoid this bar in different ways. The opinion of the Court makes the novel assumption that only direct aid financed with tax revenue is barred, and draws the erroneous conclusion that the involuntary Student Activities Fee is not a tax. . . .

CITY OF BOERNE V. FLORES (1997)

The Religious Freedom Restoration Act (RFRA; see above) not only attempted to reverse specific decisions of the Court. Congress declared that the Court had decided wrongly in Oregon v. Smith *and other cases, and set out a particular interpretation of the First Amendment for the Court to follow. Such a move, which trenched on the Court's authority to interpret the Constitution, appalled both conservatives and moderates on the bench, and it would be only a matter of time before the Court took a case testing the validity of the RFRA. In* Boerne v. Flores, *the Court chose a lower court decision that not only exposed the weaknesses of the RFRA but allowed the Court to lecture Congress on separation of powers and, in effect, warn them not to commit such a silliness again. The basic question that had existed when the RFRA passed Congress by overwhelming majorities—What source of authority did Congress have to pass such a rule?—was answered by the Court very simply: Congress had no such authority. See Gary S. Gildin, "A Blessing in Disguise . . . ,"* Harvard Journal of Law and Public Policy *23: 411 (2000); Douglas Laycock, "Federalism as a Structural Threat to Liberty,"* Harvard Journal of Law and Public Policy *22: 67 (1998); and Ronald Rotunda, "The Powers of Congress under Section Five of the Fourteenth Amendment after City of Boerne v. Flores,"* Indiana Law Review *32: 163 (1998).*

Justice Kennedy delivered the opinion of the Court.

A decision by local zoning authorities to deny a church a building permit was challenged under the Religious Freedom Restoration Act of 1993 (RFRA). The case calls into question the authority of Congress to enact RFRA. We conclude the statute exceeds Congress' power.

Situated on a hill in the city of Boerne, Texas, some 28 miles northwest of San Antonio, is St. Peter Catholic Church. Built in 1923, the church's structure replicates the mission style of the region's earlier history. The church seats about 230 worshippers, a number too small for its growing parish. Some 40 to 60 parishioners cannot be accommodated at some Sunday masses. In order to meet the needs of the congregation the Archbishop of San Antonio gave permission to the parish to plan alterations to enlarge the building.

A few months later, the Boerne City Council passed an ordinance authorizing the city's Historic Landmark Commission to prepare a preservation plan with proposed historic landmarks and districts. Under the ordinance, the Commission must preapprove construction affecting historic landmarks or buildings in a historic district.

Soon afterwards, the Archbishop applied for a building permit so construction to enlarge the church could proceed. City authorities, relying on the ordinance and the designation of a historic district (which, they argued, included the church), denied the application. The Archbishop brought this suit challenging the permit denial in the United States District Court for the Western District of Texas.

The complaint contained various claims, but to this point the litigation has centered on RFRA and the question of its constitutionality. The Archbishop relied upon RFRA as one basis for relief from the refusal to issue the permit. The District Court concluded that by enacting RFRA Congress exceeded the scope of its enforcement power under Section 5 of the Fourteenth Amendment. The court certified its order for interlocutory appeal and the Fifth Circuit reversed, finding RFRA to be constitutional. We granted *certiorari* and now reverse.

Congress enacted RFRA in direct response to the Court's decision in *Employment Div., Dept. of Human Resources of Oregon v. Smith.* There we considered a Free Exercise Clause claim brought by members of the Native American Church who were denied unemployment benefits when they lost their jobs because they had used peyote. Their practice was to ingest peyote for sacramental purposes, and they challenged an Oregon statute of general applicability which made use of the drug criminal. In evaluating the claim, we declined to apply the balancing test set forth in *Sherbert v. Verner*, under which we would have asked whether Oregon's prohibition substantially burdened a religious practice and, if it did, whether the burden was justified by a compelling government interest. We stated: "[G]overnment's ability to enforce generally applicable prohibitions of socially harmful conduct . . . cannot depend on measuring the effects of a governmental action on a religious objector's spiritual development. To make an individual's obligation to obey such a law contingent upon the law's coincidence with his religious beliefs, except where the State's interest is 'compelling' . . . contradicts both constitutional tradition and common sense." The application of the *Sherbert* test, the *Smith* decision explained, would have produced an anomaly in the law, a constitutional right to ignore neutral laws of general applicability. The anomaly would have been accentuated, the Court reasoned, by the difficulty of determining whether a particular practice was central to an individual's religion. We explained, moreover, that it "is not within the judicial ken to question the centrality of particular beliefs or practices to a faith, or the validity of particular litigants' interpretations of those creeds." . . .

Under our Constitution, the Federal Government is one of enumerated powers (*McCulloch v. Maryland* [1819]). The judicial authority to determine the constitutionality of laws, in cases and controversies, is based on the premise that the "powers of the legislature are defined and limited; and that those limits may not be mistaken, or forgotten, the constitution is written" (*Marbury v. Madison*).

Congress relied on its Fourteenth Amendment enforcement power in enacting the most far reaching and substantial of RFRA's provisions, those which impose its requirements on the States. The Fourteenth Amendment provides, in relevant part: "Section 1. . . . No State shall make or enforce any law which shall abridge the privileges or immunities of citizens of the United States; nor shall any State deprive any person of life, liberty, or property, without due process of law; nor deny to any person within its jurisdiction the equal protection of the laws. . . . Section 5. The Congress shall have power to enforce, by appropriate legislation, the provisions of this article." The parties disagree over whether RFRA is a proper exercise of Congress' Section 5 power "to enforce" by "appropriate legislation" the constitutional guarantee that no State shall deprive any person of "life, liberty, or property, without due process of law" nor deny any person "equal protection of the laws." . . .

While the line between measures that remedy or prevent unconstitutional actions and measures that make a substantive change in the governing law is not easy to discern, and Congress must have wide latitude in determining where it lies, the distinction exists and must be observed. There must be a congruence and proportionality between the injury to be prevented or remedied and the means adopted to that end. Lacking such a connection, legislation may become substantive in operation and effect. History and our case law support drawing the distinction, one apparent from the text of the Amendment.

Regardless of the state of the legislative record, RFRA cannot be considered remedial, preventive legislation, if those terms are to have any meaning. RFRA is so out of proportion to a supposed remedial or preventive object that it cannot be understood as responsive to, or designed to prevent, unconstitutional behavior. It appears, instead, to attempt a substantive change in constitutional protections. . . .

The stringent test RFRA demands of state laws reflects a lack of proportionality or congruence between the means adopted and the legitimate end to be achieved. If an objector can show a substantial burden on his free exercise, the State must demonstrate a compelling governmental interest and show that the law is the least restrictive means of furthering its interest. Claims that a law substantially burdens someone's exercise of religion will often be difficult to contest. . . . Laws valid under *Smith* would fall under RFRA without regard to whether they had the object of stifling or punishing free exercise. . . .

The substantial costs RFRA exacts, both in practical terms of imposing a heavy litigation burden on the States and in terms of curtailing their traditional general regulatory power, far exceed any pattern or practice of unconstitutional conduct under the Free Exercise Clause as interpreted in *Smith*. Simply put, RFRA is not designed to identify and counteract state laws likely to be unconstitutional because of their treatment of religion. . . .

When Congress acts within its sphere of power and responsibilities, it has not just the right but the duty to make its own informed judgment on the meaning and force of the Constitution. This has been clear from the early days of the Republic. . . .

Our national experience teaches that the Constitution is preserved best when each part of the government respects both the Constitution and the proper actions and determinations of the other branches. When the Court has interpreted the Constitution, it has acted within the province of the Judicial Branch, which embraces the duty to say what the law is (*Marbury v. Madison*). When the political branches of the Government act against the background of a judicial interpretation of the Constitution already issued, it must be understood that in later cases and controversies the Court will treat its precedents with the respect due them under settled principles, including stare decisis, and contrary expectations must be disappointed. RFRA was designed to control cases and controversies, such as the one before us; but as the provisions of the federal statute here invoked are beyond congressional authority, it is this Court's precedent, not RFRA, which must control. . . .

The judgment of the Court of Appeals sustaining the Act's constitutionality is reversed.

In a concurring opinion, Justice Stevens argued that RFRA also violated the Establishment Clause, by granting special preferences to persons who seek exemption from governmental actions on reli-

gious grounds. In a concurring opinion, Justice Scalia attacked the arguments of Justice O'Connor that Smith should be reconsidered and overruled.

Justice O'Connor, with whom Justice Breyer joins except as to a portion of Part I, dissenting.

I dissent from the Court's disposition of this case. I agree with the Court that the issue before us is whether the Religious Freedom Restoration Act (RFRA) is a proper exercise of Congress' power to enforce Section 5 of the Fourteenth Amendment. But as a yardstick for measuring the constitutionality of RFRA, the Court uses its holding in *Employment Div., Dept. of Human Resources of Oregon v. Smith,* the decision that prompted Congress to enact RFRA as a means of more rigorously enforcing the Free Exercise Clause. I remain of the view that *Smith* was wrongly decided, and I would use this case to reexamine the Court's holding there. Therefore, I would direct the parties to brief the question whether *Smith* represents the correct understanding of the Free Exercise Clause and set the case for reargument. If the Court were to correct the misinterpretation of the Free Exercise Clause set forth in *Smith,* it would simultaneously put our First Amendment jurisprudence back on course and allay the legitimate concerns of a majority in Congress who believed that *Smith* improperly restricted religious liberty. We would then be in a position to review RFRA in light of a proper interpretation of the Free Exercise Clause. . . .

In dissenting opinions, Justice Souter and Justice Breyer agreed with Justice O'Connor that Smith should be reconsidered.

AGOSTINI V. FELTON (1997)

The fears of many that a Rehnquist Court, in the name of accommodation, would tear down the wall of separation between church and state seemed groundless in the late 1980s and early 1990s. In a variety of cases the Court upheld the precedents it had developed.

In some ways the Religious Freedom Restoration Act (RFRA) was a response to what many perceived as too rigid an interpretation of the Establishment and Free Exercise clauses. But most of those cases were decided by shifting majorities, often 5–4; and given a proper case, the accommodationists on the Court stood a good chance of having their way. In Witters v. Washington Dept. of Services for the Blind *(1986), the Court permitted a recipient of a grant from a public agency to use the money to attend a religious college for the express purpose of becoming a minister. In* Zobrest v. Catalina Foothills School District *(1993), it allowed public funds to be used to pay a sign-language interpreter in a religious school. That message was not lost on the plaintiffs in* Aguilar v. Felton *(1985), in which a closely divided Court had struck down a popular New York program that used Title I money to pay for public school teachers going into parochial schools and conducting remedial programs during regular school hours, as well as a community program offering courses in these schools after hours. Following that ruling, the district court had issued an injunction against continued use of Title I monies for the programs. Using a procedural device— Rule 60(b) of the Federal Rules of Civil Procedure—to get their argument back before the high court, plaintiffs claimed that intervening decisions had effectively overruled the basis for that injunction. The slim majority of the justices that had long been unhappy with the* Lemon *test and its consequences seized upon the Rule 60(b) petition in order to overrule the earlier decision. See Robert G. Neill, "Agostini v. Felton: The Gnat Is Swallowed, but the Camel Goes Free,"* Journal of Contemporary Law *24: 192 (1998); Daniel P. Whitehead, "Agostini v. Felton: Rectifying the Chaos of Establishment Clause Jurisprudence,"* Capital University Law Review *27: 639 (1999); Jeremy Bunnow, "Reinventing the Lemon,"* Wisconsin Law Review *(1998) 1133.*

Justice O'Connor delivered the opinion of the Court.

In *Aguilar v. Felton* (1985), this Court held that the Establishment Clause of the First Amendment barred the city of New

York from sending public school teachers into parochial schools to provide remedial education to disadvantaged children pursuant to a congressionally mandated program. On remand, the [district court] entered a permanent injunction reflecting our ruling. Twelve years later, petitioners—the parties bound by that injunction—seek relief from its operation. Petitioners maintain that *Aguilar* cannot be squared with our intervening Establishment Clause jurisprudence and ask that we explicitly recognize what our more recent cases already dictate: *Aguilar* is no longer good law. We agree with petitioners that *Aguilar* is not consistent with our subsequent Establishment Clause decisions and further conclude that, on the facts presented here, petitioners are entitled under Federal Rule of Civil Procedure 60(b)(5) to relief from the operation of the District Court's prospective injunction.

Title I of the Elementary and Secondary Education Act of 1965 channels federal funds, through the States, to "local educational agencies" (LEAs) to provide remedial education, guidance, and job counseling to students who are failing, or at risk of failing, the State's student performance standards. Title I funds must be made available to all eligible children, regardless of whether they attend public schools, and the services provided to children attending private schools must be "equitable in comparison to services and other benefits for public school children." An LEA providing services to children enrolled in private schools is subject to a number of constraints that are not imposed when it provides aid to public schools. Title I services may be provided only to those private school students eligible for aid, and cannot be used to provide services on a "school-wide" basis. In addition, the LEA must retain complete control over Title I funds; retain title to all materials used to provide Title I services; and provide those services through public employees or other persons independent of the private school and any religious institution. The Title I services themselves must be "secular, neutral, and nonideological," and must "supplement, and in no case supplant, the level of services" already provided by the private school. . . .

In 1978, six federal taxpayers—respondents here—sued the Board in the District Court. The District Court granted summary judgment for the Board, but the Court of Appeals for the Second Circuit reversed. In a 5–4 decision, this Court affirmed on the ground that the Board's Title I program necessitated "an excessive entanglement of church and state in the administration of Title I benefits." On remand the District Court permanently enjoined the Board "from using public funds for any plan or program under Title I to the extent that it requires, authorizes or permits public school teachers and guidance counselors to provide teaching and counseling services on the premises of sectarian schools within New York City."

The Board reverted to its prior practice of providing instruction at public school sites, at leased sites, and in mobile instructional units (essentially vans converted into classrooms) parked near the sectarian school. The Board also offered computer-aided instruction, which could be provided "on premises" because it did not require public employees to be physically present on the premises of a religious school. It is not disputed that the additional costs of complying with *Aguilar*'s mandate are significant. Since the 1986–1987 school year, the Board has spent over $100 million providing computer-aided instruction, leasing sites and mobile instructional units, and transporting students to those sites. These "*Aguilar* costs" reduce the amount of Title I money an LEA has available for remedial education, and LEAs have had to cut back on the number of students who receive Title I benefits.

The question we must answer is a simple one: Are petitioners entitled to relief from the District Court's permanent injunction under Rule 60(b)? Rule 60(b)(5) states: "On motion and upon such terms as are just, the court may relieve a party . . . from a final judgment or order . . . when it is no longer equitable that the judgment should have prospective application." We have held that it is appropriate to grant a Rule 60(b)(5) motion when the party seeking relief from an injunction or consent decree can show "a significant change either in factual conditions or in law." Petitioners argue that there have been two significant legal developments since *Aguilar* was decided: In *Board of Education of Kiryas Joel v. Grumet* (1994), a majority of Justices have expressed their views that *Aguilar* should be reconsidered or overruled and *Aguilar* has in any event been undermined by subsequent Establishment Clause decisions, including *Witters v. Washington Department of Services for the Blind* (1986), *Zobrest v. Catalina Foothills School District* (1993), and *Rosenberger v. Rector and Visitors of the University of Virginia* (1995). The statements made by five Justices in *Kiryas Joel* do not, in themselves, furnish a basis for concluding that our Establishment Clause jurisprudence has changed. The question of *Aguilar*'s propriety was not before us there. Thus, petitioners' ability to satisfy the prerequisites of Rule 60(b)(5) hinges on whether our later Establishment Clause cases have so undermined *Aguilar* that it is no longer good law.

In order to evaluate whether *Aguilar* has been eroded by our subsequent Establishment Clause cases, it is necessary to understand the rationale upon which *Aguilar*, as well as its companion case, *School District of Grand Rapids v. Ball* (1985), rested. . . . Distilled to essentials, the Court's conclusion that the Shared Time program in *Ball* had the impermissible effect of advancing religion rested on three assumptions: (i) any public employee who works on the premises of a religious school is presumed to inculcate religion in her work; (ii) the presence of public employees on private school premises creates a symbolic union between church and state; and (iii) any and all public aid that directly aids the educational function of religious schools impermissibly finances religious indoctrination, even if the aid reaches such schools as a consequence of private decisionmaking. Additionally, in *Aguilar* there was a fourth assumption: that New York City's Title I program necessitated an excessive government entanglement with religion because public employees who teach on the premises of religious schools must be closely monitored to ensure that they do not inculcate religion.

Our more recent cases have undermined the assumptions upon which *Ball* and *Aguilar* relied. To be sure, the general principles we use to evaluate whether government aid violates the Establishment Clause have not changed since *Aguilar* was decided. For example, we continue to ask whether the government acted with the purpose of advancing or inhibiting religion and to explore whether the aid has the "effect" of advancing or inhibiting religion. What has changed since we decided *Ball* and *Aguilar* is our understanding of the criteria used to assess whether aid to religion has an impermissible effect.

As we have repeatedly recognized, government inculcation of religious beliefs has the impermissible effect of advancing religion. Our cases subsequent to *Aguilar* have, however, modified in two significant respects the approach we use to assess indoctrination. First, we have abandoned the presumption that the placement of public employees on parochial school grounds inevitably results in the impermissible effect of state-sponsored indoctrination or constitutes a symbolic union between government and religion. *Zobrest* expressly rejected the notion—relied on in *Ball* and *Aguilar*—that, solely because of her presence on private school property, a public employee will be presumed to inculcate religion in the students. *Zobrest* also implicitly repudiated the assumption that the presence of a public employee on private school property creates an impermissible "symbolic link" between government and religion. . . .

Second, we have departed from the rule relied on in *Ball* that all government aid that directly aids the educational function of religious schools is invalid. In *Witters,* we held that the Establishment Clause did not bar a State from issuing a vocational tuition grant to a blind person who wished to use the grant to attend a Christian college and become a pastor, missionary, or youth director.

We observed that the tuition grants were "made available general-ly without regard to the sectarian-nonsectarian nature of the insti-tution benefitted" and that the grants were disbursed directly to students and thus that any money that ultimately went to reli-gious institutions did so "only as a result of the genuinely inde-pendent and private choices" of individuals. The same logic applied in *Zobrest*.

Zobrest and *Witters* make clear that, under current law, the Shared Time program in *Ball* and New York City's Title I pro-gram in *Aguilar* will not, as a matter of law, be deemed to have the effect of advancing religion through indoctrination. First, there is no reason to presume that, simply because she enters a parochial school classroom, a full-time public employee such as a Title I teacher will depart from her assigned duties and instructions and embark on religious indoctrination, any more than there was a reason in *Zobrest* to think an interpreter would inculcate religion by altering her translation of classroom lectures. *Zobrest* also repudiates *Ball*'s assumption that the presence of Title I teachers in parochial school classrooms will . . . create the impression of a "symbolic union" between church and State. Justice Souter main-tains that Title I continues to foster a "symbolic union" between the Board and sectarian schools because it mandates "the involve-ment of public teachers in the instruction provided within sectar-ian schools" and "fuses public and private faculties." Justice Souter does not disavow the notion that Title I services may be provided to sectarian school students in off-campus locations. We do not see any perceptible (let alone dispositive) difference in the degree of symbolic union between a student receiving remedial instruction in a classroom on his sectarian school's campus and one receiving instruction in a van parked just at the school's curb-side. . . .

Where aid is allocated on the basis of neutral, secular criteria that neither favor nor disfavor religion, and is made available to both religious and secular beneficiaries on a nondiscriminatory basis, the aid is less likely to have the effect of advancing religion. In *Ball* and *Aguilar,* the Court gave this consideration no weight. Before and since those decisions, we have sustained programs that provided aid to all eligible children regardless of where they attended school. Applying this reasoning to New York City's Title I program, it is clear that Title I services are allocated on the basis of criteria that neither favor nor disfavor religion. The services are available to all children who meet the Act's eligibility requirements, no matter what their religious beliefs or where they go to school. The Board's program does not, therefore, give aid recipients any incentive to modify their religious beliefs or practices in order to obtain those services.

We turn now to *Aguilar*'s conclusion that New York City's Title I program resulted in an excessive entanglement between church and state.... After *Zobrest* we no longer presume that public employees will inculcate religion simply because they happen to be in a sectarian environment. Since we have abandoned the assumption that properly instructed public employees will fail to discharge their duties faithfully, we must also discard the assumption that pervasive monitoring of Title I teachers is required.

To summarize, New York City's Title I program does not run afoul of any of three primary criteria we currently use to evaluate whether government aid has the effect of advancing religion: it does not result in governmental indoctrination; define its recipients by reference to religion; or create an excessive entanglement. We therefore hold that a federally funded program providing supplemental, remedial instruction to disadvantaged children on a neutral basis is not invalid under the Establishment Clause when such instruction is given on the premises of sectarian schools by government employees pursuant to a program containing safeguards such as those present here. The same considerations that justify this holding require us to conclude that this carefully constrained program also cannot reasonably be viewed as an endorsement of religion. Accordingly, we must acknowledge that *Aguilar,* as well as the portion of *Ball* addressing Grand Rapids' Shared Time program, are no longer good law.

Stare decisis does not prevent us from overruling a previous decision where there has been a significant change in or subsequent development of our constitutional law. Our Establishment Clause jurisprudence has changed significantly since we decided *Ball* and *Aguilar,* so our decision to overturn those cases rests on far more than "a present doctrinal disposition to come out differently from the Court of 1985." We therefore overrule *Ball* and *Aguilar* to the extent those decisions are inconsistent with our current understanding of the Establishment Clause. We are only left to decide whether this change in law entitles petitioners to relief under Rule 60(b)(5). We conclude that it does. We reverse the judgment of the Court of Appeals and remand to the District Court with instructions to vacate its 1985 order.

Justice Souter, with whom Justices Stevens and Ginsburg join, and with whom Justice Breyer joins in part, dissenting.

I believe *Aguilar* was a correct and sensible decision, and my only reservation about its opinion is that the emphasis on the excessive entanglement produced by monitoring religious instructional content obscured those facts that independently called for the application of two central tenets of Establishment Clause jurisprudence. The State is forbidden to subsidize religion directly and is just as surely forbidden to act in any way that could reasonably be viewed as religious endorsement. The flat ban on subsidization antedates the Bill of Rights and has been an unwavering rule in Establishment Clause cases, qualified only by the conclusion that state exactions from college students are not the sort of public revenues subject to the ban (*Rosenberger v. Rector*). The rule expresses the hard lesson learned over and over again in the American past and in the experiences of the countries from which we have come, that religions supported by governments are compromised just as surely as the religious freedom of dissenters is burdened when the government supports religion. The ban against state endorsement of religion addresses the same historical lessons. Governmental approval of religion tends to reinforce the religious message (at least in the short run) and, by the same token, to carry a message of exclusion to those of less favored views. The human tendency, of course, is to forget the hard lessons, and to overlook the history of governmental partnership with religion when a cause is worthy, and bureaucrats have programs. That tendency to forget is the reason for having the Establishment Clause (along with the Constitution's other structural and libertarian guarantees), in the hope of stopping the corrosion before it starts.

These principles were violated by the programs at issue in *Aguilar* and *Ball*, as a consequence of several significant features common to both: each provided classes on the premises of the religious schools, covering a wide range of subjects including some at the core of primary and secondary education, like reading and mathematics; while their services were termed "supplemental," the programs and their instructors necessarily assumed responsibility for teaching subjects that the religious schools would otherwise have been obligated to provide; the public employees carrying out the programs had broad responsibilities involving the exercise of considerable discretion; while the programs offered aid to nonpublic school students generally (and Title I went to public school students as well), participation by religious school students in each program was extensive; and, finally, aid flowed directly to the schools in the form of classes and programs, as distinct from indirect aid that reaches schools only as a result of independent private choice. . . .

The Court's holding that *Aguilar* and the portion of *Ball* addressing the Shared Time program are "no longer good law" rests on mistaken reading. *Zobrest* is no sanction for overruling *Aguilar* or any portion of *Ball*. In *Zobrest* the Court did indeed recognize that the Establishment Clause lays down no absolute bar to placing public employees in a sectarian school, but the rejection of such a per se rule was hinged expressly on the nature of the employee's job, sign-language interpretation (or signing) and the circumscribed role of the signer. The Court explained: "The task of a sign-language interpreter seems to us quite different from that of a teacher or guidance counselor. . . . Nothing in this record suggests that a sign-language interpreter would do more than accurately interpret whatever material is presented to the class as a whole. In fact, ethical guidelines require interpreters to 'transmit everything that is said in exactly the same way it was intended.'" The signer could thus be seen as more like a hearing aid than a teacher, and the signing could not be understood as an opportunity to inject religious content in what was supposed to be secular instruction. *Zobrest* accordingly holds only that in these limited circumstances where a public employee simply translates for one student the material presented to the class for the benefit of all students, the employee's presence in the sectarian school does not violate the Establishment Clause. Nor did *Zobrest,* implicitly or otherwise, repudiate the view that the involvement of public teachers in the instruction provided within sectarian schools looks like a partnership or union and implies approval of the sectarian aim. On the subject of symbolic unions and the strength of their implications, the lesson of *Zobrest* is merely that less is less.

The Court next claims that *Ball* rested on the assumption that "any and all public aid that directly aids the educational function of religious schools impermissibly finances religious indoctrination, even if the aid reaches such schools as a consequence of private decisionmaking." This mischaracterizes *Ball. Ball* did not establish that "any and all" such aid to religious schools necessarily violates the Establishment Clause. It held that the Shared Time program subsidized the religious functions of the parochial schools by taking over a significant portion of their responsibility for teaching secular subjects. The Court noted that it had "never accepted the mere possibility of subsidization . . . as sufficient to invalidate an aid program," and instead enquired whether the effect of the proffered aid was "direct and substantial" (and, so, unconstitutional) or merely "indirect and incidental" (and, so, permissible), emphasizing that the question "is one of degree." *Witters* and *Zobrest* did nothing to repudiate the principle, emphasizing rather the limited nature of the aid at issue in each case as well as the fact that religious institutions did not receive it directly from the State. . . .

Finally, instead of aid that comes to the religious school indirectly in the sense that its distribution results from private decision-making, a public educational agency distributes Title I aid in the form of programs and services directly to the religious schools. In *Zobrest* and *Witters,* it was fair to say that individual students were themselves applicants for individual benefits. But under Title I, a local educational agency may receive federal funding by proposing programs approved to serve individual students who meet the criteria of need, which it then uses to provide such programs at the religious schools; students eligible for such programs may not apply directly for Title I funds. In sum, nothing since *Ball* and *Aguilar* and before this case has eroded the distinction between "direct and substantial" and "indirect and incidental." That principled line is being breached only here and now. And if a scheme of government aid results in support for religion in some substantial degree, or in endorsement of its value, the formal neutrality of the scheme does not render the Establishment Clause helpless or the holdings in *Aguilar* and *Ball* inapposite.

Justice Ginsburg dissented, joined by Justices Stevens, Souter, and Breyer. Ginsburg objected on technical grounds to the Court's use of Rule 60(b), claiming that a new majority had distorted the intent of the rule and also ignored stare decisis in order to reach a result it wanted—a result unsupported by cases following Ball *and* Aguilar.

CHRONOLOGY

1776	American Revolution; disestablishment of Anglican Church
1786	Virginia Statute for Religious Freedom
1791	First Amendment ratified
1813	Father Kohlmann case in New York
1826	Maryland passes bill giving Jews full political rights
1830s	Wave of anti-Catholic riots sweeps United States
1838	Abner Kneeland jailed for blasphemy in Massachusetts
1840s	Mormons trek to Utah
1856	Know-Nothing Party fields presidential candidate
1861	Fort Sumter fired upon; Civil War begins
1862	Morrill Anti-Polygamy Act
1868	North Carolina finally allows non-Christians to hold public office
1868	Charles Taze Russell founds Jehovah's Witnesses
1879	Court upholds Anti-Polygamy Act in *Reynolds v. United States*
1890	*Davis v. Beason* upholds disenfranchisement of Mormons
1890	Mormon Church abandons polygamy
1917	United States enters World War I
1924	Alfred E. Smith, first Catholic candidate for president
1927	Scopes trial in Dayton, Tennessee
1940	Jehovah's Witnesses win first case (*Cantwell v. Connecticut*)
1940	First flag salute case (*Minersville School District v. Gobitis*)
1940	Selective Service Act includes conscientious objector provision

1941   Pearl Harbor bombed; United States enters World War II
1943   Second flag salute case (*West Virginia Board of Education v. Barnette*)
1947   *Everson v. Board of Education* applies First Amendment to states
1952   *Zorach v. Clauson,* first accommodationist ruling
1953   Earl Warren becomes chief justice
1954   Court strikes down segregation in *Brown v. Board of Education*
1960   John F. Kennedy, first Catholic president, elected
1961   Court upholds Sunday closing laws
1962   *Engel v. Vitale* strikes down mandatory school prayer
1963   *Sherbert v. Verner* sets test of religious accommodation
1965   Elementary and Secondary Education Act begins funneling billions of federal dollars into local schools
1968   *Epperson v. Arkansas* strikes down antievolution statute
1969   Warren Burger becomes chief justice
1971   Court articulates *Lemon* test for Establishment Clause cases
1972   *Wisconsin v. Yoder* excuses Amish from compulsory school laws
1985   *Wallace v. Jaffree,* Court affirms *Engel v. Vitale*
1986   William H. Rehnquist becomes chief justice
1987   Court strikes down Louisiana Balanced Treatment Act
1990   *Oregon v. Smith* in effect overrides *Sherbert*
1992   *Lee v. Weisman* reaffirms *Engel v. Vitale*
1993   Religious Freedom Restoration Act (RFRA)
1997   Court strikes down RFRA
2001   Fundamentalist Mormon convicted of polygamy in Utah

TABLE OF CASES

ANNOTATED BIBLIOGRAPHY

GENERAL WORKS

In 1953 Leo Pfeffer published *Church, State, and Freedom* (Boston: Beacon Press), an encyclopedic overview of religious freedom and its history primarily in the United States but with chapters examining church-state relations in other countries as well. In 1964 Pfeffer revised and condensed Anson Phelps Stokes, *Church and State in the United States* (New York: Harper & Row), which while covering much of the same ground, also filled in some gaps, presented more information about the churches, and included some lesser-known documents. Although there has been a great deal of new research on the various aspects of religious freedom, no one has since attempted such a grand synthesis. In using these books, however, one should keep in mind that in addition to being a scholar, Pfeffer was one of the leading advocates of total separation of church and state in the latter twentieth century, and he successfully argued many church-state cases before the courts.

A good collection of essays on church-state relations and other issues of religious freedom is James E. Wood, Jr., ed., 1985, *Religion and the State: Essays in Honor of Leo Pfeffer* (Waco, TX: Baylor University Press). For a different perspective, see the newer but highly idiosyncratic work by John T. Noonan, Jr., 1998, *The Lustre of Our Country: The American Experience of Religious Freedom* (Berkeley: University of California Press), as well as the casebook compiled by Noonan with Edward McGlynn Gaffney, Jr., 2001, *Religious Freedom* (New York: Foundation Press), which includes documents going back to Biblical times.

There are innumerable "cases and materials" books designed for law schools, all of which have sections on the religion clauses. As interest in this area has grown, some of these sections have been expanded and published as separate books. All of these books contain lengthy excerpts from the major cases, commentaries on them, and references to law review articles that explicate those cases. Among these, see Kathleen M. Sullivan and Gerard Gunther, 1999, *First Amendment Law* (New York: Foundation Press); John T. Noonan, Jr., and Edward McGlynn Gaffney, Jr., mentioned above; Arnold H. Loewy, 1999, *Religion and the Constitution: Cases and Materials* (St. Paul, MN: West Group); and Steven H. Shiffrin and Jesse H. Choper, 2001, *The First Amendment: Cases—Comments—Questions* (3d ed., St. Paul, MN: West Group). A good, basic introduction is John Witte, Jr., 2000, *Religion and the American Constitutional Experiment: Essential Rights and Liberties* (Boulder: Westview Press).

A work that is extremely useful is Paul Finkelman, ed., 2000, *Religion and American Law: An Encyclopedia* (New York: Garland Publishing). It has entries not only on the major cases and doctrines but also on different religious groups, such as the Mormons and Catholics, and how they have fared before the courts. For an overview of American constitutional history, see Melvin I. Urofsky and Paul Finkelman, 2001, *A March of Liberty* (2 vols., rev. ed., New York: Oxford University Press).

A survey of works on religion would require a book by itself. Of special interest are the books by Martin E. Marty, including his 1984 *Pilgrims in Their Own Land: 500 Years of Religion in America* (Boston: Little, Brown); 1986 *Protestantism in the United States: Righteous Empire* (2d ed., New York: Scribner's); and 1989 *Religion and Republic: The American Circumstances* (Boston: Beacon Press). Sidney E. Ahlstrom, 1972, *A Religious History of the American People* (New Haven: Yale University Press), is also useful. Although some of the earlier volumes are a bit dated, the Chicago History of American Civilization series (ed. Daniel Boorstin) provides good overviews of different religious groups in the United States. See especially Klaus J. Hansen, 1981, *Mormonism and the American Experience;* Edwin S. Gausted, 1973, *Dissent in American Religion;* John Tracy Ellis, 1956, *American Catholicism;* Winthrop S. Hudson, 1961, *American Protestantism;* and Nathan Glazer, 1972, *American Judaism* (all Chicago: University of Chicago Press).

For more on the Baptists, see Robert G. Torbet, 1969, *A History of the Baptists* (Valley Forge, PA: Judson); James E. Wood, ed., 1976, *Baptists and the American Experience* (Valley Forge, PA: Judson); and William G. McLoughlin, 1971, *New England Dissent, 1630–1833: The Baptists and the Separation of Church and State* (2 vols., Cambridge: Harvard University Press).

On Catholicism, see Martin E. Marty, 1995, *A Short History of American Catholicism* (Allen, PA: Thomas More); Chester Gillis, 1999, *Roman Catholicism in America* (New York: Columbia University Press); and Jay P. Dolan, 1985, *The American Catholic Experience* (Garden City, NY: Doubleday).

For more on Judaism, see Naomi W. Cohen, 1992, *Jews in Christian America: The Pursuit of Religious Equality* (New York: Oxford University Press); Leonard Dinnerstein, 1994, *Anti-Semitism in America* (New York: Oxford University Press); and Howard M. Sachar, 1992, *A History of the Jews in America* (New York: Knopf).

The literature on fundamentalism is enormous and growing, but the best place to start is with the five volumes edited by Martin E. Marty and R. Scott Appleby, 1991–1995, *The Fundamentalism Project* (Chicago: University of Chicago Press).

For more on Mormonism and Jehovah's Witnesses, see the section on "The Free Exercise of Religion," below.

The Establishment Clause

Much of the debate over the Establishment Clause has dealt with whether the Framers intended that there be a strict wall of separation between church and state, or instead merely that no one church should enjoy primacy and that government could aid all religion on a nonpreferential basis. The bulk of historical research and analysis favors separation. One of the best places to start is with the prize-winning volume by Jack N. Rakove, 1996, *Original Meanings: Politics and Ideas in the Making of the Constitution* (New York: Knopf). The strongest and best-argued case for separation is Leonard W. Levy, 1994, *The Establishment Clause: Religion and the First Amendment* (2d rev. ed., Chapel Hill: University of North Carolina Press), which looks at a very broad range of Establishment Clause cases. Of especial interest is Robert S. Alley, ed., 1985, *James Madison on Religious Liberty* (Buffalo: Prometheus Books), a collection of essays on and documents by the chief drafter of the First Amendment.

There are several good books dealing with the history of religion in the colonies leading up to the First Amendment, and these all support the notion of separation as well. An older but still quite useful book is Robert Allen Rutland, 1983, *The Birth of the Bill of Rights, 1776–1791* (Rev. ed., Boston: Northeastern University Press). Both Thomas J. Curry, 1986, *The First Freedoms: Church and State in America to the Passage of the First*

Amendment (New York: Oxford University Press), and William Lee Miller, 1985, *The First Liberty: Religion and the American Republic* (New York: Knopf), are exhaustive in their treatment of religious freedom in the colonies and early Republic. An excellent collection of essays is Merrill D. Peterson and Robert C. Vaughn, eds., 1988, *The Virginia Statute for Religious Freedom: Its Evolution and Consequences in American History* (New York: Cambridge University Press). Akhil Reed Amar, 1998, *The Bill of Rights: Creation and Reconstruction* (New Haven: Yale University Press), presents a provocative view of the Bill of Rights and the Religion Clauses as part of a larger structuralist scheme to create an enduring federal republic.

A more specialized study is John G. West, Jr., 1996, *The Politics of Revelation and Reason: Religion and Civic Life in the New Nation* (Lawrence: University Press of Kansas), which argues that religion played a far larger role both in civic life and in politics, especially in the early congresses, than has been previously assumed. In contrast, Derek H. Davis, 2000, *Religion and the Continental Congress, 1774–1789: Contributions to Original Intent* (New York: Oxford University Press), looking at essentially the same materials, puts forward arguments that Congress did intend a full separation. A contemporary call for more religion in public life and for an abandonment of the wall of separation metaphor is Stephen L. Carter, 1995, *The Culture of Disbelief: How American Law and Politics Trivialize Religious Devotion* (New York: Basic Books). Richard John Neuhaus, 1986, *The Naked Square: Religion and Democracy in America* (Grand Rapids: Eerdmans) also bemoans the banishment of religion from public life.

In 1949, just two years after *Everson*, James O'Neill published *Religion and Education under the Constitution* (New York: Harper and Brothers), which put forward the thesis that aid to religion generally or to all churches without discrimination (nonpreferentialism) did not constitute an establishment of religion and therefore did not violate the First Amendment. That argument garnered practically no attention at the time, but it was later picked up and expanded upon in such works as Chester J. Antieau, Arthur T. Downey, and Edward C. Roberts, 1964, *Freedom from Federal Establishment: Formation and Early History of the First Amendment Religion Clauses* (Milwaukee, WI: Bruce Publishing Co.); Robert L. Cord, 1982, *Separation of Church and State: Historical Fact and Current Fiction* (New York: Lambeth Press); Michael J. Malbin, 1978, *Religion and Politics: The Intention of the Authors of the First Amendment* (Washington, DC: American Enterprise Institute); Walter Berns, 1976, *The First Amendment and the Future of American Democracy* (New York: Basic Books); James McClellan, "The Making and Unmaking of the Establishment Clause," in Patrick B.

McGuigan and R. R. Rader, eds., 1981, *A Blueprint for Judicial Reform* (Washington, DC: Free Congress Education and Research Foundation). See also the debate between Daniel L. Dreisbach and John D. Whaley, 1999, "What the Wall Separates: A Debate on Thomas Jefferson's 'Wall of Separation' Metaphor," *Constitutional Commentary* 16: 627. The best-known attack on the separation view is Justice Rehnquist's dissenting opinion in *Wallace v. Jaffree*, 472 U.S. 38 (1985). Efforts by the Burger and Rehnquist Courts to establish a nonpreferentialist jurisprudence are examined in Gregg Ivers, 1991, *Lowering the Wall: Religion and the Supreme Court in the 1980s* (New York: Anti-Defamation League). Robert A. Goldwin and Art Kaufman, eds., 1987, *How Does the Constitution Protect Religious Freedom?* (Washington, DC: American Enterprise Institute), includes essays that support nonpreferentialism.

Establishment Clause—Specific Cases

Everson v. Board of Education

Theodore Power, 1960, *The School Bus Law: A Case Study in Education, Religion, and Politics* (Middletown, CT: Wesleyan University Press); Tinsley E. Yarbrough, 1988, *Mr. Justice Black and His Critics* (Durham, NC: Duke University Press); Richard E. Morgan, 1972, *The Supreme Court and Religion* (New York: Free Press); and Frank J. Sorauf, 1976, *The Wall of Separation: The Constitutional Politics of Church and State* (Princeton: Princeton University Press).

Released Time

Frank Swancara, 1950, *The Separation of Religion and Government: The First Amendment, Madison's Intent, and the McCollum Decision* (New York: Truth Seeker Co.); 1948, "Tracing the 'Wall': Religion in the Public School System," *Yale Law Journal* 57: 1114; George E. Reed, 1952, "Church-State and the Zorach Case," *Notre Dame Lawyer* 27: 529; Samuel Alito, 1974, "The 'Released Time' Cases Revisited: A Study of Group Decisionmaking by the Supreme Court," *Yale Law Journal* 83: 1202.

School Prayer and Bible Reading

Kenneth M. Dolbeare and Phillip E. Hammond, 1971, *The School Prayer Decisions: From Court Policy to Local Practice* (Chicago: University of

Chicago Press); William K. Muir, 1967, *Prayer in the Public Schools* (Chicago: University of Chicago Press); Philip B. Kurland, 1962, "The Regent's Prayer Case . . . ," *Supreme Court Review* (1962) 1; John H. Laubach, 1969, *School Prayers: Congress, the Courts and the Public* (Washington, DC: Public Affairs Press); Robert K. DuPuy, 1986, "Religion, Graduation, and the First Amendment: A Threat of a Shadow?" *Drake Law Review* 35: 323; Gregory M. McAndrew, 1991, "Invocations at Graduation," *Yale Law Journal* 101: 663; Rodney K. Smith, 1986, "Now Is the Time for Reflection: *Wallace v. Jaffree* and Its Legislative Aftermath," *Alabama Law Review* 37: 345; and Suzanna Sherry, 1992, "*Lee v. Weisman:* Paradox Redux," *Supreme Court Review* (1992) 123.

Evolution

Stephen Carter, 1987, "Evolutionism, Creationism, and Treating Religion as a Hobby," *Duke Law Review* (1987) 977; Edward J. Larson, 1985, *Trial and Error: The American Controversy over Creation and Evolution* (New York: Oxford University Press); Lawrence Rosen, 1988, "Continuing the Conversation: Creationism, the Religion Clauses, and the Politics of Culture," *Supreme Court Review* (1988) 61; Garry Wills, 1990, *Under God: Religion and American Politics* (New York: Simon & Schuster).

Government Aid to Education

Richard E. Morgan, 1973, "The Establishment Clause and Sectarian Schools: A Final Installment," *Supreme Court Review* (1973) 57; Ronald Kahn, 1989, "Polity and Rights Values . . . ," *Studies in American Political Development* 3: 279; Michael W. McConnell, 1985, "Accommodation of Religion," *Supreme Court Review* (1985) 1; James M. Giacoma, 1980, "Committee for Public Education . . . : New Possibilities for State Aid to Nonpublic Schools," *St. Louis University Law Journal* 24: 406; and Donald A. Giannella, 1971, "*Lemon* and *Tilton:* The Bitter and the Sweet of Church-State Entanglement," *Supreme Court Review* (1971) 147.

Crèches, Symbols, and Speech

Norman Dorsen and Charles Sims, 1985, "The Nativity Scene Case: An Error of Judgment," *University of Illinois Law Review* (1985) 837; Kenneth Karst, 1992, "The First Amendment, the Politics of Religion, and the Symbols of Government," *Harvard Civil Liberties–Civil Rights Law*

Review 27: 503; Robert M. Slovek, 1984, "Legislative Prayer and the Establishment Clause: An Exception to Traditional Analysis," *Creighton Law Review* 17: 157; and Stephen D. Smith, 1987, "Symbols, Perceptions, and Doctrinal Illusions: Establishment Neutrality and the 'No Endorsement' Test," *Michigan Law Review* 86: 266.

THE FREE EXERCISE OF RELIGION

Although the Free Exercise Clause has not spawned a bitter historical debate akin to that surrounding the Establishment Clause, it has generated a great deal of literature on just how the clause is to be interpreted and just how far the state must go in accommodating individual religious practices. Good books to start this discussion include (but are not limited to) Nancy L. Rosenblum, ed., 2000, *Obligations of Citizenship and Demands of Faith: Religious Accommodation in Pluralist Democracies* (Princeton: Princeton University Press), which has a good sampling of articles; Steven D. Smith, 1995, *Foreordained Failure: The Quest for a Constitutional Principle of Religious Freedom* (New York: Oxford University Press), which asserts that it is impossible to find a principled way to implement free exercise; Bette Novit Evans, 1997, *Interpreting the Free Exercise of Religion: The Constitution and American Pluralism* (Chapel Hill: University of North Carolina Press), which argues that the clause both results from and makes possible a pluralist society. A somewhat similar argument is advanced in Michael S. Areiens and Robert A. Destro, 1996, *Religious Liberty in a Pluralistic Society* (Durham, NC: Duke University Press). Catherine Cookson, 2001, *Regulating Religion: The Courts and the Free Exercise Clause* (New York: Oxford University Press), argues that Free Exercise as used by the courts has been a means of regulating the tensions that might otherwise have exploded between groups. The inherent tension between the two clauses is best explicated in Jesse H. Choper, 1979, "The Religion Clauses of the First Amendment: Reconciling the Conflict," *University of Pittsburgh Law Review* 41: 673. Another worthwhile article is Douglas Laycock, 1997, "The Underlying Unity of Separation and Neutrality," 46 *Emory Law Journal* 46: 43.

Two groups that played a very important role in developing Free Exercise jurisprudence are the Mormons and the Jehovah's Witnesses. For the Church of Jesus Christ of Latter-Day Saints, see Leonard Arrington and Davis Bitton, 1979, *The Mormon Experience: A History of the Latter-Day Saints* (New York: Knopf); Gustive O. Larson, 1971, *The "Americanization" of Utah for Statehood* (San Marino, CA: Huntington Library); and

Edwin B. Firmage and Richard C. Mangrum, 1988, *Zion in the Courts: A Legal History of the Church of Jesus Christ of Latter-Day Saints, 1830–1900* (Urbana: University of Illinois Press). For Jehovah's Witnesses, see David Manwaring, 1962, *Render unto Caesar: The Flag Salute Controversy* (Chicago: University of Chicago Press); and Shawn Francis Peters, 2000, *Judging Jehovah's Witnesses: Religious Persecution and the Dawn of the Rights Revolution* (Lawrence: University Press of Kansas).

For discrimination against Jews in the early Republic, see Morton Borden, 1984, *Jews, Turks and Infidels* (Chapel Hill: University of North Carolina Press); and the highly idiosyncratic Stephen M. Feldman, 1997, *Please Don't Wish Me a Merry Christmas* (New York: New York University Press).

Free Exercise—Specific Cases

Reynolds and Mormon Polygamy

B. Carmon Hardy, 1992, *Solemn Covenant: The Mormon Polygamy Passage* (Urbana: University of Illinois Press); C. Peter McGrath, 1965, "Chief Justice Waite and the 'Twin Relic': *Reynolds v. United States*," *Vanderbilt Law Review* 18: 507; Edwin B. Firmage and Richard C. Mangrum, 1988, *Zion in the Courts: A Legal History of the Church of Jesus Christ of Latter-Day Saints* (Urbana: University of Illinois Press); Carol Weisbrod and Pamela Sheingorn, 1978, "*Reynolds v. United States:* Nineteenth-Century Forms of Marriage and the Status of Women," *Connecticut Law Review* 10: 828; and Sarah Barringer Gordon, 2001, *The Mormon Question: Polygamy and Constitutional Conflict in Nineteenth-Century America* (Chapel Hill: University of North Carolina Press).

Gobitis, *Barnette*, and the Jehovah's Witnesses

David Manwaring, 1962, *Render unto Caesar: The Flag Salute Controversy* (Chicago: University of Chicago Press); Shawn Francis Peters, 2000, *Judging Jehovah's Witnesses: Religious Persecution and the Dawn of the Rights Revolution* (Lawrence: University Press of Kansas); Michael Kent Curtis, ed., 1993, *The Flag and the Constitution, vol. 1: Flag Salute and the Law* (New York: Garland Publishing); Richard Danzig, 1984, "Justice Frankfurter's Opinions in the Flag Salute Cases: Blending Logic and Psychologic in Constitutional Decisionmaking," *Stanford Law Review* 36: 675; Peter Irons, 1988, *The Courage of Their Convictions*, pp. 15–24 (New York: Free Press).

Conscientious Objection

Ronald B. Flowers, 1993, "Government Accommodation of Religion-Based Conscientious Objection," *Seton Hall Law Review* 24: 695; Michael S. Satow, 1992, "Conscientious Objectors: Their Status, the Law and Its Development," *George Mason Civil Rights Law Journal* 3: 113; Kent Greenawalt, 1988, *Religious Convictions and Political Choice* (New York: Oxford University Press); and John A. Rohr, 1971, *Prophets Without Honor: Public Policy and the Selective Conscientious Objector* (Nashville: Abingdon Press).

Sherbert v. Verner and Unemployment Compensation

Marc Galanter, 1966, "Religious Freedom in the United States: A Turning Point?" *Wisconsin Law Review* (1966) 217; Stephen Pepper, 1986, "Taking the Free Exercise Clause Seriously," *Brigham Young University Law Review* (1986) 299.

Wisconsin v. Yoder

Albert N. Keim, ed., 1975, *Compulsory Education and the Amish: The Right Not To Be Modern* (Boston: Beacon Press); Norman Prance, 1971, "The Amish and Compulsory School Attendance: Recent Developments," *Wisconsin Law Review* (1971) 832.

Oregon v. Smith and Indian Rights

Carolyn N. Long, 2000, *Religious Freedom and Indian Rights: The Case of Oregon v. Smith* (Lawrence: University of Kansas Press); Garrett Epps, 2001, *To an Unknown God: Religious Freedom on Trial* (New York: St. Martin's Press); Douglas Laycock, 1990, "The Supreme Court's Assault on Free Exercise and the Amicus Brief That Was Never Filed," *Journal of Law and Religion* 8: 99; Chris Day, 1991, "*Employment Division v. Smith:* Free Exercise Clause Loses Balance on Peyote," *Baylor Law Review* 43: 577; John Rhodes, 1991, "An American Tradition: The Religious Persecution of Native Americans," *Montana Law Review* 52: 13; John R. Wunder, 1994, *Retained by the People: A History of American Indians and the Bill of Rights* (New York: Oxford University Press); and Jack F. Trope and Walter R. Echo-Hawk, 1992, "The Native American Graves Protection and Repatriation Act: Background and Legislative History," *Arizona State Law Journal* 24: 35.

The Religious Freedom Restoration Act and *Boerne v. Flores*

Michael W. McConnell, 1997, "Comment: Institutions and Interpretation: A Critique of *City of Boerne v. Flores*," *Harvard Law Review* 111: 153; James E. Ryan, 1992, "*Smith* and the Religious Freedom Restoration Act: An Iconoclastic Assessment," *Virginia Law Review* 78: 1407; Carolyn N. Long, 2000, *Religious Freedom and Indian Rights: The Case of Oregon v. Smith* (Lawrence: University of Kansas Press); Thomas C. Berg, 1994, "What Hath Congress Wrought: An Interpretive Guide to the Religious Freedom Restoration Act," *Villanova Law Review* 39: 1; and Marci A. Hamilton, 1994, "The Religious Freedom Restoration Act: Letting the Fox into the Henhouse . . . ," *Cardozo Law Review* 16: 357.

JUSTICES OF THE U.S. SUPREME COURT

A few justices have had a disproportionate voice in religion cases, either forging a new jurisprudence, as did Hugo Black, or arguing for what is still a minority position, as did William Rehnquist. Biographies or articles of these justices that include discussions of their religion clause jurisprudence are Roger K. Newman, 1994, *Hugo Black: A Biography* (New York: Pantheon); Tinsley E. Yarbrough, 1988, *Mr. Justice Black and His Critics* (Durham, NC: Duke University Press); Kim Isaac Eiser, 1993, *A Justice for All: William J. Brennan, Jr., and the Decisions that Transformed America* (New York: Simon & Schuster); James F. Simon, 1980, *Independent Journey: The Life of William O. Douglas* (New York: Harper & Row); Philip B. Kurland, 1971, *Mr. Justice Frankfurter and the Constitution* (Chicago: University of Chicago Press): Melvin I. Urofsky, 1991, *Felix Frankfurter: Judicial Restraint and Individual Liberty* (Boston: Twayne); Jeffrey D. Hockett, 1996, *New Deal Justice: The Constitutional Jurisprudence of Hugo L. Black, Felix Frankfurter, and Robert H. Jackson* (Lanham, MD: Rowman & Littlefield); Rodney K. Smith, 1983, "Justice Potter Stewart: A Contemporary Jurist's View of Religious Liberty," *North Dakota Law Review* 59: 183; Derek Davis, 1991, *Original Intent: Chief Justice Rehnquist and the Course of American Church/State Relations* (Buffalo, NY: Prometheus Books); and Sue Davis, 1989, *Justice Rehnquist and the Constitution* (Princeton: Princeton University Press).

INTERNET SOURCES

New Internet sites are introduced frequently. Readers who use the sites listed below are encouraged also to explore the countless links they provide to other sites.

A number of excellent sites offering information about the U.S. Supreme Court are listed below. The full text of Court decisions is available from some of these sites, but the record generally is limited to cases decided since approximately 1900.

About Atheism/Agnosticism

http://atheism.about.com: Although primarily an information source about atheism and agnosticism, this site has a very useful section that includes all court decisions relating to religious liberty.

Emory University School of Law (2 sites)

http://www.law.emory.edu/LAW/refdesk/toc.html: The electronic reference desk menu offers several useful categories of information including federal and state laws in the United States, and selected laws from more than seventy other countries. In addition to the reference option, this site offers sections on law by subject; law schools; legal periodicals; legal career information; and selected law firms.

http://www.law.emory.edu/FEDCTS: This U.S. federal courts finder site links the user to all federal appellate courts. Supreme Court links connect the user to the Legal Information Institute (LII) site. Excellent source for U.S. Court of Appeals decisions. Click any of the circuits on the U.S. maps to access rulings covering the past several years.

Findlaw

http://www.findlaw.com: Extraordinarily valuable and comprehensive. Among other assets, the site has federal and state cases and codes; U.S. and state resources; news and references; a legal subject index; and links to bar associations, lawyers, and law firms. Decisions of the U.S. Supreme Court back to 1893 can be accessed, as can federal courts of appeals rulings.

Foundation for Religious Freedom

http://www.forf.org: Keeps track of contemporary threats to religious freedom both in the United States and in countries around the world.

Jurist: The Legal Education Network

http://jurist.law.pitt.edu/supremecourt.htm: The Pittsburgh University Law School guide to the U.S. Supreme Court offers an online introduction to the "jurisprudence, structure, history and Justices of America's highest court." Links the user to sites that contain Supreme Court decisions (e.g., Legal Information Institute, Findlaw), news about the Court, biographies of the justices, the Court's procedures, and the latest media coverage of the Court.

Legal Information Institute (LII)

http://www.law.cornell.edu/index.html: Cornell Law School site containing Supreme Court decisions since 1990, U.S. and state constitutions and codes, law by source or jurisdiction (including international law), and "law about" pages providing summaries of various legal topics. The site has a "current awareness" page that contains news about the Court. LII provides a free e-mail service that distributes syllabi of Supreme Court decisions within hours of their release.

Lexis-Nexis Academic Universe

http://web.lexis-nexis.com/universe: A subscription database that covers a wide range of news, business, and reference information. Free access can be obtained to Lexis-Nexis through Academic Universe, which is available at most educational institutions.

Newspapers

A number of newspapers provide good coverage of the Supreme Court. Among the best are the *New York Times* (http://www.nytimes.com) and the *Washington Post* (http://washpostco.com).

Oyez Project

http://oyez.nwu.edu: Northwestern University's multimedia database allows users to hear oral arguments from selected cases, obtain summaries of more than 1,000 Court opinions, access biographical information on all the justices who have served on the Court, and take a virtual-reality tour of the Supreme Court building.

Religion Case Reporter

http://www.paradigmpub.com: A relatively new website, it offers monthly synopses of leading cases, organized topically.

Religious Freedom Page

http://religiousmovements.lib.Virginia.edu: An extensive and varied collection of materials about all aspects of religious freedom, created and maintained by Jeffrey K. Hadden, a professor at the University of Virginia. Includes information on legal developments, media, cults, and so on.

Religious Organizations

Many religious organizations, too numerous to list, have websites that provide information about the particular religion and about public policy issues affecting it.

Supreme Court

http://supremecourtus.gov: Overviews the Supreme Court as an institution, its functions, traditions, procedures, court rules, docket, and calendar. Also, information is available on the justices and the Supreme Court building. "Plug-in" capability is required to access information from this site.

United States Department of State

Maintains separate websites on the status of religious freedom in countries around the world.

Westlaw

http://westlaw.com: Westlaw is one of the largest and most comprehensive legal and business databases available on the Internet. Subscription is required for access, but prospective subscribers are able to fully explore the site on a "trial" basis.

INDEX

About the Author

Melvin I. Urofsky is director of the doctoral program in public policy and professor of history at Virginia Commonwealth University in Richmond. His books include ABC-CLIO's *The Warren Court: Justices, Rulings, and Legacy* (2001).